Lecture Notes in Computer Science   12527

More information about this subseries at http://www.springer.com/series/7411

Maria Carla Calzarossa ·
Erol Gelenbe · Krysztof Grochla ·
Ricardo Lent · Tadeusz Czachórski (Eds.)

Modelling, Analysis, and Simulation of Computer and Telecommunication Systems

28th International Symposium, MASCOTS 2020
Nice, France, November 17–19, 2020
Revised Selected Papers

 Springer

Editors
Maria Carla Calzarossa
Department of Industrial
and Information Engineering
University of Pavia
Pavia, Italy

Krysztof Grochla
Polish Academy of Sciences
Institute of Theoretical
and Applied Informatics
Gliwice, Poland

Tadeusz Czachórski
Institute of Theoretical
and Applied Informatics of the Polish
Academy of Sciences
Gliwice, Poland

Erol Gelenbe
Institute of Theoretical
and Applied Informatics
Gliwice, Poland

Ricardo Lent
University of Houston
Houston, TX, USA

ISSN 0302-9743 ISSN 1611-3349 (electronic)
Lecture Notes in Computer Science
ISBN 978-3-030-68109-8 ISBN 978-3-030-68110-4 (eBook)
https://doi.org/10.1007/978-3-030-68110-4

LNCS Sublibrary: SL5 – Computer Communication Networks and Telecommunications

This Springer imprint is published by the registered company Springer Nature Switzerland AG
The registered company address is: Gewerbestrasse 11, 6330 Cham, Switzerland

Preface

We are very pleased to introduce these Proceedings on the Modelling, Analysis and Simulation of Computer and Telecommunication Systems (MASCOTS 2020) workshop that was held online on November 17–19, 2020. The papers were selected from among 124 submissions by the Program Committee, based on a ranking resulting from the reports received from anonymous referees. The MASCOTS series of meetings, of which this is the 28th, has a long-standing policy of high quality, and includes a highly competent program committee composed of active researchers from Europe, Asia, Africa, New Zealand, and North and South America to whom we are very grateful.

This year's IEEE MASCOTS 2020 was a 3-day online meeting that also included two keynote talks by Professor Gabriele Kotsis of the University of Linz, our current President of the ACM, and Professor Ernesto Damiani of the University of Milan and Khalifa University in the UAE.

We are especially grateful to all those who submitted papers, from all five continents and from more than 27 countries.

To recall the beginnings of the MASCOTS series, below we give details of the proceedings of the first five Mascots conferences starting with the one in 1993, and fondly recall the pioneers who were involved in starting these symposia, especially Kallol Vijay Bagchi who energetically convinced several of us, including Erol Gelenbe, Doog de Groot, Patrick Dowd, Vijay Madisetti, Herb Schwetman, Kishor Trivedi and Jean Walrand and myself. We also recall the action of the late Professor George Riley, who contributed his energy and enthusiasm to pursuing this conference over the years.

Maria Carla Calzarossa
Erol Gelenbe
Krysztof Grochla
Ricardo Lent
Tadeusz Czachórski

Organization

Organizing Committee

General Chair

Erol Gelenbe   IITIS, Polish Academy of Sciences, Poland
and Université Côte d'Azur, France

Program Chair

Maria Carla Calzarossa   University of Pavia, Italy

Publicity Chairs

Krysztof Grochla   IITIS, Polish Academy of Sciences, Poland
Konrad Połys   IITIS, Polish Academy of Sciences, Poland

Publication Chair

Ricardo Lent   University of Houston, USA

Finance Chair

Tadeusz Czachórski   IITIS, Polish Academy of Sciences, Poland

Program Committee

Jussara Almeida	Federal University of Minas Gerais, Brazil
Jonatha Anselmi	Inria, France
Louiza Bouallouche-Medjkourne	University of Béjaïa, Algeria
Gilles Bernot	Université Côte d'Azur, France,
Andre-Luc Beylot	Institut National Polytechnique de Toulouse, France
Huibo Bi	Beijing University of Technology, China
Jalil Boukhobza	IRT, Lab-STICC, Univ. Bretagne Occidentale, France
Ivona Brandic	Technical University of Vienna, Austria
Valeria Cardellini	University of Rome Tor Vergata, Italy
Emiliano Casalicchio	Sapienza University of Rome, Italy
Suryadip Chakraborty	University of Cincinnati, USA
Claudio Cicconetti	IIT-CNR, Pisa, Italy
Tadeusz Czachórski	IITIS, Polish Academy of Sciences, Poland
Sofiene Djahel	Manchester Metropolitan University, UK
Joanna Domańska	IITIS, Polish Academy of Sciences, Poland
Lorenzo Donatiello	University of Bologna, Italy
Josu Doncel	University of the Basque Country, Spain

Contents

Network and System Optimization

Network Performance, Energy
and System Security

Performance, Energy Savings and Security: An Introduction

Ufuk Çağlayan$^{(\boxtimes)}$ (ID)

Computer Engineering Department, Yaşar University,
Üniversite Caddesi No: 37-39 Ağaçlı Yol, 35100 Bornova, Izmir, Turkey
`ufuk.caglayan@yasar.edu.tr`

Abstract. The International Symposia on the Modelling, Analysis and Simulation of Computer and Telecommunication Systems (MASCOTS) have a 28 year-long distinguished record, and we introduce the papers that were presented at the MASCOTS 2020 workshop. We also briefly review recent work of one of the founders of this series and organizer of this year's conference on the occasion of his 75th birthday, covering recent research on the Performance of Systems and Networks encompassing a broad view that includes Quality of Service, Energy Consumption and Security.

Keywords: Modelling · Analysis · Simulation of computers · Telecommunication systems · G-networks · Random neural networks · Cognitive packet networks · Quality of Service · Cyber-attacks · Energy Packet Networks

1 Modelling, Analysis and Simulation of Computer and Telecommunication Systems

We first introduce these proceedings of the MASCOTS 2020 – International Symposium on Modelling, Analysis and Simulation of Computer and Telecommunications Systems Workshop.

The meeting began with a video delivery of the Keynote by Professor Gabriele Kotsis of Linz University (Austria), and the current President of the ACM (Association for Computing Machinery) on "Intelligence? Smartness? Emotion? What do we expect from future computing machinery?"

It was followed by a session on *Traffic and Network Performance* that was chaired by Professor Kotsis, where three papers were presented. Two additional contributed papers [2,3] are included to this set since they fit with the topics of the session whose last three papers deal with the very topical issue of network and system security. These are:

- "Software Defined Network Dynamics via Diffusions," by Tadeusz Czachorski, Erol Gelenbe and Dariusz Marek [45]

© Springer Nature Switzerland AG 2021
M. C. Calzarossa et al. (Eds.): MASCOTS 2020, LNCS 12527, pp. 3–28, 2021.
https://doi.org/10.1007/978-3-030-68110-4_1

- "Network Traffic Classification Using WiFi Sensing," by Junye Li, Deepak Mishra and Aruna Seneviratne [249]
- "Performance Evaluation of the Packet Aggregation Mechanism of an N-GREEN Metro Network," by Node Tulin Atmaca, Amira Kamli, Godlove Suila Kuaban and Tadeusz Czachorski [21]
- "Random Neural Network for Lightweight Attack Detection in the IoT," by Kasia Filus, Joanna Domanska and Erol Gelenbe [4]
- "Contact Holdups and Their Impact for Overlay Delay Tolerant Networks," by Ricardo Lent [2]
- "The Random Neural Network as a Bonding Model for Software Vulnerability Prediction," by Kasia Filus, Miltiadis Siavvas, Joanna Domanska and Erol Gelenbe [3].

The next session on Computer System Performance Optimization was chaired by Dr Giuliano Casale of Imperial College London (UK), and consisted of the following papers:

- "Non-Neutrality With Users Deciding Differentiation: A Satisfying Option?" by Anne Kieffer, Patrick Maillé and Bruno Tuffin [234]
- "Measuring Performance of Fault Management in a Legacy System: An Alarm System Study," by Juri Tomak and Sergei Gorlatch [279]
- "Demonstration of SHAMan: a flexible framework for auto-tuning HPC systems," by Sophie Robert, Soraya Zertal, Philippe Couve [266].

and was followed by a session on Network and System Optimization which was chaired by Dr Josu Doncel of the University of the Basque Country (Spain), comprized of the following four papers:

- "QUIC Throughput and Fairness over Dual Connectivity," by David Hasselquist, Christoffer Lindström, Nikita Korzhitskii, Niklas Carlsson and Andrei Gurtov [226]
- "Hypothesis-based Comparison of IPv6 and IPv4 Path Distances," by David Hasselquist, Christian Wahl, Otto Bergdal and Niklas Carlsson [227]
- "LPWAN Gateway Location Selection Using Modified K-Dominating Set Algorithm," by Krzysztof Grochla, Adam Glos, Zbigniew Łaskarzewski, Jarosław Miszczak, Konrad Połys, Anna Strzoda, Artur Frankiewicz and Przemysław Sadowski [225]
- "Toolset for Run-time Dataset Collection of Deep-scene Information," by Gustav Aaro, Daniel Roos and Niklas Carlsson [5].

Finally, a last session also on Network and System Optimization, was chaired by Prof. Ivona Brandic, Technical University of Vienna (Austria), and included the following papers:

- "Measurement and Modeling of Tumblr Traffic Rachel Mclean", by Mehdi Karamollahi and Carey Williamson [251]
- "Tail Latency in Datacenter Networks," by Asaad Althoubi, Reem Alshahrani and Hassan Peyravi [18]

– "Balanced Gray Codes for Reduction of Bit-Flips in Phase Change Memories," by Arockia David Roy Kulandai, Stella J, John Rose and Thomas Schwarz [246].

2 Erol Gelenbe's Research Contributions and Analytical Models

Erol Gelenbe, who organized the 2020 MASCOTS events, was born in 1945 and is known for wide ranging pioneering work on analytical models for computer systems and networks, such the stability analysis of random access channels [63,64], the delays introduced by distributed system and database synchronization and uncertainties in the values of the data [37,140,195], the queueing effects of mass memories [144], queueing network analysis methods for packet networks [189,190], diffusion approximations applied to network admission control and the analysis of packet delay in wireless multi-hop networks [99,175], and the use of probability models to make optimal or good decisions in multi-path routing and task scheduling [36,92].

In the past much of Erol's work contributed to analytical modelling [70,71,117,128,145,153,176,233,259], and in particular he invented a new class of product form queueing networks called G-Networks [90,107,108,154,196].

Another interesting development has been Erol's incursion work into chemical master equations [102], and gene regulatory networks [100]. Another link was made to adversarial populations such as viruses in computer networks [97] and to particles in non-homogenous media [11,106], regarding the time it takes and the required energy for a set of particles to attain a designated target related to packets that travel in large multi-hop sensor networks [9,98].

However, his work shifted to machine learning very early on, well ahead of the field in general [40,42,133,228,232], including with regard to developing educational programs in regarding neural networks and machine learning [215].

2.1 The Random Neural Network

The Random Neural Network (RNN) is an analytical model for spiking neural networks [86,89,125,126,143,178], and was introduced in [76,85].

It is a biologically inspired model of spiking networks which has a recurrent structure that incorporates feedback loops [127]. It has been proved to be a universal approximator for continuous and bounded functions [177,178], and different gradient descent based learning algorithms have been suggested for the RNN [27,88,141,278].

RNNs have found application in many different areas, including combinatorial optimization [78,80], to process medical images [125], for adaptive video compression [42,200], to evaluate user satisfaction regarding network quality of service [267], as a denial of service attack detector [255], and to build virtual or enhanced reality systems [79,230,231]. It was used to evaluate voice and video quality [216,265], and for energy management in buildings [16]. RNNs were used to control downlink traffic in mobile telephony systems systems [14], for adaptive routing in packet networks [105, 133], for network intrusion detection [264], and to optimally schedule the delivery of video content [217].

Other applications can be found in [6–8, 15, 19, 20, 41, 42, 134, 148–150, 229] and several other sources can be found in [90].

In recent years new applications were developed in web search [272, 274] as well as for network routing using deep learning [273].

2.2   Auctions

Auctions have been conveniently used in web sites to advertise goods as well as for allocating resources in networks [50, 270]. In my list of unusual analytic results, let me mention his work where he considers an (economic) market composed of N English auctions [104] where customers arrive according to a random process, select some auction and bid for a product with a probability that may depend on the current value that has been attained by that product, leave the marketplace if they are successful in purchasing the product, and may go to some other auction (or may leave the market) if they are unsuccessful. This analysis leads to a closed form expression for the equilibrium prices of all the products in the market.

Variants of this model were analyzed [235] and different forms of bidding were studied in subsequent papers [139, 205]. Detailed work was conducted on the behaviour of a single auction, related not just to the price that is achieved, but also to the amount of time that is spent by the bidder or buyer to achieve a successful result [204, 280].

In recent work, these results were used to establish contracts for selling bandwidth or other resources between users of mobile networks [56] and for evaluating relevant metrics such as trustworthiness in social networks [57, 59]. Generally this work has shown that the early analytical results regarding auctions [94] can lead to many interesting results that are useful to the study of modern mobile networks [54–61].

2.3   Gene Regulatory Networks

Erol's work on Gene Regulatory Networks (GRN) [101] based on analytical models resulted from a visit to the Genopole in Evry, Paris, so as to develop a basic model about GRNs [96]. This initial work gave rise to the detection of anomalies in genetic data that can predispose to certain diseases [236, 238, 239, 243] using the GRN model to represent gene interactions and their time scale, and then estimating their parameters from normal micro-array data [240, 241] using machine learning a learning [143]. After the model's identification is complete, it is used to compare with other micro-array data, to determine whether the new data shows propensity for some disease such as cancer [237, 242]. Another line of research also arose [262] regarding protein interaction networks, and the study of the underlying chemistry [103].

2.4   Performance Modeling Motivated by New Tendencies in Networks and the Cloud

There is an increasing tendency to use Software Defined Networks (SDN) as a means to specify and control routing and quality of service in networks. However, it has shown been that though these systems provide software driven control of packet networks, they also impose frequent changes to traffic rates carried by different nodes, as well as changes in the topology of the paths that are being used [60]. Thus the usual steady-state analysis of networks loses most of its relevance since the network is constantly operating in the transient regime [46].

Indeed it has been shown that the average packet delays and node utilizations that reflect the steady-state are far from the values that these important performance metrics take in reality during the frequent state changes of the network [43], so that queueing analysis requires further attention [259], and can be used effectively to optimize multi-node packet networks that use SDN [45].

Another area which raises major performance issues and where steady-state behaviour needs to be replaced by real-time optimization techniques, including energy consumption [28], relates to the Grid and Cloud [35,245]. Thus research which deals with fast and optimal allocation of tasks to machines [162,203] has been applied to the design of a practical adaptive real-time scheduler for Fog and Cloud servers [32,206,281,283].

3   Cybersecurity

Erol's work on Cybersecurity [77] started through work on Distributed Denial of Service (DDoS) Attacks, leading to the idea of using CPN as a way to counter-attack by tracing DDoS traffic upstream and use CPN's ACK packets to provide drop commands regarding the attacking traffic at routers upstream from the target of the attack [171,256]. It was also tested on a large network to detect worm attacks and reroute connections by avoiding the nodes that are infected [268,269]. More algorithmic security issues were also considered [287], and further work was conducted on mobile network storms [12,218,219].

Starting with the EU FP7 NEMESYS Research and Innovation Project [135, 136,220], Erol's team has studied how one can improve the cybersecurity of mobile networks and wired networks, and how security interacts with Quality of Service (QoS) [224,260] and energy consumption [73]. This work has also been integrated into subsequent EU FP7 and H2020 projects which have addressed the security of E-Health systems [252,277] and home IoT services [22,39].

In the investigations concerning storms in mobile networks [12,72] Erol and his team have shown the important result that such attacks, which create a flurry of repeated attempts to establish mobile connections and bring down both the network's bandwidth and Cloud services related to mobile management, can be mitigated by an appropriate choice of time-outs in the LTE management algorithms, as well as by an optimal setting of counters which block calls when they produce repeated calls which exceed the counter value [220].

More recently, cybersecurity issues have been examined from different perspectives for the Internet of Things (IoT) [26,53,120,129,187] as part of the EU H2020 SerIoT project. The security of the transfer of data among geographically distributed European e-Health systems was also studied in the context of the EU H2020 KONFIDO project [187,253,276,277].

Security vulnerabilities in software have been studied in [275] while other recent work relates to secure IoT gateways for application such as smart homes in the context of the EU H2020 GHOST project [39]. In the context of IoT devices and gateways, Erol's work has also addressed energy limited sensor devices which can be subject to battery attacks [118], as well as deep learning techniques to detect Denial of Service Attacks against IoT devices and networks in general, especially using the Random Neural Network [4,26,33,34,62,129].

4   Energy Packet Networks (EPN)

The need to assure a sustainable usage of energy in information and communication technology (ICT) [122] had motivated Erol's work analyses the link between the random nature of harvested energy, and the random nature of the data collection activities of a wireless sensor [116], leading to an original analysis of "synchronisation" between the two resources that in this case enable wireless communications: the data packets and the energy packets, first studied in a paper published in 2014 [115].

However in some earlier work he had introduced of a novel way to view energy as a "packet-based" resource that can be modelled in discrete units which he called Energy Packets [109,110]. While Ohm's Law in the complex variable domain is a good way to analyse the steady flow of electricity in electric networks, at a nanoscopic level, say at the level of the flow of individual electrons, both the stochastic nature of the sources and the physical non-homogeneities which govern the energy transmission medium (e.g. metal) imply that different models may be needed; thus Erol recently proposed a stochastic flow model that addresses the conveyance of energy and information by the same particles [114].

At a more macroscopic level, when one deals with intermittent sources of energy so that energy must be stored in batteries or other storage units (such as compressed air cylinders) that can include conversion losses to and from the electrical storage, and energy usage itself is intermittent, models descended from G-Networks [87,90] become useful [10,111,113].

This approach has raised interesting questions about how such large networks may be analysed in the presence of flow of energy and flow of work [115,123] and some recent interesting results regarding "product form solutions" for such multi-hop networks have also been obtained [179]. However, Erol's concern for energy consumption for communications actually started a decade earlier [93,157] in the context of Wireless Ad-Hoc Networks, contributing a technique to extend overall life of a multi-hop network by using paths that have the most energy in reserve, i.e. the most full batteries. This work was pursued in papers related to network routing and admission control based on energy considerations

[172, 174, 174, 181, 197, 198, 209, 271] and this resulted in a practical design for an energy aware routing protocol.

His research group's involvement with energy consumption in information technology was also developed through their participation in EU Fit4Green Project which resulted in a widely cited paper [28] regarding the energy optimisation of Cloud Computing servers [132] and software systems [261].

Although energy consumption by ICT is an important issue, it must be viewed as a compromise between the two aspects, where a reduction in energy consumption in the manner a specific system is being operated, for instance as a function of workload or of workload distribution, is "paid for" by a loss in performance or an increase in the response times experienced by users. This issue has been studied in several of Erol's recent papers [158, 159, 162, 261].

Similar problems arise in wireless communications, but of course at far lower levels of energy consumption. Here the purpose is to minimise the amount of energy consumed per correctly received packet or bit. Indeed, in the wireless case, increasing the transmission power is often possible. This will overcome noise, but it has the opposite (negative) effect if *all* cooperating transceivers raise their power level, resulting in greater wireless signal *interference* and hence larger error probabilities for all parties. This in turn will *lengthen* the time needed to correctly receive a data unit, and hence will also increase the net energy consumed per correctly received bit or packet [132, 138, 186, 257].

5   Autonomic Communications and CPN

Intrigued by the adaptive control of computer systems and networks [24, 25, 151, 152, 155, 156, 188, 228, 263], to deal both with the very large size of the systems encountered in computer science, the imperfection of the dynamic models that describe them, and the very large size of these dynamic models themselves, Erol has long been attracted to techniques from adaptive and natural computation [112].

His main excursion in this field in the last twenty years has been the concept of the Cognitive Packet Network (CPN), which uses the RNN model quite heavily. CPN was first described in [213] as a network routing algorithm that would use paths in a network with the best observed quality of service, and hence attempt to improve the network's QoS as a whole.

However, CPN proceeded by acquiring on-line data about the success of recent decisions and actions, in order to privilege the choice of the best among them, to imrove future outcomes [194]. probes that gathered intelligence about the best paths, and the used the practical outcome of the choices that had been made, to select the best network path [164]. It was also observed that these ideas could be used to make the best choices regarding the means to protect oneself and react to Denial of Service attacks [171].

The implementation and experimentation with these ideas was summarized in an overview paper [105]. However these results also inspired further work regarding named data networking where the addresses correspond to data items rather than to IP addresses [17]. Further work has exploited this approach to the detection and mitigation of attacks in large-scale networks [124].

This in a recent economics oriented paper in the Proc. Indian Acad. Sci. Sadanha journal on "Service Provider Strategies in Telecommunications Markets: Analytical and Simulation Analysis" [38] to appear in January 2021, points to Erol's seminal work from 2001 on reinforcement learning based simulation agents, stating that *"It is typical in discrete event simulations for the designer of a simulation to pre-specify all possible transitions and closely control events, assuming fixed behavior. However, agents represent entities in the real world such as business organizations and individuals which do have the intelligence to adapt their behavior depending on the outcome of events, and take into account temporal changes in the environment. Hence, an ABM can be constructed with reinforcement learning, in which agents can be endowed with a form of intelligence. With this approach, agents learn from their observations about the simulation environment and the experience of other agents, and rely minimally on centralized control as described in [194]. In our model, the agents are passive and do not learn and react to feedback gathered from repeated simulations. Future research with learning agents that incorporate adaptive behavior of agents depending on the ever-changing data localization regime is needed."*

Starting with early work [81,131,185] that describes the Cognitive Packet Network (CPN) [105], a routing algorithm for networks with reinforcement learning that offers Quality of Service (QoS), a pioneering effort was conducted [52,95] in a clear break with traditional research that uses modeling and simulation [82–84,182,199]. Related work [194,258] suggests that decisions that have a "natural" appearance could also be incorporated in a similar manner into simulation systems where complex agent interactions occur, and agents take decisions based on their collective best interest. Similar questions have also been discussed in the context of search algorithms in dangerous environments [121].

The basic idea of CPN as it relates to networks, which has been amply tested in many experiments [163,164,167,168,170], is to use probe or "smart" Cognitive Packets (CPs) to search for paths and to measure QoS while the network is in operation. The search for paths is run via Reinforcement Learning using a Random Neural Network, based on the QoS objective of goal pursued by the end user. The CPs furnish information to the end user about the QoS offered by different paths, and in particular those actually being used by the end user, but in CPN it is the end user, which may be a representative decision maker for a QoS Class, that actually decides to switch to a new path or select a given path [105,157,169]. An extension to CPN that uses genetic algorithms to construct hitherto untested paths based on predicted QoS was also proposed [250].

More recent work has considered CPN for specific applications such as [147] web access applications where uplinks require short response times, while downloads require high bandwidth and low packet loss for video. Other recent work addresses the QoS of Voice [282], while recent work develops CPN for routing in secure IoT networks [124] and for managing Fog servers [74,75].

CPN was also used for energy minimizing routing [172,173], as well as admission control [191] and denial of service defense [130,171]. Adaptive techniques for wireless sensor networks are discussed in [180,183,184,254], and adaptivity for secondary memory systems is analyzed in [288].

6 Emergency Management Systems

Erol was personally affected by the major earthquake that took place near Istanbul, in Izmit and Yalova. He was at the sites in order to try to locate two family members who had gone missing and had perished during the event. The rudimentary technology used to seek, locate and try to evacuate the victims meant that only rudimentary means were used by rescuers who flocked to the area in the days after the earthquake. Thus Erol has devoted time to understanding research on emergency management technologies [31,210,212], and developing relevant models and algorithms [48,49,137,211], many of which overlap with planning in military operations [146,207,208]. He has investigated simulations [66,142,146] to represent the fast changing emergency events, developing a novel agent based simulator DBES [51] for evacuation simulation. Distributed techniques that do not require expensive infrastructures are needed [68], and he has organised several workshops in this area [65,192,193].

Optimal rescuer allocation [69,201,202], and best matches between available resources and the emergency situation have been studied, as well as disruption tolerant techniques for robust communications in emergencies [223], together with relevant modelling techniques [67,221,222,247,284]. Autonomic routing techniques based on CPN with directional techniques have been studied to manage evacuees without centralised decision agents [29,29,30,119,244].

7 Conclusions

Finally, we would like to recall the International Symposia on Computer and Information Sciences (ISCIS) with a hopeful note for the future regarding these series of conferences were started by Erol 35 years ago to provide the Turkish academic community in Computer Science with a means to disseminate their research and meet their international peers through quality publications that were refereed and published internationally.

Since 1998, the venues have included many successful locations both in Turkey and abroad:

- 32. ISCIS 2018-2: Poznan, Poland [47],
- 31. ISCIS 2018-1: London, UK [214],
- 30. ISCIS 2015: [13],
- 29. ISCIS 2014: Krakow, Poland [44],
- 28. ISCIS 2013: Paris, France [161],
- 27. ISCIS 2012: Paris, France [160],
- 26. ISCIS 2011: London, UK [165],

- 25. ISCIS 2010: London, UK [166],
- 24. ISCIS 2009: North Cyprus [1],
- 23. ISCIS 2008: Istanbul, Turkey,
- 22. ISCIS 2007: Ankara, Turkey,
- 21. ISCIS 2006: Istanbul, Turkey [248],
- 20. ISCIS 2005: Istanbul, Turkey [286],
- 19. ISCIS 2004: Antalya, Turkey [23],
- 18. ISCIS 2003: Antalya, Turkey [285],
- 17. ISCIS 2002: Orlando, Florida, USA [91],
- 15. ISCIS 2000: Istanbul, Turkey,
- 14. ISCIS 1999: Ege University, Turkey,
- 13. ISCIS 1998: Ankara, Turkey.

We therefore conclude by indicating that we look forward to further conferences of the quality of Mascots 2020, and more in the ISCIS series, as we look hopefully to the years 2021 and 2022 in the post-covid world.

References

1. The 24th International Symposium on Computer and Information Sciences, ISCIS 2009, North Cyprus, 14–16 September 2009. IEEE (2009)
2. Lent, R.: Contact holdups and their impact for overlay delay tolerant networks. In: Calzarossa, M.C., et al. (eds.) MASCOTS 2020. LNCS, vol. 12527, pp. 92–101. Springer, Cham (2021)
3. Filus, K., Siavvas, M., Domanska, J., Gelenbe, E.: The random neural network as a bonding model for software vulnerability prediction. In: Calzarossa, M.C., et al. (eds.) MASCOTS 2020. LNCS, vol. 12527, pp. 102–116. Springer, Cham (2021)
4. Filus, K., Domanska, J., Gelenbe, E.: A random neural network for attack detection. In: Calzarossa, M.C., et al. (eds.) MASCOTS 2020. LNCS, vol. 12527, pp. 79–91. Springer, Cham (2021)
5. Aaro, G., Roos, D., Carlsson, N.: Toolset for run-time dataset collection of deep-scene information. In: Calzarossa, M.C., et al. (eds.) MASCOTS 2020. LNCS, vol. 12527, pp. 224–236. Springer, Cham (2021)
6. Abdelbaki, H., Gelenbe, E., El-Khamy, S.E.: Random neural network decoder for error correcting codes. In: International Joint Conference on Neural Networks, IJCNN 1999, vol. 5, pp. 3241–3245. IEEE (1999)
7. Abdelbaki, H., Gelenbe, E., Kocak, T.: Matched neural filters for EMI based mine detection. In: International Joint Conference on Neural Networks, IJCNN 1999, vol. 5, pp. 3236–3240. IEEE (1999)
8. Abdelbaki, H., Gelenbe, E., Koçak, T., El-Khamy, S.E.: Random neural network filter for land mine detection. In: Proceedings of the Sixteenth National Radio Science Conference, NRSC 1999, pp. C43–1. IEEE (1999)
9. Abdelrahman, O.H., Gelenbe, E.: Search in non-homogenous random environments? ACM SIGMETRICS Per. Eval. Rev. **39**(3), 37–39 (2011)
10. Abdelrahman, O.H., Gelenbe, E.: Packet delay and energy consumption in non-homogeneous networks. Comput. J. **55**(8), 950–964 (2012)
11. Abdelrahman, O.H., Gelenbe, E.: Time and energy in team-based search. Phys. Rev. E **87**(3), 032125 (2013)

12. Abdelrahman, O.H., Gelenbe, E.: Signalling storms in 3g mobile networks. In: 2014 IEEE International Conference on Communications, ICC 2014, Sydney, Australia, 10–14 June 2014, pp. 1017–1022. IEEE (2014). https://doi.org/10.1109/ICC.2014.6883453

13. Abdelrahman, O.H., Gelenbe, E., Gorbil, G., Lent, R. (eds.): Information Sciences and Systems 2015. LNEE, vol. 363. Springer, Cham (2016). https://doi.org/10.1007/978-3-319-22635-4

14. Adeel, A., Larijani, H., Ahmadinia, A.: Random neural network based cognitive engines for adaptive modulation and coding in LTE downlink systems. Comput. Electr. Eng. **57**, 336–350 (2017). https://doi.org/10.1016/j.compeleceng.2016.11.005

15. Aguilar, J., Gelenbe, E.: Task assignment and transaction clustering heuristics for distributed systems. Inf. Sci. **97**(1), 199–219 (1997)

16. Ahmad, J., Larijani, H., Emmanuel, R., Mannion, M., Javed, A., Phillipson, M.: Energy demand prediction through novel random neural network predictor for large non-domestic buildings. In: 2017 Annual IEEE International Systems Conference, SysCon 2017, Montreal, QC, Canada, 24–27 April 2017, pp. 1–6. IEEE (2017). https://doi.org/10.1109/SYSCON.2017.7934803

17. Akinwande, O., Gelenbe, E.: A reinforcement learning approach to adaptive forwarding in named data networking. In: Czachórski, T., Gelenbe, E., Grochla, K., Lent, R. (eds.) ISCIS 2018. CCIS, vol. 935, pp. 211–219. Springer, Cham (2018). https://doi.org/10.1007/978-3-030-00840-6_23

18. Asaad Althoubi, R.A., Peyravi, H.: Tail latency in datacenter networks. In: Calzarossa, M.C., et al. (eds.) MASCOTS 2020. LNCS, vol. 12527, pp. 254–272. Springer, Cham (2021)

19. Atalay, V., Gelenbe, E.: Parallel algorithm for colour texture generation using the random neural network model. Int. J. Pattern Recogn. Artif. Intell. **6**(02n03), 437–446 (1992)

20. Atalay, V., Gelenbe, E., Yalabik, N.: The random neural network model for texture generation. Int. J. Pattern Recogn. Artif. Intell. **6**(01), 131–141 (1992)

21. Atmaca, T., Kamli, A., Kuaban, G.S., Czachorski, T.: Performance evaluation of the packet aggregation mechanism of an N-green metro network node. In: Calzarossa, M.C., et al. (eds.) MASCOTS 2020. LNCS, vol. 12527, pp. 62–78. Springer, Cham (2021)

22. Augusto-Gonzalez, J., et al.: From internet of threats to internet of things: a cyber security architecture for smart homes. In: 2019 IEEE 24th International Workshop on Computer Aided Modeling and Design of Communication Links and Networks (CAMAD), pp. 1–6. IEEE (2019)

23. Aykanat, C., Dayar, T., Körpeoğlu, İ. (eds.): ISCIS 2004. LNCS, vol. 3280. Springer, Heidelberg (2004). https://doi.org/10.1007/b101749

24. Badel, M., Gelenbe, E., Leroudier, J., Potier, D., Lenfant, J.: Adaptive optimization of the performance of a virtual memory computer. ACM SIGMETRICS Perf. Eval. Rev. **3**(4), 188 (1974)

25. Badel, M., Gelenbe, E., Leroudier, J., Potier, D.: Adaptive optimization of a time-sharing system's performance. Proc. IEEE **63**(6), 958–965 (1975)

26. Baldini, G., et al.: IoT network risk assessment and mitigation: the SerIoT approach (2020)

27. Basterrech, S., Mohamed, S., Rubino, G., Soliman, M.A.: Levenberg-Marquardt training algorithms for random neural networks. Comput. J. **54**(1), 125–135 (2011). https://doi.org/10.1093/comjnl/bxp101

28. Berl, A., et al.: Energy-efficient cloud computing. Comput. J. **53**(7), 1045–1051 (2010)
29. Bi, H., Desmet, A., Gelenbe, E.: Routing emergency evacuees with cognitive packet networks. In: Gelenbe, E., Lent, R. (eds.) Information Sciences and Systems 2013. LNEE, vol. 264, pp. 295–303. Springer, Cham (2013). https://doi.org/10.1007/978-3-319-01604-7_29
30. Bi, H., Gelenbe, E.: A cooperative emergency navigation framework using mobile cloud computing. In: Czachórski, T., Gelenbe, E., Lent, R. (eds.) Information Sciences and Systems 2014, pp. 41–48. Springer, Cham (2014). https://doi.org/10.1007/978-3-319-09465-6_5
31. Bi, H., Gelenbe, E.: A survey of algorithms and systems for evacuating people in confined spaces. Electronics **8**(6), 711 (2019)
32. Brun, O., Wang, L., Gelenbe, E.: Big data for autonomic intercontinental overlays. IEEE J. Sel. Areas Commun. **34**(3), 575–583 (2016)
33. Brun, O., Yin, Y., Augusto-Gonzalez, J., Ramos, M., Gelenbe, E.: IoT attack detection with deep learning. In: ISCIS Security Workshop (2018)
34. Brun, O., Yin, Y., Gelenbe, E.: Deep learning with dense random neural network for detecting attacks against IoT-connected home environments. Proc. Comput. Sci. **134**, 458–463 (2018)
35. Buyya, R., et al.: A manifesto for future generation cloud computing: research directions for the next decade. ACM Comput. Surv. (CSUR) **51**(5), 1–38 (2019)
36. Chabridon, S., Gelenbe, E.: Scheduling of distributed tasks for survivability of the application. Inf. Sci. **97**(1&2), 179–198 (1997). https://doi.org/10.1016/S0020-0255(96)00177-6
37. Chesnais, A., Gelenbe, E., Mitrani, I.: On the modeling of parallel access to shared data. Commun. ACM **26**(3), 196–202 (1983)
38. Chouhan, A.S., Sridhar, V., Rao, S.: Service provider strategies in telecommunications markets: analytical and simulation analysis. Sadanha **46**(1), 2333–2335 (2021)
39. Collen, A., et al.: GHOST - safe-guarding home IoT environments with personalised real-time risk control. In: Gelenbe, E., et al. (eds.) Euro-CYBERSEC 2018. CCIS, vol. 821, pp. 68–78. Springer, Cham (2018). https://doi.org/10.1007/978-3-319-95189-8_7
40. Cramer, C., Gelenbe, E.: Video quality and traffic QoS in learning-based sub-sampled and receiver-interpolated video sequences. IEEE J. Sel. Areas Commun. **18**(2), 150–167 (2000). https://doi.org/10.1109/49.824788
41. Cramer, C., Gelenbe, E., Bakircioglu, H.: Video compression with random neural networks. In: International Workshop on Neural Networks for Identification, Control, Robotics, and Signal/Image Processing. Proceedings, pp. 476–484. IEEE (1996)
42. Cramer, C., Gelenbe, E., Bakircloglu, H.: Low bit-rate video compression with neural networks and temporal subsampling. Proc. IEEE **84**(10), 1529–1543 (1996)
43. Czachorski, T., Gelenbe, E., Kuaban, G.S., Marek, D.: A time-dependent routing model of software defined networks. In: The Second International Workshop on Stochastic Modeling and Applied Research of Technology: SMARTY 2020, 16–20 August 2020. Karelian Research Center, Russian Academy of Sciences, Petrozavodsk (2020)
44. Czachórski, T., Gelenbe, E., Lent, R. (eds.): Information Sciences and Systems 2014. Springer, Cham (2014). https://doi.org/10.1007/978-3-319-09465-6

45. Czachorski, T., Gelenbe, E., Marek, D.: Software defined network dynamics via diffusions. In: Calzarossa, M.C., et al. (eds.) MASCOTS 2020. LNCS, vol. 12527, pp. 29–47. Springer, Cham (2021)
46. Czachorski, T., Gelenbe, E., Sulla, K.G., Marek, D.: Transient behaviour of a network router. In: 2020 43rd International Conference on Telecommunications and Signal Processing (TSP), pp. 1–5. IEEE (2020)
47. Czachórski, T., Gelenbe, E., Grochla, K., Lent, R. (eds.): ISCIS 2018. CCIS, vol. 935. Springer, Cham (2018). https://doi.org/10.1007/978-3-030-00840-6
48. Desmet, A., Gelenbe, E.: Graph and analytical models for emergency evacuation. In: 2013 IEEE International Conference on Pervasive Computing and Communications Workshops (PERCOM Workshops), pp. 523–527. IEEE (2013)
49. Desmet, A., Gelenbe, E.: Interoperating infrastructures in emergencies. In: Gelenbe, E., Lent, R. (eds.) Computer and Information Sciences III, pp. 123–130. Springer, London (2013). https://doi.org/10.1007/978-1-4471-4594-3_13
50. Di Ferdinando, A., Lent, R., Gelenbe, E.: A framework for autonomic networked auctions. In: Proceedings of the 2007 Workshop on INnovative SERvice Technologies, pp. 1–10 (2007)
51. Dimakis, N., Filippoupolitis, A., Gelenbe, E.: Distributed building evacuation simulator for smart emergency management. Comput. J. **53**(9), 1384–1400 (2010)
52. Dobson, S., et al.: A survey of autonomic communications. ACM Trans. Auton. Adap. Syst. (TAAS) **1**(2), 223–259 (2006)
53. Domanska, J., Gelenbe, E., Czachorski, T., Drosou, A., Tzovaras, D.: Research and innovation action for the security of the internet of things: the SerIoT project. In: Gelenbe, E., et al. (eds.) Euro-CYBERSEC 2018. CCIS, vol. 821, pp. 101–118. Springer, Cham (2018). https://doi.org/10.1007/978-3-319-95189-8_10
54. Du, J., Gelenbe, E., Jiang, C., Han, Z., Ren, Y.: Auction-based data transaction in mobile networks: data allocation design and performance analysis. IEEE Trans. Mobile Comput. **19**(5), 1040–1055 (2019)
55. Du, J., Gelenbe, E., Jiang, C., Zhang, H., Han, Z., Ren, Y.: Data transaction modeling in mobile networks: contract mechanism and performance analysis. In: GLOBECOM 2017-2017 IEEE Global Communications Conference, pp. 1–6. IEEE (2017)
56. Du, J., Gelenbe, E., Jiang, C., Zhang, H., Ren, Y.: Contract design for traffic offloading and resource allocation in heterogeneous ultra-dense networks. IEEE J. Sel. Areas Commun. **35**(11), 2457–2467 (2017)
57. Du, J., Gelenbe, E., Jiang, C., Zhang, H., Ren, Y., Poor, H.V.: Peer prediction-based trustworthiness evaluation and trustworthy service rating in social networks. IEEE Trans. Inf. Foren. Sec. **14**(6), 1582–1594 (2018)
58. Du, J., Jiang, C., Gelenbe, E., Han, Z., Ren, Y., Guizani, M.: Networked data transaction in mobile networks: a prediction-based approach using auction. In: 2018 14th International Wireless Communications & Mobile Computing Conference (IWCMC), pp. 201–206. IEEE (2018)
59. Du, J., Jiang, C., Gelenbe, E., Xu, L., Li, J., Ren, Y.: Distributed data privacy preservation in IoT applications. IEEE Wirel. Commun. **25**(6), 68–76 (2018)
60. Du, J., Jiang, C., Gelenbe, E., Zhang, H., Ren, Y.: Traffic offloading in software defined ultra-dense networks. In: Ultra-Dense Networks: Principles and Applications, p. 164 (2020)
61. Du, J., Jiang, C., Gelenbe, E., Zhang, H., Ren, Y., Quek, T.Q.: Double auction mechanism design for video caching in heterogeneous ultra-dense networks. IEEE Trans. Wireless Commun. **18**(3), 1669–1683 (2019)

62. Evmorfos, S., Vlachodimitropoulos, G., Bakalos, N., Gelenbe, E.: Neural network architectures for the detection of SYN flood attacks in IoT systems. In: Proceedings of the 13th ACM International Conference on PErvasive Technologies Related to Assistive Environments, pp. 1–4. No. 69. ACM (2020). https://doi.org/10.1145/3389189.3398000

63. Fayolle, G., Gelenbe, E., Labetoulle, J.: Stability and optimal control of the packet switching broadcast channel. J. ACM (JACM) **24**(3), 375–386 (1977)

64. Fayolle, G., Gelenbe, E., Labetoulle, J., Bastin, D.: The stability problem of broadcast packet switching computer networks. Acta Informatica **4**(1), 49–53 (1974)

65. Filippoupolitis, A., et al.: PerNEM 2014: the fourth international workshop on pervasive networks for emergency management, 2014-welcome and committees welcome message from the PernEM'14 co-chairs. In: Proceedings PerCOM 2014 (2014)

66. Filippoupolitis, A., et al.: Distributed agent-based building evacuation simulator (2012)

67. Filippoupolitis, A., Gorbil, G., Gelenbe, E.: Spatial computers for emergency management. In: 2011 Fifth IEEE Conference on Self-Adaptive and Self-Organizing Systems Workshops, pp. 61–66. IEEE (2011)

68. Filippoupolitis, A., Gorbil, G., Gelenbe, E.: Pervasive emergency support systems for building evacuation. In: 2012 IEEE International Conference on Pervasive Computing and Communications Workshops, pp. 525–527. IEEE (2012)

69. Filippoupolitis, A., Hey, L., Loukas, G., Gelenbe, E., Timotheou, S.: Emergency response simulation using wireless sensor networks. In: AMBI-SYS 2008: Proceedings of the 1st International Conference on Ambient Media and Systems, pp. 1–7, February 2008

70. Fourneau, J.M., Gelenbe, E.: G-networks with adders. Future Internet **9**(3), 34 (2017)

71. Fourneau, J., Gelenbe, E., Suros, R.: G-networks with multiple classes of negative and positive customers. Theor. Comput. Sci. **155**(1), 141–156 (1996). https://doi.org/10.1016/0304-3975(95)00018-6

72. Francois, F., Abdelrahman, O.H., Gelenbe, E.: Impact of signaling storms on energy consumption and latency of LTE user equipment. In: 2015 IEEE 17th International Conference on High Performance Computing and Communications, 2015 IEEE 7th International Symposium on Cyberspace Safety and Security, and 2015 IEEE 12th International Conference on Embedded Software and Systems, pp. 1248–1255. IEEE (2015)

73. Francois, F., Abdelrahman, O.H., Gelenbe, E.: Towards assessment of energy consumption and latency of LTE UEs during signaling storms. In: Abdelrahman, O.H., Gelenbe, E., Gorbil, G., Lent, R. (eds.) Information Sciences and Systems 2015. LNEE, vol. 363, pp. 45–55. Springer, Cham (2016). https://doi.org/10.1007/978-3-319-22635-4_4

74. Fröhlich, P., Gelenbe, E.: Optimal fog services placement in SDN IoT network using random neural networks and cognitive network map. In: Rutkowski, L., Scherer, R., Korytkowski, M., Pedrycz, W., Tadeusiewicz, R., Zurada, J.M. (eds.) ICAISC 2020. LNCS (LNAI), vol. 12415, pp. 78–89. Springer, Cham (2020). https://doi.org/10.1007/978-3-030-61401-0_8

75. Frohlich, P., Gelenbe, E., Nowak, M.P.: Smart SDN management of fog services. In: GIOTS 2020: Global IoT Summit 2020, IEEE Communications Society, Dubin, Ireland, 1–5 June 2020. TechRxiv (2020)

76. Gelenbe, E.: Réseaux neuronaux aléatoires stables. Comptes rendus de l'Académie des sciences. Série 2, Mécanique, Physique, Chimie, Sciences de l'univers, Sciences de la Terre **310**(3), 177–180 (1990)
77. Gelenbe, E.: Current research on cybersecurity in Europe. In: Gelenbe, E., et al. (eds.) Recent Cybersecurity Research in Europe: Proceedings of the 2018 ISCIS Security Workshop, Imperial College London. Lecture Notes CCIS No. 821. Springer (2018)
78. Gelenbe, E., Batty, F.: Minimum graph vertex covering with the random neural network. In: Computer Science and Operations Research, pp. 139–147. Pergamon, Amsterdam (1992)
79. Gelenbe, E., Hussain, K.F., Kaptan, V.: Simulating autonomous agents in augmented reality. J. Syst. Softw. **74**(3), 255–268 (2005)
80. Gelenbe, E., Koubi, V., Pekergin, F.: Dynamical random neural network approach to the traveling salesman problem. Proc. IEEE Syst. Man Cybern. Conf. **2**, 630–635 (1993)
81. Gelenbe, E., Lent, R.: Mobile ad-hoc cognitive packet networks. In: Proceedings of the IEEE ASWN, pp. 2–4 (2002)
82. Gelenbe, E.: A unified approach to the evaluation of a class of replacement algorithms. IEEE Trans. Comput. **100**(6), 611–618 (1973)
83. Gelenbe, E.: On approximate computer system models. J. ACM (JACM) **22**(2), 261–269 (1975)
84. Gelenbe, E.: Probabilistic models of computer systems. Acta Informatica **12**(4), 285–303 (1979)
85. Gelenbe, E.: Random neural networks with negative and positive signals and product form solution. Neural Comput. **1**(4), 502–510 (1989)
86. Gelenbe, E.: Stability of the random neural network model. Neural Comput. **2**(2), 239–247 (1990)
87. Gelenbe, E.: G-nets and learning recurrent random networks. In: Proceedings of the International Conference on Artificial Neural Networks, Brighton, England (1992)
88. Gelenbe, E.: Learning in the recurrent random neural network. Neural Comput. **5**(1), 154–164 (1993)
89. Gelenbe, E.: G-networks: a unifying model for neural and queueing networks. Ann. Oper. Res. **48**(5), 433–461 (1994)
90. Gelenbe, E.: The first decade of G-networks. Eur. J. Oper. Res. **126**(2), 231–232 (2000)
91. Gelenbe, E. (ed.): International Symposium on Computer and Information Sciences. CRC Press (2002)
92. Gelenbe, E.: Sensible decisions based on QoS. Comput. Manage. Sci. **1**(1), 1–14 (2003)
93. Gelenbe, E.: Quality of service in ad hoc networks. Ad Hoc Netw. **2**(3), 203 (2004)
94. Gelenbe, E.: Analysis of automated auctions. In: Levi, A., Savaş, E., Yenigün, H., Balcısoy, S., Saygın, Y. (eds.) ISCIS 2006. LNCS, vol. 4263, pp. 1–12. Springer, Heidelberg (2006). https://doi.org/10.1007/11902140_1
95. Gelenbe, E.: Users and services in intelligent networks. IEE Proc. Intell. Transp. Syst. **153**(3), 213–220 (2006)
96. Gelenbe, E.: Analytical solution of gene regulatory networks. In: 2007 IEEE International Fuzzy Systems Conference, pp. 1–6. IEEE (2007)
97. Gelenbe, E.: Dealing with software viruses: a biological paradigm. Inf. Secur. Tech. Rep. **12**(4), 242–250 (2007)

98. Gelenbe, E.: A diffusion model for packet travel time in a random multi-hop medium. ACM Trans. Sensor Netw. **3**(2), 10-es (2007)
99. Gelenbe, E.: A diffusion model for packet travel time in a random multihop medium. ACM Trans. Sensor Netw. (TOSN) **3**(2), 10 (2007)
100. Gelenbe, E.: Steady-state solution of probabilistic gene regulatory networks. Phys. Rev. E **76**(1), 031903 (2007)
101. Gelenbe, E.: Steady-state solution of probabilistic gene regulatory networks. Phys. Rev. E **76**(3), 031903 (2007)
102. Gelenbe, E.: Network of interacting synthetic molecules in steady-state. Proc. Royal Soc. A **464**, 2219–2228 (2008)
103. Gelenbe, E.: Network of interacting synthetic molecules in steady state. Proc. Royal Soc. A Math. Phys. Eng. Sci. **464**(2096), 2219–2228 (2008)
104. Gelenbe, E.: Analysis of single and networked auctions. ACM Trans. Internet Technol. (TOIT) **9**(2), 8 (2009)
105. Gelenbe, E.: Steps toward self-aware networks. Commun. ACM **52**(7), 66–75 (2009)
106. Gelenbe, E.: Search in unknown random environments. Phys. Rev. E **82**, 061112 (2010)
107. Gelenbe, E.: Special issue on G-networks and their applications. Perform. Eval. **67**, 415–416 (2010)
108. Gelenbe, E.: Introduction to the special issue on G-networks and the random neural network (2011)
109. Gelenbe, E.: Energy packet networks: adaptive energy management for the cloud. In: CloudCP 2012: Proceedings of the 2nd International Workshop on Cloud Computing Platforms, pp. 1–5. ACM (2012). https://doi.org/10.1145/2168697.2168698
110. Gelenbe, E.: Energy packet networks: ICT based energy allocation and storage. In: Rodrigues, J.J.P.C., Zhou, L., Chen, M., Kailas, A. (eds.) GreeNets 2011. LNICST, vol. 51, pp. 186–195. Springer, Heidelberg (2012). https://doi.org/10.1007/978-3-642-33368-2_16
111. Gelenbe, E.: Energy packet networks: smart electricity storage to meet surges in demand. In: Proceedings of the 5th International ICST Conference on Simulation Tools and Techniques, pp. 1–7. ICST (Institute for Computer Sciences, Social-Informatics and Telecommunications Engineering) (2012)
112. Gelenbe, E.: Natural computation. Comput. J. **55**(7), 848–851 (2012)
113. Gelenbe, E.: Adaptive management of energy packets. In: 2014 IEEE 38th International Computer Software and Applications Conference Workshops, pp. 1–6. IEEE (2014)
114. Gelenbe, E.: Error and energy when communicating with spins. In: 2014 IEEE Global Conference on Signal and Information Processing (GlobalSIP), pp. 784–787. IEEE, December 2014. https://doi.org/10.1109/GlobalSIP.2014.7032226
115. Gelenbe, E.: A sensor node with energy harvesting. ACM SIGMETRICS Perform. Eval. Rev. **42**(2), 37–39 (2014)
116. Gelenbe, E.: Synchronising energy harvesting and data packets in a wireless sensor. Energies **8**(1), 356–369 (2015). https://doi.org/10.3390/en8010356
117. Gelenbe, E.: Agreement in spins and social networks. ACM SIGMETRICS Perform. Eval. Rev. **44**(2), 15–17 (2016)
118. Gelenbe, E., Abdelrahman, O.H.: An energy packet network model for mobile networks with energy harvesting. Nonlinear Theory Appl. **9**(3), 1–15 (2018). https://doi.org/10.1587/nolta.9.1. IEICE 2018

119. Gelenbe, E., Bi, H.: Emergency navigation without an infrastructure. Sensors **14**(8), 15142–15162 (2014)
120. Gelenbe, E., Campegiani, P., Czachórski, T., Katsikas, S.K., Komnios, I., Romano, L., Tzovaras, D.: Security in computer and information sciences: First international ISCIS security workshop 2018, EURO-CYBERSEC 2018, London, UK, 26–27 February 2018, revised selected papers (2018)
121. Gelenbe, E., Cao, Y.: Autonomous search for mines. Eur. J. Oper. Res. **108**(2), 319–333 (1998)
122. Gelenbe, E., Caseau, Y.: The impact of information technology on energy consumption and carbon emissions. Ubiquity **2015**, 1–15 (2015)
123. Gelenbe, E., gce Ceran, E.T.: Central or distributed energy storage for processors with energy harvesting. In: The Fourth International Conference on Sustainable Internet and ICT for Sustainability. IEEE, April 2015
124. Gelenbe, E., Domanska, J., Frohlich, P., Nowak, M., Nowak, S.: Self-aware networks that optimize security, QoS and energy. Proc. IEEE **108**(7) (2020, accepted for publication)
125. Gelenbe, E., Feng, Y., Krishnan, K.R.R.: Neural network methods for volumetric magnetic resonance imaging of the human brain. Proc. IEEE **84**(10), 1488–1496 (1996)
126. Gelenbe, E., Feng, Y., Ranga, K., Krishnan, R.: Neural networks for volumetric MR imaging of the brain. In: International Workshop on Neural Networks for Identification, Control, Robotics, and Signal/Image Processing. Proceedings, pp. 194–202. IEEE (1996)
127. Gelenbe, E., Fourneau, J.M.: Random neural networks with multiple classes of signals. Neural Comput. **11**(4), 953–963 (1999). https://doi.org/10.1162/089976699300016520
128. Gelenbe, E., Fourneau, J.: G-networks with resets. Perform. Eval. **49**(1/4), 179–191 (2002)
129. Gelenbe, E., et al.: IoT network attack detection and mitigation. In: The 9th Mediterranean Conference on Embedded Computing (MECO 2020), Budva, Montenegro, 8–11 June 2020, pp. 1–6 (2020). https://ieeexplore.ieee.org/stamp/stamp.jsp?tp=&arnumber=9134241&isnumber . . .
130. Gelenbe, E., Gellman, M., Loukas, G.: An autonomic approach to denial of service defence. In: Sixth IEEE International Symposium on a World of Wireless Mobile and Multimedia Networks, WoWMoM 2005, pp. 537–541. IEEE (2005)
131. Gelenbe, E., Gellman, M., Su, P.: Self-awareness and adaptivity for quality of service. In: Proceedings of the Eighth IEEE International Symposium on Computers and Communication (ISCC 2003), pp. 3–9. IEEE (2003)
132. Gelenbe, E., Gesbert, D., Gunduz, D., Külah, H., Uysal-Biyikoglu, E.: Energy harvesting communication networks: optimization and demonstration (the e-crops project). In: 2013 24th Tyrrhenian International Workshop on Digital Communications-Green ICT (TIWDC), pp. 1–6. IEEE (2013)
133. Gelenbe, E., Ghanwani, A., Srinivasan, V.: Improved neural heuristics for multicast routing. IEEE J. Sel. Areas Commun. **15**(2), 147–155 (1997). https://doi.org/10.1109/49.552065
134. Gelenbe, E., Ghanwani, A., Srinivasan, V.: Improved neural heuristics for multicast routing. IEEE J. Sel. Areas Commun. **15**(2), 147–155 (1997)
135. Gelenbe, E., et al.: NEMESYS: enhanced network security for seamless service provisioning in the smart mobile ecosystem. In: Gelenbe, E., Lent, R. (eds.) Information Sciences and Systems 2013. LNEE, vol. 264, pp. 369–378. Springer, Cham (2013). https://doi.org/10.1007/978-3-319-01604-7_36

136. Gelenbe, E., et al.: Security for smart mobile networks: the NEMESYS approach. In: 2013 International Conference on Privacy and Security in Mobile Systems (PRISMS), pp. 1–8. IEEE (2013)

137. Gelenbe, E., Gorbil, G., Wu, F.J.: Emergency cyber-physical-human systems. In: 2012 21st International Conference on Computer Communications and Networks (ICCCN), pp. 1–7. IEEE (2012)

138. Gelenbe, E., Gündüz, D.: Optimum power level for communications with interference. In: 2013 24th Tyrrhenian International Workshop on Digital Communications-Green ICT (TIWDC), pp. 1–6. IEEE (2013)

139. Gelenbe, E., Györfi, L.: Performance of auctions and sealed bids. In: Bradley, J.T. (ed.) EPEW 2009. LNCS, vol. 5652, pp. 30–43. Springer, Heidelberg (2009). https://doi.org/10.1007/978-3-642-02924-0_3

140. Gelenbe, E., Hebrail, G.: A probability model of uncertainty in data bases. In: Proceedings of the Second International Conference on Data Engineering, pp. 328–333. IEEE Computer Society (1986)

141. Gelenbe, E., Hussain, K.: Learning in the multiple class random neural network. IEEE Trans. Neural Netw. 13(6), 1257–1267 (2002). https://doi.org/10.1109/TNN.2002.804228

142. Gelenbe, E., Hussain, K., Kaptan, V.: Simulating autonomous agents in augmented reality. J. Syst. Softw. 74(3), 255–268 (2005)

143. Gelenbe, E., Hussain, K.F.: Learning in the multiple class random neural network. IEEE Trans. Neural Netw. 13(6), 1257–1267 (2002)

144. Gelenbe, E., Iasnogorodski, R.: A queue with server of walking type (autonomous service). Annales de l'institut Henri Poincaré (B) Probabilités et Statistiques 16(1), 63–73 (1980)

145. Gelenbe, E., Kammerman, P., Lam, T.: Performance considerations in totally mobile wireless. Perform. Eval. 36, 387–399 (1999)

146. Gelenbe, E., Kaptan, V., Wang, Yu.: Biological metaphors for agent behavior. In: Aykanat, C., Dayar, T., Körpeoğlu, İ. (eds.) ISCIS 2004. LNCS, vol. 3280, pp. 667–675. Springer, Heidelberg (2004). https://doi.org/10.1007/978-3-540-30182-0_67

147. Gelenbe, E., Kazhmaganbetova, Z.: Cognitive packet network for bilateral asymmetric connections. IEEE Trans. Indus. Inform. 10(3), 1717–1725 (2014). https://doi.org/10.1109/TII.2014.2321740

148. Gelenbe, E., Koçak, T.: Area-based results for mine detection. IEEE Trans. Geosci. Remote Sens. 38(1), 12–24 (2000)

149. Gelenbe, E., Koçak, T., Wang, R.: Wafer surface reconstruction from top-down scanning electron microscope images. Microelectron. Eng. 75(2), 216–233 (2004)

150. Gelenbe, E., Koubi, V., Pekergin, F.: Dynamical random neural network approach to the traveling salesman problem. In: International Conference on Systems, Man and Cybernetics. Systems Engineering in the Service of Humans, Conference Proceedings, pp. 630–635. IEEE (1993)

151. Gelenbe, E., Kurinckx, A.: Random injection control of multiprogramming in virtual memory. IEEE Trans. SE Softw. Eng. 4(1), 2–17 (1978)

152. Gelenbe, E., Labed, A.: ESPRIT LTR project 8144 LYDIA load balancing and G-networks: design, implementation and evaluation. Technical report, IHEI, Univ. René Descartes, Paris V (1996)

153. Gelenbe, E., Labed, A.: G-networks with multiple classes of signals and positive customers. Eur. J. Oper. Res. 108(2), 293–305 (1998). https://doi.org/10.1016/S0377-2217(97)00371-8

154. Gelenbe, E., Labed, A.: G-networks with multiple classes of signals and positive customers. Eur. J. Oper. Res. **108**(2), 293–305 (1998)
155. Gelenbe, E., Lenfant, J., Potier, D.: Analyse d'un algorithme de gestion simultanée mémoire centrale - disque de pagination. Acta Informatica **3**, 321–345 (1974). https://doi.org/10.1007/BF00263587
156. Gelenbe, E., Lenfant, J., Potier, D.: Response time of a fixed-head disk to transfers of variable length. SIAM J. Comput. **4**(4), 461–473 (1975). https://doi.org/10.1137/0204039
157. Gelenbe, E., Lent, R.: Power-aware ad hoc cognitive packet networks. Ad Hoc Netw. **2**(3), 205–216 (2004)
158. Gelenbe, E., Lent, R.: Optimising server energy consumption and response time. Theoret. Appl. Inform. **24**, 257–270 (2012)
159. Gelenbe, E., Lent, R.: Trade-offs between energy and quality of service. In: 2012 Sustainable Internet and ICT for Sustainability (SustainIT), pp. 1–5. IEEE (2012)
160. Gelenbe, E., Lent, R. (eds.): Computer and Information Sciences III. 27th International Symposium on Computer and Information Sciences, Paris, France, October 3–4, 2012. Springer, London (2013). https://doi.org/10.1007/978-1-4471-4594-3
161. Gelenbe, E., Lent, R. (eds.): Information Sciences and Systems 2013. 2013 - Proceedings of the 28th International Symposium on Computer and Information Sciences, ISCIS 2013, Paris, France, October 28–29, Lecture Notes in Electrical Engineering, vol. 264. Springer, London (2013). https://doi.org/10.1007/978-3-319-01604-7
162. Gelenbe, E., Lent, R., Douratsos, M.: Choosing a local or remote cloud. In: 2012 Second Symposium on Network Cloud Computing and Applications, pp. 25–30. IEEE (2012)
163. Gelenbe, E., Lent, R., Montuori, A., Xu, Z.: Cognitive packet networks: QoS and performance. In: 10th IEEE International Symposium on Modeling, Analysis and Simulation of Computer and Telecommunications Systems, MASCOTS 2002. Proceedings, pp. 3–9. IEEE (2002)
164. Gelenbe, E., Lent, R., Nunez, A.: Self-aware networks and QoS. Proc. IEEE **92**(9), 1478–1489 (2004)
165. Gelenbe, E., Lent, R., Sakellari, G. (eds.): Computer and Information Sciences II. Springer, London (2012). https://doi.org/10.1007/978-1-4471-2155-8
166. Gelenbe, E., Lent, R., Sakellari, G., Sacan, A., Toroslu, I.H., Yazici, A. (eds.): Computer and Information Sciences - Proceedings of the 25th International Symposium on Computer and Information Sciences, London, UK, 22–24 September 2010. LNEE, vol. 62. Springer, London (2010). https://doi.org/10.1007/978-90-481-9794-1
167. Gelenbe, E., Lent, R., Xu, Z.: Design and performance of cognitive packet networks. Perform. Eval. **46**(2), 155–176 (2001)
168. Gelenbe, E., Lent, R., Xu, Z.: Measurement and performance of a cognitive packet network. Comput. Netw. **37**(6), 691–701 (2001)
169. Gelenbe, E., Lent, R., Xu, Z.: Towards networks with cognitive packets. In: Goto, K., Hasegawa, T., Takagi, H., Takahashi, Y. (eds.) Performance and QoS of Next Generation Networking, pp. 3–17. Springer, London (2001). https://doi.org/10.1007/978-1-4471-0705-7_1
170. Gelenbe, E., Liu, P.: QoS and routing in the cognitive packet network. In: Sixth IEEE International Symposium on a World of Wireless Mobile and Multimedia Networks, WoWMoM 2005, pp. 517–521. IEEE (2005)
171. Gelenbe, E., Loukas, G.: A self-aware approach to denial of service defence. Comput. Netw. **51**(5), 1299–1314 (2007)

172. Gelenbe, E., Mahmoodi, T.: Energy-aware routing in the cognitive packet network. Energy, pp. 7–12 (2011)
173. Gelenbe, E., Mahmoodi, T.: Distributed energy-aware routing protocol. In: Gelenbe, E., Lent, R., Sakellari, G. (eds.) Computer and Information Sciences II, pp. 149–154. Springer, London (2012). https://doi.org/10.1007/978-1-4471-2155-8_18
174. Gelenbe, E., Mahmoodi, T., Morfopoulou, C.: Energy aware routing in packet networks. E-Energy (2010)
175. Gelenbe, E., Mang, X., Önvural, R.: Diffusion based statistical call admission control in ATM. Perform. Eval. **27**, 411–436 (1996)
176. Gelenbe, E., Mang, X., Onvural, R.: Bandwidth allocation and call admission control in high-speed networks. IEEE Commun. Mag. **35**(5), 122–129 (1997)
177. Gelenbe, E., Mao, Z.H., Li, Y.D.: Function approximation by random neural networks with a bounded number of layers. Differ. Equ. Dynam. Syst. **12**(1–2), 143–170 (2004)
178. Gelenbe, E., Mao, Z.W., Li, Y.D.: Function approximation with spiked random networks. IEEE Trans. Neural Netw. **10**(1), 3–9 (1999)
179. Gelenbe, E., Marin, A.: Interconnected wireless sensors with energy harvesting. In: Gribaudo, M., Manini, D., Remke, A. (eds.) ASMTA 2015. LNCS, vol. 9081, pp. 87–99. Springer, Cham (2015). https://doi.org/10.1007/978-3-319-18579-8_7
180. Gelenbe, E., Morfopoulou, C.: Routing and G-networks to optimise energy and quality of service in packet networks. In: Hatziargyriou, N., Dimeas, A., Tomtsi, T., Weidlich, A. (eds.) E-Energy 2010. LNICST, vol. 54, pp. 163–173. Springer, Heidelberg (2011). https://doi.org/10.1007/978-3-642-19322-4_18
181. Gelenbe, E., Morfopoulou, C.: A framework for energy-aware routing in packet networks. Comput. J. **54**(6), 850–859 (2011)
182. Gelenbe, E., Muntz, R.R.: Probabilistic models of computer systems. Part I Exact Results. Acta Informatica **7**(1), 35–60 (1976)
183. Gelenbe, E., Ngai, E.: Adaptive random re-routing for differentiated QoS in sensor networks. Comput. J. **53**(7), 1052–1061 (2010)
184. Gelenbe, E., Ngai, E.C.H.: Adaptive QoS routing for significant events in wireless sensor networks. In: 2008 5th IEEE International Conference on Mobile Ad Hoc and Sensor Systems, pp. 410–415. IEEE (2008)
185. Gelenbe, E., Núñez, A.: Self-aware networks and quality of service. In: Kaynak, O., Alpaydin, E., Oja, E., Xu, L. (eds.) ICANN/ICONIP -2003. LNCS, vol. 2714, pp. 901–908. Springer, Heidelberg (2003). https://doi.org/10.1007/3-540-44989-2_107
186. Gelenbe, E., Oklander, B.: Cognitive users with useful vacations. In: 2013 IEEE International Conference on Communications Workshops (ICC), pp. 370–374. IEEE (2013)
187. Gelenbe, E., Pavloski, M.: Performance of a security control scheme for a health data exchange system. In: IEEE International Black Sea Conference on Communications and Networking, 26–29 May 2020. Virtual Conference (2020)
188. Gelenbe, E., Potier, D., Brandwajn, A., Lenfant, J.: Gestion Optimale d'un Ordinateur Multiprogramme a Memoire Virtuelle. In: Conti, R., Ruberti, A. (eds.) Optimization Techniques, Part II. LNCS, vol. 4, pp. 132–143. Springer, Heidelberg (1973). https://doi.org/10.1007/3-540-06600-4_12
189. Gelenbe, E., Pujolle, G.: Introduction aux réseaux de files d'attente. Eyrolles (1982)
190. Gelenbe, E., Rosenberg, C.: Queues with slowly varying arrival and service processes. Manage. Sci. **36**(8), 928–937 (1990)

191. Gelenbe, E., Sakellari, G., D'arienzo, M.: Admission of QoS aware users in a smart network. ACM Trans. Auton. Adap. Syst. (TAAS) **3**(1), 1–28 (2008)
192. Gelenbe, E., Sakellari, G., Filippoupolitis, A.: PerNEM 2012: second international workshop on pervasive networks for emergency management 2012, committees and welcome. In: Proceedings of the PerCOM 2012 (2012)
193. Gelenbe, E., Sakellari, G., Filippoupolitis, A.: PerNEM 2013: third international workshop on pervasive networks for emergency management 2013-committees and welcome. In: Proceedings of the PerCOM 2013 (2013)
194. Gelenbe, E., Seref, E., Xu, Z.: Simulation with learning agents. Proc. IEEE **89**(2), 148–157 (2001)
195. Gelenbe, E., Sevcik, K.: Analysis of update synchronization for multiple copy data bases. IEEE Trans. Comput. **28**(10), 737–747 (1979)
196. Gelenbe, E., Shachnai, H.: On g-networks and resource allocation in multimedia systems. Eur. J. Oper. Res. **126**(2), 308–318 (2000)
197. Gelenbe, E., Silvestri, S.: Optimisation of power consumption in wired packet networks. In: Bartolini, N., Nikoletseas, S., Sinha, P., Cardellini, V., Mahanti, A. (eds.) QShine 2009. LNICST, vol. 22, pp. 717–729. Springer, Heidelberg (2009). https://doi.org/10.1007/978-3-642-10625-5_45
198. Gelenbe, E., Silvestri, S.: Reducing power consumption in wired networks. In: 2009 24th International Symposium on Computer and Information Sciences, pp. 292–297. IEEE (2009)
199. Gelenbe, E., Stafylopatis, A.: Global behavior of homogeneous random neural systems. Appl. Math. Model. **15**(10), 534–541 (1991)
200. Gelenbe, E., Sungur, M., Cramer, C., Gelenbe, P.: Traffic and video quality with adaptive neural compression. Multimedia Syst. **4**(6), 357–369 (1996)
201. Gelenbe, E., Timotheou, S.: Random neural networks with synchronized interactions. Neural Comput. **20**(9), 2308–2324 (2008)
202. Gelenbe, E., Timotheou, S.: Synchronized interactions in spiked neuronal networks. Comput. J. **51**(6), 723–730 (2008)
203. Gelenbe, E., Timotheou, S., Nicholson, D.: Fast distributed near-optimum assignment of assets to tasks. Comput. J. **53**(9), 1360–1369 (2010)
204. Gelenbe, E., Velan, K.: An approximate model for bidders in sequential automated auctions. In: Håkansson, A., Nguyen, N.T., Hartung, R.L., Howlett, R.J., Jain, L.C. (eds.) KES-AMSTA 2009. LNCS (LNAI), vol. 5559, pp. 70–79. Springer, Heidelberg (2009). https://doi.org/10.1007/978-3-642-01665-3_8
205. Gelenbe, E., Velan, K.: Mathematical models of automated auctions. In: Hakansson, A., Hartung, R. (eds.) Agent and Multi-Agent Systems in Distributed Systems-Digital Economy and E-Commerce, pp. 137–161. Springer, Heidelberg (2013). https://doi.org/10.1007/978-3-642-35208-9_8
206. Gelenbe, E., Wang, L.: Tap: a task allocation platform for the EU FP7 PANACEA project. In: Advances in Service-Oriented and Cloud Computing: Workshops of ESOCC 2015, Taormina, Italy, 15–17 September 2015, Revised Selected Paper, vol. 567, p. 425 (2016)
207. Gelenbe, E., Wang, Y.: A mathematical approach for mission planning and rehearsal. In: Defense and Security Symposium, pp. 62490Q–62490Q. International Society for Optics and Photonics (2006)
208. Gelenbe, E., Wang, Y.: Modelling large scale autonomous systems. In: 2006 9th International Conference on Information Fusion, pp. 1–7. IEEE (2006)
209. Gelenbe, E., Wu, F.J.: Distributed networked emergency evacuation and rescue. In: 2012 IEEE International Conference on Communications (ICC), pp. 6334–6338. IEEE (2012)

210. Gelenbe, E., Wu, F.J.: Large scale simulation for human evacuation and rescue. Comput. Math. Appl. **64**(12), 3869–3880 (2012)
211. Gelenbe, E., Wu, F.J.: Sensors in cyber-physical emergency systems. In: IET Conference on Wireless Sensor Systems (WSS 2012), pp. 1–7. IET (2012)
212. Gelenbe, E., Wu, F.J.: Future research on cyber-physical emergency management systems. Future Internet **5**(3), 336–354 (2013)
213. Gelenbe, E., Xu, Z., Seref, E.: Cognitive packet networks. In: 11th IEEE International Conference on Conference Tools with Artificial Intelligence. Proceedings, pp. 47–54. IEEE (1999)
214. Gelenbe, E., et al. (eds.): Euro-CYBERSEC 2018. CCIS, vol. 821. Springer, Cham (2018). https://doi.org/10.1007/978-3-319-95189-8
215. Georgiopoulos, M., et al.: A sustainable model for integrating current topics in machine learning research into the undergraduate curriculum. IEEE Trans. Educ. **52**(4), 503–512 (2009)
216. Ghalut, T., Larijani, H.: Non-intrusive method for video quality prediction over LTE using random neural networks (RNN). In: 9th International Symposium on Communication Systems, Networks & Digital Signal Processing, CSNDSP 2014, Manchester, UK, 23–25 July 2014, pp. 519–524. IEEE (2014). https://doi.org/10.1109/CSNDSP.2014.6923884
217. Ghalut, T., Larijani, H.: Content-aware and QOE optimization of video stream scheduling over LTE networks using genetic algorithms and random neural networks. J. Ubiquit. Syst. Perv. Netw. **9**(2), 21–33 (2018). https://doi.org/10.5383/JUSPN.09.02.003
218. Gorbil, G., Abdelrahman, O.H., Gelenbe, E.: Storms in mobile networks. In: Proceedings of the 10th ACM Symposium on QoS and Security for Wireless and Mobile Networks, pp. 119–126. ACM (2014)
219. Görbil, G., Abdelrahman, O.H., Gelenbe, E.: Storms in mobile networks. In: Mueller, P., Foschini, L., Yu, R. (eds.) Proceedings of the 10th ACM Symposium on QoS and Security for Wireless and Mobile Networks, Q2SWinet 2014, Montreal, QC, Canada, 21–22 September 2014, pp. 119–126. ACM (2014). http://doi.acm.org/10.1145/2642687.2642688
220. Gorbil, G., Abdelrahman, O.H., Pavloski, M., Gelenbe, E.: Modeling and analysis of RRC-based signalling storms in 3G networks. IEEE Trans. Emerg. Topics Comput. **4**(1), 113–127 (2016)
221. Gorbil, G., Filippoupolitis, A., Gelenbe, E.: Intelligent navigation systems for building evacuation. In: Gelenbe, E., Lent, R., Sakellari, G. (eds.) Computer and Information Sciences II, pp. 339–345. Springer, London (2011). https://doi.org/10.1007/978-1-4471-2155-8_43
222. Görbil, G., Gelenbe, E.: Design of a mobile agent-based adaptive communication middleware for federations of critical infrastructure simulations. In: Rome, E., Bloomfield, R. (eds.) CRITIS 2009. LNCS, vol. 6027, pp. 34–49. Springer, Heidelberg (2010). https://doi.org/10.1007/978-3-642-14379-3_4
223. Gorbil, G., Gelenbe, E.: Opportunistic communications for emergency support systems. Procedia Comput. Sci. **5**, 39–47 (2011)
224. Gorbil, G., Gelenbe, E.: Disruption tolerant communications for large scale emergency evacuation. In: 2013 IEEE International Conference on Pervasive Computing and Communications Workshops (PERCOM Workshops), pp. 540–546. IEEE (2013)
225. Grochla, K., et al.: LP WAN gateway location selection using modified k-dominating set algorithm. In: Calzarossa, M.C., et al. (eds.) MASCOTS 2020. LNCS, vol. 12527, pp. 209–223. Springer, Cham (2021)

226. Hasselquist, D., Lindström, C., Korzhitskii, N., Carlsson, N., Gurtov, A.: Quic throughput and fairness over dual connectivity. In: Calzarossa, M.C., et al. (eds.) MASCOTS 2020. LNCS, vol. 12527, pp. 175–190. Springer, Cham (2021)

227. Hasselquist, D., Wahl, C., Bergdal, O., Carlsson, N.: Hypothesis-based comparison of ipv6 and ipv4 path distances. In: Calzarossa, M.C., et al. (eds.) MASCOTS 2020. LNCS, vol. 12527, pp. 191–208. Springer, Cham (2021)

228. Hey, L., Gelenbe, E.: Adaptive packet prioritisation for large wireless sensor networks. Telecommun. Syst. **48**(1–2), 125–150 (2011)

229. Hocaoglu, A.K., Gader, P.D., Gelenbe, E., Kocak, T.: Optimal linear combination of order statistics filters and their relationship to the delta-operator. In: AeroSense 1999, pp. 1323–1329. International Society for Optics and Photonics (1999)

230. Hussain, K.F., Kaptan, V.: Modeling and simulation with augmented reality. Int. J. Oper. Res. **38**(2), 89–103 (2004)

231. Hussain, K.F., Radwan, E., Moussa, G.S.: Augmented reality experiment: drivers' behavior at an unsignalized intersection. IEEE Trans. Intell. Transp. Syst. **14**(2), 608–617 (2013)

232. Hussain, K.F., Bassyouni, M.Y., Gelenbe, E.: Accurate and energy-efficient classification with spiking random neural network. Probability in the Engineering and Informational Sciences (2019)

233. Jr., E.G.C., Gelenbe, E., Plateau, B.: Optimization of the number of copies in a distributed data base. IEEE Trans. Softw. Eng. **7**(1), 78–84 (1981). https://doi.org/10.1109/TSE.1981.234510. http://doi.ieeecomputersociety.org/10.1109/TSE.1981.234510

234. Kieffer, A., Maillé, P., Tuffin, B.: Non-neutrality with users deciding differentiation: a satisfying option?'. In: Calzarossa, M.C., et al. (eds.) MASCOTS 2020. LNCS, vol. 12527, pp. 119–128. Springer, Cham (2021)

235. Kim, G., Gelenbe, E.: Analysis of an automated auction with concurrent multiple unit acceptance capacity. In: Al-Begain, K., Fiems, D., Knottenbelt, W.J. (eds.) ASMTA 2010. LNCS, vol. 6148, pp. 382–396. Springer, Heidelberg (2010). https://doi.org/10.1007/978-3-642-13568-2_27

236. Kim, H.S., Gelenbe, E.: G-networks based two layer stochastic modeling of gene regulatory networks with post-translational processes. Interdisc. Bio Central **3**(2), 8-1 (2011)

237. Kim, H., Atalay, R., Gelenbe, E.: G-network modelling based abnormal pathway detection in gene regulatory networks. In: Gelenbe, E., Lent, R., Sakellari, G. (eds.) Computer and Information Sciences II, pp. 257–263. Springer, London (2011). https://doi.org/10.1007/978-1-4471-2155-8_32

238. Kim, H., Gelenbe, E.: Stochastic gene expression model base gene regulatory networks. In: Lee, J.H., Lee, H., Kim, J.S. (eds.) EKC 2009, pp. 235–244. Springer, Berlin (2010). https://doi.org/10.1007/978-3-642-13624-5_22

239. Kim, H., Gelenbe, E.: Reconstruction of large-scale gene regulatory networks using Bayesian model averaging. In: 2011 IEEE International Conference on Bioinformatics and Biomedicine (BIBM), pp. 202–207. IEEE (2011)

240. Kim, H., Gelenbe, E.: Reconstruction of large-scale gene regulatory networks using Bayesian model averaging. IEEE Trans. NanoBiosci. **11**(3), 259–265 (2012). https://doi.org/10.1109/TNB.2012.2214233

241. Kim, H., Gelenbe, E.: Stochastic gene expression modeling with hill function for switch-like gene responses. IEEE/ACM Trans. Comput. Biol. Bioinform. **9**(4), 973–979 (2012). https://doi.org/10.1109/TCBB.2011.153

242. Kim, H., Park, T., Gelenbe, E.: Identifying disease candidate genes via large-scale gene network analysis. Int. J. Data Mining Bioinform. **10**(2), 175–188 (2014). https://doi.org/10.1504/IJDMB.2014.064014

243. Kim, H., Park, T., Gelenbe, E.: Identifying disease candidate genes via large-scale gene network analysis. Int. J. Data Mining Bioinform. **10**(2), 175–188 (2014)

244. Kokuti, A., Gelenbe, E.: Directional navigation improves opportunistic communication for emergencies. Sensors **14**(8), 15387–15399 (2014)

245. Kolodiej, J., Khan, S., Gelenbe, E., Talbi, E.: Scalable optimization in grid, cloud, and intelligent network computing. Concur. Comput. Pract. Experience **25**(12), 1719–1721 (2013)

246. Kulandai, A.D.R., J, S., Rose, J., Schwarz, T.: Balanced gray codes for reduction of bit-flips in phase change memories. In: Calzarossa, M.C., et al. (eds.) MASCOTS 2020. LNCS, vol. 12527, pp. 159–171. Springer, Cham (2021)

247. Lent, R., Abdelrahman, O.H., Gorbil, G., Gelenbe, E.: Fast message dissemination for emergency communications. In: 2010 8th IEEE International Conference on Pervasive Computing and Communications Workshops (PERCOM Workshops), pp. 370–375. IEEE (2010)

248. Levi, A., Savaş, E., Yenigün, H., Balcısoy, S., Saygın, Y. (eds.): ISCIS 2006. LNCS, vol. 4263. Springer, Heidelberg (2006). https://doi.org/10.1007/11902140

249. Li, J., Mishra, D., Seneviratne, A.: Network traffic classification using wifi sensing. In: Calzarossa, M.C., et al. (eds.) MASCOTS 2020. LNCS, vol. 12527, pp. 48–61. Springer, Cham (2021)

250. Liu, P., Gelenbe, E.: Recursive routing in the cognitive packet network. In: 3rd International Conference on Testbeds and Research Infrastructure for the Development of Networks and Communities, TridentCom 2007, pp. 1–6. IEEE (2007)

251. Mclean, R., Karamollahi, M., Williamson, C.: Measurement and modeling of tumblr traffic. In: Calzarossa, M.C., et al. (eds.) MASCOTS 2020. LNCS, vol. 12527, pp. 237–253. Springer, Cham (2021)

252. Nalin, M.: The European cross-border health data exchange roadmap: case study in the Italian setting. J. Biomed. Inform. **94**, 103183 (2019)

253. Natsiavas, P., et al.: Comprehensive user requirements engineering methodology for secure and interoperable health data exchange. BMC Med. Inform. Decis. Mak. **18**(1), 85 (2018)

254. Ngai, E.C.H., Gelenbe, E., Humber, G.: Information-aware traffic reduction for wireless sensor networks. In: 2009 IEEE 34th Conference on Local Computer Networks, pp. 451–458. IEEE (2009)

255. Oeke, G., Loukas, G.: A denial of service detector based on maximum likelihood detection and the random neural network. Comput. J. **50**(6), 717–727 (2007)

256. Oke, G., Loukas, G., Gelenbe, E.: Detecting denial of service attacks with bayesian classifiers and the random neural network. In: 2007 IEEE International Fuzzy Systems Conference, pp. 1–6. IEEE (2007)

257. Oklander, B., Gelenbe, E.: Optimal behaviour of smart wireless users. In: Gelenbe, E., Lent, R. (eds.) Information Sciences and Systems 2013, pp. 87–95. Springer, Cham (2013). https://doi.org/10.1007/978-3-319-01604-7_9

258. Ören, T.I., Numrich, S.K., Uhrmacher, A.M., Wilson, L.F., Gelenbe, E.: Agent-directed simulation: challenges to meet defense and civilian requirements. In: Proceedings of the 32nd Conference on Winter Simulation, pp. 1757–1762. Society For Computer Simulation International (2000)

259. Pankratova, E., Farkhadov, M., Gelenbe, E.: Research of heterogeneous queueing system SM—M$^{(n)}|\infty$. In: Dudin, A., Nazarov, A., Kirpichnikov, A. (eds.) ITMM

2017. CCIS, vol. 800, pp. 122–132. Springer, Cham (2017). https://doi.org/10.1007/978-3-319-68069-9_10

260. Pavloski, M., Görbil, G., Gelenbe, E.: Bandwidth usage—based detection of signaling attacks. In: Abdelrahman, O.H., Gelenbe, E., Gorbil, G., Lent, R. (eds.) Information Sciences and Systems 2015. LNEE, vol. 363, pp. 105–114. Springer, Cham (2016). https://doi.org/10.1007/978-3-319-22635-4_9

261. Pernici, B., Aiello, M., Vom Brocke, J., Donnellan, B., Gelenbe, E., Kretsis, M.: What is can do for environmental sustainability: a report from CAiSE'11 panel on green and sustainable is. Commun. Assoc. Inf. Syst. **30**(1), 18 (2012)

262. Phan, H.T., Stemberg, M.J., Gelenbe, E.: Aligning protein-protein interaction networks using random neural networks. In: 2012 IEEE International Conference on Bioinformatics and Biomedicine, pp. 1–6. IEEE (2012)

263. Potier, D., Gelenbe, E., Lenfant, J.: Adaptive allocation of central processing unit quanta. J. ACM **23**(1), 97–102 (1976). https://doi.org/10.1145/321921.321932

264. Qureshi, A., Larijani, H., Ahmad, J., Mtetwa, N.: A novel random neural network based approach for intrusion detection systems. In: 2018 10th Computer Science and Electronic Engineering Conference, CEEC 2018, University of Essex, Colchester, UK, 19–21 September 2018, pp. 50–55. IEEE (2018). https://doi.org/10.1109/CEEC.2018.8674228

265. Radhakrishnan, K., Larijani, H.: Evaluating perceived voice quality on packet networks using different random neural network architectures. Perform. Eval. **68**(4), 347–360 (2011). https://doi.org/10.1016/j.peva.2011.01.001

266. Robert, S., Zertal, S., Couve, P.: Demonstration of shaman: a flexible framework for auto-tuning hpc systems. In: Calzarossa, M.C., et al. (eds.) MASCOTS 2020. LNCS, vol. 12527, pp. 147–158. Springer, Cham (2021)

267. Rubino, G., Tirilly, P., Varela, M.: Evaluating users' satisfaction in packet networks using random neural networks. In: Kollias, S.D., Stafylopatis, A., Duch, W., Oja, E. (eds.) ICANN 2006, Part I. LNCS, vol. 4131, pp. 303–312. Springer, Heidelberg (2006). https://doi.org/10.1007/11840817_32

268. Sakellari, G., Gelenbe, E.: Adaptive resilience of the cognitive packet network in the presence of network worms. In: Proceedings of the NATO Symposium on C3I for Crisis, Emergency and Consequence Management, pp. 11–12 (2009)

269. Sakellari, G., Hey, L., Gelenbe, E.: Adaptability and failure resilience of the cognitive packet network. In: DemoSession of the 27th IEEE Conference on Computer Communications (INFOCOM 2008), Phoenix, Arizona, USA (2008)

270. Sakellari, G., Leung, T., Gelenbe, E.: Auction-based admission control for self-aware networks. In: Gelenbe, E., Lent, R., Sakellari, G. (eds.) Computer and Information Sciences II, pp. 223–230. Springer, London (2011). https://doi.org/10.1007/978-1-4471-2155-8_28

271. Sakellari, G., Morfopoulou, C., Mahmoodi, T., Gelenbe, E.: Using energy criteria to admit flows in a wired network. In: Gelenbe, E., Lent, R. (eds.) Computer and Information Sciences III, pp. 63–72. Springer, London (2013). https://doi.org/10.1007/978-1-4471-4594-3_7

272. Serrano, W., Gelenbe, E.: The random neural network in a neurocomputing application for web search. Neurocomputing **280**, 123–134 (2018)

273. Serrano, W., Gelenbe, E.: Deep learning clusters in the cognitive packet network. Neurocomputing **396**, 406–428 (2020)

274. Serrano, W., Gelenbe, E., Yin, Y.: The random neural network with deep learning clusters in smart search. Neurocomputing **396**, 394–405 (2020)

275. Siavvas, M., Gelenbe, E., Kehagias, D., Tzovaras, D.: static analysis-based approaches for secure software development. In: Gelenbe, E., et al. (eds.) Euro-CYBERSEC 2018. CCIS, vol. 821, pp. 142–157. Springer, Cham (2018). https://doi.org/10.1007/978-3-319-95189-8_13

276. Staffa, M., et al.: KONFIDO: an OpenNCP-based secure eHealth data exchange system. In: Gelenbe, E., et al. (eds.) Euro-CYBERSEC 2018. CCIS, vol. 821, pp. 11–27. Springer, Cham (2018). https://doi.org/10.1007/978-3-319-95189-8_2

277. Staffa, M., et al.: An openNCP-based solution for secure eHealth data exchange. J. Netw. Comput. Appl. **116**, 65–85 (2018)

278. Timotheou, S.: A novel weight initialization method for the random neural network. Neurocomputing **73**(2), 160–168 (2009)

279. Tomak, J., Gorlatch, S.: Measuring performance of fault management in a legacy system: An alarm system study. In: Calzarossa, M.C., et al. (eds.) MASCOTS 2020. LNCS, vol. 12527, pp. 129–146. Springer, Cham (2021)

280. Velan, K., Gelenbe, E.: Analysing bidder performance in randomised and fixed-deadline automated auctions. In: Jędrzejowicz, P., Nguyen, N.T., Howlet, R.J., Jain, L.C. (eds.) KES-AMSTA 2010. LNCS (LNAI), vol. 6071, pp. 42–51. Springer, Heidelberg (2010). https://doi.org/10.1007/978-3-642-13541-5_5

281. Wang, L., Brun, O., Gelenbe, E.: Adaptive workload distribution for local and remote clouds. In: 2016 IEEE International Conference on Systems, Man, and Cybernetics (SMC), pp. 003984–003988. IEEE (2016)

282. Wang, L., Gelenbe, E.: An implementation of voice over IP in the cognitive packet network. In: Czachórski, T., Gelenbe, E., Lent, R. (eds.) Information Sciences and Systems 2014, pp. 33–40. Springer, Cham (2014). https://doi.org/10.1007/978-3-319-09465-6_4

283. Wang, L., Gelenbe, E.: Adaptive dispatching of tasks in the cloud. IEEE Trans. Cloud Comput. **6**(1), 33–45 (2018)

284. Witkowski, M., White, G., Louvieris, P., Gorbil, G., Gelenbe, E., Dodd, L.: High-level information fusion and mission planning in highly anisotropic threat spaces. In: 2008 11th International Conference on Information Fusion, pp. 1–8. IEEE (2008)

285. Yazıcı, A., Şener, C. (eds.): ISCIS 2003. LNCS, vol. 2869. Springer, Heidelberg (2003). https://doi.org/10.1007/b14229

286. Yolum, I., Güngör, T., Gürgen, F., Özturan, C. (eds.): ISCIS 2005. LNCS, vol. 3733. Springer, Heidelberg (2005). https://doi.org/10.1007/11569596

287. Yu, C.M., Ni, G.K., Chen, I.Y., Gelenbe, E., Kuo, S.Y.: Top-k query result completeness verification in tiered sensor networks. IEEE Trans. Inf. Forensics Secur. **9**(1), 109–124 (2014)

288. Zhu, Q., Gelenbe, E., Qiao, Y.: Adaptive prefetching algorithm in disk controllers. Perform. Eval. **65**(5), 382–395 (2008)

Software Defined Network Dynamics via Diffusions

Tadeusz Czachórski[1(✉)], Erol Gelenbe[1], and Dariusz Marek[2]

[1] Institute of Theoretical and Applied Informatics, Polish Academy of Sciences,
ul. Bałtycka 5, 44-100 Gliwice, Poland
`tadek@iitis.pl`
[2] The Silesian University of Technology,
Akademicka 16, 44-100 Gliwice, Poland

Abstract. Software-Defined Networks (SDN) dynamically modify the paths of Internet flows in response to the quality of service or security needs, and hence frequently modify traffic levels at network routers. Thus network routers often operate in the transient regime, rather than at steady-state, with significant impact on packet loss probabilities and delay. We, therefore, investigate the time-dependent performance of a small network of routers, modelled as G/G/1/N queueing stations. A diffusion approximation is developed to predict the quality of service of the routers in the transient regime. Numerical examples show that the results in the transient regime can differ very significantly from the steady-state results, and therefore that the transient analysis must be taken into account in evaluating the performance of routers in a SDN network.

1 Introduction

The performance of computer networks since its beginnings, was investigated [1,2] via networks of node queues that contain packets, representing interconnected routers that forward packets from source to a destination over several hops or routers. These models are used to compute in steady-state, the network delays and loss probabilities in routers, and to predict or optimise the overall transmission quality of service. The evolution of computer networks has resulted in new architectures, methods and models have been adapted and new parameters introduced.

The increased use of the Internet to carry voice traffic [3], as well as the Internet of Things, Cloud, Fog and Edge computing [4] brings new challenges by increasing the variety of network architectures and the complex stochastic nature of the transmitted flows. Also, the increased use of SDN controllers inside networks [5–7] creates frequent changes in traffic patterns and paths, and hence dynamic changes also in the traffic intensity of different paths and of the traffic carried by routers in the network.

M. C. Calzarossa et al. (Eds.): MASCOTS 2020, LNCS 12527, pp. 29–47, 2021.
https://doi.org/10.1007/978-3-030-68110-4_2

These changes raise a new need for transient analysis since the network is seldom operating at "steady-state". In this context, queueing networks [1] diffusion approximations [8], fluid approximations [9], and network calculus [10,11] are some of the mathematical techniques that may be used.

Earlier analytical studies of SDN networks are based on steady-state models based on discrete Markov chain analysis [12–17] with Poisson flows, or on network calculus [18,19] which only provides a rough estimate of network delays, especially when frequent controller decisions modify the traffic load. To address this concern, in recent work, we have considered a single SDN forwarder and modelled it with diffusion approximations [20] to determine its transient behaviour. The accuracy of the diffusion approximation has been examined in several studies such as [21], and was found to be acceptable with regard to other forms of analysis such as discrete event simulations which are subject to statistical confidence intervals and long simulation runs. Therefore in this paper, we will not present comparisons of the diffusion results with discrete event simulation.

The large scale deployment of the IoT [22] together with Cloud Services [4], where measured data from sensors is transported to the cloud for decision making and the control of cyber-physical systems, has increased the complexity and challenges of networks that must now ensure better security [23] of the traffic flows, acceptable quality of service, flexible network management, and energy optimisation [24]. The introduction of artificial intelligence into network routing and management [25,26] also provides greater variability in the flows that traverse the network. Besides, the decoupling of the data plane, the control plane and the application plane through Software Defined Networks (SDN) [5] gives carriers, service providers and enterprises more significant control over the way traffic moves around networks [27,28] and simplifies network operation, management and administration. However, it imposes frequent updates of network paths and of the traffic levels that are carried by the routers, so that the transient behaviour of network components becomes of great interest.

Recent studies have analyzed SDN networks to optimize steady-state performance using queueing [12–17,29] and network calculus [18,19,30]. However, SDN Controllers modify the state of the network quite frequently, and these issues require the analysis of the transient behaviour of a router. However, the usual tools for network performance are not well adapted to this requirement since the transient analysis of queueing network models is particularly difficult, and the discrete event simulation of the transient behaviour of networks is very time-consuming due to the large number of randomised repetitions that are needed to achieve a reasonable level of statistical accuracy.

Therefore, in this paper, we address the time-dependent behaviour of a router using diffusion approximations which offer two essential advantages: packet interarrival and service times distributions do not depend on the usual "Poisson and exponential" assumptions, and they lead to computationally efficient results concerning the system's transient behaviour. Additionally, the diffusion model only requires the first two moments of the interarrival and service times, so that relatively realistic parameters can be based on measured traffic data, and it provides numerical results which are difficult to obtain with other techniques [31]. While the approach for steady-state distributions was introduced decades ago [32,33] and applied to numerous problems, including to admission control in industrial telecommunication systems [34], and active queue management for non-integer PID controllers in IP routers [35], the transient analysis is more challenging and requires carefully crafted analytical techniques which we use in this paper.

The features which are in favour of the method are that the diffusion model of a single server allows general interarrival and service time distributions for realistic network data, going beyond conventional discrete Markov models. Results are obtained as queue length and waiting time distributions, simplifying the analysis of QoS parameters such as delay, jitter and loss probability. Also, networks may be hierarchical with any topology and number of nodes, fitting well the diffusion approximation, which is scalable and decomposes network analysis into individual nodes.

The numerical examples that we exhibit show that the transient regime can differ very significantly from the steady-state results. Since SDN controllers frequently change the state of the network paths, including the resulting traffic intensities and the load of each router, our numerical results show that the transient analysis will be indispensable in evaluating the performance of routers in a SDN network.

1.1   Contributions of This Paper

In this paper, we develop the transient analysis of the diffusion approximation approach for small multi-node networks in which SDN controllers' decisions cause frequent changes of the paths of flows and hence of the traffic carried by different forwarders or routers. We compute the dynamics of queue length distributions, queueing delays, and loss probabilities as a function of changes in traffic intensity, based on solving a system of partial differential equations for the queue length distributions and the delays of several interconnected nodes as a function of time. The analysis we develop allows us to compute a network's transient behaviour, and the time it takes for a network to reach its new steady-state after the input traffic rates change. We can also compute the transient and steady-state packet loss probabilities in cases when they may be small, and hence very difficult to obtain via discrete event simulations.

We compute the diffusion transient state step-by-step in short time intervals with parameters which are specific to each of these intervals. Thus SDN routing traffic decisions can easily be reflected in successive changes to time-dependent and state-dependent diffusion parameters. Transient path delay averages can also be computed from transient node delay averages.

The use of these results are illustrated with two applications:

- In all networks, and in particular those carrying IoT traffic, short and intermittent packet sequences carrying measurement data need to be conveyed rapidly towards a destination. At the same time, when SDN controllers are used, long traffic sequences at higher traffic rates may be re-allocated between paths for purposes of traffic balancing and may disrupt the QoS of the short sequences. The question then is to determine when the short sequences should be forwarded, e.g. just after a major long connection ends, or just when it begins. Intuitively speaking, one may wish to wait for the end of the longer and higher traffic sequence in order to obtain a better QoS for the short packet sequence. The transient analysis recommends that the short sequence be superposed on the longer higher rate traffic just as the latter begins, which is counterintuitive, as discussed in Sect. 4.1.

– The second example is given in Sect. 4.2, and shows how Service Level Agreements (SLA) are strongly affected by the use of precise transient analysis rather than steady-state analysis.

2 Transient Analysis

The diffusion approximation replaces the number of packets in a queueing system by the real-valued valued diffusion process $X(t) \in [0, N]$ where N is the maximum size of the queue. Following the approach in [8], resulting in equations (1), at the extremities of the interval $x = 0$ and $x = N$, two absorbing barriers are placed so that when $X(t)$ reaches a barrier, it stays there for a random time and jumps from $x = 0$ to $x = 1$ with intensity λ and from $x = N$ to $x = N-1$ with intensity μ. The resulting diffusion equation is:

$$\frac{\partial f(x,t;x_0)}{\partial t} = \frac{\alpha}{2}\frac{\partial^2 f(x,t;x_0)}{\partial x^2} - \beta\frac{\partial f(x,t;x_0)}{\partial x}$$
$$+\lambda p_0(t)\delta(x-1) + \mu p_N(t)\delta(x-N+1),$$
$$\frac{dpp_N(t)0(t)}{dt} = \lim_{x\to 0}[\frac{\alpha}{2}\frac{\partial f(x,t;x_0)}{\partial x} - \beta f(x,t;x_0)] - \lambda p_0(t),$$
$$\frac{dp_N(t)}{dt} = \lim_{x\to N}[\frac{\alpha}{2}\frac{\partial f(x,t;x_0)}{\partial x} - \beta f(x,t;x_0)] - \mu p_N(t), \qquad (1)$$

where $\delta(x)$ is the Dirac delta function, and $f(x,t;x_0) = P[x \leq X(t) < x + dx \mid X(0) = x_0]$ of $X(t)$; $p_0(t)$ and $p_N(t)$ denote probabilities that at time t the process is in barriers at $x = 0$, $x = N$, respectively. The incremental changes of $X(t)$, $dX(t) = X(t+dt) - X(t)$ are normally distributed with mean βdt and variance αdt where β, α are coefficients of the diffusion equation, where $\beta = (\lambda - \mu)$ and $\alpha = (\sigma_A^2\lambda^3 + \sigma_B^2\mu^3)$; $1/\lambda$ and $1/\mu$ are the mean interarrival and service times, and σ_A^2, σ_B^2 are the variances of the interarrival and service time, respectively.

To determine the solution of (1) we use the following approach from [36]. First we consider a diffusion process with two *absorbing* barriers at $x = 0$ and $x = N$, started at $t = 0$ from $x = x_0$. Its probability density function $\phi(x,t;x_0)$ has the following form [37]:

$$\phi(x,t;x_0) = \begin{cases} \delta(x-x_0) & \text{for } t = 0, \\ \dfrac{1}{\sqrt{2\Pi\alpha t}}\displaystyle\sum_{n=-\infty}^{\infty}\{a(t)+b(t)\} & \text{for } t > 0, \end{cases} \qquad (2)$$

where

$$a(t) = \exp\left[\frac{\beta x_n'}{\alpha} - \frac{(x - x_0 - x_n' - \beta t)^2}{2\alpha t}\right],$$

$$b(t) = \exp\left[\frac{\beta x_n''}{\alpha} - \frac{(x - x_0 - x_n'' - \beta t)^2}{2\alpha t}\right],$$

and $x_n' = 2nN$, $x_n'' = -2x_0 - x_n'$.

If the initial condition is defined by a function $\psi(x)$, $x \in (0, N)$, $\lim_{x\to 0} \psi(x) = \lim_{x\to N} \psi(x) = 0$, then the probability density function (pdf) of the process is $\phi(x, t; \psi) = \int_0^N \phi(x, t; \xi)\psi(\xi)d\xi$.

The probability density function $f(x, t; \psi)$ of the diffusion process with elementary returns is composed of the function $\phi(x, t; \psi)$ referring to the diffusion process before it reaches any barrier, and of a spectrum of functions $\phi(x, t-\tau; 1)$, $\phi(x, t-\tau; N-1)$. The latter functions represent diffusion processes with absorbing barriers at $x = 0$ and $x = N$, started with densities $g_1(\tau)$ and $g_{N-1}(\tau)$ at time $\tau < t$ at points $x = 1$ and $x = N - 1$ due to jumps from the barriers:

$$f(x, t; \psi) = \phi(x, t; \psi) + \int_0^t g_1(\tau)\phi(x, t - \tau; 1)d\tau$$

$$+ \int_0^t g_{N-1}(\tau)\phi(x, t - \tau; N - 1)d\tau \tag{3}$$

where the densities $g_1(\tau)$, $g_{N-1}(\tau)$, as well as $p_0(t)$ and $p_N(t)$, are obtained from the probability balance equations at the barriers.

The delay through the queue, including waiting and service time, is then obtained as a first passage time from an initial point taken with probability given by $f(x, t; \psi)$ to the absorbing barrier placed at $x = 0$.

3   Transient Analysis of a Network

Consider a network of M stations with general service time distributions and routing probabilities r_{ij}. We first decompose the network by determining the input flows at each station and then apply the single server model to each station separately.

In the transient state the input flow $\lambda_{i-in}(t)$ of any station i and its output flow $\lambda_{i-out}(t) = (1 - p_0(t))\mu_i$ are different. The traffic equations balancing the flows of stations are

$$\lambda_{i-in}(t) = \lambda_{0i}(t) + \sum_{j=1}^M \lambda_{j-out}(t)r_{ji}, \quad i = 1, \ldots, M, \tag{4}$$

where the first term λ_{0i} represents traffic flow coming directly to station i from the outside of the network. Denote by $f_{Aj}(x, t)$ and $f_{Bj}(x, t)$ the density functions of interarrival and service times at station j; the pdf $f_{Dj}(x, t)$ of the inter-departure times from this node at time t is

$$f_{Dj}(x, t) = \varrho_j(t)f_{Bj}(x, t) + [1 - \varrho_j(t)]f_{Aj}(x, t) * f_{Bj}(x, t), \quad i = 1, \ldots, M \tag{5}$$

where $*$ denotes the convolution and $i = 1, \ldots, M$. The first term of (5) represents the interdeparture times of packets when the node is busy, and the second term gives the interdeparture times when it is idle. The formula (5), known as Burke's theorem, is exact for Poisson input and approximate in other cases. From (5) we have:

$$C_{Dj}^2(t) = \varrho_j^2(t) C_{Bj}^2(t) + C_{Aj}^2(t)(1 - \varrho_j(t)) + \varrho_j(t)[1 - \varrho_j(t)]. \qquad (6)$$

Packets leaving the node j according to the distribution $f_{Dj}(x, t)$ choose any node i with probability r_{ji} and the times between packets routed from node j to i has pdf:

$$f_{ji}(x, t) = f_{Dj}(x, t) r_{ji} + f_{Dj}(x, t) * f_{Dj}(x, t)(1 - r_{ji}) r_{ji} + \cdots \qquad (7)$$

The variance of $f_{ji}(x, t)$ allows us to determine the variance of the number of customers going from station j to i, and after summing over all stations sending packets to station i we receive

$$C_{Ai}^2(t) = \frac{1}{\lambda_{i-in}(t)} \sum_{j=1}^{M} r_{ji} \lambda_{i-out}(t)[(C_{Dj}^2(t) - 1) r_{ji} + 1] + \frac{C_{0i}^2(t) \lambda_{0i}(t)}{\lambda_{i-in}(t)}, \qquad (8)$$

where the parameters λ_{0i} and C_{0i}^2 refer to the flow coming to i from outside of the network, and (6), (8) form a system of linear equations yilding $C_{Ai}^2(t)$ and, in consequence, the diffusion parameters $\beta_i(t)$, $\alpha_i(t)$ for every node i.

If $f_{Ri}(x, t)$ is the response time pdf at node i, then the response time pdf for the path $1, \ldots, n$ is $f_R = f_{R1}(x, t) * f_{R2}(x, t) * f_{R3}(x, t) * \cdots * f_{Rn}(x, t)$.

3.1   Packet Service Time for a SDN Data Plane Router

In SDN, routes are selected by one or more SDN controllers, while the SDN data plane routers are forwarding devices that follow the rules given by the controller. The centralisation of network intelligence and management in the controller enables a global network view, network programmability and deployment of innovative approaches such as smart cognitive routing [27].

Since the input and output hardware of an SDN forwarder is fast, the actual forwarding time between nodes can be neglected. However, the main component of service time that needs to be considered is the time during which the node's hardware identifies – for each successive packet – the flow to which the packet belongs, and in which output port the packet must be placed:

– Assume that the identification of the flow is conducted as a linear search in a flow table with K entries (i.e. the number of flows), and that T is the time to check one entry. If p is the probability that *the router's flow table does not contain the flow rule for a given packet*, this will be discovered after going through all K positions, i.e. after time KT which is a constant service time with zero variance.

- Otherwise, with probability $(1 - p)$, the time to find the existing entry is uniformly distributed in $[T, KT]$ for a simple linear search, since the packet is equally likely to belong to any of the flows, with mean $\frac{(K+1)T}{2}$ and variance $\frac{(K^2-1)T^2}{12}$.
- As a result, the service time S has the following mean and variance:

$$E[S] = T[pK + (1 - p)\frac{K+1}{2}], \quad V(S) = (1 - p)\frac{(K^2 - 1)T^2}{12}.$$

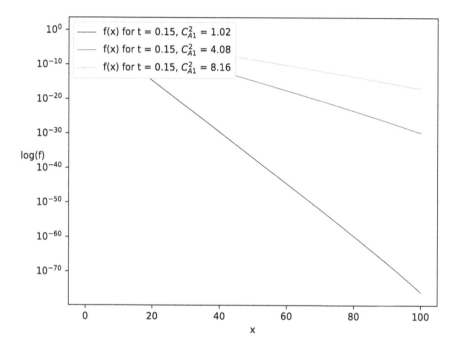

Fig. 1. Queue length Probability Density Function for node S1 at time $t = 0.15$ with different values of C_{A1}^2. (Color figure online)

4   Numerical Examples

We consider a network composed of 4 forwarders. Host 1 is sending packets to Host 2 through forwarders S1-S2-S4 or S1-S3-S4, with routing probabilities $r_{12} = 0.15$, $r_{13} = 0.85$. The packet traffic rate from Host 1 is denoted $\lambda(t)$ in the range of 500 to 2500 packets/sec, and the changes in the traffic rate the pattern of is displayed in blue in all the figures. It is the total flow sent by S1; the flows of S2 and S3 are defined by the routing probabilities. The duration of the time interval being considered is 1 s.

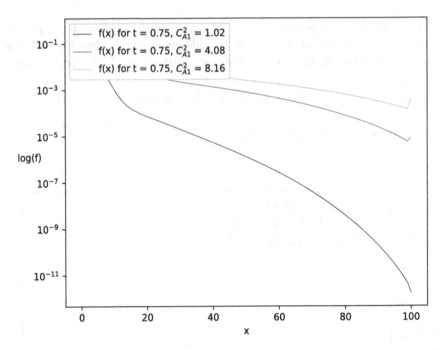

Fig. 2. Queue length pdf for node S1 at time $t = 0.75$ with different values of C_{A1}^2. (Color figure online)

Traffic data from the CAIDA traces [38] concerning IPv4 packet interarrival times from the Equinix Chicago link, collected during one hour on 18 February 2016, gave $C_{A1}^2 = 1.02$ with over 22 million packets belonging to over 1:17 million IPv4 flows. The computations were also carried out for four and eight times larger, values C_{A1}^2 to see how these variations influence the network's performance. We assume that the switches store $K = 950$ flows and that the time to examine one flow in the flow table is $T = 8 \cdot 10^{-7}$ s with $p = 0$. The resulting mean service time is $S = 1/\mu = 0.038$ ms or $\mu = 2,631.5$ packets/sec and $C_B^2 = 0.33$. The buffer capacity per flow is $N = 100$. These values are compatible with existing equipment but may vary with the type of router.

The transient solution is obtained numerically for 100 successive sub-intervals of the length 10 ms in 100 sub-intervals with fixed diffusion parameters in each sub-interval. At the end of each sub-interval (4), (8) are solved to determine new parameters of the flow for the single station models in the next interval. The density function $f_i(x)$ obtained for any station i at the end of an interval gives the initial conditions for the diffusion equation at the next interval.

Figure 1 and 2 present $f(x, t : \psi)$ given by (3) for station S1. In the first case, the buffer is relatively empty, i.e. the probability of the queue size being close to N is of the order of 10^{-30} or 10^{-70}. Note that the probability scale is logarithmic, and the method has no difficulty to compute such small values, which would be impossible in a simulation model. We see also the impact of C_{A1}^2

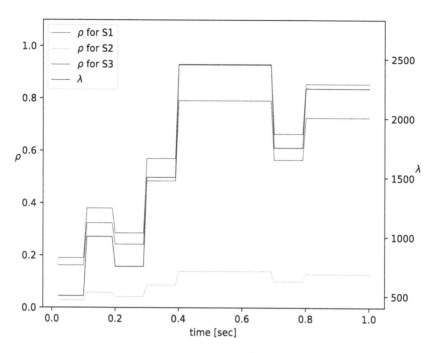

Fig. 3. The utilisation $\varrho(t) = 1 - p(0,t)$ and $C_{A1}^2 = 1.02$ for nodes S1, S2, S3, S4. (Color figure online)

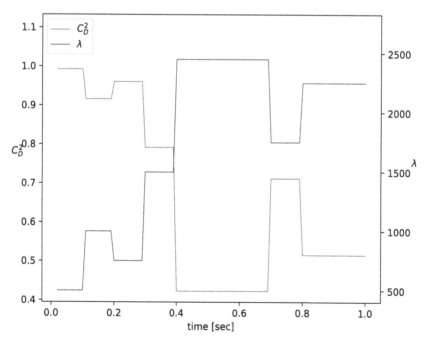

Fig. 4. $C_{D1}^2(t)$ for node S1. (Color figure online)

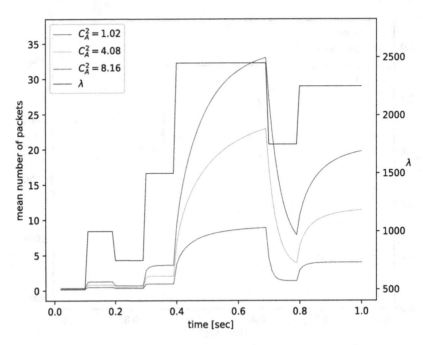

Fig. 5. Station S1, mean number of packets, for different values of C_{A1}^2. (Color figure online)

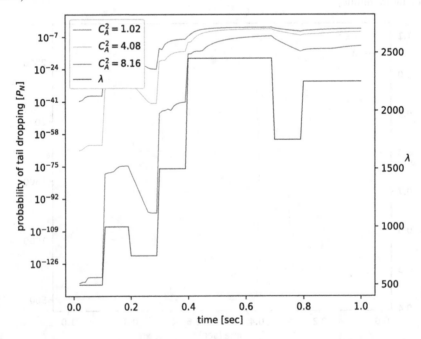

Fig. 6. Station S1, loss probability $p(N)$, for different values of C_{A1}^2. (Color figure online)

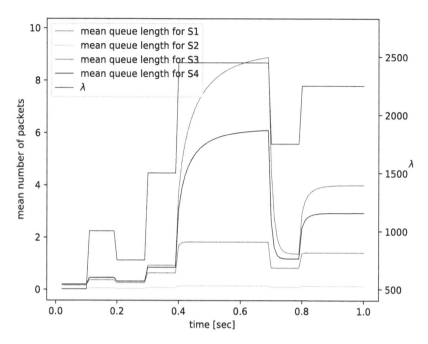

Fig. 7. Mean number of packets at S1, S2, S3, S4, for paths S1-S2-S4 and S1-S3-S4 paths. (Color figure online)

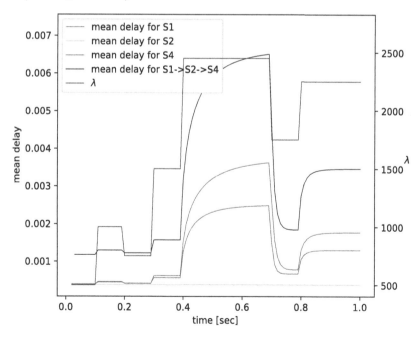

Fig. 8. Mean delays at S1, S3, S4 and total mean delay for the path S1-S2-S4, for $C_{A1}^2 = 1.02$ (Color figure online)

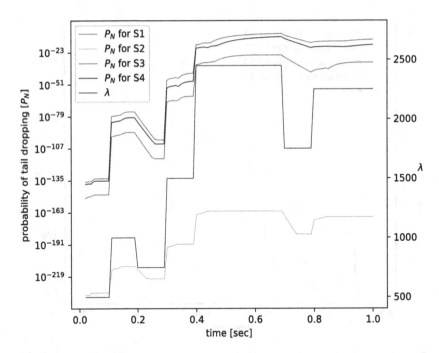

Fig. 9. Packet Loss Probability with $C_{A1}^2 = 1.02$, for nodes S1, S2, S3, S4, $p(N,t)$ (Color figure online)

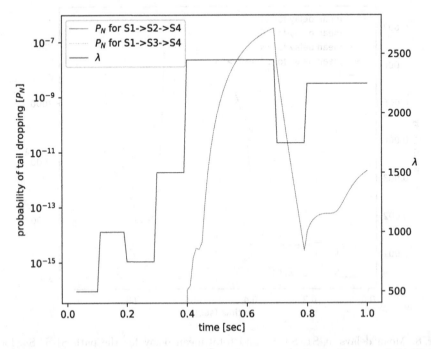

Fig. 10. Packet Loss Probability with $C_{A1}^2 = 1.02$, for paths S1-S2-S4 and S1-S3-S4 paths (Color figure online)

which affects α in the diffusion equation; a greater C_{A1}^2 increases the probability of larger queue lengths. Figures 3 and 4 show the changes in the utilisation rate $\varrho_i(t)$ of stations and the interdeparture time C_{D1}^2 from (6), as $\lambda(t)$ is varied, showing that $\varrho(t)$ and C_{D1}^2 follow the variations in $\lambda(t)$ closely.

Figures 5 and 6 refer to station S1 and shows the variation of mean queue length for various values of C_{A1}^2. The queue length increases considerably with the variance of interarrival times, and the duration of the transient period also increases. Higher utilisation rates due to larger λ lead to a longer transient period. For large λ, the steady-state is not attained before the next change of the input flow rate. The right-hand figure illustrates the significant influence of C_{A1}^2 on the loss probabilities, which are presented in logarithmic scale.

Figures 7 and 8 present the dynamics of the average queue length and delay at stations S1, S2, S4, and the total average delay along the path S1-S2-S4. Again, we see the influence of the traffic rate on the queue length and the duration of the transient period. For higher traffic rates, the transient time is, in general, longer than the periods between changes in λ so that steady-state is never reached.

Figures 9 and 10 display the loss probabilities for each station separately, and the total loss probability for two paths S1-S2-S4, S1-S3-S4, which are practically the same and they superimpose. These figures also illustrate the method's ability to compute very small probabilities of the order of 10^{-200}.

4.1   Scheduling Short Sequences of Packets

Consider a short sequence of a few packets (of very low traffic rate) containing measurement traffic, emanating for instance from some IoT sensor, which is very sensitive to packet loss. Suppose the SDN controller establishes a connection, to be able to forward these packets at time 0.4 s along path $S1- > S2- > S4$. At the same time, the SDN controller also establishes a connection for another flow totalling 1000 packets/sec. Suppose also that when this connection was established this same path was already carrying 1500 packets/sec.

The question then is whether the source of the low data rate measurement traffic should wait for the high data rate traffic to end before forwarding its traffic. Of course, waiting has the disadvantage of incurring the waiting delay, which may be quite long. However, if the data traffic is very sensitive to losses, it may be better to wait for the high traffic rate flow to end.

The analysis that is illustrated in Fig. 10 tells us that the low data rate IoT source should not wait at all. It should send its traffic *right away* as soon as the path $S1- > S2- > S4$ is established for the IoT traffic at time 0.4 s, simply because of the transient behaviour of the packet loss probability which is less than 10^{-13} in the period just after time 0.4 s. In addition to avoiding the wait for the high traffic rate to end, the instant when the high traffic rate ends at time 0.7 s and the following 0.1 s will have a much higher packet loss probability of the order of 10^{-7} due to the transient effect in packet loss. In addition, the transient analysis of Fig. 8 also tells us that the mean wait delay incurred by the packets is of the order of 0.004 s, rather than the 0.3 s that would be wasted waiting for the high traffic rate to subside.

Obviously, this type of very useful insight about the transients in packet loss and delay can only be obtained via the transient analysis tools developed in this paper.

4.2   The Effect of Transients on Service Level Agreements

A high priority customer of the network needs to send a flow of packets every 30 min from node 1 to node 4 during a short time window of $\Delta = 200$ ms. The customer indicates that the traffic rate λ_1 may take a fixed value between 2500 and 3200 packets/second, and that the inter-arrival time distribution for packets will have a squared coefficient of variation which does not exceed $C = 2$.

- The customer has stringent QoS constraints so that the network operator must abide by a Service Level Agreement (SLA): the total average packet delay through the path must not exceed $W_m = 0.01$ during the connection, and the total average packet loss over the path must not exceed $L_m = 150$.
- Due to the existing network topology, to reach node 4, the traffic must travel through the three identical router s$S1-> S2-> S4$. The network operator will program a SDN controller to set up a private 3-node path $S1-> S2->$ $S4$ for this flow, at the beginning of each successive 30 min interval, and reserve it (empty of other traffic) for 200 ms. After 100 ms, this flow stops sending packets, and the SDN controller can re-allocate the path to other flows.
- The operator's current routers have a 2000 packet/second forwarding capacity. The operator would like to know if this is sufficient, or whether she/he should upgrade the hardware to higher available speeds of 2300, or 2600 or 2900 packet/second.

Let $t = 0$ be the beginning of an interval of length Δ, and $N_i(t)$ be the average number of packets from the flow in router i, at t seconds after the beginning of the flow. Let:

$$W_{max} = S \max_{t \in \Delta}[N_1(t) + N_2(t) + N_4(t)], \tag{9}$$

$$L_{max} = \max_{t \in \Delta}[L_1(t) + L_2(t) + L_4(t)], \tag{10}$$

where W_{max}, L_{max} are the worst case values of the packet delay and loss for the flow rate, starting at $t \in [0, \Delta]$ Due to the existing network topology, to reach Node 4 the traffic must travel through the three identical routers $S1->$ $S2-> S4$. After $\Delta = 200$ ms this particular flow stops sending packets, and the SDN controller can re-allocate these nodes to other flows. We compute $L_i(t) = \lambda_i Prob[f_i(N, t)]$, where N is the router buffer size, and obtain W_{max}, L_{max} as a function of λ_1 for the worst case value $C_{A1}^2 = 2$, and different router speeds, to see which speed is needed.

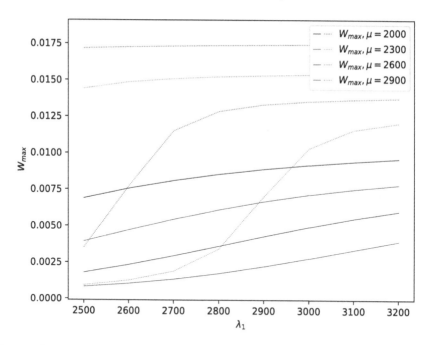

Fig. 11. W_{max} as in Eq. (12) for various λ_1 (solid line) compared with steady state solution (dotted line) (Color figure online)

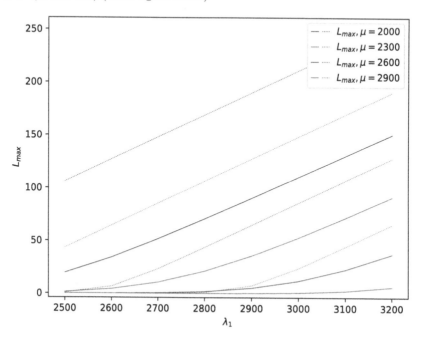

Fig. 12. L_{max} as in Eq. (12) for various λ_1 (solid line) compared with steady state solution (dotted line) (Color figure online)

The transient diffusion model yields W_{max}, L_{max} as shown in Figs. 11 and 12, (in full lines) plotted against λ_1 for different values of $S = \mu^{-1}$. The figures also show (in dotted lines) the values of the steady-state values of average delay and loss rate.

$$W = \frac{1}{\mu} \lim_{t \to \infty} [N_1(t) + N_2(t) + N_4(t)], \tag{11}$$

$$L_{max} = \lim_{t \to \Delta} [L_1(t) + L_2(t) + L_4(t)], \tag{12}$$

We see that the transient analysis allows us to operate safely with routers having a capacity of $\mu = 2000\,packets/sec$, while the steady-state analysis over-estimates the average delay and loss probability by over 100%, and recommends upgrading the routers to a packet processing capacity of at least 2600 packets/sec.

5   Conclusions

This paper considers a small network of routers or forwarders in a network con-trolled by a SDN controller which makes changes to paths through the network, and regularly modifies traffic rates at different routers. Our purpose is to evalu-ate the effect of transient effects and in particular their importance relative to usual steady-state analyses which have been studied. We, therefore, develop a computationally efficient diffusion approximation method, present its analytical solution, and implement the numerical techniques needed for the transient com-putations. Using realistic parameters, including relatively low-frequency changes of paths by SDN controllers every 100 ms, we show that the system may seldom reach steady-state when the network is moderately to heavily loaded – which is the region of interest for performance modelling and optimisation studies. Though at light loads transients are short, at moderate to heavy loads transients are significant for individual node and path delays, and packet loss probabilities. The method we have developed is operational and gives quantitative results for models with realistic parameters.

Numerical examples for single and multiple node models provide the dynam-ics of queue lengths, delays and packet loss and their dynamics in response to changes in the flow intensity and the variance of interarrival times. Through numerical examples, we also show how transient analysis provides insights that are more accurate and cover cases where the steady-state analysis would pro-vide wrong or incomplete results. Thus we conclude that transient analysis can play a major role in the performance evaluation of SDN networks and should be incorporated into SDN controls and that diffusion approximations can be useful and computationally efficient for this purpose.

Acknowledgements. This research was supported by the SerIoT Research and Innovation Action, funded by the European Commission (EC) under the H2020-IOT-2017 Program, Grant Agreement 780139. The EC's support does not constitute an endorsement of this paper, which reflects the views only of the authors.

References

1. Kleinrock, L.: Queueing Systems, Vol. 1: Theory. Wiley, Hoboken (1975)
2. Kleinrock, L.: Queueing Systems, Vol. 2: Computer Applications. Wiley, Hoboken (1976)
3. Toral-Cruz, H., Pathan, A.S.K., Pacheco, J.C.R.: Accurate modeling of VoIP traffic QoS parameters in current and future networks with multifractal and Markov models. Math. Comput. Model. **57**(11–12), 2832–2845 (2013)
4. Buyya, R., et al.: A manifesto for future generation cloud computing: research directions for the next decade. ACM Comput. Surv. (CSUR) **51**(5), 1–38 (2019)
5. McKeown, N., et al.: Openflow: enabling innovation in campus networks. ACM SIGCOMM Comput. Commun. Rev. **38**(2), 69–74 (2008)
6. Tuncer, D., Charalambides, M., Clayman, S., Pavlou, G.: Adaptive resource management and control in software defined networks. IEEE Trans. Netw. Serv. Manag. **12**(1), 18–33 (2015)
7. Xia, W., Wen, Y., Foh, C.H., Niyato, D., Xie, H.: A survey on software-defined networking. IEEE Commun. Surv. Tutor. **17**(1), 27–51 (2015)
8. Gelenbe, E.: On approximate computer systems models. J. ACM **22**(2), 261–269 (1975)
9. Kurtz, T.G.: Limit theorems for sequences of jump Markov processes approximating ordinary differential processes. J. Appl. Probab. **8**(2), 344–356 (1971)
10. Fidler, M.: Survey of deterministic and stochastic service curve models in the network calculus. IEEE Commun. Surv. Tutor. **12**(1), 59–86 (2010)
11. Fidler, M., Rizk, A.: A guide to the stochastic network calculus. IEEE Commun. Surv. Tutor. **17**(1), 92–105 (2015)
12. Mahmood, K., Chilwan, A., Osterbo, O., Jarschel, M.: Modelling of OpenFlow-based software-defined networks: the multiple node case. Inst. Eng. Technol. J. **4**(5), 278–284 (2015)
13. Ansell, J., Seah, W.K.G., Ng, B., Marshall, S.: Making queueing theory more palatable to SDN/OpenFlow-based network practitioners. In: Proceeding of the 2016 IEEE/IFIP Network Operations and Management Symposium, Istanbul, Turkey, pp. 1119–1124. IEEE (2016)
14. Singh, D., Ng, B., Lai, Y.-C., Lin, Y.-D., Seah, W.K.G.: Modelling software-defined networking: software and hardware switches. J. Comput. Netw. Comput. Appl. **122**, 24–36 (2018)
15. Lai, Y.-C., Ali, A., Hassan, M., Hossain, S., Lin, Y.-D.: Performance modeling and analysis of TCP connections over software defined networks. In: Proceeding of the 2017 IEEE Global Communications Conference, Singapore, pp. 1–6. IEEE (2017)
16. Fahmin, A., Lai, Y.-C., Hossain, S., Lin, Y.-D., Saha, D.: Performance modeling of SDN with NFV under or aside the controller. In: Proceeding of the 5th International Conference on Future Internet of Things and Cloud Workshops, Prague, pp. 211–216. IEEE (2017)
17. Miao, W., Min, G., Wu, Y., Wang, H., Hu, J.: Performance modelling and analysis of software defined networking under bursty multimedia traffic. ACM Trans. Multimedia Comput. Commun. Appl. **12**(55), 24–36 (2018)

18. Azodolmolky, S., Wieder, P., Yahyapour, R.: Performance evaluation of a scalable software-defined networking deployment. In: Proceeding of the 2013 Second European Workshop on Software Defined Networks, Berlin, Germany, pp. 68–74. IEEE (2013)

19. Azodolmolky, S., Nejabati, R., Pazouki, M., Wieder, P., Yahyapour, R., Simeonidou, D.: An analytical model for software defined networking: a network calculus-based approach. In: Proceeding of the IEEE Global Communications Conference, Atlanta, USA, pp. 1397–1402. IEEE (2013)

20. Czachórski, T., Gelenbe, E., Kuaban, G.S., Marek, D.: Transient behaviour of a network router, accepted. In: Herencsár, N., Benedetto, F., Hosek, J. (eds.) Proceedings of International Conference on Telecommunications and Signal Processing TSP 2020, Milano. IEEE (2020)

21. Czachórski, T., Pekergin, F.: Diffusion approximation as a modelling tool. In: Kouvatsos, D.D. (ed.) Network Performance Engineering. LNCS, vol. 5233, pp. 447–476. Springer, Heidelberg (2011). https://doi.org/10.1007/978-3-642-02742-0_20

22. Lee, S.K., Bae, M., Kim, H.: Future of IoT networks: a survey. Appl. Sci. **7**(10), 1072 (2017)

23. Gelenbe, E., Domanska, J., Frohlich, P., Nowak, M., Nowak, S.: Self-aware networks that optimize security, QoS and energy. Proc. IEEE **108**(7) (2020, accepted for publication)

24. Gelenbe, E.: Energy packet networks: adaptive energy management for the cloud. In: CloudCP 2012: Proceedings of the 2nd International Workshop on Cloud Computing Platforms, pp. 1–5. ACM (2012). https://doi.org/10.1145/2168697.2168698

25. Dobson, S., et al.: A survey of autonomic communications. ACM Trans. Auton. Adapt. Syst. (TAAS) **1**(2), 223–259 (2006)

26. Gelenbe, E., Liu, P., Lainé, J.: Genetic algorithms for route discovery. IEEE Trans. Syst. Man Cybern. Part B (Cybern.) **36**(6), 1247–1254 (2006)

27. Francois, F., Gelenbe, E.: Towards a cognitive routing engine for software defined networks. In: Proceeding of the 2016 IEEE International Conference on Communications, Kuala Lumpur, pp. 1–6. IEEE (2016)

28. Goto, Y., Ng, B., Seah, W.K.G., Takahashi, Y.: Queueing analysis of software defined network with realistic openflow-based switch model. Comput. Netw. **164**, 106892 (2019)

29. Sood, K., Yi, S., Xiang, Y.: Performance analysis of software-defined network router using M/Geo/1. IEEE Commun. Lett. **20**(12), 27–51 (2016)

30. Bozakov, Z., Rizk, A.: Taming SDN controllers in heterogeneous hardware environments. In: Proceeding of the 2013 Second European Workshop on Software Defined Networks, Berlin, Germany, pp. 50–55. IEEE (2013)

31. Bisnik, N., Abouzeid, A.A.: Queuing network models for delay analysis of multihop wireless ad hoc networks. Ad Hoc Netw. **7**(1), 79–97 (2009)

32. Gelenbe, E., Pujolle, G.: The behaviour of a single-queue in a general queueing network. Acta Informatica **7**, 123–136 (1976). https://doi.org/10.1007/BF00265766

33. Gelenbe, E.: Probabilistic models of computer systems part ii: Diffusion approximations, waiting times and batch arrivals. Acta Informatica **12**, 285–303 (1979). https://doi.org/10.1007/BF00268317

34. Marin, G.A., Mang, X., Gelenbe, E., Önvural, R.O.: Statistical call admission control. US Patent 6,222,824 (2001)

35. Domański, A., Domańska, J., Czachórski, T., Klamka, J., Szygula, J., Marek, D.: Diffusion approximation model of TCP NewReno congestion control mechanism. SN Comput. Sci. **1**, 43 (2020)

36. Czachórski, T.: A method to solve diffusion equation with instantaneous return processes acting as boundary conditions. Bull. Polish Acad. Sci. Tech. Sci. **41**(4), 417–451 (1993)
37. Cox, R.P., Miller, H.D.: The Theory of Stochastic Processes. Chapman and Hall, London (1965)
38. https://data.caida.org/datasets/passive-2016/equinix-chicago/20160218-130000. UTC/

Network Traffic Classification Using WiFi Sensing

Junye Li$^{(\boxtimes)}$, Deepak Mishra, and Aruna Seneviratne

School of Electrical Engineering and Telecommunications, University of New South
Wales, Sydney, NSW 2052, Australia
{junye.li,d.mishra,a.seneviratne}@unsw.edu.au

Abstract. With the ubiquity of WiFi-enabled devices, WiFi Channel
State Information (CSI) based sensing of the physical environment has
been researched broadly, and for network management and monitoring,
advanced measures for Network Traffic Classification (NTC) have been
called. This paper proposes a novel CSI-based NTC model using off-the-
shelf WiFi sensing tools. We conducted experiments in both controlled
environment and real-world environment. Experiment results have shown
that the frequency-selective CSI signatures can be used to distinguish
four common NTC classes: ping, music streaming, buffered video streaming, and live video streaming. CSI features for NTC include the number of
prominent CSI amplitude bins, locations of bins and relevant prominence
of bins on the amplitude histogram over time for different subcarriers. We
conclude with a clear WiFi sensing-based distinction of different network
types where it is observed that ping and music streaming have similarities in their features, while buffered and live video streaming resemble
each other in their CSI amplitude features.

Keywords: Classification · Network traffic · Frequency selectiveness ·
Probability mass function · Hardware experiments

1 Introduction

With the recent development of Internet of Things (IoT) [4], and the need for network monitoring and management [7], ubiquitous commodity devices with WiFi
capability provide an opportunity for target monitoring and network management. Additionally, a lot of attention has been given to the Channel State Information (CSI) based WiFi sensing applications such as human/target detection
and classification. The passivity of CSI-based WiFi sensing provides an unob-
trusive, low-cost method compared with other dedicated sensor-based methods
which might be controversial in terms of user privacy. On the other hand, Network Traffic Classification (NTC) has been the focus for privacy and network
management purposes. By employing effective and robust NTC techniques, it is
possible to optimise the network management as well as detecting potentially
hostile intruders.

© Springer Nature Switzerland AG 2021
M. C. Calzarossa et al. (Eds.): MASCOTS 2020, LNCS 12527, pp. 48–61, 2021.
https://doi.org/10.1007/978-3-030-68110-4_3

Therefore, in this paper, we present a novel possibility for NTC employing CSI-based WiFi sensing techniques using off-the-shelf low-cost devices, providing a unique insight into this matter.

1.1 Literature Survey

NTC aims to distinguish the network traffic by protocol (HTTP, DNS, NTP etc.), application (gaming, video streaming etc.), and other classes for network monitoring and Quality of Service (QoS) purposes. Packet-header features, such as source and destination ports, packet size are also used with combined Convolutional Neural Network (CNN) and Recurrent Neural Network (RNN) for NTC in [6]. To examine the potential of NTC without predefined classes, autoencoder with time interval based feature vector to classify network traffic without relying on predefined classes, achieving about 80% precision in [5]. Also, the application of NTC in malware traffic detection is examined in [9] using CNN with automatic feature learning from the packet layer.

On a different path, some WiFi sensing techniques, especially WiFi CSI signatures, have been utilised for detection and classification applications for targets in physical environments. [11] uses temporal and spatial domain CSI signature with CNN achieving an average above 90% accuracy for vehicle classification. [1] applies Moving Variance Segmentation (MVS) to CSI signatures for human motion classification in different environments, namely flat floor and staircase. [12] identifies persons with their walking CSI signature with 80% to 92% accuracies. Additionally, [13] firstly demonstrates that CSI can be used to infer the text and pattern-based mobile phone password with up to 92% of accuracy, and then shows that with channel interference as protection the password inference drops to as low as 22%.

1.2 Motivation and Scope

In the previous studies utilising CSI-based WiFi sensing, the main focus is to identify changes in the physical environment. To our best knowledge, no research has been done to examine the impact of the network traffic content on the generated CSI signatures. Traditional network traffic classification relies on packet capturing, analysis and modelling to differentiate data traffics to classes such as text, multimedia streaming or online gaming. This motivates our research to bridge the gap to utilise WiFi-based sensing with CSI signatures for data type classification, with the goal to provide a better understanding into CSI and improved performance for traffic type classification. Our research echoes the rising demand for security and privacy [4], in the era of IoT and wireless communications, and could be extended to the relevant fields.

1.3 Contribution

This research makes the following contributions:

1. we have proposed a novel framework exploiting WiFi sensing-based CSI signatures for network traffic classification;
2. the experiments are conducted in both controlled and real-world environments to qualify the distinguishing features empirically using off-the-shelf devices with the latest customised firmware;
3. we propose a novel statistical analysis tool for examining CSI amplitude and identify the prominent distinguishing features for CSI amplitudes of different cases;
4. this research has provided non-trivial insights from a unique perspective of network traffic into understanding the determining factors of CSI signature.

The following of this paper is organised as follows: Sect. 2 describes the CSI-based NTC framework and method; Sect. 3 introduces the experiment environment and hardware/software setup; Sect. 4 presents the results and Sect. 5 concludes the results and makes remarks about potential improvements and extensions of this study.

2   Proposed Framework

This section presents the foundations of CSI-based WiFi sensing, Network Traffic Classification (NTC), the theoretical foundation of our study, and the objective of this study.

2.1   CSI-based WiFi Sensing

In the IEEE 802.11n/ac/ax standards, CSI is measured from the WiFI PHY layer using the Orthogonal Frequency Division Multiplexing (OFDM), which enables the frame-by-frame measurement of the frequency response of a channel [2].

Generally, CSI-based WiFi sensing involves the following:

1. collect CSI with supported hardware;
2. CSI outlier removal and noise filtering;
3. using CSI pattern/established machine learning models for environment sensing.

Specifically, CSI samples are calculated by using the change in the preamble of each wireless frame received by the receiver from the transmitter. This calculated CSI takes the form of complex numbers, $a_n \cdot \exp(j\theta_n)$, where a_n is the CSI amplitude, θ_n is the phase, and n indicates the OFDM WiFi carrier index. Each subcarrier of a given wireless link between a transmitter and a receiver antenna pair (as denoted by Tx-Rx) generates a CSI complex number. Here we would like to recall that the amplitude of each CSI number actually indicates the signal attenuation after multi-path effect, which is similar to the Received Signal Strength Indicator (RSSI, [10]).

CSI-based WiFi sensing, includes human behaviour monitoring, user profile construction, localisation, object identification etc. These applications utilise the statistical features extracted from the CSI amplitude and phase information for classification. In particular, statistical time-domain features like mean, variance, and skewness, along with frequency-domain features like spectrogram and percentile frequency components are exploited together with pattern, model, or deep learning-based models for classification.

2.2 Network Traffic Classification

In general, network traffic classification (NTC) aims at categorising the network traffic into coarse categories, such as audio call, website interaction, buffered video streaming, or the ones to/from specific websites or applications, such as Facebook, Twitter and BitTorrent. The classified traffic information can then be used for network management, Quality of Service (QoS), as well as other malicious activity identification [5,6,9]. There are several methods for NTC [9]:

1. port-based;
2. deep packet inspection-based (DPI-based);
3. statistic-based;
4. behavioural-based.

Mostly, NTC relies on the packet source and destination for distinguishing the data traffic, along with the underlying traffic duration, protocol type and packet size. Thereafter, rule-based or model-based classifiers are applied.

2.3 Objective and Performance Metric

Specifically, this paper aims to distinguish the network traffic types of ping, music streaming, buffered video streaming and live video streaming using the CSI signatures collected between the client and the CSI extractor. Additionally, we would like to identify the key CSI-based statistical parameters that help in this classification. Lastly, we target to empirically characterise the role of external environmental factors and the device-specific characteristics.

We propose to capture the temporal variation of CSI samples by a new metric defined as:

$$F_{|H(f,t)|}(x;f) = \frac{\#(x_{low} < |H(f,t)| \leq x_{up})}{Number\ of\ CSI\ Amp.\ Frames} \qquad (1)$$

where $F_{|H(f,t)|}$ denotes the Probability Mass Function (PMF) of the amplitude $|H(f,t)|$ of CSI at a time instant t of subcarrier f, with $\#(x_{low} < |H(f,t)| \leq x_{up})$ denoting the number of CSI frames that fall within the xth bin $(x_{low}, x_{up}]$. For examination, The denominator term normalises the result to its distribution probability. We will investigate the number of prominent CSI amplitude bins, the value of each bin along with their respective spread, and the robustness of the proposed metric $F_{|H(f,t)|}$ for NTC.

As for continuous-valued CSI samples, it is unusual to have identical values, we, therefore, find different modes by dividing the n obtained CSI amplitudes into k bins. This histogram of the underlying CSI amplitudes is more commonly known as the probability mass function for the discrete values of CSI amplitudes as defined respectively by the bin centres. Thus, now, the tallest bar in the Probability Mass Function (PMF) histogram yields the mode of the CSI amplitudes for each subcarrier.

3   Experiment Setup

This section outlines the lab environment in which the experimented is conducted and the hardware and software setup details.

3.1   Experiment Environment

The experiments are conducted in two different environments as listed in Table 1. In each of the environments, experiments are conducted without human presence to minimise the channel interference.

As shown in Fig. 1, the setup in the computer lab mimics that of normal user scenario with other WiFi devices and computers present, with the WiFi router AP and client set up as shown, about 2.5 m apart. The Tx and Rx of CSI are about 0.5 m from each other. During the experiment there is no change of the physical environment in the lab, albeit interference from other WiFi signals are still present.

For the setup in the chamber shown in Fig. 2, there is no other device present, and the chamber is metallically shielded to minimised interference from outside. The Tx and Rx of CSI are set up about 1.5 m apart. During the experiment there is no change in the physical environment of the chamber.

Table 1. Experiment environment

Environment	Characteristics
Computer Lab	Reflects real-world scenario, where other WiFi signals and devices are present
RF-shield chamber	A more controlled, interference-free environment

3.2   Hardware and Software Details

The hardware devices used for the experiments are listed in Table 2. There are two sets of Access Point(AP)/Client pairs used for the experiments, namely Router AP/Wireless Adaptor pair, and the Raspberry Pi Hotspot AP and Raspberry Pi client pair, set up as shown in Fig. 1 and 2.

As shown in Fig. 3, CSI is collected using Raspberry Pi 4B with Nexmon CSI [8], an open-source customised firmware installed (the Pi acts as the Rx of CSI). Compared with the previously used Linux CSI Tool [3] that uses an outdated Intel NIC 5300 network adaptor, where CSI is measured actively, Nexmon CSI

Table 2. List of experimental hardware

Device Name	Role	Specifications
Raspberry Pi 4B	Rx	Nexmon CSI customised firmware installed, single antenna, supports CSI measurement of 802.11a/g/n/ac WiFi
	AP/Client(Tx)	Ad-hoc 802.11n 2.4 GHz WiFi @ Channel 2, single antenna
TP-Link Outdoor CPE 210	AP	802.11n 2.4 GHz 20 MHz WiFi @ Channel 2, single antenna
Netgear AC2100 WiFi Adaptor	Client(Tx)	Single antenna 802.11a/b/n/ac USB WiFi adaptor

Fig. 1. Lab setup

on Raspberry Pi allows for passive CSI collection. That is, CSI of the channel between the Rx and the transmitter (Tx) is generated without the Tx directly communicating with the Rx (Tx is connected to the WiFi router). Nexmon CSI is written primarily in C, allowing for further changes as needed. The transmitter used is a desktop with Netgear AC6100 USB WiFi adaptor, which is connected to the WiFi router.

For the experiment, WiFi frames are generated by the desktop Tx with different kinds of network activities: ping, music streaming, buffered video streaming and live video streaming. The CSI is then measured by the Rx and processed to extract the PMF of each network traffic type. It should be noted that for the PMF, only the data subcarriers (as defined in IEEE 802.11n) are plotted. Also, for both PMF across subcarriers and the subcarrier-level PMF, the probability value is normalised.

Fig. 2. Chamber setup

3.3   Network Traffic Generation

With the aforementioned experiment setup, several experiments are conducted in both the computer lab and the RF-shielded chamber. Experiments are all conducted with minimal change in the environment (that is, no human presence, no physical movement). Each experiment consists of several trials of different network activities at Tx: pinging from the terminal, music streaming using Spotify, buffered video streaming on YouTube, and live video streaming using Twitch. All the activities are pre-configured remotely, and each trial lasts from 5 min to 30 min on a rolling basis (ping, Spotify, YouTube, Twitch, ping and so on) For each type of network traffic, at least 10,000 CSI frames are measured and analysed.

4   Experiment Results and Observations

This section presents the results that we collected and analysed, and is divided into two subsections following two different experiment environments as listed in Table 1.

4.1   Measurement and Observation Parameters

Table 3 summarises the experimental and data processing parameters for CSI amplitude, following the process in Fig. 3. The *Hampel Filter Window Length*

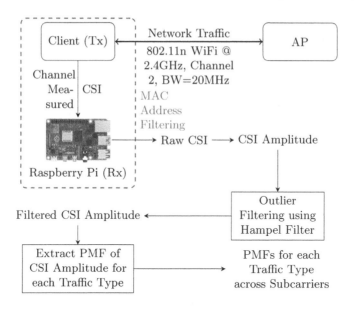

Fig. 3. CSI extraction illustration

specifies the window length used for outlier filtering; *PMF Number of Bins* specifies the number of amplitude bins configured for PMF plots; *Number of CSI Frames* indicates the number of CSI frames measured for each traffic type.

Table 3. CSI amplitude processing parameters

Parameter	Value
Hampel Filter Window Length	11
PMF Number of Bins	75
Number of CSI Frames for Each Traffic Type	>10000
Tx-Rx Distance (Lab)	≈0.5 m
Tx-Rx Distance (Chamber)	≈1.5 m

We choose the Probability Mass Function to statistically analyse the CSI amplitude, which allows the visualisation of the statistical features of the CSI amplitude, such as mean, variance, the number of clusters, and the location of clusters. Further, we can utilise a combined PMF across all the subcarriers to identify the commonly present trend in the CSI amplitude statistics. Also, in one particular experiment, we used two Raspberry Pi Rxs to measure the CSI while recording the CPU core temperature of each of them. This provides a possible cause for the differences in the CSI signature for different traffic types.

It can be observed that the change of CSI amplitude is relatively negligible over time, whereas the CSI amplitude varies more pronounced across subcarriers, as shown in Fig. 4. This indicates the relatively small change of CSI amplitude over time, justifying our choice to examine the CSI frames.

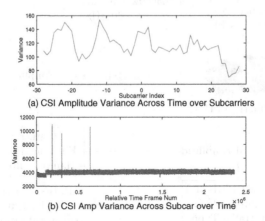

Fig. 4. CSI amplitude variance across time and subcarrier

For each data type, as shown in Fig. 3, the CSI amplitudes are recorded and filtered for outliers. The CSI amplitude consists of all the CSI frames of the same data type for each experiment, and are sorted in the relative time order, consisting of 48 data subcarriers, as shown in Fig. 5(a). Then, the PMF of all the data subcarriers is calculated and analysed, and put into a density plot, shown in Fig. 5(b), which comprises the PMF of the subcarriers corresponding to Fig. 5(a). The PMF across subcarriers visualises the statistical features of CSI amplitude across time, such as the number of prominent CSI amplitude bins, the location of bins, and the relative prominence of bins. For more detailed, subcarrier-level analysis, the PMF of each subcarrier, for example, the PMF of subcarrier 5, as shown in Fig. 5(c), are presented and analysed. The patterns and features of the PMF will be discussed in details in Sect. 4.3.

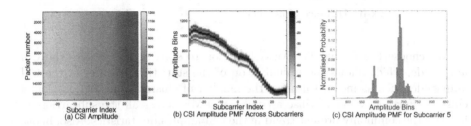

Fig. 5. CSI PMF Flow

4.2   Observations from Lab Experiments

As listed in Fig. 1, for this experiment carried out in the computer lab, we use a TP-Link WiFi router as the AP, a workstation with a wireless adaptor as the client for internet activities and as the Tx for CSI, and a Raspberry Pi as the Rx for CSI measurement. The client (Tx) generates network traffic and sends wireless packets for Ping, Spotify, YouTube and Twitch traffic. For the experiments carried out in the computer lab, there are two different sets of AP and client (Tx) used to ensure the remove possible device dependencies, as listed in Table 2, to ensure the applicability of the traffic classification across hardware devices.

Workstation as Client, Router as AP. The first AP and client pair is the workstation with a wireless adaptor as the client, whereas a WiFi router is used as the AP. It can be observed in Fig. 6 that, firstly, the CSI amplitude of ping resembles that of the Spotify, whereas YouTube and Twitch share more similarities. In particular, for subcarrier -28 of both Ping and Spotify have the most likely amplitude value of 1050, while for YouTube and Twitch are located around 950 amplitude bin at subcarrier -28. Regardless of the probability of particular CSI amplitude, the amplitude versus subcarrier trend is very similar for Ping and Spotify, or for Twitch and YouTube. For the lower subcarrier indices, the probabilities are the least for the lower amplitude values for ping, whereas the higher amplitudes of Spotify have lower probability.

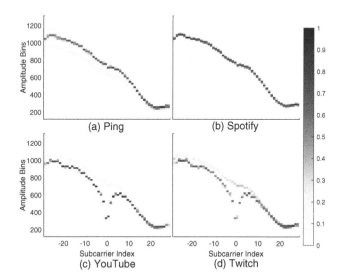

Fig. 6. Lab experiment workstation/router pmfs across subcarriers

Raspberry Pi Ad-Hoc Network. Similarly, the same experiment is repeated with the Raspberry Pi Ad-Hoc AP/client pair. However, Spotify is not supported on Raspberry Pi, so it is not tested. Following the same procedure as outlined in Fig. 3, the PMFs across subcarriers are generated for Ping, YouTube, and Twitch.

As the traffic types are not very distinguishable on the PMFs across subcarriers, shown in Fig. 7, the PMFs of subcarrier -10 are shown in Fig. 8. It can be observed that for Ping traffic the CSI amplitude is spread relatively evenly at two levels; for YouTube, the CSI amplitudes concentrate mainly at three levels, while for Twitch there are only two main CSI amplitude clusters.

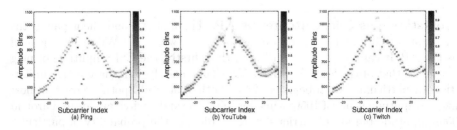

Fig. 7. Lab experiment Raspberry Pi Ad-Hoc PMFs across Subcarriers

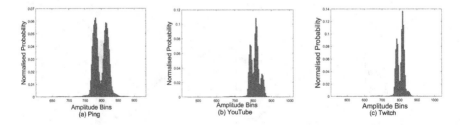

Fig. 8. Lab experiment Raspberry Pi Ad-Hoc PMFs for Subcarrier -10

4.3   Interference-Free NTC Performance Inside Chamber

As stated in Sect. 3.1, the experiment is also conducted in an RF-shielded chamber.

Results. It can be observed that Spotify and YouTube share similar CSI amplitude PMF shape, while Twitch and Ping are more uniquely distinguishable with the shape of the dominant CSI amplitude bins.

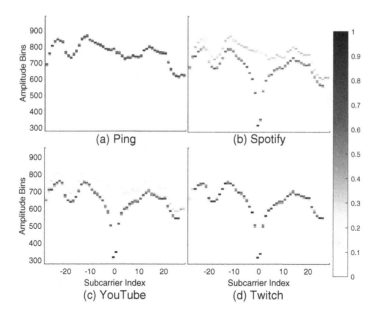

Fig. 9. Chamber experiment workstation/router pmfs across subcarriers

Temperature. The CPU core temperature of the Raspberry Pi Rx is also recorded using the *vcgencmd measure_temp* utility for all the traffic types. For this experiment, two Raspberry Pi Rxs are used to measure CSI simultaneously, and as shown in Fig. 10.

Although the temperature measurement precision with the *vcgencmd measure_temp* utility is to $1\,°C$, this measurement could still be insightful nonetheless. It is speculated that the device temperature varies as the rate of receiving CSI frames change (Generally Twitch traffic generates the most number of frame, followed by YouTube/Ping, and Spotify has the least), hence the slight variation in the measured CSI. Additionally, due to possible ventilation and cooling differences, the Raspberry Pi Rx devices might experience different CPU temperatures for CSI measurement. This observation could lead to further investigations into the relationship between the status and the characteristics of the CSI measurement device and CSI signatures.

4.4   Performance Comparison

We would like to conclude with comparing the characteristics of the traffic types with different hardware setups as described in Sect. 4.2 and 4.3. It can be seen from Fig. 6 that for the workstation/router setup, there is only one prominent amplitude bin on Ping and Twitch PMF across subcarriers, and two prominent amplitude bins for Spotify and YouTube. Whereas in Fig. 7 for Pi Ad-Hoc setup, all three traffic types have two prominent bins and the differences between different traffic types are more subtle, as shown in Fig. 8. It is speculated that

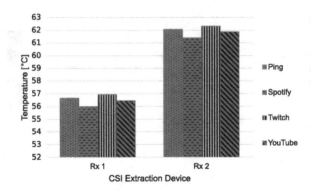

Fig. 10. Measured Rx CPU temperature mean

different devices have different performance in term of traffic classification, and in this case, the workstation/router setup traffic is more distinctive.

Next, for different experimental environments, namely in the lab and the chamber, as shown in Fig. 1 and 2, we compare the relative NTC performance as respectively plotted in Fig. 6 and 9. It can be observed that the NTC performance between different traffic types is more visible in the case of chamber, as compared to the lab scenario, because the former is more immune to interference and possible environmental changes.

5   Conclusion

In conclusion, we have introduced a new metric for CSI signature analysis, namely the PMF, and used it for NTC applications. In particular, we collected CSI for different network traffic in different environments, i.e. a computer lab and an isolated RF-chamber. Our experimental observations corroborated the fact that CSI could be used for NTC. We also noted the similarities between different network traffics, such as that of Spotify and YouTube in Fig. 9, and that of YouTube and Twitch in Fig. 6. It is possible that the classification performance might be better in the chamber than in the lab, and the network traffic of workstation/router pair is more easily distinguishable than Raspberry Pi pair. However, this requires further verification. During our experiment, we also noted device temperature as a possible cause for the difference in the CSI signature.

For future works, several aspects could be examined: the relationship between the CSI frame rate, device temperature and the CSI signature; the probability of combining our methods with existing NTC methods; evaluate the CSI-based NTC performance while trying to classify network traffic of multiple devices at once; the CSI signature difference of more subtle differences in the data traffic, such as video type, music type rather than that of different applications, which leads to privacy, secrecy, security applications.

References

1. Dong, Z., Li, F., Ying, J., Pahlavan, K.: Indoor motion detection using wi-fi channel state information in flat floor environments versus in staircase environments. Sensors **18**, 2177 (2018). https://doi.org/10.3390/s18072177
2. Gringoli, F., Schulz, M., Link, J., Hollick, M.: Free your csi: a channel state information extraction platform for modern Wi-Fi Chipsets. In: Proceedings of International Workshop. Wireless Network Testbeds, Experimental Evaluation & Characterization (WiNTECH), p. 21–28. Los Cabos, Mexico (2019). https://doi.org/10.1145/3349623.3355477
3. Halperin, D., Hu, W., Sheth, A., Wetherall, D.: Tool Release: Gathering 802.11n Traces with Channel State Information. ACM SIGCOMM CCR **41**(1), 53 (2011)
4. Hameed, A., Alomary, A.: Security Issues in IoT: A Survey. In: Proceedings of International Conference on Innovation and Intelligence for Informatics, Computing, and Technologies (3ICT), pp. 1–5 (2019). https://doi.org/10.1109/3ICT.2019.8910320
5. Höchst, J., Baumgärtner, L., Hollick, M., Freisleben, B.: Unsupervised traffic flow classification using a neural autoencoder. In: Proceedings of IEEE 42nd Conference on Local Computer Networks (LCN), pp. 523–526 (2017). https://doi.org/10.1109/LCN.2017.57
6. Lopez-Martin, M., Carro, B., Sanchez-Esguevillas, A., Lloret, J.: Network traffic classifier with convolutional and recurrent neural networks for internet of things. IEEE Access **5**, 18042–18050 (2017). https://doi.org/10.1109/ACCESS.2017.2747560
7. Pacheco, F., Exposito, E., Gineste, M., Baudoin, C., Aguilar, J.: Towards the deployment of machine learning solutions in network traffic classification: a systematic survey. IEEE Commun. Surv. Tutor. **21**(2), 1988–2014 (2019). https://doi.org/10.1109/COMST.2018.2883147
8. Schulz, M., Wegemer, D., Hollick, M.: Nexmon: The C-based Firmware Patching Framework (2017). https://nexmon.org
9. Wang, W., Zhu, M., Zeng, X., Ye, X., Sheng, Y.: Malware traffic classification using convolutional neural network for representation learning. In: Proceedings of International Conference on Information Networking (ICOIN), pp. 712–717 (2017). https://doi.org/10.1109/ICOIN.2017.7899588
10. Wang, Z., Jiang, K., Hou, Y., Dou, W., Zhang, C., Huang, Z., Guo, Y.: A survey on human behavior recognition using channel state information. IEEE Access **7**, 155986–156024 (2019). https://doi.org/10.1109/ACCESS.2019.2949123
11. Won, M., Sahu, S., Park, K.J.: DeepWiTraffic: Low Cost WiFi-Based Traffic Monitoring System Using Deep Learning. ArXiv abs/1812.08208 (2018)
12. Zeng, Y., Pathak, P.H., Mohapatra, P.: WiWho: wifi-based person identification in smart spaces. In: Proceedings of ACM/IEEE International Conference on Information Processing in Sensor Networks (IPSN), pp. 1–12 (2016). https://doi.org/10.1109/IPSN.2016.7460727
13. Zhang, J., Tang, Z., Li, R., Chen, X., Gong, X., Fang, D., Wang, Z.: Protect Sensitive information against channel state information based attacks. In: Proceedings of IEEE International Conference on Computational Science and Engineering (CSE) and IEEE International Conference on Embedded and Ubiquitous Computing (EUC), vol. 2, pp. 203–210 (2017). https://doi.org/10.1109/CSE-EUC.2017.221

Performance Evaluation of the Packet Aggregation Mechanism of an N-GREEN Metro Network Node

Tülin Atmaca[1], Amira Kamli[1], Godlove Suila Kuaban[2], and Tadeusz Czachórski[2(✉)]

[1] Samovar, Télécom Sud Paris. Institut Polytechnique de Paris, Evry, France
{tulin.atmaca,amira.kamli}@lecom-sudparis.eu
[2] Institute of Theoretical and Applied Informatics Polish Academy of Sciences, ul. Bałtycka 5, 44-100 Gliwice, Poland
{gskuaban,tadek}@iitis.pl

Abstract. Today's telecommunication network infrastructure and services are dramatically changing due partially to the rapid increase in the amount of traffic generation and its transportation. This rapid change is also caused by the increased demand for a high quality of services and the recent interest in green networking strengthened by cutting down carbon emission and operation cost. Access networks generate short electronic packets of different sizes, which are aggregated into larger optical packets at the ingress edge nodes of the optical backbone network. It is transported transparently in the optical domain, reconverted into the electronic domain at the egress edge nodes, and delivered to the destination access networks. Packet aggregation provides many benefits at the level of MAN, and core networks such as, increased spectral efficiency, energy efficiency, optimal resource utilisation, simplified traffic management which significantly reduces protocol and signalling overhead. However, packet aggregation introduces performance bottleneck at the edge node as the packets from the access networks are temporarily stored in the aggregation buffers during the packet aggregation process. In this article, we apply the diffusion approximation model and other stochastic modelling methods to analytically evaluate the performance of a new packet aggregation mechanism which was developed specifically for an N-GREEN (Next Generation of Routers for Energy Efficiency) metro network. We obtain the distribution of the packets' queue in the aggregation buffer, which influences the distribution of the waiting time (delay) experienced by packets in the aggregation buffer. We then, demonstrate the influence of the probability p of successfully inserting the packet data units from the aggregation queue to the optical ring within a defined timeslot Δ. We also discuss the performance evaluation of the complete ring by deriving the utilisation of each link.

1 Introduction

Different access networks such as Digital Subscriber Line (DSL), Ethernet local area networks (LANs), wireless LANs, mobile networks (e.g. 3G, 4G, and 5G),

© Springer Nature Switzerland AG 2021
M. C. Calzarossa et al. (Eds.): MASCOTS 2020, LNCS 12527, pp. 62–78, 2021.
https://doi.org/10.1007/978-3-030-68110-4_4

and the Internet of Things (IoT) generate packets of different sizes which are usually aggregated into larger packets. The main objective behind these methods is to leverage on the large optical bandwidth in the core network and to reduce processing overhead. This mechanism is called packet aggregation and it involves the assembly of smaller packets into larger ones. It provides many benefits at the level of core and MAN networks, such as increased spectral efficiency, energy efficiency, optimal resource utilisation [1], simplified traffic management, and significantly reduces protocol and signalling overhead. It notably influences the overall performance of the network in terms of packet latency, packet losses, and bandwidth utilisation. Therefore, packet aggregation mechanisms and transmission queue management must be carefully designed and parameterised.

The application of packet aggregation in 5G networks was studied in [1], where the short packets from the 5G access networks are aggregated into larger ones before they are inserted into the core network for transportation. Also, the authors in [2] applied packet aggregation at the edge router of a software-defined network (SDN) to aggregate smaller packets from IoT networks into larger ones before they are transported in the internet core network to the IoT cloud servers. It is expected that 5G and IoT networks will generate vast amounts of traffic of smaller packet sizes to be transported over IP or optical backbone networks. These packets need to be aggregated to larger IP or optical packets to avoid both increased processing overhead and energy consumption. Packet aggregation was extensively applied in the grooming of electronic packets at the electronic domain of the edge node of optical networks, e.g. optical burst switching (OBS) networks [3]. More efficient packet aggregation algorithms have been developed for NGREEN metro networks. An N-GREEN metro network is a cost-effective and energy-efficient optical network which consists of ring typologies of over-dimensioned switches and router nodes. Ring typologies are very common in the Metro networks. They enable the deployment of ring protection mechanisms which ensure the survivability of the core network during failures. Therefore, N-GREEN is an attractive network solution for emerging Metro and core networks, and it is also provided with SDN functionalities [4].

To transport electronic packets over optical networks, the smaller electronic packets are aggregated, converted into optical bursts or packets, and then inserted into the core network. The optical signals are then transported transparently from the ingress edge node to the egress edge node, without conversion opto/electro/opto (O/E/O) to perform routing. Therefore, the elimination of O/E/O conversions significantly reduces the energy consumption as the packets are switched in the optical domain, and the optical signals are boosted using optical amplifiers which are relatively energy efficient. In classical IP over optical networks, e.g. OBS networks, smaller packets are collected in aggregation buffers, and the contents of the buffers are framed into lager packets, and then sent to a transmission queue. The most popular packet aggression mechanisms implemented in commercial network nodes are the time-based, the size-based and the hybrid packet aggregation algorithms [3].

The drawback of these aggregation mechanisms is that the generated bursts are sometimes of variable sizes which may be very large, resulting in burst dropping at the core network or sometimes small, resulting in poor resource utilisation [5]. Also, under low traffic conditions, the arriving electronic packets may experience longer delays in the aggregation buffer, which are not desirable for real-time traffic. The edge node is therefore, considered to be the performance bottleneck of the network. The performance evaluations of the time-based, size-based, and hybrid packet aggregation mechanisms were studied in [3,6], assuming that the arrival of electronic packets into the buffer follows a Poisson process. The authors in [7] compared the Poisson-based interarrival times distribution with the measured distribution from the Center for Applied Internet Data Analysis (CAIDA) repositories, and realised that even though the Poisson assumption simplifies the performance analysis, it differs from reality. The authors, therefore, used diffusion approximation with CAIDA traffic to evaluate the performance of time-based, size-based, and hybrid packet aggregation mechanisms. In this paper, we propose the use of diffusion approximation to evaluate a novel packet aggregation mechanism that was recently proposed in [8,9]. In this mechanism, smaller electronic packets called service data units (SDU) are continuously collected in an over-dimensioned aggregation buffer. The accumulated packets in the buffer are then framed into fixed-sized larger packet data unit (PDU). The PDUs are then inserted into the metro optical ring using a slot reservation insertion method, timer-based, or an opportunistic insertion method.

In this paper, we analytically evaluate the performance of the packet aggregation mechanism of an N-GREEN metro network node. We use diffusion approximation model with reflecting barrier to analytically study the dynamic changes in the content of the buffer, as the PDUs are inserted into the optical ring from the aggregation buffer. We obtain the distribution of the content of the queue of SDUs in the aggregation buffer for different values of p (the probability of inserting a PDU into the optical packet within a given timeslot Δ). We also obtained the distribution of the delay experienced by the SDUs within the aggregation buffer and then investigated the influence of p. We discussed the performance evaluation of the complete ring by deriving the link utilisation.

2   Description of the N-GREEN Packet Aggregation Mechanism

The N-GREEN project proposed two technological innovations for optical networks such as the WDM Slotted Add/Drop Multiplexer (WSADM) technology, and a Modular and Self Protected Backplane. It exploits the benefits of WDM or multicoloured optical packets, which enable the use of low cost commercially available components, integration of SDN technology, compliance with 5G performance requirements, and relatively low energy consumption. An N-GREEN metro network ring consists of the optical switch node (also called an electrical bridge) and the bridge nodes as shown in Fig. 1. The optical switch node (node 1 in the figure) aggregates smaller electronic packets from access networks into

larger packets which are converted into optical packets and inserted into the
metro ring. It also connects the metro ring to other metro rings. The bridge
nodes bypass or relays transit optical packets transparently without optical-
electrical-optical conversions and add/drop optical packets. The transmission of
optical packets between the bridge nodes does not pass through the switch node
in order to avoid O/E/O conversions and hence, a relative reduction in energy
consumption [8]. Capital expenditure (CAPEX) comparisons of WSADM technology with the optical packet switching (OPS) or optical burst switching (OBS)
technologies indicate that WSADM could compete favourably with existing technologies in terms of cost, energy consumption and performance [10,11].

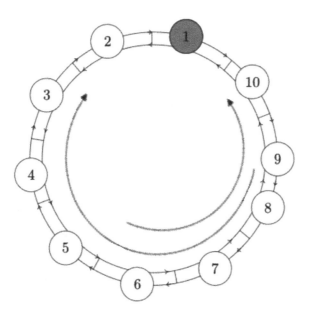

Fig. 1. An N-GREEN optical metro ring [8]

In the considered packet aggregation mechanism, multiple electronic packets
or service data units (SDUs), e.g. IP packets from various access networks, form
a first-in-first-out queue waiting to be inserted into the optical packet at any
available timeslot. The size of the optical packet is fixed and equal to L bytes.
New optical packets circulating in the ring appear at each constant time interval
Δ, but some of them are already occupied and cannot be used, Fig. 2. Denote
by p probability that an optical packet is empty and the content of the queue
may be transferred to it. Consider two ways of filling optical packets.

Case 1: Every empty packet is loaded. If the queue is smaller than L bytes,
the whole its content is inserted; if the queue is larger then the optical packet,
L bytes are inserted, and the rest stays waiting for the next available packet.

Case 2: If the content of the queue is smaller than L, the optical buffer is not filled; otherwise, L bytes are loaded, and the rest is waiting for the next opportunity.

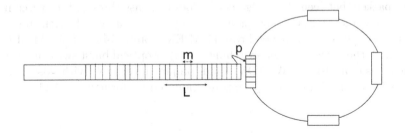

Fig. 2. The N-GREEN packet aggregation system

The optical packets are circulating inside the ring and transport messages among stations. Each station has a similar queue of electronic packets waiting to be transported by the optical ring. First, we will study a single queue, and then we will try to model the queue interactions inside the ring.

3   Diffusion Model of the Queue

We approximate the size of the content of the buffer by a diffusion process. Diffusion approximation, since its very beginning [12–14] is applied in queueing problems and performance evaluation, appears also in a patent [15]. The models are often related to G/G/1, G/G/1/N or G/G/m/M+K stations and their networks, cf. [16], it was also used recently for modelling, e.g. energy harvesting sensor nodes [17], Clouds [18] and routers in Software Defined Networks, [19].

The size of the queue of SDUs in the aggregation buffer is represented by a diffusion process $X(t)$, and its evolution is given by the diffusion equation

$$\frac{\partial f(x,t;x_0)}{\partial t} = \frac{\alpha}{2}\frac{\partial^2 f(x,t;x_0)}{\partial x^2} - \beta\frac{\partial f(x,t;x_0)}{\partial x} \tag{1}$$

where βdt and αdt represent the mean and variance of the changes of the diffusion process at dt. The equation defines the conditional probability density function (pdf) of the diffusion process $X(t)$

$$f(x,t;x_0)dx = P[x \le X(t) < x + dx \mid X(0) = x_0].$$

The diffusion approximation applied to queueing systems is based on the assumption that the number of arrivals of customers joining the queue during a time T has a distribution which is close to normal and does not depend on the distribution of interarrival times but only on its two first moments. The mean and variance of this normal distribution are λT and $\lambda^3 \sigma_A^2 T$ where $1/\lambda$ and σ_A^2, are mean and variance of interarrival times, [12]. Here, the position x of the process $X(t)$ corresponds to the number of bytes currently in the buffer. The number of bytes received at a unit of time is a product of two independent random variables: X – the number of packets and Y – the size of packets. The mean of a product variable XY is $E(XY) = E(X)E(Y)$ and the variance is

$$
\begin{aligned}
Var(XY) &= E(X^2Y^2) - (E(XY))^2 \\
&= Var(X)Var(Y) + Var(X)(E(Y))^2 \\
&+ Var(Y)(E(X))^2,
\end{aligned}
$$

the mean number of arrived at a time unit packets is $E(X) = \lambda$ and the variance is $Var(X) = \lambda^3 \sigma_A^3$, and we denote by m the mean size of a packet (in bytes) and by σ_m^2 the variance of its size, therefore the mean number of arrived at a time unit bytes is

$$
\beta = \lambda m
$$

and the variance of number of arrived at a time unit bytes defining α in Eq. (1) is

$$
\alpha = \lambda^3 \sigma_A^2 \sigma_m^2 + \lambda^3 \sigma_A^2 m^2 + \sigma_m^2 \lambda^2. \tag{2}
$$

We consider the unlimited queue; therefore, the diffusion process is limited only by a reflecting barrier at $x = 0$ (the queue is never negative).

Without any barrier, the density of the unrestricted process defined by Eq. (1) and started at x_0 is

$$
f(x,t;x_0) = \frac{1}{\sqrt{2\Pi \alpha t}} \exp\left[-\frac{(x - x_0 - \beta t)^2}{2\alpha t}\right];
$$

with the reflecting barrier at $x = 0$ it becomes, see e.g. [20]

$$
f(x,t;x_0) = \frac{1}{\sqrt{2\Pi \alpha t}} [a(t) - \exp(2\beta x/\alpha)b(t)] \tag{3}
$$

where

$$
a(t) = \exp\left[-\frac{(x - x_0 - \beta t)^2}{2\alpha t}\right]
$$

and

$$
b(t) = \exp\left[-\frac{(-x - x_0 - \beta t)^2}{2\alpha t}\right]
$$

We may also define the initial condition in a more general way, the starting point is not only at x_0 but it is at any point ξ given by a distribution $\psi(\xi)$, in this case

$$
f(x,t;\psi) = \int_0^\infty f(x,t;\xi)\psi(\xi)d\xi. \tag{4}
$$

Loading the optical packet with the queue content, i.e. decreasing the queue, corresponds to the jumps back of the process $X(t)$. However, the jumps may occur only at discrete moments, at the end of the interval Δ. Therefore we concentrate on the diffusion description during constant intervals Δ and the definition of immediate changes in the process between these intervals.

Two ways of charging the optical packet are considered:

3.1   Case 1

The process is decreased by jumps back occurring with probability p after each fixed time-interval Δ. If $x \leq L$ jumps are to $x = 0$, the entire content of the queue is loaded to the optical packet, the queue becomes empty, and the filling process is started again when the first electronic packet arrives into the buffer. If $x > L$, the jump is performed to $x = x - L$ (distance L back): the size of the queue is larger than the size of the optical packet and the queue is emptied only partially. Denote by $f^{(i)}(x, \Delta; \psi^{(i)})$ the pdf of the process during ith interval Δ. At the beginning of each interval, the time is set to zero, hence always $t \in [0, \Delta]$. The distribution of the queue at the end of each Δ, after the jump, if it occurs, defines the initial distribution of the queue for the next time slot. Assume that the initial value of the process is $x_0 = 0$, the queue is empty.

At the end of the first interval, the position of the process, before a possible jump, is given by $f^{(1)}(x, \Delta; 0)$. The jump occurs with probability p giving the initial distribution for the next interval

$$\psi^{(2)}(0) = \int_m^L f^{(1)}(x, \Delta; m)dx \tag{5}$$

and for $\xi > 0$

$$\psi^{(2)}(\xi) = f^{(1)}(\xi + L, \Delta; 0) \tag{6}$$

or with probability $1 - p$ there is no jump and the new initial condition is given by the position of the process at the end of previous time-slot

$$\psi^{(2)}(\xi) = f^{(1)}(\xi, \Delta; 0). \tag{7}$$

Therefore, the complete initial condition for the second time slot is defined as

$$\psi^{(2)}(0) = p \int_m^L f^{(1)})(x, \Delta; m)dx,$$
$$\psi^{(2)}(\xi) = pf^{(1)}(\xi + L, \Delta; 0) \tag{8}$$
$$+ (1 - p)f^{(1)}(\xi, \Delta; 0), \xi > 0$$

and these initial conditions determine the movement of the process during the second time slot and its position at the end of it, $f^{(2)}(\xi, \Delta; \psi^{(2)})$.

In the same way for the next slots,

$$\psi^{(n+1)}(0) = p \int_0^L f^{(n)}(x, \Delta; \psi^{(n)})dx,$$
$$\psi^{(n+1)}(\xi) = pf^{(n)}(\xi + L, \Delta; \psi^{(n)}) \tag{9}$$
$$+ (1 - p)f^{(n)}(\xi, \Delta; \psi^{(n)}), \xi > 0$$

until the convergence, when $\psi^{(n+1)}(\xi) = \psi^{(n+1)}(\xi)$ and $f^{(n+1)}(x,t;\psi^{(n+1)}) \approx f^{(n)}(x,t;\psi^{(n)})$. This convergence is illustrated later in Figs. 3, 4, 5 and 6 for various valuess of p.

3.2 Case 2

In this case, we try to fill the optical packet at the end of Δ only if the queue size is greater than L. The equations of Case 1 are adapted in the following way. As previously, at the end of the first interval Δ the queue distribution has density $f^{(1)}(x, \Delta; 0)$. and for any slot $n \geq 1$

$$
\begin{aligned}
\psi^{(n+1)}(\xi) &= f^{(n)}(\xi, \Delta; \psi^{(n)}), \quad \xi < L, \\
\psi^{(n+1)}(\xi) &= p f^{(n)}(\xi + L, \Delta; \psi^{(n)}), \\
&+ (1 - p) f^{(n)}(\xi, \Delta; \psi^{(n)}), \quad \xi \geq L.
\end{aligned}
\tag{10}
$$

When the steady state is reached, the initial distribution $\psi = \lim_{n \to \infty} \psi^{(n)}$ and the state of the queue at the end of Δ is the same $f(x, \Delta; \psi) = \psi(x)$.

In both cases, the manner how the optical packets are filled causes that their volume L is not used in 100%. The packet is filled entirely with the probability that the size of the queue at the end of the interval is equal or higher than L, i.e. $\int_L^\infty f(x, \Delta; \psi) dx$. The partial filling of the optical packet (probability of loading x bytes) is given by $f(x, \Delta; \psi)$, $x < L$. The mean effective size of the packet is

$$
L_{\mathit{eff}} = L \int_L^\infty f(x, \Delta; \psi) dx + \int_0^L f(x, \Delta; \psi) x dx.
\tag{11}
$$

4 Queueing Delays

A packet coming at $t \in (t, \Delta)$ sees the queue distribution $f(x, t; \psi)$. With the probability

$$
p_1 = \int_0^L f(x, t, \psi) dx
$$

the queue is smaller than L, and therefore the packet will be loaded during the nearest filling of the optical packet (this is an approximation as we do not consider the size of the incoming packet). Its waiting time will be therefore $\Delta - t$ with probability p or $\Delta - t + \Delta$ with probability $(1 - p)p$, or $\Delta - t + 2\Delta$ with probability $(1 - p)^2 p$, ... $\Delta - t + n\Delta$ with probability $(1 - p)^n p$ depending when the first empty slot will be available. Denote its distribution density function as

$$
\begin{aligned}
f_{W1}(w, t) =\ & p\delta\left(w - (\Delta - t)\right) + (1 - p)p\delta(w - (2\Delta - t)) \\
& + (1 - p)^2 p \delta(w - (3\Delta - t)) + \dots \\
& + (1 - p)^n p \delta(w - ((n + 1)\Delta - t)) + \dots
\end{aligned}
\tag{12}
$$

where $\delta(x)$ is Dirac delta function. Assuming that the packet arrival may happen at any moment t of the time slot with the same density $1/\Delta$, we determine $f_{W1}(w)$ as

$$f_{W1}(w) = \int_0^{\Delta} \frac{1}{\Delta} f_{W1}(w, t) dt. \tag{13}$$

Similarily, if the queue size is between L and $2L$ which will happen with probability

$$p_2 = \int_L^{2L} f(x, t; \psi) dx$$

then we should have two empty optical packets to put the packet inside. It means that we add the delay of waiting for the second empty optical packet to the waiting time defined above, This delay is equal Δ with probability p if just the next optical packet is empty, 2Δ if the next packet is occupied but the one after it is empty – with probability $(1-p)p$, etc. The distribution of this additional delay $f_\Delta(w)$ is

$$\begin{aligned} f_\Delta(w) = {} & p\delta(w - \Delta) + (1-p)p\delta(w - 2\Delta) \\ & + (1-p)^2 p\delta(w - 3\Delta) + \dots \\ & + (1-p)^n p\delta(w - (n+1)\Delta) + \dots \end{aligned} \tag{14}$$

Therefore the waiting time for a packet arriving at time t and seeing the queue size between L and $2L$ is determined by the convolution

$$f_{W2}(w) = f_{W1}(w) * f_\Delta(w)$$

and the waiting time for the arriving packet seeing the queue size between $2L$ and $3L$ is determined by

$$f_{W3}(w) = f_{W1}(w) * f_\Delta(w) * f_\Delta(w)$$

and the unconditional waiting time distribution $f_W(w, t)$ for a packet coming at a time t is

$$f_W(w) = \sum_{n=1}^{\infty} p_n f_{Wn}(w) \tag{15}$$

where

$$p_n = \int_{(n-1)L}^{nL} f(x, t; \psi) dx \tag{16}$$

and

$$f_{Wn}(w) = f_{W1}(w) * f_\Delta(w)^{*(n-1)} \tag{17}$$

Equation (15) presents the probability distribution function of the delay introduced by the aggregation queue.

5   Numerical Examples

In numerical examples we use PDUs of length $L = 12.5$ KB (12500 bytes) and the time slots $\Delta = 10$ μs at 10 Gb/s, the same realistic parameters as considered in [8,9].

The interarrival times have a general distribution with mean $1/\lambda$, variance σ_A^2, and the size of electronic packets is determined by a general distribution having density with mean m and variance σ_m^2.

Assume $\lambda = 1$ packet/μs, the average packet size $m = 700$ bytes, squared coefficients of variation $C_A^2 = \sigma_A^2\lambda^2 = 1$ and $C_m^2 = \sigma_m^2/m^2 = 1$.

It means that the parameters of the diffusion equation are: arrival rate $\beta = \lambda m = 0.7$ kB/μs and $\alpha = 1.47$, as defined by Eq. (2)

Naturally, the variances C_A^2, C_m^2 may be different and represent any distribution, that is the advantage of diffusion approximation. Note that the squared coefficient of variation close to one does not mean necessarily that a distribution is resembling the exponential one. When analysing the distributions of packet sizes and times between packets given by CAIDA (Center for Applied Internet Data Analysis) repositories, we met distributions which are far away from exponential ones, but with $C^2 \approx 1$.

The PDUs are uploaded following Case 1 procedure.

Figures 3, 4, 5 and 6 illustrate the convergence of the solution formulated in Eq. (10) for various values of p, it is visible that at each case, 25 iterations give satisfactory results. Figure 7 presents the impact of probability p on the final distribution $f(x,t;\psi)$ of the queue length in bytes.

Table 1. Probabilities p_n, $n = 1,\ldots,5$ that arriving electronic packet sees queue size $x \in [(n-1)L, nL]$, as in Eq. (16)

p_n	$p = 0.25$	$p = 0.5$	$p = 0.75$	$p = 1$
$n = 1$	0.000422	0.011993	0.085542	0.5581957
$n = 2$	0.004069	0.066236	0.287785	0.430287
$n = 3$	0.016506	0.130243	0.276826	0.011427
$n = 4$	0.049166	0.183986	0.185722	$8.86 * 10^{-5}$
$n = 5$	0.119076	0.210541	0.100210	$3.66 * 10^{-7}$

The Table 1 presents probabilities p_n that n empty optical packets will be needed to allow the transport of a packet joining the queue.

Figures 8, 9 and 10 refer to the waiting time distributions. Figure 8 presents $f_{Wn}(w)$ as defined in Eq. (17), we see he waiting time depends on the number n of empty slots needed to evacuate the queue before the considered packet may be sent.

Figure 9 displays $f_{W5}(w)$ and illustrates how the probability p of an empty optical packet changes, for a fixed $n = 5$, the waiting time distribution.

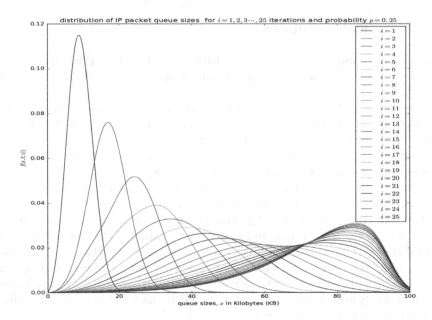

Fig. 3. The distribution of the aggregation queue size, $f(x, t; \psi)$ if $p = 0.25$ for consecutive iterations as in Eq. (10) $i = 1 \ldots 25$

Figure 10 gives the unconditional waiting time probability density distribution $f_W(w)$ following Eq. (15).

6   The Ring Performance

Let us evaluate the performance of the whole ring having n stations. Assume that each of the stations is delivering a flow of the same intensity λ of packets or $m\lambda$ of bytes. Assume also that the ring has n stations, the destination of flows is equiprobable, the traffic is one-way and the station receiving its flow after making a round deletes it.

It means that the whole flow λ packets generated by a station i is transmitted entirely between i and $i+1$, at $i+1$ station a $1/(n-1)$ part of it is subtracted and the rest, i.e. $(n-2)/(n-1)\lambda$ is sent further, on the next station again $1/(n-1)$ part of the original traffic is deleted, etc. and there is no traffic at all between station $i-1$ and i. If the traffic of each station is behaving in the same way, the total traffic between stations is $\lambda_{tot} = \lambda n/2$.

The total capacity of the ring assured by optical packets is L/Δ, but packets are not filled entirely, the effective mean content of a packet is L_{eff}, Eq. (11), hence the real capacity is $\mu = L_{eff}/\Delta$.

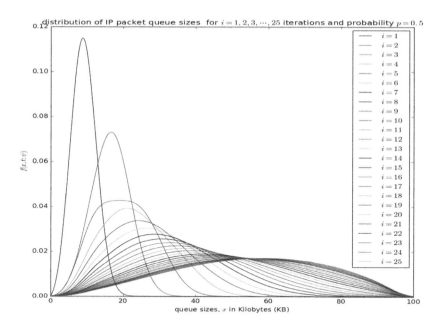

Fig. 4. The distribution of the aggregation queue size, $f(x, t; \psi)$ if $p = 0.5$ for consecutive iterations as in Eq. (10) $i = 1 \dots 25$

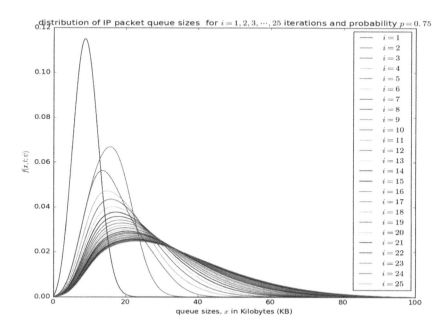

Fig. 5. The distribution of the aggregation queue size, $f(f(x, t; \psi))$ if $p = 0.75$ for consecutive iterations as in Eq. (10) $i = 1 \dots 25$

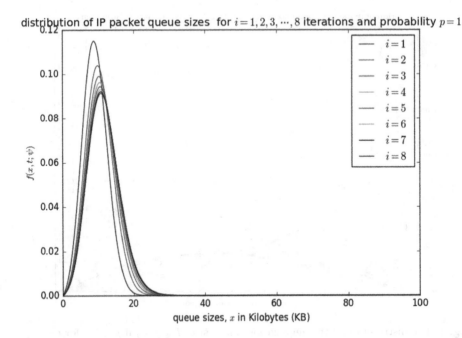

Fig. 6. The distribution of the aggregation queue size, $f(x, t; \psi)$ if $p = 1$ for consecutive iterations as in Eq. (10) $i = 1 \ldots 25$

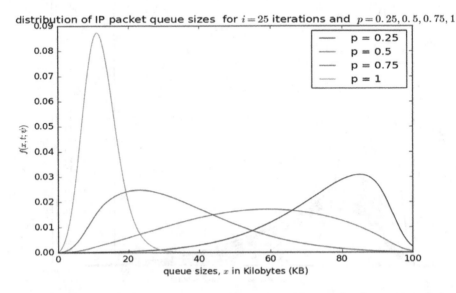

Fig. 7. The distribution of the aggregation queue size, $f(x, t; \psi)$ for the $i = 25$ iterations and different values p

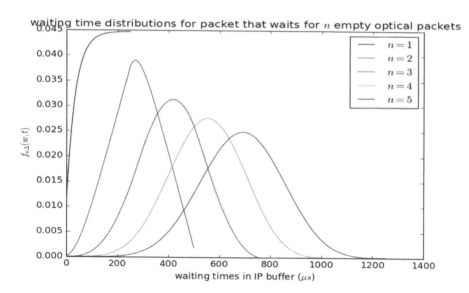

Fig. 8. $f_{Wn}(w)$ as defined in Eq. (17) – the influence of the number of empty optical packets n needed to complete the transfer on the waiting time distribution, $p = 0.25$

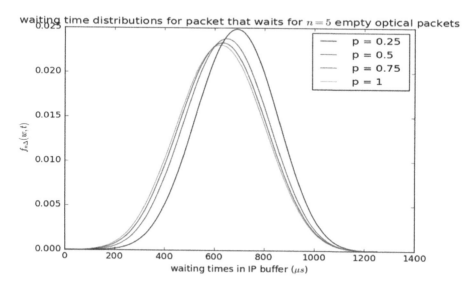

Fig. 9. $f_{W5}(w)$ as defined in Eq. (17) – the influence of the probability p of the empty optical packet on the distribution of waiting time if $n = 5$.

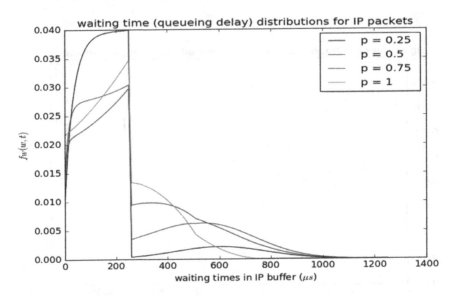

Fig. 10. The unconditional waiting time (queueing delay) density function $f_W(w)$ as in Eq. 13; $p = 0.25, 0.50, 0.75, 1$

Let us define the utilisation factor of the link as

$$\varrho = \lambda_{tot} m/\mu = \frac{\lambda_{tot} m \Delta}{L_{eff}} \tag{18}$$

and take it as an estimation of the probability that an optical packet is occupied $\varrho = (1 - p)$.

In the multicasting mode, where the traffic generated by a station i makes nearly the entire loop and is deleted only by the station $i - 1$, the ring traffic is $\lambda_{tot} = n\lambda$, the rest of the reasoning remains the same.

The evaluation of p, in Eq. (18) is based on L_{eff} in Eq. (11) which in turn is given by the diffusion model where p is a parameter. Therefore we should use iteratively the diffusion model and Eq. (18) looking for convergence of p for a given λ.

7   Conclusion

We have applied diffusion approximation modelling to analytically evaluate the performance of the packet aggregation mechanism of an N-GREEN metro network node. We compared the distribution of the queue size of SDUs in the aggregation buffer (distribution of the content of the buffer) for different values of p (the probability of loading a PDU into the optical packet within a given timeslot Δ or the probability that an empty optical packet is available within the timeslot Δ) as shown in Fig. 7 . For large values of p, the queue size of SDUs in the aggregation buffer is small. However, for small values of p, the queue size of SDUs in the aggregation buffer is significantly large. Even though we have assumed that the aggregation buffer is over-dimensioned to ensure that it does not overflow, it can overflow if the value of p is low and the arrival of packets into the aggregation buffer is fast. We also investigate the influence of p on the distribution of the waiting time (delay) experienced by the SDUs in the aggregation buffer, as shown in Fig. 9. The higher the value of p, the smaller the delay, but the smaller the value of p, the longer the delay.

Therefore, we have demonstrated the influence of the probability of successfully inserting the aggregated packets from the aggregation buffer to the optical transmission ring on the distribution of the queue size in the aggregation buffer and on the distribution of the delay experienced by the SDUs in the aggregation buffer. We have also discussed the performance evaluation of the complete ring by deriving the link utilisation. The designer can optimise the throughput and delay by tunning the design parameters such as the size of the aggregated packet (PDU) L, the timeslot Δ and the probability p of successfully inserting the packet.

References

1. Akyurek, A.S., Rosing, T.S.: Optimal packet aggregation scheduling in wireless networks. IEEE Trans. Mob. Comput. **17**(12), 2835–2852 (2018)
2. Lin, Y., Wang, S., Huang, C., Wu, C.: The SDN approach for the aggregation/disaggregation of sensor data. Sensors **18**(7), 2025 (2018)
3. Hermandéz, J.A., Aracil, J., López, V., de Vergara, J.L.: On the analysis of burst-assembly delay in obs networks and applications in delay-based service differentiation. Photon Netw. Commun. **14**, 49–62 (2007)
4. Gravey, A., Amar, D., Gravey, P., Morvan, M., Uscumlic, B., Chiaroni, D.: Modeling packet insertion on a wsadm ring. In: Proceedings of the 22nd International Conference on Optical Network Design and Modeling (ONDM), (Dublin), pp. 82–87. IEEE (2018)
5. Choi, J.Y., Le Vu, H., Cameron, C.W., Zukerman, M., Kang, M.: The effect of burst assembly on performance of optical burst switched networks. In: Kahng, H.-K., Goto, S. (eds.) ICOIN 2004. LNCS, vol. 3090, pp. 729–739. Springer, Heidelberg (2004). https://doi.org/10.1007/978-3-540-25978-7_73
6. Suila, K.G., Czachórski, T., Rataj, A.: A queueing model of the edge node in IP over all-optical networks. In: Gaj, P., Sawicki, M., Suchacka, G., Kwiecień, A. (eds.) CN 2018. CCIS, vol. 860, pp. 258–271. Springer, Cham (2018). https://doi.org/10.1007/978-3-319-92459-5_21
7. Kuaban, G.S., Anyam, E., Czachórski, T., Rataj, A.: Performance of a buffer between electronic and all-optical networks, diffusion approximation model. In: Czachórski, T., Gelenbe, E., Grochla, K., Lent, R. (eds.) ISCIS 2018. CCIS, vol. 935, pp. 68–75. Springer, Cham (2018). https://doi.org/10.1007/978-3-030-00840-6_8
8. Kamli, X., Atmaca, T., Lepers, C., Rataj, A., Amar, D.: Performance improvement of colored optical packet switching thanks to time slot sharing. In: Proceedings of the 14th Advanced International Conference on Telecommunications, Barcelona, Spain, pp. 12–31, IARIA (2018)

9. Kamli, A.: Analysis and Optimisation of a new futuristic optical network architecture. PhD thesis, Ecole doctorale n = 580 Sciences et technologies de l'information et del communication (STIC), Université Paris-Saclay, France (2020)

10. Chiaroni, D., Uscumlic, B.: Potential of WDM packets.: In: Proceedings of the 2017 International Conference on Optical Network Design and Modeling (ONDM), (Budapest), pp. 1–6. IEEE (2018)

11. Triki, A. Gravey, A., Gravey, P., Morvan, M.: Long-term capex evolution for slotted optical packet switching in a metropolitan network. In: Proceedings of the 2017 International Conference on Optical Network Design and Modeling (ONDM), (Budapest), pp. 1–6, IEEE (2018)

12. Gelenbe, E.: On approximate computer systems models. J. ACM **22**(2), 261–269 (1975)

13. Kobayashi, H.: Modeling and Analysis: An Introduction to System Performance Evaluation Methodology. Addison-Wesley, Reading, Massachusetts (1978)

14. Gelenbe, E.: Probabilistic models of computer systems part ii: diffusion approximations, waiting times and batch arrivals. Acta Informatica **12**(4), 285–303 (1979)

15. Gelenbe, E., Mang, X., Onvural, R.O.: Diffusion based statistical call admission control in ATM. Perform. Eval. **27**(12), 411–436 (1996)

16. Czachórski, T., Pekergin, F.: Diffusion approximation as a modelling tool. In: Kouvatsos, D.D. (ed.) Network Performance Engineering. LNCS, vol. 5233, pp. 447–476. Springer, Heidelberg (2011). https://doi.org/10.1007/978-3-642-02742-0_20

17. Abdelrahman, O., Gelenbe, E.: Diffusion model for energy harvesting sensor nodes. In: Proceedings of 24th IEEE International Symposium on Modeling, Analysis and Simulation of Computer and Telecommunication Systems (MASCOTS), pp. 154–158, IEEE (2016)

18. Czachorski, T., Grochla, K.: Diffusion approximation models for cloud computations with task migrations. In: Proceedings of the 2019 IEEE International Conference on Fog Computing (ICFC), Prague. IEEE (2019)

19. Czachorski, T., Gelenbe, E., Kuaban, S.G., Marek, D.: Transient behaviour of a network router. In: Proceedings of the 43th International Conference on Telecommunications and Signal Processing. Milano, Italy. IEEE (2020)

20. Cox, R.P., Miller, H.D.: The Theory of Stochastic Processes. Chapman and Hall, London, UK (1965)

Random Neural Network for Lightweight Attack Detection in the IoT

Katarzyna Filus[✉], Joanna Domańska, and Erol Gelenbe

Institute of Theoretical and Applied Informatics, IITIS-PAN,
Polish Academy of Sciences, ul. Baltycka 5, 44100 Gliwice, Poland
kfilus@iitis.pl
https://www.iitis.pl

Abstract. Cyber-attack detection has become a basic component of all information processing systems, and once an attack is detected it may be possible to block or mitigate its effects. This paper addresses the use of a learning recurrent Random Neural Network (RNN) to build a lightweight detector for certain types of Botnet attacks on IoT systems. Its low computational cost based on a small 12-neuron recurrent architecture makes it particularly attractive for edge devices. The RNN can be trained off-line using a fast simplified gradient descent algorithm, and we show that it can lead to high detection rates of the order of 96%, with false alarm rates of a few percent.

Keywords: IoT Attack detection · Random neural network · Machine learning · Lightweight attack detection

1 Introduction

Cyberattacks are increasingly common, sophisticated and malignant, while we constantly increase our reliance on Internet connected devices in almost every area of life: smart homes, cities, health monitoring, industry, military, agriculture etc. Also, the rapid increase in the number of IoT devices, their functionality and connectivity, has introduced additional security threats [12] because such simple devices are more prone to vulnerabilities that can lead to data theft, power supply drainage [34], and compromises that lead to their use in Botnets for Distributed Denial of Service (DDoS) attacks [38].

Since they are often Internet accessible and interconnected for machine-to-machine (M2M) communications, IoT devices are a natural "doorway" for attackers, and the use of wireless communications also increases their vulnerability [40].

This research was supported by the EU H2020 IoTAC Research and Innovation Action, funded by the European Commission (EC) under Grant Agreement ID: 952684. The EC's support does not constitute an endorsement of this paper, which reflects the views only of the authors.

M. C. Calzarossa et al. (Eds.): MASCOTS 2020, LNCS 12527, pp. 79–91, 2021.
https://doi.org/10.1007/978-3-030-68110-4_5

IoT devices are often embedded with microcontrollers powered by batteries; therefore energy saving is important and complex attack detection techniques that require a large amount of computation cannot be installed on such systems [59]. Thus much work has been done on creating simple yet accurate intrusion detection techniques for IoT platforms and evaluating them on representative datasets [11, 19].

Over the years, many different techniques have been used for attack detection. In [43] it is indicated that the major algorithms used in the last decade for intrusion detection are based on the Artificial Neural Networks (ANNs), including Deep Learning based approaches that have gained popularity due to their ability to extract patterns better than shallow learning methods despite their need for additional computational resources [64]. While for some IoT devices security is crucial, for others energy-efficiency is critical; thus the trade-off between security-effectiveness and energy-efficiency needs to be considered [40].

Hence we propose a recurrent Random Neural Network (RNN) for lightweight attack detection which can be trained off-line, creating a small but effective network that produces satisfactory results with a minimum of computationally demanding operations, and potentially low energy consumption. The small size of the RNN leads to less storage space and energy consumption for storage, as well as to lower computation times for detection which also save energy. We initialize the network weights in such a way as to establish the "neutrality" of the network prior to the learning process for faster and more accurate learning. We also reduce the number of computationally demanding operations during learning by fixing the total value of the RNN excitatory and inhibitory weights, so that only excitatory weights need to be updated with an automatic effect on the inhibitory weights.

In the sequel, Sect. 2 discusses the area of Intrusion Detection and provides a literature overview. In Sect. 3 we discuss the RNN and summarize its initialization and the simplified learning algorithm. Section 4 describes our experimental results based on training the RNN with attack data and testing it using disjoint attack data. Finally we draw some conclusions and suggest future work.

2   Related Work on CyberAttack Datasets and Detection

Over the years, many different cyberattack datasets have been created such as the DARPA datasets [16, 17], the KDDCup'99 datasets [42], and their successors. However, since the time when these datasets were created more than twenty years ago, attacks have changed and detectors that were trained with that data have become less reliable [43]. Thus in recent years, datasets with IoT traffic have been created such as N-Baiot [53], IoT host-based datasets for IDS research [9], the IoT Network Intrusion Dataset [50], the BoT-IoT dataset [51] and MedBIoT [38].

The Bot-IoT dataset was created in the Cyber Range Laboratory of the University of New South Wales' Canberra Cyber Center (Australia). Their testbed consists of network platforms and simulated IoT services. The network platforms include normal and attacking virtual machines with additional network devices such as a packet filtering firewall and Network Interface Cards. The Ostinato software [55] is used to generate realistic normal network traffic, and four Kali Linux machines are used to simulate a set of standard Botnet attacks. The IoT sensors are simulated and use MQTT, the machine-to machine connectivity protocol, to transfer messages to a Cloud Service provider (AWS). The MQTT protocol runs over TCP/IP. The network protocol analyser (tshark) is used to capture the normal and attack raw data. Packet capturing is performed with the pcap library. The pcap files that are collected, are 69.3 GB in size and consist of 72 million records.

While in some datasets [9,50,53] only a very limited range of IoT multimedia devices are used, the Bot-IoT dataset [51] uses a variety of devices such as smart lights, a smart thermostat, a weather monitoring station, smart garage doors and a refrigerator, and it has been used in many recent papers [10,20–22,39].

In the sequel we will use the Bot-IoT dataset which consists of real and simulated IoT traffic, and contains three main types of attacks: both DoS and DDoS attacks, information gathering, and information theft.

2.1 Attack Detection

Many different approaches have been used for attack detection. Signature-based detection [13,52] utilizes known patterns of the attacks to detect abnormal behaviours in the network traffic. This type of detection does not have a strong generalization power and can be easily bypassed by novel types of attacks [38].

Anomaly-based detection systems operate by identifying the patterns that define normal and abnormal traffic, and can be divided into three main groups: knowledge-based, statistical and Machine Learning (ML) based. Knowledge-based systems use a set of rules and finite state machines. Statistically based techniques [5] are typically based on time series. The ML approaches covers include clustering techniques [63], Genetic Algorithms [60], and ANNs [41] and Deep Learning.

As indicated in [43], the most popular approach in the last decade has been to use ML based algorithms, especially ANNs that are successful because of their classification power and their ability to generalize to datasets for which they have not been specifically trained. A recent trend is also the increased usage of Deep Learning techniques for IDS [20,22,65].

Attack detection aims to identify within a given traffic stream, those sub-streams that are viewed as being "normal", and those sub-streams that are likely to contain various forms of attacks. Typically, a binary classification into "normal" and "attack" traffic is preferred because of its simplicity [49]. Indeed, detectors that attempt to seek more detailed classifications for instance into different types of attacks, tend to be more error prone, leading to a decrease in classification accuracy [64].

3   The Random Neural Network

The Random Neural Network (RNN) was introduced in [23]. It is a biologically inspired spiking neural network model, which has a recurrent structure that incorporates feedback loops. It has been proved to be a universal approximator for continuous and bounded functions [30,31]. Different gradient descent based learning algorithms have been suggested for the RNN [8,24].

RNNs have found application in many different fields, including modelling, optimization, image processing, communication systems, pattern recognition and classification [61]. For instance, they have been used for combinatorial optimization [25,29]. In [6,7] it has been shown that RNNs can be utilized to generate textures.

Other applications include the detection of explosive mines [1,35], medical image segmentation [27], the detection and classification of vehicles [45], video compression [14], the evaluation of subjective metrics of user satisfaction regarding the quality of service in networks [58], and as a detector of DDoS Attacks [54]. The image texture recognition capability of the RNN exhibited in [33], was used to accurately insert 3-D images into moving virtual reality scenes [28,44] and applied to the augmented reality simulation of transportation systems [46].

The RNN has also been used to evaluate the voice and video quality [36,57] of multimedia data streams. In smart buildings they have been used for the dynamic management of energy [3,4] and of heating, ventilation, air conditioning and cooling systems [47,48].

In the field of communications, RNNs have been used to control the modulation of downlink traffic in LTE systems [2], to construct adaptive network routing algorithms [32] in smart networks [18], to design intrusion detection in networks [56], and to optimally schedule video sequences for content delivery [37].

3.1   The Random Neural Network

In this section, we present the notation for the RNN [23]. The RNN with N neurons is represented by a vector of non-negative integers $K(t)$ and by a probability distribution $P[K(t) = k]$:

$$K(t) = (K_1(t), \ ... \ K_N(t)), \ K_i(t) \geq 0, \tag{1}$$

$$p(k, t) = Prob[K(t) = k], \ where \tag{2}$$
$$k = (k_1, \ ... \ , k_N), \ k_i \geq 0,$$

and k is a specific value taken by $K(t)$, where $K_i(t)$ represents the excitation level of neuron i in the network, and it is non-negative (as already indicated) and unbounded. Each neuron in a RNN receives *external excitatory and inhibitory spikes* according to independent Poisson processes of rate $\Lambda_i \geq 0$ and λ_i, respectively.

If $K_i(t) > 0$, neuron i can "fire" or spend a spike after an exponentially distributed interval of parameter $r_i \geq 0$, either to some other neuron j with probability p_{ij}^+ as an excitatory spike, or with probability p_{ij}^- as an inhibitory spike. We denote by $w_{i,j}^+ = r_i p_{ij}^+$ and $w_{i,j}^- = r_i p_{ij}^-$ the excitatory and inhibitory outgoing weights of neuron i. The spike leaving neuron i when it is excited, may also leave the network as a whole with probability $d_i \geq 0$ so that $d_i + \sum_{j=1}^{N}[p_{ij}^+ + p_{ij}^-] = 1$ for all neurons i.

When neuron i receives an excitatory spike at time t, it state increases by one, i.e. $K_i(t^+) = K_i(t)+1$. If it receives an inhibitory spike then it decreases by one, but only if it was previously positive, i.e. : $K_i(t^+) = max\ [0,\ K_i(t)-1]$. The key theoretical result that was proved in [24] regarding the RNN is as follows:

Theorem. Define $p(k) = \lim_{t \to \infty} p(k,t)$. If:

$$q_i = \frac{\Lambda_i + \sum_{j=1}^{N} q_j w_{j,i}^+}{r_i + \lambda_i + \sum_{j=1}^{N} q_j w_{j,i}^-} < 1, \tag{3}$$

It follows that for $k = (k_1,\ ...\ k_N)$

$$p(k) = \prod_{i=1}^{N} q_i^{k_i}(1 - q_i), \ and$$

$$q_i = \lim_{t \to \infty} Prob[K_i(t) > 0].$$

The conditions under which for all neurons we have $q_i < 1$ are discussed in [24].

3.2   Initialization of the Network Weights

It is quite common to initialize a neural network with randomly generated weights, or to select them using some other method that may optimize some criterion [62]. Here we select network weights so that prior to learning, the excitation probability of each neuron is given by the "neutral" value $q_i = 0.5$ for $i = 1,\ ...\ ,N$ when the input to each neuron is also set to a neutral value. In particular the neutral input value is selected as $\lambda_i = 0$, $\Lambda_i = \Lambda^o > 0$ and $w_{ij}^+ = w_{ij}^- = w$, for $i, j = 1,\ ...\ ,N$, so that:

$$q_i = \frac{\Lambda^o + wQ}{2Nw + wQ}, \tag{4}$$

$$where\ Q = \sum_{i=1}^{N} q_i = Nq, \tag{5}$$

$$so\ that\ if\ q_i = q = 0.5,\ we\ have\ w = \frac{4\Lambda^o}{3N}.$$

3.3   Learning

The biggest asset of ANNs is their ability to adapt by learning from a given set of examples. An ANN learning algorithm typically sets the network weights in such a way as to map the values of the output neurons in a manner that matches the requirements of a classification or decision scheme, as a function of the input values received by the ANN. In a recurrent network, which is obviously not going to be "feedforward" with data going from a set of inputs to a set of outputs, even though still we distinguish the input and output values of the network, some or all of the neurons may act as both input and output neurons.

The ANNs' ability to learn is closely related to their property of being universal approximators for bounded and continuous functions [15], which was also established for the RNN in [30,31]. Of the many different types of learning algorithms, the ones based on Gradient Descent – that also include most Deep Learning Algorithms – are commonly used. In particular, the RNN's Gradient Descent learning algorithm was introduced in [24] and extended in [33], both for feedforward and recurrent (feedback) networks. In [8] a further extension was presented for feedforward RNNs.

Denote by $\Lambda = (\Lambda_1, \ldots, \Lambda_N)$ and $\lambda = (\lambda_1, \ldots, \lambda_N)$ positive and negative input signal vectors respectively. Denote by $\iota = (\Lambda, \lambda)$ the set of input pairs and let the output vector $Y = (y_1, \ldots, y_N)$ be such that $y_i \in [0, 1]$. Suppose we are given a data set D which is composed of pairs (ι, Y). Then a simple objective of a learning algorithm can be stated as follows. Let W be the set of all weights of the network $W = \{w_{i,j}^+, w_{i,j}^- : 1 \leq i, j \leq N\}$. Then the learning algorithm approximates the following optimization problem:

$$\arg \min_W C, \; where \; C = \frac{1}{2} \sum_{(\iota,Y) \in D} a_i[q_i(\iota, W) - y_i]^2, \tag{6}$$

and $a_i \geq 0$ is a constant which determines the relative importance of neuron i. In the experiments presented in the sequel, the network has just one output neuron, so that we will set $a_i = 1$ only for that neuron, while $a_j = 0$ for all other neurons.

Note that we have written $q_i(\iota, W)$ to stress the fact that q_i depends only on the inputs and on the weights of the network. The learning carries out this optimization iteratively, by iterating through all the weights for a given (ι, Y), and repeating this process for all the $(\iota, Y) \in D$.

After the initialization we maintain the equality $W_{i,j} = w_{i,j}^+ + w_{i,j}^- = 2w$ so that we only need to compute each $w_{i,j}^+$ using the gradient iterations for k and each pair of neurons (u, v):

$$w_{u,v}^{+,(k+1)} = w_{u,v}^{+,(k)} - \eta \frac{\partial C}{\partial w_{u,v}^+}\Big|_{W=W^k,(\iota,Y)}, \tag{7}$$

where $\eta > 0$ is known as the learning rate. The details of the computational algorithm can be found in [24].

4   Experimental Results and Conclusions

We use the "10-best features version" of the Bot-IoT dataset [51] and limit the number of samples to 1177. To generate these features, the authors of [51] used data gathered in pcap files, and applied Correlation Coefficient and Entropy techniques to chose the best training features. Our testing dataset includes 589 samples with 350 attack instances and 239 non-attack instances.

The learning algorithm is implemented using Python, and the RNN used in the experiments consists of $N = 12$ neurons. 10 neurons receive external signals, and we have one output neuron. We also tried using a minimal network with eleven neurons, as well as a larger one, but achieved the best results using twelve neurons. When the number of neurons was smaller, the results were worse, and for bigger topologies the results did not improve. The weight updates are carried out after determining the output for every individual input data item sample, in contrast to batch learning.

In Table 1 we show the precision that is obtained with Random Intitalization, as compared to the initialization with "neutral weights", and thirdly the advantage of also using the additional feature of just learning the excitatory weights and maintaining the inhibitory weights so that the sum of the two remains constant (Weight Restriction or WR). We clearly see that the third approach is the best, both for training and testing recall.

The computation times presented in Table 2 are the average time values for training the network. Introducing the "neutral" initialization significantly speeds up the learning time from the 488.48 s to 166.16 s on average. When only the excitatory weights need to be learned, the learning time drops to 100.78 s. Thus the most accurate learning approach is also the fastest.

In Fig. 1 we present the evaluation (on the training and validation datasets) during the learning process. In these figures, the "number of iterations" is the number of samples that were used in the training. The accuracy curves with neutral initialization have the desired shape - the increase in the accuracy is visible almost from the beginning of the training. As can be seen in Fig. 1a it took more that 100 iterations to initiate the increase in the accuracy. After this slow start, a rapid increase occurs and then it stops and no further increase in the accuracy can be observed. Introducing WR optimizes the learning process not only by limiting the number of calculations needed but also by decreasing the number of iterations needed to achieve results comparable with those of the RNN without it. Also, it can be observed that the RNN with WR is also much better at generalization.

Table 1. Comparison of Accuracy, Precision and Recall for the best models achieved with the two weight initializations

Random		'Neutral'		'Neutral'+WR	
Train	Valid	Train	Valid	Train	Valid
Accuracy					
86.29	83.71	96.90	96.09	96.80	96.09
Precision					
100.0	100.0	99.79	100.0	99.48	100.0
Recall					
77.83	75.0	94.80	94.00	95.33	94.00

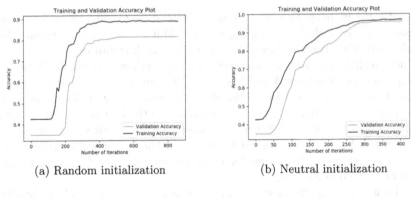

(a) Random initialization   (b) Neutral initialization

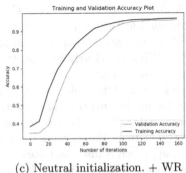

(c) Neutral initialization. + WR

Fig. 1. Accuracy plots for the networks with different types of weight handling implemented after the stabilization of the learning process

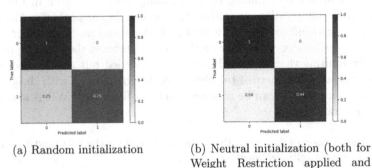

(a) Random initialization   (b) Neutral initialization (both for Weight Restriction applied and without it)

Fig. 2. Confusion matrices of the networks with different types of weight handling approaches implemented after the stabilization of the learning process

In Fig. 2 a graphical representation of the results is shown in the form of confusion matrices. It is clearly visible that using 'neutral' initialization we can also improve the RNN's accuracy for attack detection.

Table 2. Comparison of average execution times [s] for the models achieved with different types of weight handling implemented

Random	'Neutral'	'Neutral'+WR
488.48	166.16	100.78

In future work we will examine the design of attack detectors that can identify multiple forms of attacks simultaneously. This is a very challenging task that needs to be addressed with more sophisticated techniques including the use of multiple simultaneously operating neural networks.

We also plan to integrate these attack detection techniques in our existing test-bed which has been reported recently [26], so that we may evaluate the capacity of an integrated system not only to detect attacks, but also to react in a manner which mitigates or eliminates their effects.

References

1. Abdelbaki, H., Gelenbe, E., Kocak, T.: Neural algorithms and energy measures for EMI based mine detection. J. Differ. Eqn. Dyn. Syst. **13**(1–2), 63–86 (2005)
2. Adeel, A., Larijani, H., Ahmadinia, A.: Random neural network based cognitive engines for adaptive modulation and coding in LTE downlink systems. Comput. Electr. Eng. 57, 336–350 (2017). https://doi.org/10.1016/j.compeleceng.2016.11.005
3. Ahmad, J., Larijani, H., Emmanuel, R., Mannion, M., Javed, A., Phillipson, M.: Energy demand prediction through novel random neural network predictor for large non-domestic buildings. In: 2017 Annual IEEE International Systems Conference, SysCon 2017, Montreal, QC, Canada, 24–27 April 2017, pp. 1–6. IEEE (2017). https://doi.org/10.1109/SYSCON.2017.7934803
4. Ahmad, J., et al.: Energy demand forecasting of buildings using random neural networks. J. Intell. Fuzzy Syst. 38(4), 4753–4765 (2020). https://doi.org/10.3233/JIFS-191458
5. Aldribi, A., Traoré, I., Moa, B., Nwamuo, O.: Hypervisor-based cloud intrusion detection through online multivariate statistical change tracking. Comput. Secur. **88**, 101646 (2020)
6. Atalay, V., Gelenbe, E.: Parallel algorithm for colour texture generation using the random neural network model, pp. 227–236. World Scientific Publishing Co., Inc, USA (1992)
7. Atalay, V., Gelenbe, E., Yalabik, N.: The random neural network model for texture generation. Int. J. Pattern Recogn. Artif. Intell. **6**(1), 131–141 (1992)
8. Basterrech, S., Mohamed, S., Rubino, G., Soliman, M.A.: Levenberg-marquardt training algorithms for random neural networks. Comput. J. 54(1), 125–135 (2011). https://doi.org/10.1093/comjnl/bxp101

9. Bezerra, V.H., da Costa, V.G.T., Martins, R.A., Junior, S.B., Miani, R.S., Zarpelao, B.B.: Providing IoT host-based datasets for intrusion detection research. In: Anais do XVIII Simpósio Brasileiro em Segurança da Informação e de Sistemas Computacionais, pp. 15–28 (2018)

10. Brandon, A., Seekins, M., Joshua, B.V., Samuel, C., Haller, J.: Network data analysis to support risk management in an IoT environment. In: 2019 IEEE 10th Annual Ubiquitous Computing, Electronics & Mobile Communication Conference (UEMCON), pp. 0063–0068 (2019)

11. Brun, O., Yin, Y., Gelenbe, E.: Deep learning with dense random neural network for detecting attacks against iot-connected home environments. Proc. Comput. Sci. 134, 458–463 (2018). https://doi.org/10.1016/j.procs.2018.07.183

12. Cisco 2018 annual cybersecurity report (Cisco 2018). https://www.cisco.com/c/dam/en_us/about/annual-report/2018-annual-report-full.pdf. Accessed 26 Jul 2020

13. Cortés, F.M., Gómez, N.G.: A hybrid alarm management strategy in signature-based intrusion detection systems. In: 2019 IEEE Colombian Conference on Communications and Computing (COLCOM), pp. 1–6 (2019)

14. Cramer, C.E., Gelenbe, E.: Video quality and traffic QoS in learning-based sub-sampled and receiver-interpolated video sequences. IEEE J. Sel. Areas Commun. 18(2), 150–167 (2000)

15. Cybenko, G.: Approximations by superpositions of sigmoidal functions. Math. Control Signals Syst. 2(4), 303–314 (1989)

16. DARPA intrusion detection evaluation data set. MIT Lincoln Laboratory (1998). https://www.ll.mit.edu/r-d/datasets/1998-darpa-intrusion-detection-evaluation-dataset. Accessed 26 Jul 2020

17. DARPA Intrusion Detection Evaluation Data Set. MIT Lincoln Laboratory (1999). https://www.ll.mit.edu/r-d/datasets/1999-darpa-intrusion-detection-evaluation-dataset. Accessed 26 Jul 2020

18. Dobson, S., et al.: A survey of autonomic communications. ACM Trans. Autonom. Adap. Syst. (TAAS) 1(2), 223–259 (2006)

19. Evmorfos, S., Vlachodimitropoulos, G., Bakalos, N., Gelenbe, E.: Neural network architectures for the detection of SYN flood attacks in IoT systems. In: Proceedings of the 13th ACM International Conference on PErvasive Technologies Related to Assistive Environments. PETRA 2020, New York, NY, USA, Association for Computing Machinery (2020). https://doi.org/10.1145/3389189.3398000

20. Ferrag, M.A., Maglaras, L.: Deepcoin: a novel deep learning and blockchain-based energy exchange framework for smart grids. IEEE Trans. Eng. Manage. 67, 1285–1297 (2019)

21. Galeano-Brajones, J., Cortés-Polo, D., Valenzuela-Valdés, J.F., Mora, A.M., Carmona-Murillo, J.: Detection and mitigation of DoS attacks in SDN. an experimental approach. In: 2019 Sixth International Conference on Internet of Things: Systems, Management and Security (IOTSMS), pp. 575–580. IEEE (2019)

22. Ge, M., Fu, X., Syed, N., Baig, Z., Teo, G., Robles-Kelly, A.: Deep learning-based intrusion detection for IoT networks. In: 2019 IEEE 24th Pacific Rim International Symposium on Dependable Computing (PRDC), pp. 256–25609 (2019)

23. Gelenbe, E.: Random neural networks with negative and positive signals and product form solution. Neural Comput. 1(4), 502–510 (1989)

24. Gelenbe, E.: Learning in the recurrent random neural network. Neural Comput. 5, 154–164 (1993)

25. Gelenbe, E., Batty, F.: Minimum graph vertex covering with the random neural network. In: Computer Science and Operations Research, pp. 139–147. Pergamon, Amsterdam (1992)
26. Gelenbe, E., Domańska, J., Fröhlich, P., Nowak, M.P., Nowak, S.: Self-aware networks that optimize security, QoS, and energy. Proc. IEEE **108**(7), 1150–1167 (2020)
27. Gelenbe, E., Feng, Y., Krishnan, K.R.R.: Neural network methods for volumetric magnetic resonance imaging of the human brain. Proc. IEEE **84**(10), 1488–1496 (1996)
28. Gelenbe, E., Hussain, K.F., Kaptan, V.: Simulating autonomous agents in augmented reality. J. Syst. and Softw. **74**(3), 255–268 (2005)
29. Gelenbe, E., Koubi, V., Pekergin, F.: Dynamical random neural network approach to the traveling salesman problem. Proceedings of IEEE Systems Man and Cybernetics Conference **2**, 630–635 (1993)
30. Gelenbe, E., Mao, Z.H., Li, Y.: Function approximation with spiked random networks. IEEE Trans. Neural Netw. **10**(1), 3–9 (1999)
31. Gelenbe, E., Mao, Z.H., Li, Y.: Function approximation by random neural networks with a bounded number of layers. J. Differ. Eqn. Dyn. Syst. **12**(1–2), 143–170 (2004)
32. Gelenbe, E.: Steps toward self-aware networks. Commun. ACM **52**(7), 66–75 (2009)
33. Gelenbe, E., Hussain, K.F.: Learning in the multiple class random neural network. IEEE Trans. Neural Netw. **13**(6), 1257–1267 (2002)
34. Gelenbe, E., Kadioglu, Y.M.: Energy life-time of wireless nodes with network attacks and mitigation. In: 2018 IEEE International Conference on Communications Workshops, ICC Workshops 2018, Kansas City, MO, USA, 20–24 May 2018, pp. 1–6. IEEE (2018). https://doi.org/10.1109/ICCW.2018.8403561
35. Gelenbe, E., Kocak, T.: Area-based results for mine detection. IEEE Trans. Geosci. Remote Sens. **38**(1), 12–24 (2000)
36. Ghalut, T., Larijani, H.: Non-intrusive method for video quality prediction over LTE using random neural networks (RNN). In: 9th International Symposium on Communication Systems, Networks & Digital Signal Processing, CSNDSP 2014, Manchester, UK, 23–25 July 2014, pp. 519–524. IEEE (2014). https://doi.org/10.1109/CSNDSP.2014.6923884
37. Ghalut, T., Larijani, H.: Content-aware and QOE optimization of video stream scheduling over LTE networks using genetic algorithms and random neural networks. J. Ubiquitous Syst. Pervasive Netw. 9(2), 21–33 (2018). https://doi.org/10.5383/JUSPN.09.02.003
38. Guerra-Manzanares, A., Medina-Galindo, J., Bahsi, H., Nõmm, S.: MedBIoT: generation of an IoT botnet dataset in a medium-sized IoT network. In: 6th International Conference on Information Systems Security and Privacy, pp. 207–218 (2020)
39. Guizani, N., Ghafoor, A.: A network function virtualization system for detecting malware in large IoT based networks. IEEE J. Sel. Areas Commun. **38**(6), 1218–1228 (2020)
40. Hamdi, M., Abie, H.: Game-based adaptive security in the Internet of Things for ehealth. In: 2014 IEEE International Conference on Communications (ICC), pp. 920–925 (2014)
41. Hanif, S., Ilyas, T., Zeeshan, M.: Intrusion detection in IoT using artificial neural networks on UNSW-15 dataset. In: 2019 IEEE 16th International Conference on Smart Cities: Improving Quality of Life Using ICT & IoT and AI (HONET-ICT), pp. 152–156 (2019)

42. Hettich, S., Bay, S.: The UCI KDD Archive. Irvine, CA: University of California, Department of Information and Computer Science (1999). http://kdd.ics.uci.edu. Accessed 26 Jul 2020

43. Hindy, H., et al.: A taxonomy and survey of intrusion detection system design techniques, network threats and datasets. arXiv preprint arXiv:1806.03517 (2018)

44. Hussain, K.F., Kaptan, V.: Modeling and simulation with augmented reality. Int. J. Oper. Res. **38**(2), 89–103 (2004)

45. Hussain, K.F., Moussa, G.S.: On road vehicle classification based on random neural network and bag of visual words. Probabil. Eng. Inform. Sci. **30**, 403–412 (2016)

46. Hussain, K.F., Radwan, E., Moussa, G.S.: Augmented reality experiment: Drivers' behavior at an unsignalized intersection. IEEE Trans. Intell. Transp. Syst. **14**(2), 608–617 (2013)

47. Javed, A., Larijani, H., Ahmadinia, A., Emmanuel, R., Mannion, M., Gibson, D.: Design and implementation of a cloud enabled random neural network-based decentralized smart controller with intelligent sensor nodes for HVAC. IEEE Internet Things J. 4(2), 393–403 (2017). https://doi.org/10.1109/JIOT.2016.2627403

48. Javed, A., Larijani, H., Ahmadinia, A., Gibson, D.: Smart random neural network controller for HVAC using cloud computing technology. IEEE Trans. Ind. Inform. 13(1), 351–360 (2017). https://doi.org/10.1109/TII.2016.2597746

49. Jeatrakul, P., Wong, K.W.: Comparing the performance of different neural networks for binary classification problems. In: 2009 Eighth International Symposium on Natural Language Processing, pp. 111–115 (2009)

50. Kang, H., Ahn, D.H., Lee, G.M., Yoo, J.D., Park, K.H., Kim, H.K.: IoT network intrusion dataset (2019). http://dx.doi.org/10.21227/q70p-q449

51. Koroniotis, N., Moustafa, N., Sitnikova, E., Turnbull, B.: Towards the development of realistic botnet dataset in the internet of things for network forensic analytics: Bot-IoT dataset. Future Generation Comput. Syst. **100**, 779–796 (2019)

52. Li, W., Tug, S., Meng, W., Wang, Y.: Designing collaborative blockchained signature-based intrusion detection in IoT environments. Future Generation Comput. Syst. **96**, 481–489 (2019)

53. Meidan, Y., et al.: N-baiot-network-based detection of IoT botnet attacks using deep autoencoders. IEEE Pervasive Comput. **17**(3), 12–22 (2018)

54. Oeke, G., Loukas, G.: A denial of service detector based on maximum likelihood detection and the random neural network. Comput. J. **50**(6), 717–727 (2007)

55. Ostinato Traffic Generator for Network Enzineers. https://ostinato.org/. Accessed 08 Sept 2020

56. Qureshi, A., Larijani, H., Ahmad, J., Mtetwa, N.: A novel random neural network based approach for intrusion detection systems. In: 2018 10th Computer Science and Electronic Engineering Conference, CEEC 2018, University of Essex, Colchester, UK, 19–21 September 2018, pp. 50–55. IEEE (2018). https://doi.org/10.1109/CEEC.2018.8674228

57. Radhakrishnan, K., Larijani, H.: Evaluating perceived voice quality on packet networks using different random neural network architectures. Perform. Eval. 68(4), 347–360 (2011). https://doi.org/10.1016/j.peva.2011.01.001

58. Rubino, G., Tirilly, P., Varela, M.: Evaluating Users' Satisfaction in Packet Networks Using Random Neural Networks. In: Kollias, S.D., Stafylopatis, A., Duch, W., Oja, E. (eds.) ICANN 2006. LNCS, vol. 4131, pp. 303–312. Springer, Heidelberg (2006). https://doi.org/10.1007/11840817_32

59. Saeed, A., Ahmadinia, A., Javed, A., Larijani, H.: Intelligent intrusion detection in low-power IoTs. ACM Trans. Internet Technol. (TOIT) **16**(4), 1–25 (2016)

60. Shon, T., Kovah, X., Moon, J.: Applying genetic algorithm for classifying anomalous TCP/IP packets. Neurocomputing **69**(16), 2429–2433 (2006)
61. Timotheou, S.: The random neural network: a survey. Comput. J. **53**(3), 251–267 (2010)
62. Timotheou, S.: A novel weight initialization method for the random neural network. Neurocomputing **73**(2), 160–168 (2009)
63. Xiang, C., Yong, P.C., Meng, L.S.: Design of multiple-level hybrid classifier for intrusion detection system using Bayesian clustering and decision trees. Pattern Recogn. Lett. **29**(7), 918–924 (2008)
64. Yin, C., Zhu, Y., Fei, J., He, X.: A deep learning approach for intrusion detection using recurrent neural networks. IEEE Access **5**, 21954–21961 (2017)
65. Yin, Y.: Deep learning with the random neural network and its applications. ArXiv abs/1810.08653 (2018)

Contact Holdups and Their Impact for Overlay Delay Tolerant Networks

Ricardo Lent[(✉)] [iD]

University of Houston, Houston, TX 77204, USA
rlent@uh.edu

Abstract. The standard approach to bundle routing in delay-tolerant networks with predictable contacts uses a graph traversal algorithm to search for paths where the graph's nodes represent the presumed and non-expired contact opportunities and the edges the waiting time for the next contact to occur. However, unforeseen systemic issues may introduce random contact holdups, i.e., the start time of certain contacts may be delayed, which may lead to lower performance than anticipated. An analysis of random contact holdups and their impact on the probabilistic optimal routing of bundles over parallel, non-overlapping substrate paths are provided. The study brings new insight into the consequences of unforeseen divergences between the planned contacts and their realization, which may help to improve the design of future DTN protocols.

Keywords: Delay tolerant networking · Performance evaluation · Optimal routing · Data communications

1 Introduction

One property of challenged networks is that their topologies are continually changing, which in general prevents the permanent end-to-end connectivity for at least a subset of the nodes. This observation has motivated the introduction of new networking protocols and the delay (or disruption) tolerant approach for application where the core internet-design assumptions no longer hold as node-to-node communications are not always possible. Delay-tolerant networking (DTN) defines the means for the transmission of data pieces (i.e., data bundles) over a dynamically changing network. A DTN operates as an overlay on top of a network substrate and commonly comprises mobile nodes and wireless links using a store-carry-forward transmission approach. A bundle transmission can only proceed during a contact, i.e., when the location of both and receiver and transmitter, the state of the operational environment, and the network management policy permits. Therefore, a bundle delivery to the intended destination can involve the use of multiple contacts along a selected path.

In many applications, the contacts are predictable or at least assumed to be predictable. In wireless sensor networks, where the duty cycle of the nodes is known in advance, it is possible to estimate the future contact opportunities. Likewise, the detailed planning of space missions allows determining the expected contact plan for future bundle transmissions. DTN routing algorithms,

© Springer Nature Switzerland AG 2021
M. C. Calzarossa et al. (Eds.): MASCOTS 2020, LNCS 12527, pp. 92–101, 2021.
https://doi.org/10.1007/978-3-030-68110-4_6

such as the CCSDS standard Schedule Aware Routing (CCSDS 734.3-B-1), make use of the contact plan to determine the forwarding path for bundles, which can be computed using the Contact Graph Routing algorithm. It consists of the path search using a graph whose nodes represent the presumed non-expired contacts. Rather than focusing on DTNs with deterministic contacts, which involve knowledge of the exact timing of the contact events, this the study addresses the random contact case with predictable parameters, i.e., contacts with known probability distribution.

In either case, despite the presumed contact plan or contact properties are expected to be available to the routing decision engine, the realization of each contact may be subject to delays (holdups). For instance, a contact over a satellite link may involve mechanically aligning the transmitter and receiver antennas which may take longer than initially expected. If so, the setup time will add unexpected delay to the start time of the contact, negatively impacting the bundles scheduled to be transmitted during that contact event. This study provides a performance evaluation of these random contact holdups.

2   Background

This work is related to the recent efforts that have been devoted to defining new protocols for DTN communications. For example, the Licklider Transmission Protocol (LTP) [8] defines a convergence layer protocol for links that are either, or both, characterized by long propagation delay and long-term disconnections. When a link disruption occurs, LTP allows pausing an ongoing bundle transmission that can be later resumed on the next contact event. Prior work has evaluated the retransmission mechanism of LTP that ensures reliable bundle deliveries [3,7,9,10]. The experimental performance measurement of the reference DTN protocols has received good attention in the past through the the open-source implementation provided by NASA's ION-DTN. Representative works include [6,11]. Contact graph routing is in practice the routing approach selected for DTNs with predictable contacts [1] and the foundation of the Schedule-Aware Bundle Routing standard (CCSDS 734.3-B-1). Various extensions have been proposed to improve different protocol aspects [2,5] including the possibility of opportunistic routing. This paper extends prior work on the probabilistic optimal routing over parallel DTN links [4].

3   Response Time with Contact Holdups

The links of a delay-tolerant overlay network are defined by substrate paths that involve one or more transmissions. The performance of a single overlay link is first analyzed by abstracting away the dynamics of the underlay into a contact model. This approach is appropriate as the overlay link becomes available only after the whole substrate path is connected. The results are then used to determine the probabilistic optimal routing where multiple substrate paths are assumed to be available to carry bundles to the destination node.

It is assumed that the (overlay) contacts occur randomly. The expectation is that the contacts will last C seconds on average, providing link-up time for the transmission of bundles. The interarrival rate of the contacts is $\alpha = (C+V)^{-1}$, where V is the anticipated mean disruption time of the overlay link.

The contact arrivals are independent of the transmission state of the link and therefore, a contact may end while a bundle is still being transmitted. In such a case, the DTN protocols can pause the bundle transmission for the duration of the disruption and resume it as soon as the next contact starts. The bundles are processed on a first-come-first-serve basis and arrive at a rate λ with each bundle transmission requiring S seconds on average without link disruptions.

3.1   Average Response Time with Contact Holdups

While it is anticipated that contacts will occur with an average duration C, random holdups are modeled as occurring with probability h delaying the start of contacts by fC seconds on average, where f is the holdup factor, $0 \le f < 1$. Therefore, contacts occur with an average duration of $C_h = C(1 - hf)$. The interarrival rate of the contacts is unchanged by the holdups. so the disruptions occur with average length $V_h = V + hfC$.

The overlay link is modeled as an M/G/1 queue with multiple vacations with the vacations (i.e., link disruptions) occurring without regard to the number of bundles in the system [4]. Likewise, the bundle arrivals to the system occur regardless of the link availability. A new bundle arrival can be transmitted immediately as long as the system is not busy with another transmission and no other bundles are queued.

A convergence-layer protocol that supports link disruptions, such as LTP, is assumed. Since a link disruption does not cause a bundle drop, but an extension of the transmission time of the bundle, let X denote the extended average service time with random link disruptions, $X \ge S$. The average bundle response time T is the sum of the average waiting time of bundles W and the extended service time X. The former term is in turn given by the residual time of any ongoing transmission and the product $N_q X$, where N_q is the average number of bundles in the buffer: $W = N_q X + R$. Using the mean residual time method $R = \lim_{t \to \infty} \left\{ \frac{1}{t} \int_0^t r(t)dt + \frac{1}{t} \int_0^t v_h(t)dt \right\}$, where $r(t)$ and $v_h(t)$ are the residual work and residual disruption times respectively, and after applying Little's law, lead to:

$$T = X + \lambda \frac{X^2 + Var(X)}{2(1 - X\lambda)} + \alpha \frac{V_h^2 + Var(V_h)}{2(1 - X\lambda)} \tag{1}$$

where $Var(X)$ and $Var(V_h)$ are the variances of the extended service time and interruption duration respectively. Since no restrictions on the transmission buffer length of the node have been assumed, the condition $\lambda X < \alpha C_h$ must hold for stability.

3.2   Exponential Assumptions

With exponential distribution assumptions for the service, contact, and disruption times, the service time S is extended as follows depending on the ratio of the disruption and contact times:

$$X = S\left(1 + \frac{V_h}{C_h}\right) = \frac{S}{a(1 - fh)C} \tag{2}$$

Using (2) in (1) with $Var(X) = X^2$ and $Var(V_h) = V_h^2$ yields the mean bundle response time over a link (substrate path) with random disruptions:

$$T = T^{(H)} \approx \frac{SV^2 + CV(2S + (1 - H)V) + C^2(S + 2HV)}{(C + V)(C((1 - H) - S\lambda) - SV\lambda)} \tag{3}$$

where $H = fh$ is a parameter that weights the severity of the contact holdups through a single value. This approximation results after disregarding the high-order terms of H as both f and h are expected to be small in practice. The extra latency brought by the contact holdups to the average bundle response time is given by $T^{(H)} - T^{(0)}$, where $T^{(0)}$ denotes the average response time for the $H = 0$ case:

$$T^{(H)} - T^{(0)} = \frac{CH(CSV(2 - V\lambda) + SV^2(1 + V\lambda) + C^2(S + 2V - 2SV\lambda))}{(C + V)(C - S(C + V)\lambda)(C(1 - H) - S(C + V)\lambda)} \tag{4}$$

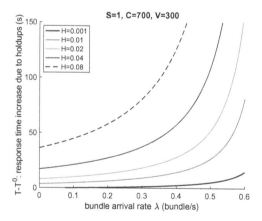

Fig. 1. Average latency increase in the bundle response time due to random contact holdups. $H = hf$, where the average duration of the holdups is fC, which occur with probability h.

To illustrate, Fig. 1 depicts the value of $T^{(H)} - T^{(0)}$ for an arbitrary case with the service time without interruptions set to 1s, average contact duration 700s, and average disruption time 300s.

3.3   Model Validation

The model (3) was validated using results from an event-driven simulation of a single queuing system with vacations. The start times of selected contacts were delayed with probability h by a random amount with a mean value fC. The mean bundle service time without disruptions was fixed to 1s, while the duration of the contact and disruption lengths were randomly selected from an exponential distribution with average durations 700 s and 300 s respectively. The simulation was evaluated for a range of values for the bundle arrival rate up to 0.4 bundle/s. The evaluation consists of the repetition of the simulation runs for at least 20 times for each set of parameter choices, each simulation generating the arrival and transmission of 100,000 bundles.

The values depicted in Fig. 2 show the average response times calculated from the simulation samples along with the theoretical results. A close match between the model and the simulation results can be observed. The differences between the results, which appear to be larger as h increases, were produced by the larger variability introduced by the higher number of random holdup events occurring in the simulation for large h.

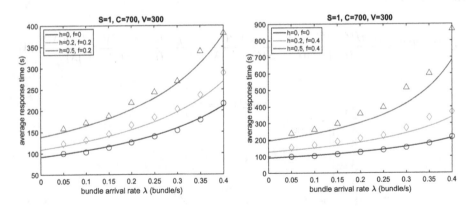

Fig. 2. Validation of the model by comparison with simulation results. Model results are represented by the oblique lines. The average simulation results are represented as points in the chart. The test was repeated for a range of bundle arrival rates and contact holdup parameters.

4   Contact Holdups and Optimal Routing

Consider that $\mathcal{N}$ overlay links, which involve an equal number of non-overlapping substrate paths, are available to carry bundles for a certain bundle flow. Each link can transmit bundles with an average service time S_i, $i = 1, 2 \ldots, \mathcal{N}$. The source generates bundles at a rate λ bundles/s towards a certain destination node. The actual contact plan is not known, i.e., the exact start and end times of the future contacts are unknown. However, the contact rate and the average duration of the random contacts are assumed to be known although they may occur with some deviation as examined in the previous section.

Routing optimality is defined probabilistically. The objective is to split the input flow into $\mathcal{N}$ subflows that concurrently carry the bundles over the parallel substrate paths with minimum delay. That is, the goal is to find the bundle forwarding probability $p_i \in P$ for the i-th overlay link, $\sum_i p_i = 1$, which minimizes the average bundle response time of the flow. Each overlay link i handles $p_i \lambda$ bundles/s on average. The values p_i can be found by solving the following expression where (3) was applied to find the mean response time for each link i. Furthermore, for the calculation is assumed that $H_i = 0$ since the future contact holdups of the links are not known nor expected by the routing decision engine, so that the optimal flow split is decided with only knowledge of the mean service time, contact duration, disruption duration, and flow rate:

$$\underset{p_i \in P}{\text{minimize}} \quad \sum_{i=1}^{\mathcal{N}} p_i T_i^{(0)}(p_i \lambda)$$

$$\text{subject to:}$$

$$p_i \lambda X_i < \alpha_i C_i (1 - H_i).$$

(5)

It is interesting to note that the term H_i was left on purpose in the constraint that appears in (5). Despite those values are assumed to be zero in the calculation of the $T^{(0)}$ term, the actual values of H_i should be used in the constraint to prevent the possibility of unstable queues. If T_i denotes the average response time of the overlay link i after including the effects of the contact holdups, then the extra mean delay brought by those events is given by: $\sum_{i=1}^{\mathcal{N}} p_i (T_i^{(H)}(p_i \lambda) - T_i^{(0)}(p_i \lambda))$.

5 Evaluation

To facilitate the presentation of results, consider that only two non-overlapping substrate paths, A and B, connect the source and destination nodes of a single bundle flow of λ bundles/s. The flow is split between the two paths using probability p, which represents the routing policy: path A is assigned $p\lambda$ bundles/s and path B the remaining $(1 - p)\lambda$ bundles/s.

5.1 Test Cases

A set of selected cases show the impact of the contact holdups under different assumptions for the disruption pattern and service time of the overlay links. In all cases, the average interarrival time of the contacts was set to 1,000s. As explained in the previous section, the routing probability p is determined using knowledge of the service time S, the bundle rate λ, and the expected disruption pattern given by C and V. The routing is decided without awareness of the contact holdups, which does occur on one of the links (link A), that is, one link does not operate as expected, but the other does.

Firstly, identical service times ($S = 1$) for both overlay links are considered. The mean contact time that is expected by the routing engine is the same for both links with the time equally split between contacts and disruptions ($C = V = 500$). The lowest response time depicted in Fig. 3 (a) corresponds to the expected results (i.e., without contact holdups). The holdup factor was kept at 0.2 while the holdup probability was set to 0.1, 0.3, or 0.5. As expected, increasing probabilities for contact holdups produce an increase in the average response time as the carrying capacity of the network is reduced. Figure 4 depicts the optimal routing probability for the overlay link A. Because both links A and B are identical and the expected disruption patterns have the same parameter values, the flow is split equally between the two links.

In the second case, the service rate of the overlay link A is twice as fast as that of B, but the contact holdup factor is large ($f_A = 0.5$), that is, when a contact holdup occurs, the contact start time is severely delayed by half of the contact duration of average. As in the first case, the contact pattern is expected to be equally divided into contacts and disruptions ($C = V = 500$). The optimal routing probability (Fig. 4) forwards a larger proportion of the flow traffic through link A ($p \approx 0.66$) than through the second link because the former link is known to be faster. This situation creates a large performance impact as link A is subject to severe contact holdups as depicted in Fig. 3(b).

In another case, the service times of both overlay links are set to the same value $S_A = S_B = 1$, but link A is expected to offer larger contacts than link B ($C_A = 800, C_B = 500$). The contact holdup factor for link A was fixed to 0.2. Similar to the previous case, the optimal routing probability p remains above 0.5, which makes the majority of traffic flow through link A. This situation causes a large increase in the average bundle response time as shown in Fig. 3(c).

In the last case, the contact holdup probability for link A was fixed to $h_A = 0.1$ and different values for the holdup factor (0.01, 0.1, 0.5) were studied. Unlike the previous cases, the contact duration of link A was expected to be smaller than that of link B ($C_A = 400, C_B = 500$), which makes the optimal routing probability p remain below 0.5 as depicted in Fig. 4. As shown in Fig. 3(d), the contact holdups produced a large increase in the average response time of bundles but the different choices for the holdup factors did not lead to major performance differences.

5.2   Routing with Knowledge of the Contact Holdups

One question that remains is regarding the possible performance benefits of an arbitrary mitigation strategy that could be purposely designed to deal with contact holdups. A possibility is that the contact holdups could be predicted or that the bundles that are currently queued for transmission and that are affected by a contact holdup event are re-routed. To evaluate the optimal case, (5) was evaluated using $T^{(H)}$ in place of $T^{(0)}$, i.e., with the awareness of the contact holdup parameter at the time of making the routing decision. Figure 5 depicts the mean response time of bundles for the test case with 2 overlay links with $S_A = S_B = 1$. The expected contact durations were set to $800\,s$ and $500\,s$

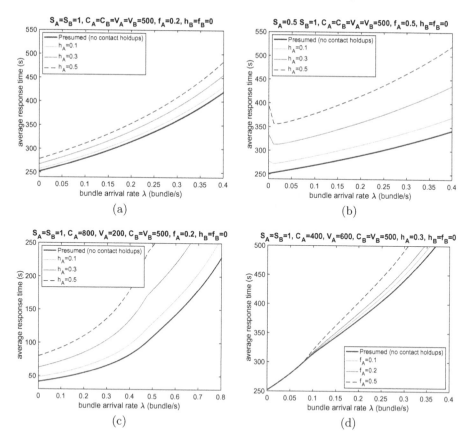

Fig. 3. Optimal average response times for four representative cases and the performance impact of random contact misses.

respectively for each of the two links. As before, the contacts occurred with identical contact interarrival times of 1000 s, and only link A was affected by contact holdups with $H_A = 0.1$. The results indicate that the implementation of a mitigation strategy can help to improve the flow performance by reducing the mean response time of bundles under medium-to-heavy traffic. This is achieved by routing a larger proportion of the traffic through the unaffected overlay link. No significant differences were observed under low traffic levels or smaller values of H than the one observed.

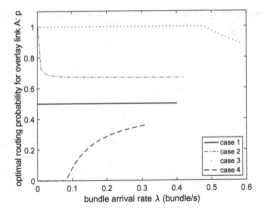

Fig. 4. Optimal routing probability (p) for path A, for the four evaluation scenarios. The routing probability for path B is $(1 - p)$.

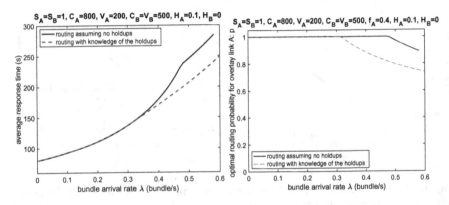

Fig. 5. Optimal response time (left) and routing probability for path A (right) contrasting the results obtained with and without awareness of the contact holdup parameter when deciding the routing policy.

6   Conclusion

In this paper, a delay-tolerant network with random contact holdups was investigated. To this end, an M/G/1 model with multiple vacations with unrestricted bundle arrivals and vacations, as well as the possibility of work interruptions was used. The model was validated using event-driven simulation results. With contact holdups occurring with a certain probability, the reduction in the mean contact length contributes to increasing the response time of data bundles. The model allowed quantifying the performance impact of these random contact holdups to the optimal routing policy with or without awareness of the features of the holdup events.

Acknowledgment. The author would like to thank Prof. Erol Gelenbe for encouraging the submission of this paper. This work was supported by an *Early Career Faculty* grant from NASA's Space Technology Research Grants Program #80NSSC17K0525.

References

1. Araniti, G., et al.: Contact graph routing in DTN space networks: overview, enhancements and performance. IEEE Commun. Mag. **53**(3), 38–46 (2015). https://doi.org/10.1109/MCOM.2015.7060480
2. Burleigh, S., Caini, C., Messina, J.J., Rodolfi, M.: Toward a unified routing framework for delay-tolerant networking. In: 2016 IEEE International Conference on Wireless for Space and Extreme Environments (WiSEE), pp. 82–86 (2016)
3. Lent, R.: Analysis of the block delivery time of the Licklider transmission protocol. IEEE Trans. Commun. (2018). https://doi.org/10.1109/TCOMM.2018.2875717
4. Lent, R.: Performance evaluation of the probabilistic optimal routing in delay tolerant networks. In: 2020 IEEE International Conference on Communications (ICC). Dublin, IE, June 2020
5. Sanchez Net, M., Burleigh, S.: Evaluation of opportunistic contact graph routing in random mobility environments. In: 2018 6th IEEE International Conference on Wireless for Space and Extreme Environments (WiSEE), pp. 183–188 (2018)
6. Wang, R., Burleigh, S.C., Parikh, P., Lin, C.J., Sun, B.: Licklider transmission protocol (LTP)-based DTN for cislunar communications. IEEE/ACM Trans. Netw. **19**(2), 359–368 (2011). https://doi.org/10.1109/TNET.2010.2060733
7. Wu, H., Li, Y., Jiao, J., Cao, B., Zhang, Q.: LTP asynchronous accelerated retransmission strategy for deep space communications. In: 2016 IEEE International Conference on Wireless for Space and Extreme Environments (WiSEE), pp. 99–104, September 2016.https://doi.org/10.1109/WiSEE.2016.7877312
8. Wu, Y., Li, Z.: Queueing analysis for delay/disruption tolerant networks with random link interruptions. In: 2016 IEEE International Conference on Internet of Things (iThings) and IEEE Green Computing and Communications (GreenCom) and IEEE Cyber, Physical and Social Computing (CPSCom) and IEEE Smart Data (SmartData), pp. 94–99, December 2016. https://doi.org/10.1109/iThings-GreenCom-CPSCom-SmartData.2016.42
9. Yang, Z., et al.: Analytical characterization of licklider transmission protocol (LTP) in cislunar communications. IEEE Trans. Aerosp. Electron. Syst. **50**(3), 2019–2031 (2014)
10. Yu, Q., Burleigh, S.C., Wang, R., Zhao, K.: Performance modeling of licklider transmission protocol (LTP) in deep-space communication. IEEE Trans. Aerosp. Electron. Syst. **51**(3), 1609–1620 (2015)
11. Zhao, K., Wang, R., Burleigh, S., Qiu, M., Sabbagh, A., Hu, J.: Modeling memory-variation dynamics for the licklider transmission protocol in deep-space communications. IEEE Trans. Aerosp. Electron. Syst. **51**(4), 2510–2524 (2015). https://doi.org/10.1109/TAES.2015.140907

The Random Neural Network as a Bonding Model for Software Vulnerability Prediction

Katarzyna Filus[1]([✉]), Miltiadis Siavvas[2], Joanna Domańska[1],
and Erol Gelenbe[1]

[1] Institute of Theoretical and Applied Informatics, Polish Academy of Sciences,
Baltycka 5, 44-100 Gliwice, Poland
{kfilus,joanna,seg}@iitis.pl
[2] Information Technologies Institute, Centre for Research and Technology Hellas,
6th km Harilaou - Thermi, 57001 Thessaloniki, GR, Greece
siavvasm@iti.gr

Abstract. Software vulnerability prediction is an important and active area of research where new methods are needed to build accurate and efficient tools that can identify security issues. Thus we propose an approach based on mixed features that combines text mining features and the features generated using a Static Code Analyzer. We use a Random Neural Network as a bonding model that combines the text analysis that is carried out on software using a Convolutional Neural Network, and the outputs of Static Code Analysis. The proposed approach was evaluated on commonly used datasets and led to 97% training accuracy, and 93%–94% testing accuracy, with a 1% reduction in false positives with respect to previously published results on similar data sets.

Keywords: Random neural networks · Software vulnerability prediction · Machine learning · Convolutional neural networks · Text mining

1 Introduction

The cost of building secure software is high but the results of not meeting security requirements may be much more severe. Cyberattacks occur on a daily basis and threaten the security and privacy of valuable and sensitive information. Indeed, the Cisco Consumer Privacy Survey shows that a significant majority of 84% of respondents care about data privacy [10]. Thus security was stated to be "foundational" and a "top IT priority" in the Cisco 2019 Annual Report [9].

This research was funded by the European Commission (EC) through the EU H2020 IoTAC Research and Innovation Action under Grant Agreement ID: 952684, and through the EU H2020 SDK4ED Research and Innovation Action under Grant Agreement ID: 780572. The EC's financial support does not constitute an endorsement of this paper, which reflects the views only of the authors.

M. C. Calzarossa et al. (Eds.): MASCOTS 2020, LNCS 12527, pp. 102–116, 2021.
https://doi.org/10.1007/978-3-030-68110-4_7

Security of software is mostly based on carefully written source code, and software vulnerabilities are the consequence of defects that are hard to find [89]. Most vulnerabilities are caused by common programming mistakes introduced by programmers in the early stages of the Software Development Life Cycle (SDLC) [79]. Programmers often lack the security expertise and their testing resources are limited. Hence, Static Code Analyzers based on software security standards, e.g. SonarQube [80] and Veracode [87] are often used in the software production cycle. It has also become common to use binary classifiers to prioritize testing efforts [69].

Despite the fact that modern programming languages focus on security and that many software security guidelines are available, vulnerabilities are still rife. Referring to Veracode's software security report [86], more than 85% of all applications scanned using the Veracode's application security platform between April 1, 2017 and March 31, 2018, had at least one software vulnerability. More than 13% of the applications contained at least one critical flaw. Approximately 85.7% of .NET applications, 87.5% of Java applications and 92% of C++ applications contain at least one vulnerable component.

Unfortunately, code analysis in terms of security is time-consuming and expensive [50], and thus researchers should commit their efforts to create accurate and efficient Vulnerability Predictors based on new approaches. In recent years, results based on heterogeneous features suggest that it is a good approach to follow [15,99], while the application of deep learning to Vulnerability Prediction is increasing [12,62,69], and it would also be beneficial to establish guiding principles regarding the representation and utilization of software components with such models [59]. The currently used methodologies presented in Sect. 2 offer a panorama in this respect.

1.1 Scope of the Present Work

The aim of our work is to create a software vulnerability prediction model based on Random Neural Networks (RNN) and Convolutional Neural Networks (CNN) that uses both text mining features and metrics generated from a Static Code Analyzer.

Over the years, RNNs have found application to video compression [41], medical image segmentation [25], the search for buried explosive devices [35], vehicle classification [46], in the field of virtual reality [33,52], in augmented reality [34,48], and network attack detection and mitigation [4,17,39,65,70].

Other areas where RNNs have been successful include deep learning [98], smart network management [14,31,36,37,40], emergency management and cyberphysical systems [42,43], the dynamic management of Cloud and Fog services [21,22,90], the use of machine learning in smart search [75,76] and network routing including the use of Software Defined Networks [5,19,20,29,30,38,91].

The CNN has also been successfully used in many fields [1,58], including for Magnetic Resonance Image reconstruction [94], automatic road segmentation [57], music generation [93] and relation extraction from plain text [45].

This wide usage and success of both the RNN and the CNN in a variety of applications justifies their use for Software Vulnerability Prediction in this paper, where text data processing and dimensionality reduction is carried out with a small CNN, and the RNN is used as a model that bonds both parts of the analysis. We utilize transfer learning: feature maps generated by a hidden layer of the CNN are provided as input to the RNN model and additional features that are obtained via metrics generated from a static analysis tool are used to improve the identification of vulnerabilities and the reduction of false positives.

Section 2 describes the background and work regarding Software Vulnerability Prediction. It also describes the approaches used in this field. Section 3 makes a brief introduction to the Random Neural Network. Section 4 presents the methodology used based on machine learning, and the dataset that was used for training the network. In Sect. 5 we describe our experimental results, while Sect. 6 concludes the article and discusses future work.

2   Software Vulnerability Prediction

Security plays a crucial role in modern information systems, and has become a primary concern in programming language design and implementation [71]. Modern programming languages focus on safety and reliability, because weaknesses in language models can be exploited by attackers, and compilers are used as control mechanisms on program execution.

To enhance software security, languages such as OCaml, Java, and C# use static analysis and dynamic checks [71]. RUST is a system programming language recommended for safety critical domains, which assumes memory-safety and thread-safety [13]. Additionally, software-oriented organizations such as the Open Web Application Security Project (OWASP) [66], SANS Institute [72] and the Computer Emergency Response Team Coordination Center (CERT/CC) [7] create standards concerning software security and publish guidelines, e.g. OWASP Secure Coding Practices Guide [67], on how to create secure software components.

Many critical software vulnerabilities are grouped into rankings such as OWASP Top10 [68] and CWE/25 [11]. To produce secure code, developers focus on static security tests [86] that help eliminate vulnerabilities in the coding stage of the Software Development Life Cycle (SDLC), offered by some of the Integrated Development Environments (IDEs) themselves, e.g. Visual Studio (C/C++) [88], IntelliJ IDEA (Java) [49] and Eclipse (Java) [16]. Dedicated applications that focus on static analysis have also been created, e.g. SonarQube [80] and Veracode [87].

Two types of software analysis are generally used for vulnerability detection: static and dynamic analysis, each with testing methodologies that differ significantly from each other. Static analysis is usually applied in the early stages of the SDLC. It can be based on Text Mining, Software Metrics, or security-related Automated Static Analysis (ASA) alerts [79]. It is successful in detecting leaks of private data, unauthorised access to resources, permission misuse, intent injection, clone detection, code verification, cryptography implementation issues and test generation [3]. Dynamic testing is much more time consuming; it needs an executable version of the software, and is therefore used later in the life cycle. It is perceived to be more complex than static analysis [3] because it not only requires an executable version of the software, but also requires additional resources and the ability to simulate user behaviour.

Dynamic testing can be divided into Fuzz testing [54], Concolic Testing [92] and Search Based Testing [73]. It is important to highlight that none of these methods should be treated as being superior. They offer different testing methodologies and environments. Some vulnerabilities are easier to find using static analysis, and for some of them one must apply dynamic analysis, as they simply cannot be found before the program is actually executed [86]. It is generally a good practice to use both of them, because using a single testing technique is not sufficient to identify all vulnerabilities and address all the problems that may be encountered [85].

Software metrics can be used to discriminate between vulnerable and non-vulnerable software components [2]. In [61] complexity metrics are used, while in [8] metrics named complexity, coupling and cohesion have been used as early indicators of vulnerabilities. In [78] the Complexity, Code Churn and Developer Activity metrics are used to indicate the potential presence of vulnerabilities.

ASA alerts which apply Singular Value Decomposition, have been used to identify fault-prone software components [77]. In [23], ASA alerts have been used for early identification of vulnerability-prone and attack-prone software components, and this approach can be used for prioritizing re-design, as well as for verification and validation efforts.

Text Mining for Software Vulnerability Prediction has also generated much interest. In [63] software components were represented as a list of extracted "includes" and "function calls" with information about whether a file incorporates them. In [51] function calls have been retrieved from Abstract Syntax Trees. As a result, a single component can be represented as a binary vector of features. Some approaches from Natural Language Processing (NLP) have been applied as well. In [59] the software components were represented as a series of terms. Using this approach, the order of the terms is also taken into consideration. Alternatively, the components can be treated as a Bag-Of-Words (i.e. a set of tokens or unit terms) with associated frequencies [74] or using term-weighing called the Term Frequency-Inverse Gravity Moment [56].

As an alternative to a high-level representation of the program, in [50] cleaned java bytecode lines were treated as a set of words, together with n-grams, a popular NLP technique. Using this method, bigger groups of terms are also treated as unit terms. In [69], an approach that combines n-grams and statistical feature selection is presented.

In some works, mixed features are used to build Vulnerability Prediction models. In [100] Text Mining features are used along with Software Metrics. In [99] traditional software metrics are used along with Developer Metrics, Software Property Metrics, Popularity Metrics and Security Metrics which are alerts generated by a static code analyzer. In [15], besides the Complexity Metrics

(Software Metrics), special Vulnerability Metrics such as Dependency Metrics, Pointer Metrics and Control Structures are used.

Other works have compared different approaches to vulnerability prediction. In [89] and [81] the approaches based on Software Metrics and Text Mining are compared. In a paper [51] three approaches have been discussed, namely: using the presence of includes and function calls (text mining based on regex expressions and Abstract Syntax Trees), traditional text mining using tokens with corresponding frequencies of occurrence, and software metrics. The results in [51] suggest that the performance of models based only on software metrics is insufficient. On the contrary, the results presented in [81] suggest that from a practical perspective, the performance of models based on software metrics is comparable to text mining techniques.

Apart from the form of the training features, many different prediction models have been used in this field: Support Vector Machines (SVM) [63], Random Forests [50,56,74,81,89], Bayesian Networks [78], Linear Discriminant Analysis [78], Decision Trees [56,99], Boosted Trees [99], Linear Regression [99], Naïve Bayes Classifier [74], K-Nearest Neighbours [56], Artificial Neural Networks [6,99] with Deep Learning in particular [12,59,62,69].

This paper proposes an approach based on mixed features, i.e. the text mining features and the features generated using a Static Code Analyzer. To build our model we use Convolutional Neural Networks and, novel in this field, Random Neural Networks.

3   Random Neural Networks

The Random Neural Network (RNN) is a specific type of Artificial Neural Network introduced in [26,27], whose purpose was to mimic the spiking behaviour of neurons in the mammalian brain. A gradient based learning algorithm for the RNN was introduced for both feedforward and recurrent (feedback) networks [24]. The RNN has been considerably extended to develop the theory of G-Networks [18,28] in queueing theory and stochastic processes, and from a machine learning perspective it has also resulted in deep learning algorithms [44].

In the RNN, each neuron's internal state is represented by a non-negative integer, and information is exchanged between neurons using positive and negative spikes which play opposite roles: a positive spike received by a neuron will increase its internal state by 1 representing excitation, while the arrival of a negative spike will reduce its state by 1 (provided its state is non-zero) representing inhibition. If a neuron's potential is strictly positive, we will say that it is "excited" and it is then able to "fire" or send out spikes at exponentially distributed intervals, while if it potential is zero the neuron is quiescent and it cannot send spikes to other neurons or to entities that are external to the network. When a neuron fires, its internal state drops by one for each outgoing spike.

RNNs have been shown to exhibit a great classification power and are able to outperform other traditional methods in many different areas [47,95–97]. They have been successfully used in the fields of vehicle classification [46], medical image segmentation [25], inserting 3-D images in moving virtual reality scenes [33], augmented reality simulation of transportation systems [48], determining the state of servers in a dynamic network Cloud environment [96] and attack detection [4,64,70]. Many different models of RNNs have been introduced: multiple signal class random neural networks [32], the Dense Random Neural Network [4], the Spiking Random Neural Network Function Approximator [95].

In this paper we use a modification of the RNN's training process with a Weight Restriction that reduces the number of computationally-demanding operations by considering only the derivatives of positive weights during the Gradient Descent algorithm. Since in this case the sum of the outgoing excitatory and inhibitory weights of a neuron to another neuron is fixed, the change of the excitatory weights will imply an identical but opposite change in the inhibitory weights. Also, as an alternative to random weight initialization [24,46] or some other computationally-demanding approaches [24,83,84], we use a "neutral" initialization that sets the weights to such values which set the initial excitation probability of each neuron in the network to 0.5, when the input values to the network are also neutral.

4   Methodology

In our approach, we propose a system that combines text mining features with metrics obtained from a Static Code Analyzer. To predict the labels of the examined software components we utilize Artificial Neural Networks, namely Random Neural Networks and Convolutional Neural Networks. We used 70% of the data for training and 30% for testing. To eliminate the imbalance of the data, we down-sampled the majority class (i.e. the non vulnerable class) for the training set and left the original number of samples in the testing dataset. We select five best features out of all the metrics generated by the Static Code Analyzer using the χ^2 ranking technique. Additionally, we performed feature analysis using a visualization method called the $t - distributed$ stochastic neighbour embedding (t-SNE) which is a non-linear algorithm used to decrease the dimensionality of data [55]. It is a good choice for examining whether a local structure exists in high-dimensional data, and as a means to visualise it in a two-dimensionalbreak space [60].

4.1   Dataset

We have used a dataset introduced in [59] for our experiments that consists of $61,638$ source code components, of which $43,913$ are not vulnerable and $17,725$ are vulnerable. The software elements are written in C/C++. Two types of vulnerabilities are considered in this dataset: CWE-119 - buffer error vulnerabilities ($10,440$ components) and CWE-399 - resource management error vulnerabilities ($7,285$ components), and we only consider CWE-399 vulnerabilities.

To achieve the text mining features, we follow a method described in [74]. This approach is based on the assumption that the programming language can be treated as an natural language, so that common text mining techniques can be applied to represent the information that it contains. Using the Bag-Of-Words techniques, the elements can be represented as tokens with associated frequencies. To obtain the desired metrics, we utilize a static code analyzer named SonarQube [80]. The tool allows to extract a broad number of metrics, including size (e.g. lines of code) and complexity. The number of instances in the classes and the whole dataset has been presented in Table 1.

Table 1. The number of instances in non-vulnerable and vulnerable classes of the examined data

Category	Instances	
Non-vulnerable	815	1499
Vulnerable	684	

4.2 Proposed System

The predictive part of the proposed system is composed of two parts: the first one is used for dimensionality reduction and extracting the information from text features, the second one is a bonding model for the extracted feature maps and metrics generated from a static analysis tool. The first part is built on a small CNN neural network. The text mining model has been built using the Keras functional API [53], and the second part is a computationally-efficient RNN. The workflow of the system is presented in Fig. 1.

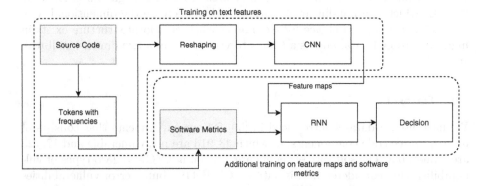

Fig. 1. The workflow of a software vulnerability prediction system based on both text mining features and metrics generated from a static analysis tool using Convolutional neural networks and random neural networks

The feature maps we take from the CNN part are 1-dimensional with 10 features. To enhance the result,s we use additional features generated using SonarQube tool [80]. The best features are chosen with a popular ranking technique - χ^2, and we take the five best features to estimate how the feature diverges from the expected distribution [82].

5   Experimental Results

We first examine the generated dataset using the t-SNE algorithm as presented in Fig. 2. It is clearly visible that the algorithm can find a local structure in high-dimensional data in both the feature maps generated using a CNN and the software metrics (all the metrics have been taken under consideration). Although it is harder to divide features generated in the Static Analysis tool, a local structure exists there and it can suggest that additional information can be extracted by adding these features to the overall analysis. Using both sets of

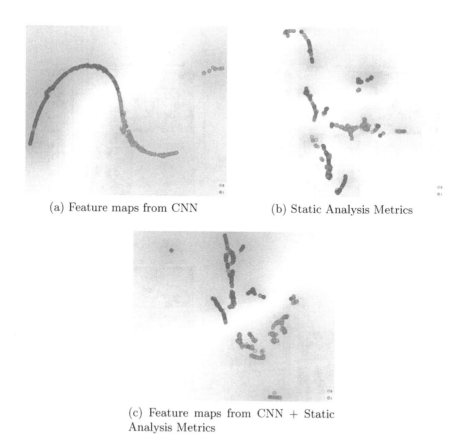

(a) Feature maps from CNN   (b) Static Analysis Metrics

(c) Feature maps from CNN + Static Analysis Metrics

Fig. 2. t-SNE visualization of vulnerable and not vulnerable classes on the basis of different types of features

features, an almost linear separation of vulnerable and non-vulnerable instances can be achieved.

The best model created during the experiments for text mining, and the hybrid model both achieved 97% training accuracy, while they achieved 93% and 94% testing accuracy, respectively, for both the CNN model based on text mining and the hybrid model using the RNN. The results for the text mining model and the hybrid model are shown in the form of normalized confusion matrices in Fig. 3.

Although the Hybrid model achieves 1% lower recall or True Positive Rate for the training set, the value is this same for the testing set for both the text mining model and the hybrid model. Using a model that utilizes both feature maps obtained using CNN and metrics obtained from SonarQube static code analyzer, we managed to decrease the False Positive Rate for both training and testing data by 1%. We notice that the model is good at generalizing and despite the fact that data in the testing set is distributed differently than in the training set (since we used down-sampling to balance the vulnerable and non-vulnerable instances) it achieves satisfactory results in terms of Recall and False Positive Rate.

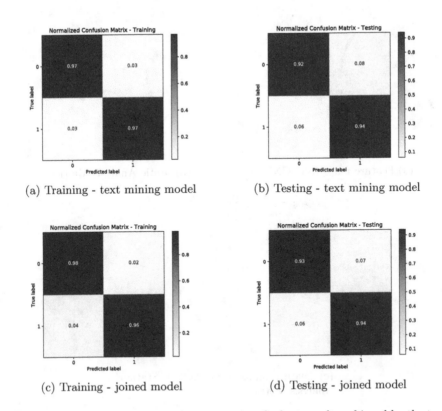

(a) Training - text mining model   (b) Testing - text mining model

(c) Training - joined model   (d) Testing - joined model

Fig. 3. Normalized confusion matrices presenting the best results achieved by the text mining model and the hybrid model

6   Conclusions and Future Work

In this paper, we have exploited the successful usage in a wide variety of applications of two neural network models with their respective learning algorithms, namely the RNN and the CNN, to address the challenging issue of Software Vulnerability Prediction. In our proposed approach, text data processing and dimensionality reduction is accomplished by a small CNN, while an RNN operates as a bonding model for both parts of the analysis. Feature maps obtained from a CNN hidden layer are given to the RNN as input, while additional features obtained from metrics generated by static analysis, help to improve the correct determination of vulnerabilities and to reduce the false alarms.

The analysis performed using the t-SNE algorithm have shown that high-dimensional features used for training the neural networks contain a local structure that can be used for Software Vulnerability Prediction. Although this local structure obtained using features from a Static Code Analyzer is not as marked as the features obtained from the text mining, it is reasonable to assume that the information contained in these features can help improve the approaches based on text mining. It also appears that the biggest challenge in many Software Vulnerability Prediction techniques and Static Analysis tools is a significant number of false positives. Our experiments show that by using text features as well as metrics generated by a static code analyzer, false positives can be reduced.

To fully evaluate the proposed method, more tests need to be performed. More complex neural network architectures may also provide us with even better results. Such models should be tested on larger datasets containing different types of vulnerabilities, possibly leading to a general Vulnerability Prediction approach. As an alternative, the use of multiple predictors that address different types of vulnerabilities, rather than a tool that predicts the occurrence of vulnerabilities in general, could be implemented.

In future work we will also consider a more exhaustive set of statistical features that are generated by a static analyzer, with features extracted by different feature selection methods. Different Static Code Analyzers could also be used to identify the best features, which can then be compared and evaluated with respect to their usefulness in building Software Vulnerability Prediction tools.

References

1. Ajit, A., Acharya, K., Samanta, A.: A review of convolutional neural networks. In: 2020 International Conference on Emerging Trends in Information Technology and Engineering (ic-ETITE), Vellore, India. pp. 1–5. IEEEXpress (2020). https://doi.org/10.1109/ic-ETITE47903.2020.049
2. Alves, H., Fonseca, B., Antunes, N.: Software metrics and security vulnerabilities: dataset and exploratory study. In: 2016 12th European Dependable Computing Conference (EDCC), pp. 37–44 (2016)

3. Amin, A., Eldessouki, A., Magdy, M.T., Abdeen, N., Hindy, H., Hegazy, I.: Androshield: automated android applications vulnerability detection, a hybrid static and dynamic analysis approach. Information 10(10), 326 (2019)

4. Brun, O., Yin, Y., Gelenbe, E.: Deep learning with dense random neural network for detecting attacks against IoT-connected home environments. Procedia Comput. Sci. 134, 458–463 (2018)

5. Brun, O., Wang, L., Gelenbe, E.: Big data for autonomic intercontinental overlays. IEEE J. Sel. Areas Commun. 34(3), 575–583 (2016)

6. Catal, C., Akbulut, A., Ekenoglu, E., Alemdaroglu, M.: Development of a software vulnerability prediction web service based on artificial neural networks. In: Kang, U., Lim, E.-P., Yu, J.X., Moon, Y.-S. (eds.) PAKDD 2017. LNCS (LNAI), vol. 10526, pp. 59–67. Springer, Cham (2017). https://doi.org/10.1007/978-3-319-67274-8_6

7. Computer Emergency Response Team Coordination Center. https://www.kb.cert.org/vuls/ Accessed 05 Aug 2020

8. Chowdhury, I., Zulkernine, M.: Using complexity, coupling, and cohesion metrics as early indicators of vulnerabilities. J. Syst. Architect. 57(3), 294–313 (2011)

9. Cisco 2019 Annual Report. (Cisco 2019). https://www.cisco.com/c/dam/en_us/about/annual-report/cisco-annual-report-2019.pdf Accessed 05 Aug 2020

10. Cisco Cybersecurity Series 2019. Consumer Privacy Survey. (Cisco 2019). https://www.cisco.com/c/dam/en_us/about/annual-report/cisco-annual-report-2019.pdf Accessed 05 Aug 2020

11. CWE Top 25 Most Dangerous Software Errors. https://cwe.mitre.org/top25/archive/2019/2019_cwe_top25.html Accessed 05 Aug 2020

12. Dam, H.K., Tran, T., Pham, T., Ng, S.W., Grundy, J., Ghose, A.: Automatic feature learning for vulnerability prediction. arXiv preprint arXiv:1708.02368 (2017)

13. Ding, Y., et al.: Poster: Rust SGX SDK: Towards memory safety in intel SGX enclave. In: Proceedings of the 2017 ACM SIGSAC Conference on Computer and Communications Security, pp. 2491–2493 (2017)

14. Dobson, S., et al.: A survey of autonomic communications. ACM Trans. Auton. Adapt. Syst. (TAAS) 1(2), 223–259 (2006)

15. Du, X., et al.: Leopard: Identifying vulnerable code for vulnerability assessment through program metrics. In: 2019 IEEE/ACM 41st International Conference on Software Engineering (ICSE), pp. 60–71 (2019)

16. Enabling Open Innovation & Collaboration — The Eclipse Foundation. https://www.eclipse.org/ Accessed 05 Aug 2020

17. Evmorfos, S., Vlachodimitropoulos, G., Bakalos, N., Gelenbe, E.: Neural network architectures for the detection of SYN flood attacks in IoT systems. In: Proceedings of the 13th ACM International Conference on PErvasive Technologies Related to Assistive Environments, no. 69, pp. 1–4. ACM (2020) https://doi.org/10.1145/3389189.3398000

18. Fourneau, J.M., Gelenbe, E.: G-networks with adders. Future Internet 9(3), 34 (2017)

19. Francois, F., Gelenbe, E.: Optimizing secure SDN-enabled inter-data centre overlay networks through cognitive routing. In: 2016 IEEE 24th International Symposium on Modeling, Analysis and Simulation of Computer and Telecommunication Systems (MASCOTS), pp. 283–288. IEEE (2016)

20. Francois, F., Gelenbe, E.: Towards a cognitive routing engine for software defined networks. In: 2016 IEEE International Conference on Communications (ICC), pp. 1–6. IEEE (2016)

21. Fröhlich, P., Gelenbe, E.: Optimal fog services placement in SDN IoT network using random neural networks and cognitive network map. In: Rutkowski, L., Scherer, R., Korytkowski, M., Pedrycz, W., Tadeusiewicz, R., Zurada, J.M. (eds.) ICAISC 2020. LNCS (LNAI), vol. 12415, pp. 78–89. Springer, Cham (2020). https://doi.org/10.1007/978-3-030-61401-0_8

22. Frohlich, P., Gelenbe, E., Nowak, M.P.: Smart SDN management of fog services. In: GIOTS 2020: Global IoT Summit 2020, IEEE Communications Society, pp. 1–5 June 2020, Dubin, Ireland. TechRxiv (2020)

23. Gegick, M., Williams, L.: Toward the use of automated static analysis alerts for early identification of vulnerability-and attack-prone components. In: Second International Conference on Internet Monitoring and Protection (ICIMP 2007), pp. 18–18. IEEE (2007)

24. Gelenbe, E.: Learning in the recurrent random neural network. Neural Comput. **5**, 154–164 (1993)

25. Gelenbe, E., Feng, Y., Krishnan, K.R.R.: Neural network methods for volumetric magnetic resonance imaging of the human brain. Proc. IEEE **84**(10), 1488–1496 (1996)

26. Gelenbe, E.: Random neural networks with negative and positive signals and product form solution. Neural Comput. **1**(4), 502–510 (1989)

27. Gelenbe, E.: Stability of the random neural network model. Neural Comput. **2**(2), 239–247 (1990)

28. Gelenbe, E.: G-networks with signals and batch removal. Probab. Eng. Inf. Sci. **7**(3), 335–342 (1993)

29. Gelenbe, E.: Steps toward self-aware networks. Commun. ACM **52**(7), 66–75 (2009)

30. Gelenbe, E.: Machine learning for network routing. In: 2020 9th Mediterranean Conference on Embedded Computing (MECO), pp. 1–1. IEEE (2020)

31. Gelenbe, E., Domanska, J., Frohlich, P., Nowak, M., Nowak, S.: Self-aware networks that optimize security, Qos and energy. In: Proceedings of the IEEE, accepted for publication, vol. 108 no. 7 (2020)

32. Gelenbe, E., Fourneau, J.M.: Random neural networks with multiple classes of signals. Neural Comput. **11**(4), 953–963 (1999)

33. Gelenbe, E., Hussain, K., Kaptan, V.: Simulating autonomous agents in augmented reality. J. Syst. Softw. **74**(2), 255–268 (2005)

34. Gelenbe, E., Hussain, K., Kaptan, V.: Simulating autonomous agents in augmented reality. J. Syst. Softw. **74**(3), 255–268 (2005)

35. Gelenbe, E., Koçak, T.: Area-based results for mine detection. IEEE Trans. Geosci. Remote Sens. **38**(1), 12–24 (2000)

36. Gelenbe, E., Lent, R., Nunez, A.: Self-aware networks and Qos. Proc. IEEE **92**(9), 1478–1489 (2004)

37. Gelenbe, E., Lent, R., Xu, Z.: Measurement and performance of a cognitive packet network. Comput. Netw. **37**(6), 691–701 (2001)

38. Gelenbe, E., Liu, P., Laine, J.: Genetic algorithms for route discovery. IEEE Trans. Syst. Man Cybern. Part B (Cybernetics) **36**(6), 1247–1254 (2006)

39. Gelenbe, E., Loukas, G.: A self-aware approach to denial of service defence. Comput. Netw. **51**(5), 1299–1314 (2007)

40. Gelenbe, E., Montuori, A., Nunez, A., Lent, R., Xu, Z.: Experiments with Qos driven learning packet networks. Internet Process Coordination, CRC Press, Boca Raton, pp. 215–233 (2020)

41. Gelenbe, E., Sungur, M., Cramer, C.: Learning random networks for compression of still and moving images. JPL: A Decade of Neural Networks; Practical Applications and Prospects, pp. 171–189 (1994)

42. Gelenbe, E., Wu, F.J.: Large scale simulation for human evacuation and rescue. Comput. Math. Appl. **64**(12), 3869–3880 (2012)

43. Gelenbe, E., Wu, F.J.: Future research on cyber-physical emergency management systems. Future Internet **5**(3), 336–354 (2013)

44. Gelenbe, E., Yin, Y.: Deep learning with dense random neural networks. In: Gruca, A., Czachórski, T., Harezlak, K., Kozielski, S., Piotrowska, A. (eds.) Gelenbe, E., Yin, Y.: Deep learning with dense random neural networks. In: International Conference on Man-Machine Interactions. pp. 3–18. Springer, Cham (2017). AISC, vol. 659, pp. 3–18. Springer, Cham (2018). https://doi.org/10.1007/978-3-319-67792-7_1

45. He, Z., Chen, W., Li, Z., Zhang, W., Shao, H., Zhang, M.: Syntax-aware entity representations for neural relation extraction. Artif. Intell. **275**, 602–617 (2019)

46. Hussain, K., Moussa, G.: On-road vehicle classification based on random neural network and bag-of-visual words. Probab. Eng. Inf. Sci. **30**(3), 403–412 (2016)

47. Hussain, K., Yousef, M., Gelenbe, E.: Accurate and energy-efficient classification with spiking random neural network. Probab. Eng. Inf. Sci., 1–11 (2019). https://doi.org/10.1017/S0269964819000147

48. Hussain, K.F., Radwan, E., Moussa, G.S.: Augmented reality experiment: Drivers' behavior at an unsignalized intersection. IEEE Trans. Intell. Trans. Syst. **14**(2), 608–617 (2013)

49. IntelliJ IDEA: The Java IDE for Professional Developers by JetBrains. https://www.jetbrains.com/idea/ Accessed 05 Aug 2020

50. Jackson, K.A., Bennett, B.T.: Locating SQL injection vulnerabilities in java byte code using natural language techniques. SoutheastCon **2018**, 1–5 (2018)

51. Jimenez, M., Papadakis, M., Le Traon, Y.: Vulnerability prediction models: A case study on the linux kernel. In: 2016 IEEE 16th International Working Conference on Source Code Analysis and Manipulation (SCAM), pp. 1–10 (2016)

52. Kaptan, V., Gelenbe, E.: Fusing terrain and goals: agent control in urban environments. In: Multisensor, Multisource Information Fusion: Architectures, Algorithms, and Applications 2006. vol. 6242, p. 624208. International Society for Optics and Photonics (2006)

53. Keras Functional API. https://keras.io/guides/functional_api/ Accessed 06 Aug 2020

54. Klees, G., Ruef, A., Cooper, B., Wei, S., Hicks, M.: Evaluating fuzz testing. In: Proceedings of the 2018 ACM SIGSAC Conference on Computer and Communications Security, pp. 2123–2138 (2018)

55. Kobak, D., Berens, P.: The art of using t-SNE for single-cell transcriptomics. Nature Commun. **10**(1), 1–14 (2019)

56. Kudjo, P.K., Chen, J., Zhou, M., Mensah, S., Huang, R.: Improving the accuracy of vulnerability report classification using term frequency-inverse gravity moment. In: 2019 IEEE 19th International Conference on Software Quality, Reliability and Security (QRS), pp. 248–259 (2019)

57. Lan, M., Zhang, Y., Zhang, L., Du, B.: Global context based automatic road segmentation via dilated convolutional neural network. Inf. Sci. **535**, 156–171 (2020)

58. Li, Z., Yang, W., Peng, S., Liu, F.: A survey of convolutional neural networks: Analysis, applications, and prospects (2020)

59. Li, Z., et al.: Vuldeepecker: A deep learning-based system for vulnerability detection. arXiv preprint arXiv:1801.01681 (2018)
60. Liu, J., Li, Q., Yang, H., Han, Y., Jiang, S., Chen, W.: Sequence fault diagnosis for PEMFC water management subsystem using deep learning with t-SNE. IEEE Access **7**, 92009–92019 (2019)
61. Moshtari, S., Sami, A., Azimi, M.: Using complexity metrics to improve software security. Comput. Fraud Secur. **2013**(5), 8–17 (2013)
62. Nafi, K.W., Roy, B., Roy, C.K., Schneider, K.A.: A universal cross language software similarity detector for open source software categorization. J. Syst. Softw. **162**, 110491 (2020)
63. Neuhaus, S., Zimmermann, T., Holler, C., Zeller, A.: Predicting vulnerable software components. In: Proceedings of the 14th ACM Conference on Computer and Communications Security, pp. 529–540 (2007)
64. Öke, G., Loukas, G.: A denial of service detector based on maximum likelihood detection and the random neural network. Comput. J. **50**(6), 717–727 (2007)
65. Oke, G., Loukas, G., Gelenbe, E.: Detecting denial of service attacks with bayesian classifiers and the random neural network. In: 2007 IEEE International Fuzzy Systems Conference, pp. 1–6. IEEE (2007)
66. Open Web Application Security Project (OWASP). https://owasp.org/ Accessed 05 Aug 2020
67. OWASP Secure Coding Practices Quick Reference Guide. https://owasp.org/www-pdf-archive/OWASP_SCP_Quick_Reference_Guide_v1.pdf Accessed 05 Aug 2020
68. OWASP Top Ten. https://owasp.org/www-project-top-ten/ Accessed 05 Aug 2020
69. Pang, Y., Xue, X., Wang, H.: Predicting vulnerable software components through deep neural network. In: Proceedings of the 2017 International Conference on Deep Learning Technologies, pp. 6–10 (2017)
70. Saeed, A., Ahmadinia, A., Javed, A., Larijani, H.: Intelligent intrusion detection in low-power IoTs. ACM Trans. Internet Technol. (TOIT) **16**(4), 1–25 (2016)
71. Salka, C.: Programming languages and systems security. IEEE Secur. Priv. **3**(3), 80–83 (2005)
72. Information Security Training - SANS Cyber Security Certifications & Research. https://www.sans.org/ Accessed 05 Aug 2020
73. Scalabrino, S., Grano, G., Di Nucci, D., Oliveto, R., De Lucia, A.: Search-based testing of procedural programs: iterative single-target or multi-target approach? In: International Symposium on Search Based Software Engineering, pp. 64–79 (2016)
74. Scandariato, R., Walden, J., Hovsepyan, A., Joosen, W.: Predicting vulnerable software components via text mining. IEEE Trans. Softw. Eng. **40**(10), 993–1006 (2014)
75. Serrano, W., Gelenbe, E.: Deep learning clusters in the cognitive packet network. Neurocomputing **396**, 406–428 (2020)
76. Serrano, W., Gelenbe, E., Yin, Y.: The random neural network with deep learning clusters in smart search. Neurocomputing **396**, 394–405 (2020)
77. Sherriff, M., Heckman, S.S., Lake, M., Williams, L.: Identifying fault-prone files using static analysis alerts through singular value decomposition. In: Proceedings of the 2007 conference of the center for advanced studies on Collaborative research, pp. 276–279 (2007)
78. Shin, Y., Meneely, A., Williams, L., Osborne, J.A.: Evaluating complexity, code churn, and developer activity metrics as indicators of software vulnerabilities. IEEE Trans. Softw. Eng. **37**(6), 772–787 (2010)

79. Siavvas, M., Gelenbe, E., Kehagias, D., Tzovaras, D.: Static analysis-based approaches for secure software development. In: International ISCIS Security Workshop, pp. 142–157 (2018)
80. SonarQube. https://www.sonarqube.org/ Accessed 03 Aug 2020
81. Tang, Y., Zhao, F., Yang, Y., Lu, H., Zhou, Y., Xu, B.: Predicting vulnerable components via text mining or software metrics? an effort-aware perspective. In: 2015 IEEE International Conference on Software Quality, Reliability and Security, pp. 27–36 (2015)
82. Thaseen, I.S., Kumar, C.A.: Intrusion detection model using fusion of chi-square feature selection and multi class SVM. J. King Saud Univ. Comput. Inf. Sci. **29**(4), 462–472 (2017)
83. Timotheou, S.: A novel weight initialization method for the random neural network. Neurocomputing **73**(1), 160–168 (2009)
84. Timotheou, S.: The random neural network: a survey. Comput. J. **53**(3), 251–267 (2010)
85. Veracode: State of software security. Technical Report (2016)
86. Veracode: State of software security, vol. 9, Technical Report (2018)
87. Veracode. https://www.veracode.com/ Accessed 05 Aug 2020
88. Visual Studio IDE, Code Editor, Azure DevOps, & App Center - Visual Studio. https://visualstudio.microsoft.com/ Accessed 05 Aug 2020
89. Walden, J., Stuckman, J., Scandariato, R.: Predicting vulnerable components: software metrics vs text mining. In: 2014 IEEE 25th International Symposium on Software Reliability Engineering, pp. 23–33 (2014)
90. Wang, L., Brun, O., Gelenbe, E.: Adaptive workload distribution for local and remote clouds. In: 2016 IEEE International Conference on Systems, Man, and Cybernetics (SMC), pp. 003984–003988. IEEE (2016)
91. Wang, L., Gelenbe, E.: Real-time traffic over the cognitive packet network. In: Gaj, P., Kwiecień, A., Stera, P. (eds.) CN 2016. CCIS, vol. 608, pp. 3–21. Springer, Cham (2016). https://doi.org/10.1007/978-3-319-39207-3_1
92. Wang, X., Sun, J., Chen, Z., Zhang, P., Wang, J., Lin, Y.: Towards optimal concolic testing. In: Proceedings of the 40th International Conference on Software Engineering, pp. 291–302 (2018)
93. Wu, J., Liu, X., Hu, X., Zhu, J.: Popmnet: generating structured pop music melodies using neural networks. Artif. Intell. **286**, 103303 (2020)
94. Wu, Y., Ma, Y., Liu, J., Du, J., Xing, L.: Self-attention convolutional neural network for improved MR image reconstruction. Inf. Sci. **490**, 317–328 (2019)
95. Yin, Y., Gelenbe, E.: A classifier based on spiking random neural network function approximator (2018)
96. Yin, Y., Wang, L., Gelenbe, E.: Multi-layer neural networks for quality of service oriented server-state classification in cloud servers. In: 2017 International Joint Conference on Neural Networks (IJCNN), pp. 1623–1627. IEEE (2017)
97. Yin, Y.: Deep learning with the random neural network and its applications. ArXiv abs/1810.08653 (2018)
98. Yin, Y., Gelenbe, E.: Deep learning in multi-layer architectures of dense nuclei. arXiv preprint arXiv:1609.07160 (2016)
99. Zhang, M., de Carnavalet, X.D.C., Wang, L., Ragab, A.: Large-scale empirical study of important features indicative of discovered vulnerabilities to assess application security. IEEE Trans. Inf. Forensics Secur. **14**(9), 2315–2330 (2019)
100. Zhang, Y., et al.: Combining software metrics and text features for vulnerable file prediction. In: 2015 20th International Conference on Engineering of Complex Computer Systems (ICECCS), pp. 40–49 (2015)

Computer System Performance
and Reliability

Non-neutrality with Users Deciding Differentiation: A Satisfying Option?

Anne Kieffer[1], Patrick Maillé[2], and Bruno Tuffin[3(✉)]

[1] INSA, Rennes, France
anne.kieffer@insa-rennes.fr
[2] IMT Atlantique, IRISA, UMR CNRS 6074, 35700 Rennes, France
patrick.maille@imt.fr
[3] Inria, Univ Rennes, CNRS, IRISA, Rennes, France
bruno.tuffin@inria.fr

Abstract. The network neutrality debate has been raging worldwide for around fifteen years now. Our goal in this paper is to model and discuss a quite recent option which could be seen as a trade-off between neutrality and differentiation operated by Internet service providers (ISPs), and satisfy both ends of the world: differentiation potentially chosen by end users. By using a model from the literature, we compare the outcomes of three scenarios: neutrality, non-neutrality with differentiation decided by ISPs, and non-neutrality decided by users. We illustrate that, depending on network parameters, letting end users decide may end up as a fair and viable solution, and that non-neutrality imposed by ISPs is not necessarily bad for all actors.

1 Introduction

The success of the Internet is based on the notion of packets treated equally and routed through the network in a "best-effort" way. The *network neutrality debate* [18] started with Internet service providers (ISPs) claiming that they are supporting the infrastructure development and maintenance while content providers (CPs) send an increasing traffic and get an increasing share of the revenue generated by the network activity. ISPs were asking for the possibility to request payments for services and to differentiate traffic. This raised complaints from user associations and CPs arguing among other things that it would prevent innovation [7–10,14]. The debate has been raging, with neutrality rules defined and imposed by regulators worldwide (see as examples [4] for the FCC in the USA and [2] for BEREC in Europe). The debate is even exacerbated with the recent decision to repeal neutrality in the USA [5,11].

There have been many models to analyze the pros and cons of neutrality and/or service differentiation; see among others [1,3,10,13] and the references therein. The goal is in general to discuss (using tools from game theory) whether service differentiation can be beneficial or hurtful to the society, and whether introducing regulation would improve the outcomes.

© Springer Nature Switzerland AG 2021
M. C. Calzarossa et al. (Eds.): MASCOTS 2020, LNCS 12527, pp. 119–128, 2021.
https://doi.org/10.1007/978-3-030-68110-4_8

It would indeed be interesting to find a trade-off satisfying all actors, CPs, users and ISPs. Quoting [16]:

> Rather than focusing on network behavior only, it may be more helpful to consider end-user choice as the principle for deciding whether a particular traffic management or other policy is reasonable if it cannot be readily justified as protecting the network against attack or abuse.

In other words, i) service differentiation is often seen as a restraint to innovation, but users should be able to choose to favor new services if they find them relevant, and innovative CPs could also gain from this; ii) with user-driven differentiation, the ISP stays "neutral" in the sense that it does not choose to differentiate; iii) such an approach would allow ISPs to operate some differentiation, release the necessity to invest on capacity and get a reasonable share of revenue.

The purpose of this paper is to apply a mathematical model to investigate whether the option of allowing differentiation, operated by users, is worthwhile with respect to neutrality or differentiation operated by the ISP. This is studied in the context of actors (here users, an ISP and CPs) making decisions to optimize their own interest. (Therefore the mathematical framework is that of non-cooperative game theory [10,15].) We propose to use the model and results in [12] where users want to access two types of services, video (it was voice in [12] but we "update" it) and data, through a network modeled by an $M/M/1$ queue. We assume an infinity of potential *infinitesimal* users sensitive to price and delay and asking for service as soon as they get a non-negative utility: the user equilibrium notion is then called *Wardrop equilibrium* [17]. The three scenarios we compare are: a unique class of service (neutral scenario) for which packets are served in a first-come-first-served manner; a situation with two priority classes but for which the ISP decides which class should get priority, and the same two-priority classes but for which each user decides its service class. On top of that, the ISP optimizes its price(s) for service, anticipating the users' response, for the three scenarios. Our comparison of the outcomes shows that letting users decide the differentiation is a viable and balanced solution, since it allows both CPs to be served, and may also satisfy all actors with respect to a neutral situation. Similarly, letting the ISP differentiate may actually be beneficial for users, a conclusion consistent with other analyses in standard revenue management theory.

The remaining of the paper is organized as follows. Section 2 presents the basic model we are taking from [12], the relevant results therein, and the scenarios with the structure of the game that is played. Section 3 compares the outputs of the three scenarios to discuss if results are surprising, and conclusions and recommendations are made in Sect. 4.

2 Model

2.1 Basic Model

We recall in this subsection the model and results first introduced in [12].

The model considers two classes of (infinitesimal) customers, say video (indexed by v) and data (indexed by d) users, each one generating packets with an average rate λ_d (resp. λ_v) per unit of mass of customers. If p is the per-packet price charged to users, the respective (per-packet) utilities of type-d and type-v users are

$$U_d(\mathbb{E}[D]) = u_d(\mathbb{E}[D]) - p \ \text{ with } u_d(y) = y^{-\alpha_d}$$
$$U_v(\mathbb{E}[D]) = u_v(\mathbb{E}[D]) - p \ \text{ with } u_v(y) = y^{-\alpha_v},$$

where $u_i(\mathbb{E}[D])$ for $i \in \{d, v\}$ is the willingness to pay for a packet transmission in the network if the expected delay is $\mathbb{E}[D]$. It is assumed that $0 < \alpha_d < \alpha_v$, meaning that video users are more sensitive to congestion than data users. The curves intersect to highlight that voice users give more value to small delays.

Let N_d (resp. N_v) be the number (or more precisely, mass since users are assumed infinitesimally small) of data (resp. video) users. It is assumed that there is a potential unlimited number of video and data customers coming in as soon as their utility is positive, or leaving if negative. The equilibrium notion in terms of the actual mass of customers is the Wardrop equilibrium [17], where users of a given type either do not use at all a class of service because of a non-positive utility, or use a class of service but have a zero utility (otherwise new users would enter or leave).

The network is represented by its bottleneck modeled as an M/M/1 queue. In the neutral case without differentiation,

$$\mathbb{E}[D] = \frac{1}{\mu - (\lambda_d N_d + \lambda_v N_v)}$$

where μ is the network service rate. In the case of two priority classes H for high and L for low, with packet rates (to be more clearly defined later) λ_H and λ_L,

$$\mathbb{E}[D_H] = \frac{1}{\mu - \lambda_H}$$

$$\mathbb{E}[D_L] = \frac{1}{(\mu - \lambda_H)(1 - (\lambda_H + \lambda_L)/\mu)}.$$

See [6] if a proof of those formulas is needed.

2.2 Scenarios and Goal

We will consider three different scenarios:

– The neutral scenario for which the ISP proposes a single class of service;

- The non-neutral scenario for which the ISP decides which type of users will use which priority class;
- The non-neutral scenario for which each infinitesimal user will selfishly decide its priority class.

In each case, the decisions are taken in the following order:
1) The ISP first determines (revenue-maximizing) price(s).
2) Customers use the service or not: given the price(s) and the service policy, the mass of users of each type asking for service satisfies the Wardrop principle. Even if the ISP plays first, it plays anticipatively, taking into account the reaction of users.

We will compare the output of the game for the three types of actors: users, CPs and the ISP, in order to determine if a strategy should be favored by regulators, in particular the recent proposition to let users decide their service class. This type of comparison was not the purpose in [12]. More precisely, we are going to compare for the three scenarios: i) the ISP revenue to see if and why the ISP is pushing for a solution; ii) the CPs individual revenue $a_j \lambda_j N_j$, $j \in \{v, d\}$ (a_j being a per-unit-of-volume advertisement revenue), and cumulated revenue $a_d \lambda_d N_d + a_v \lambda_v N_v$ to evaluate if differentiation necessarily means a loss for CPs and the type of preferred differentiation; iii) user satisfaction/demand N_j and total demand $N_v + N_d$.

In the next subsections, we describe the user equilibria for our three scenarios that were computed in [12] but called differently and for a different analysis.

2.3   User Equilibrium from the Literature

No Differentiation/neutrality. The Wardrop equilibrium in the case with no differentiation is such that:

1. If $p > 1$, only type-v users join, with a mass $N_v(p) = \frac{\mu - \alpha_v \sqrt[\alpha_v]{p}}{\lambda_v}$.
2. If $p < 1$, only type-d users join, $N_d(p) = \frac{\mu - \alpha_d \sqrt[\alpha_d]{p}}{\lambda_d}$ and the ISP revenue is $\Pi(p) = \lambda_d N_d(p)$.
3. If $p = 1$, there is an infinite number of equilibria, type-d and v users having the same sensitivity to price, but we will consider in that case that only type-v users will be present.

The optimal revenue in the neutral case is $\Pi^{(n)} = \max \left(p_d \frac{\mu}{\alpha_d + 1}, p_v \frac{\mu}{\alpha_v + 1} \right)$ with $p_d = \left(\frac{\mu \alpha_d}{\alpha_d + 1} \right)^{\alpha_d}$ and $p_v = \left(\frac{\mu \alpha_v}{\alpha_v + 1} \right)^{\alpha_v}$.

The type of users present at the revenue-maximizing price therefore depends on the value of the service rate μ. More specifically, there is a threshold

$$\mu^* = \left(\left(\frac{\alpha_d}{\alpha_d + 1} \right)^{\alpha_d} \left(\frac{\alpha_v + 1}{\alpha_v} \right)^{\alpha_v} \frac{\alpha_v + 1}{\alpha_d + 1} \right)^{\frac{1}{\alpha_v - \alpha_d}} \tag{1}$$

such that if $\mu < \mu^*$, we are in the case with type-d users only, whereas if $\mu \geq \mu^*$ we are in the scenario with only type-v users.

Dedicated Classes/ISP Deciding Differentiation. The case when the ISP decides which type of users gets which priority class is called the *dedicated class scenario* in [12].

Define p_H and p_L as the respective prices for the high and low priority service classes. The output of the case with dedicated classes (with type-v users being assigned the high-priority class) is:

- The mass of class-H is $N_H = N_v(p_H, p_L) = \frac{\mu - \alpha\sqrt[\alpha]{p_H}}{\lambda_v}$ if $p_H < \mu^{\alpha_v}$ and 0 otherwise.
- The mass of class-L is

$$N_L = N_d(p_H, p_L) = \begin{cases} \lambda_d^{-1}(\alpha\sqrt[\alpha]{p_H} - \mu\frac{\alpha\sqrt[\alpha]{p_L}}{\alpha\sqrt[\alpha]{p_H}}) & \text{if } p_L \leq \frac{p_H^{2\frac{\alpha_d}{\alpha_v}}}{\mu^{\alpha_d}} \text{ and } p_H \leq \mu^{\alpha_v} \\ \lambda_d^{-1}(\mu - \alpha\sqrt[\alpha]{p_L}) & \text{if } p_L < \mu^{\alpha_d} \text{ and } p_H > \mu^{\alpha_v} \\ 0 & \text{otherwise.} \end{cases}$$

Price optimization is tricky, with non-informative formulas provided in [12], hence we will perform a numerical optimization.

Open Classes/user-Defined Differentiation. Users deciding which priority class to use is called the *open class scenario* in [12]. The user equilibrium (that is, masses of customers) with open classes is:
- If $p_L, p_H > 1$, we only have type-v users, with

$$N_H = \frac{\mu - \alpha\sqrt[\alpha]{p_H}}{\lambda_v} \text{ and } N_L = \frac{\alpha\sqrt[\alpha]{p_H} - \mu\,\alpha\sqrt[\alpha]{\frac{p_L}{p_H}}}{\lambda_v}$$

- If $p_L, p_H < 1$, we only have type-d users, with

$$N_H = \frac{\mu - \alpha\sqrt[\alpha]{p_H}}{\lambda_d} \text{ and } N_L = \frac{\alpha\sqrt[\alpha]{p_H} - \mu\,\alpha\sqrt[\alpha]{\frac{p_L}{p_H}}}{\lambda_d};$$

- If $p_L < 1$ and $p_H > 1$, the low-priority queue will be used by data customers, and the high-priority queue by video customers; $N_H = N_v = \left[\frac{\mu - \alpha\sqrt[\alpha]{p_H}}{\lambda_v}\right]^+$ and

$$N_L = N_d(p_H, p_L) = \begin{cases} \lambda_d^{-1}(\alpha\sqrt[\alpha]{p_H} - \mu\frac{\alpha\sqrt[\alpha]{p_L}}{\alpha\sqrt[\alpha]{p_H}}) & \text{if } p_L \leq \frac{p_H^{2\frac{\alpha_d}{\alpha_v}}}{\mu^{\alpha_d}} \text{ and } p_H \leq \mu^{\alpha_v} \\ \lambda_d^{-1}(\mu - \alpha\sqrt[\alpha]{p_L}) & \text{if} p_L < \mu^{\alpha_d} \text{ and } p_H > \mu^{\alpha_v} \\ 0 & \text{otherwise.} \end{cases}$$

Similarly to the case with dedicated classes, choosing the prices optimizing the ISP revenue will be performed numerically.

3   Numerical Results

We now compute and compare the revenues and demand in the three scenarios. To start, Fig. 1 displays, for the neutral case (only one class), all values on the

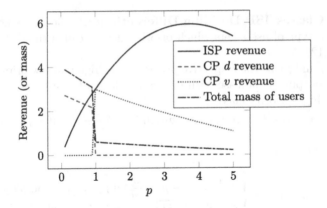

Fig. 1. Revenues and demand in the neutral case when $\mu = 4$, $a_d = 0.7$, $a_v = 1$, $\alpha_d = 1$, $\alpha_v = 1.5$, $\lambda_d = 1$, $\lambda_v = 5$

same graph when varying the price p charged by packet by the ISP. (Note that units are different for demand and revenues.) When $p < 1$ only type-d users are served, while there are only type-v users when $p > 1$. We can check that there is an optimal price to be charged if the ISP wishes to maximize its revenue. As could be expected, that price does not correspond to an optimum for users or CPs.

The outputs at prices optimizing the ISP revenue for the three scenarios are displayed in Fig. 2 (optimal price), Fig. 3 (corresponding ISP revenue), Fig. 4 (CPs revenue), and Fig. 5 (demand) when varying the service rate μ of the M/M/1 queue.

It can be readily checked in Fig. 2 that prices increase with the service rate μ; in other words, a scarce resource does not correspond to a price increase. When μ is small, the price p_L when the ISP decides the classes is equal to the optimal

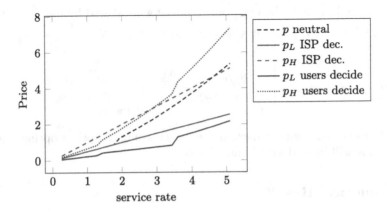

Fig. 2. Optimal prices in terms of μ when $\alpha_d = 1$, $\alpha_v = 1.5$, $\lambda_d = 1$, $\lambda_v = 5$

neutral price, but that class is not served. If users decide differentiation, p_L is smaller. The price p_H of the high priority class is larger if users decide than if the ISP does when μ is large, and, it may be counter-intuitive, for the largest values of μ, the neutral price is larger than the high-class price when ISP decides differentiation; it is due to type-d users in service in the former case and type-v in the latter.

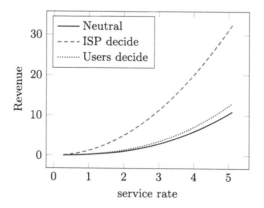

Fig. 3. Optimal ISP revenues in terms of μ when $a_d = 0.7$, $a_v = 1$, $\alpha_d = 1$, $\alpha_v = 1.5$, $\lambda_d = 1$, $\lambda_v = 5$

On Fig. 3, the ISP revenue is as expected larger if it decides differentiation, but letting users decide is a better solution for the ISP than a fully neutral scenario. The larger the network capacity, the larger the revenue differences.

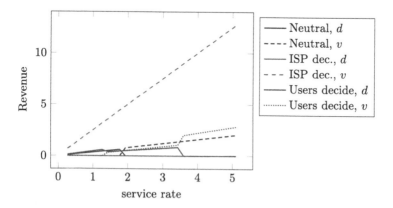

Fig. 4. Optimal CP revenues in terms of μ when $a_d = 0.7$, $a_v = 1$, $\alpha_d = 1$, $\alpha_v = 1.5$, $\lambda_d = 1$, $\lambda_v = 5$

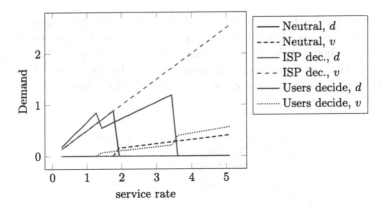

Fig. 5. Demand at optimal prices in terms of μ when $\alpha_d = 1$, $\alpha_v = 1.5$, $\lambda_d = 1$, $\lambda_v = 5$

Now let us look at CP revenues in Fig. 4 and demands N_d, N_v in Fig. 5: note that they do not always increase with μ. Remark also that letting users decide differentiation is the only case when both types of service will be active in the network for a range of service rates; in this sense it is an interesting and fair scenario.

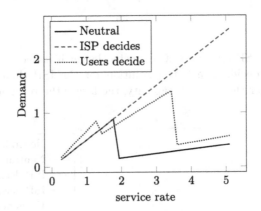

Fig. 6. Total demand at optimal prices in terms of μ when $\alpha_d = 1$, $\alpha_v = 1.5$, $\lambda_d = 1$, $\lambda_v = 5$

Looking at total demand in Fig. 6, letting users decide is the best option when μ is small, and is always better than the neutral case. As μ increases, differentiation decided by the ISP is better, but it hides that only one type of service is used, which is again not the case when users decide for a range of values.

4 Conclusions

As the neutrality debate is still raging, we have discussed in this paper the option of letting users choose a service class for each application. This way, innovation would not be slowed down with users asking for good quality for new and good quality applications; it would also reduce the load on ISPs, with no requirement to provide a good quality for all services. The network would stay neutral because not interfering (except for the price decision) on service class choices.

We have used a model from the literature to discuss and compare the output with a neutral situation and a fully non-neutral one where the ISP decides how to differentiate traffic. According to our results, letting users decide seems a nice trade-off in terms of demand and revenues for CPs and ISPs.

As future works, we would like to analyze other types of models and check whether they corroborate the results we have obtained here. Another issue is how to implement this promising option in practice, from a technical point of view.

References

1. Altman, E., Legout, A., Xu, Y.: Network non-neutrality debate: an economic analysis. In: Domingo-Pascual, J., Manzoni, P., Palazzo, S., Pont, A., Scoglio, C. (eds.) NETWORKING 2011. LNCS, vol. 6641, pp. 68–81. Springer, Heidelberg (2011). https://doi.org/10.1007/978-3-642-20798-3_6
2. BEREC: Berec guidelines on the implementation by national regulators of european net neutrality rules. Document number: BoR (16) 127 (2016). https://berec.europa.eu/eng/document_register/subject_matter/berec/regulatory_best_practices/guidelines/6160-berec-guidelines-on-the-implementation-by-national-regulators-of-european-net-neutrality-rules
3. Coucheney, P., Maillé, P., Tuffin, B.: Network neutrality debate and ISP interrelations: Traffic exchange, revenue sharing, and disconnection threat. Netnomics 1(3), 155–182 (2014)
4. Federal Communications Commission: protecting and promoting the open internet (2015). https://www.federalregister.gov/documents/2015/04/13/2015-07841/protecting-and-promoting-the-open-internet
5. Federal Communications Commission: restoring internet freedom (2018). https://docs.fcc.gov/public/attachments/FCC-17-166A1.pdf
6. Kleinrock, L.: Queueing Systems, vol. 2. Wiley, New York (1976)
7. Lenard, T., May, R.E.: Net Neutrality or Net Neutering: Should Broadband Internet Services be Regulated. Springer US (2006) https://doi.org/10.1007/0-387-33928-0
8. Maillé, P., Reichl, P., Tuffin, B.: Internet governance and economics of network neutrality. In: Hadjiantonis, A.M., Stiller, B. (eds.) Telecommunication Economics. LNCS, vol. 7216, pp. 108–116. Springer, Heidelberg (2012). https://doi.org/10.1007/978-3-642-30382-1_15
9. Maillé, P., Simon, G., Tuffin, B.: Toward a net neutrality debate that conforms to the 2010s. IEEE Commun. Mag. 54(3), 94–99 (2016)
10. Maillé, P., Tuffin, B.: Telecommunication Network Economics: From Theory to Applications. Cambridge University Press (2014)

11. Maillé, P., Tuffin, B.: Neutral and non-neutral countries in a global internet: what does it imply? In: Djemame, K., Altmann, J., Bañares, J.Á., Agmon Ben-Yehuda, O., Naldi, M. (eds.) GECON 2019. LNCS, vol. 11819, pp. 111–123. Springer, Cham (2019). https://doi.org/10.1007/978-3-030-36027-6_10

12. Mandjes, M.: Pricing strategies under heterogeneous service requirements. Comput. Netw. **42**(2), 231–249 (2003)

13. Njoroge, P., Ozdaglar, A., Stier-Moses, N., Weintraub, G.: Investment in two-sided markets and the net neutrality debate. Rev. Netw. Econ. **12**(4), 355–402 (2010)

14. Odlyzko, A.: Network neutrality, search neutrality, and the never-ending conflict between efficiency and fairness in markets. Rev. Netw. Econ. **8**(1), 40–60 (2009)

15. Osborne, M., Rubinstein, A.: A Course in Game theory. MIT Press (1994)

16. Schulzrinne, H.: Network neutrality is about money, not packets. IEEE Internet Comput. **22**(6), 8–17 (2018). https://doi.org/10.1109/MIC.2018.2877837

17. Wardrop, J.: Some theoretical aspects of road traffic research. Proc. Inst. Civ. Eng. **1**, 325–378 (1957)

18. Wu, T.: Network neutrality, broadband discrimination. J. Telecommun. High Technol. **2**, 141 (2003)

Measuring Performance of Fault Management in a Legacy System: An Alarm System Study

Juri Tomak$^{(\boxtimes)}$ and Sergei Gorlatch

University of Muenster, Muenster, Germany
{jtomak,gorlatch}@uni-muenster.de

Abstract. A challenging aspect in distributed systems is managing faults, i.e., detecting failures and reacting to them, especially when strict real-time constraints must be met. In this paper, we address the problem of measuring the performance of the fault management mechanism in a complex legacy system with hard real-time requirements. We propose a novel approach to performance evaluation of the fault management mechanism in distributed real-time legacy software systems by developing a performance testing infrastructure, implemented based on the load testing tool *Locust*. Our use case is a commercial alarm system in productive use that is provided and further developed by the GS company group in Germany. We show in extensive experiments that our approach to performance measurement allows to adequately estimate to what degree the fault management mechanism of a legacy real-time system comply with the strict time constraints. We provide an open-source repository with our measurement infrastructure which allows to reproduce our experiments.

Keywords: Alarm systems · Performance evaluation · Legacy system · Real-time requirements · Fault management · Performance testing

1 Introduction

In distributed systems, a complex and challenging aspect is managing faults, i.e., detecting failures and reacting to them, especially if real-time constraints must be met [9].

In this paper, we address the problem of measuring the performance of the fault management mechanism in a complex distributed system with real-time requirements. The problem is exacerbated by the fact that we deal with a large, legacy system [10], i.e., its technical documentation is incomplete, there are remaining bugs, and the system remains continuously under development, often not by the original designers of the system. Our use case is a commercial alarm system in productive use that is provided and further developed by the GS company group in Germany [6].

We thank the GS company group for the opportunity to perform our case study with their alarm system. This work was supported by the BMBF project HPC2SE at the University of Muenster.

M. C. Calzarossa et al. (Eds.): MASCOTS 2020, LNCS 12527, pp. 129–146, 2021.
https://doi.org/10.1007/978-3-030-68110-4_9

There are two commonly used approaches to performance evaluation: performance modeling and performance measurement [1,12]. Because commercial software systems are quite complex, simplified analytical models are created, based on abstract characteristics of the system. To find those characteristics, an in-depth analysis of the system has to be performed [4]. However, creating even a simplified model requires the support from application experts who know the software system and its internal details [8]. Moreover, as in our case the system contains bugs and is continuously under development, it is quite probable that the performance model will not represent the system well enough, especially as time passes.

Therefore, as alternative to models, we employ performance measurement (also known as performance testing [8]) by generating artificial workloads and measuring performance characteristics of the system, like the response time [12].

In this paper, we propose an approach to performance measurement in distributed real-time legacy software systems. Our approach develops a novel performance testing infrastructure based on the load testing tool Locust [2]. Compared to the successful approach [4], we test the legacy system from a black box perspective, ignoring the internal behavior of the system. Therefore, we do not depend on the technical documentation necessary to identify the characterizing variables. Furthermore, we do not require tools to collect data in the production system version, which is not always accessible. Thus, when the system changes, we can still perform our measurements without having to change our approach or adapt our model. We evaluate our approach on the case study of a real-world industrial alarm system designed and provided by the GS company group [6], with strict requirements regarding the real-time behavior of the system.

The short-term goal of our work is to better understand the timing behavior of the fault detection mechanism and to find out if and when the real-time constraints might be unsatisfied. Our long-term goal is to create a uniform performance testing infrastructure to support the envisaged system refactoring process, in which the fault management will be redesigned and improved.

In the remainder of the paper, Sect. 2 describes the typical architecture and performance requirements of an alarm system, and how our target alarm system of the GS company group works. Sect. 3 describes our experimental approach to measuring the performance of the alarm system and finding out if the system complies with the real-time requirements under faults. In Sect. 4, we conclude the paper and outline future work.

2   Case Study: An Alarm System

2.1   Alarm System Architecture

Figure 1 shows a high-level overview of a typical alarm system and its components. An Alarm Device (AD) is installed at the customer's home. If the AD detects a breach of the safety criteria, like a fire or a burglary, or a technical malfunction of the AD itself, it transmits an alarm message to the Alarm Receiving

Software (ARS) running within the Alarm Receiving Center (ARC)—a computer center which acts as the endpoint for incoming alarm messages.

The ARS is responsible for receiving and processing alarm messages and forwarding them to the Risk Management Software (RMS) running within the Emergency and Service control Center (ESC). Once the ARS has processed the alarm message, an acknowledgment is sent to the AD, confirming that no retransmission of the alarm message is required. The ESC-Employees then coordinate appropriate actions according to an intervention plan agreed in advance with the customer.

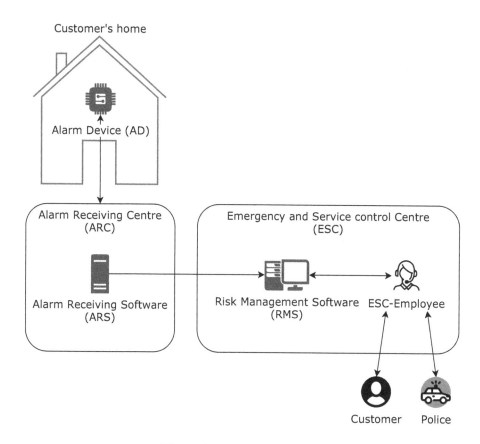

Fig. 1. A typical alarm system

For example, in case of a burglary, the AD registers an intrusion and transmits the respective message to the ARS. After processing the message, the ARS sends it to the RMS. An employee then handles the intrusion by calling the police and the customer.

2.2 The Legacy System of the GS Company Group

Our particular use case is a production-quality software for alarm system designed and implemented by the GS company group [6] which is a leading alarm system provider in Germany. The company owns three ARCs and three ESCs located in the north-western part of Germany, that handle about 13.000 alarms per day from about 82.000 alarm devices located all over Germany around the clock.

The current alarm software system provided by the company is a large, complex, and largely undocumented distributed system consisting of around 80 executable software components (programs) and libraries written in BASIC, C++, C#, and Java. The size of most of them ranges between 1500 and 76000 Lines of Code (LoC); some programs consist of more than 100.000 LoC, altogether summing up to over 1.5 million LoC. One developer was solely responsible for developing multiple programs and libraries over ten to twenty years, but the majority of the original developers are no longer in the company or will leave soon. Moreover, the software system lacks automated testing mechanisms like unit tests. Therefore, our current system is a legacy system in the classical meaning, i.e., "a large software system that we don't know how to cope with but that is vital to our organization" [10].

Our legacy system uses component and data replication as its fault management approach [9]: the whole software system including the database is replicated to different geographically separated colocations—computing centers where the programs, executed within virtual machines (VM), share computing resources like network bandwidth, CPU, storage, and so on. One of the colocations is designated as the master and the others as slaves. This architecture is commonly referred to as master-slave architecture.

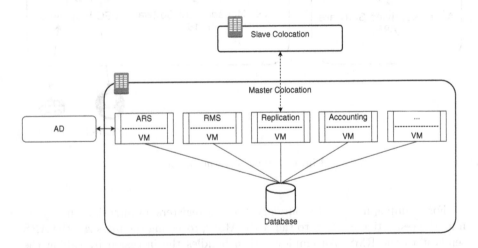

Fig. 2. The colocation architecture

Figure 2 shows the high-level architecture of a colocation: The AD sends alarm messages to the ARS of the master colocation using a proprietary transmission protocol. At all times only one colocation, for the production and the staging environment respectively, is actively receiving alarm messages, while the others are idle. A colocation is a resource-sharing environment [8]. The drawback of a resource-sharing environment is that programs unrelated to the ARS, like the RMS or Accounting, can adversely affect the performance of the ARS. The reason is that all programs produce load independently from each other, either triggered by alarm messages or user input, or by periodic tasks. The combination of resource-sharing and non-deterministic load pose a great challenge to measure performance in a reliable and reproducible manner.

The company GS employs altogether five colocations, of which three serve as the production environment, and two as the staging environment. A staging environment is a replica of the production environment meant for software testing under production-like conditions. Therefore, every colocation runs the same software, although the colocations of the staging environment sometimes have newer versions. Our architecture in Fig. 2 is database-centric [8]: all programs use a shared database per colocation in order to: 1) read and write data that are shared between the programs, and 2) build a processing pipeline for interprocess communication, where the ARS stores alarm messages in a certain table, the RMS periodically reads from the table, produces more data in different tables, where other programs read from, and so on.

In our application case study, we focus on the ARS as the central endpoint for all alarm devices, thus being also a potential bottleneck: if the ARS is not running properly, no alarm message can reach the ESC. For simplicity, we view the ARS as a single piece of software (in our use case, the ARS consists of around 15 programs and libraries).

Practical observations by the GS company group's employees identified that the current version of the ARS has a performance problem in case of a fault in the colocation. A fault may have different reasons, such as: the software is not responding (for example because of a software bug), the network has a link failure, the computer that runs the ARS has a defect, or a power failure shuts down the whole system. A possible classification of faults is given in [9].

The fault management mechanism consists of fault detection and fault recovery. Listing 1.1 shows and explains a simplified pseudocode of the RMS's fault detection mechanism as documented by the company.

```
1 repeat every checkInterval seconds:
2   for each colocation in colocationsList:
3     if anyProgramIsFaultedOn(colocation, timeout):
4       errorCounter += 1
5       colocation.isFaulted = errorCounter >= errorThreshold
```

Listing 1.1. Pseudocode of the RMS's fault detection mechanism: Every checkInterval seconds, RMS checks the status of all programs running in a colocation, including ARS (lines 1–2). Function anyProgramIsFaultedOn sends a network request to every program running in the colocation. If any program running in a colocation does not reply within `timeout` ms, an `errorCounter` is incremented (lines 3-4). If `errorCounter` exceeds `errorThreshold`, it is marked as faulted (line 5) and an employee of the ESC can see the status in RMS, although he is not actively notified.

Usually, two fault recovery techniques are used: restarting faulted software and failover—switching to another colocation.

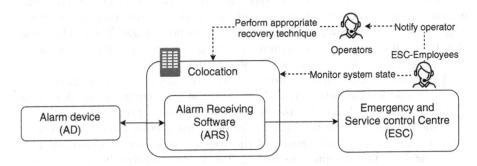

Fig. 3. Alarm system and its operators

Figure 3 shows two operators that are involved in performing a recovery in the current GS legacy system: the employees working in the ESC, and the technical operators qualified for restarting faulted software or switching to another colocation. The ESC employees notice a fault in the ARC: usually, they see a warning in the Risk Management Software (RMS). However, faults are sometimes subtle, e.g., RMS is running unusually slow, requiring the employees to judge each particular situation and make decisions based on their experience. Especially at night, they must decide if there is a serious fault, such that they wake one of the operators who has to boot up his computer, establish a remote connection to a server, and perform an appropriate recovery technique.

The whole recovery process usually takes at least several minutes (up to 15 min is not unusual) to perform, because the ESC employees need time to notice the fault and decide the next action, and the operators are not available around the clock.

2.3   Performance Requirements of Alarm System

Figure 4 shows a simplified view of an alarm system regarding its timing behavior. The main relevant timing metric is the *response time* $t_{response}$ between the AD and the ARS: it indicates how quickly the system responds to a request. Commonly, response time is understood as the time between a request and *any* response, according to [7]. We, however, use the definition of the EN 50136 standard [5] for alarm systems that defines the response time as the time between sending an alarm message (request) and receiving a *positive* acknowledgment (response). Timeouts or negative responses are not treated as acknowledgments.

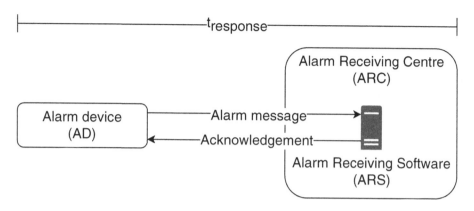

Fig. 4. Response time according to EN 50136 in an alarm system

That means that the ARS has to comply with the specified real-time requirements under any circumstances, including high workloads and failures.

The EN 50136 standard [5] specifies the real-time requirements for the
response time of an alarm system as follows: the arithmetic mean of all response
times measured in any time interval must not exceed 10 s, and the maximum
response time must not exceed 30 s.

3   Case Study: Measuring the Performance of the Fault Management of GS Legacy System

This section explains how we use the load-testing tool Locust [2] to measure the
response time in case of faults and, as a result, find out how much time the fault
management mechanism of the legacy Alarm Receiving Software (ARS) of the
GS group requires. We present how we use Locust to simulate alarm devices,
which software changes we made to prepare the ARS for performance testing,
and how we measure the performance of the fault management mechanism.

Figure 5 shows our test setup: Locust sends alarms to the ARS and measures
the response time $t_{response}$. Note that, compared to Fig. 4, the Locust load
generation – by simulating one or many ADs – takes the place of the real ADs.

In this section, we use the following terminology to distinguish between one
execution of Locust and a set of executions: A *performance test* refers to one
execution of Locust, while an *experiment* is a series of performance tests together
with supplemental actions that we perform while a performance test is executed.

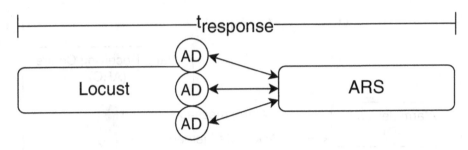

Fig. 5. Using Locust to simulate ADs to measure the response time $t_{response}$ of ARS.

3.1 Using the Locust Tool

Figure 6 shows the generic architecture of our performance testing infrastructure. This infrastructure is adaptable to other kinds of systems by changing corresponding scripts.

We use altogether three Python scripts to evaluate the performance of a software system (often referred to as System under Test) The executor.py script executes a load testing tool – in our case Locust. The load testing tool performs the actual performance measurement and produces a logfile written in our custom format. In our case, Locust produces aggregated metrics like average and maximum response time as .csv files. This, however, does not deliver the amount of details we require for our evaluation, so we rather write every response time into the logfile. Finally, script loadtest_plotter.py takes the logfile, visualizes the measurements and the respective real-time requirements, so that we can evaluate the results.

In our performance testing infrastructure for evaluating the performance of the ARS, we rely on the load testing tool *Locust* [2] that provides the following useful features:

1) it can be quickly and easily installed by using the pip tool: `python -m pip install locust`;
2) it provides a Command-Line-Interface (CLI) through the `locust` command available in the shell after installation, so that we can automate executing Locust in different configurations;
3) we can implement additional request/response based protocols that are not supported by Locust out-of-the-box [3], because the alarm devices usually employ a variety of proprietary transmission protocols and transmission protocols standardized by different vendors.

Figure 7 shows our performance testing infrastructure, adapted for Locust. When using Locust, we implement performance tests as Python scripts—we refer to them as Locust scripts—and the CLI tool to execute the Locust scripts:

1) executor.py: executes the shell-command in Listing 1.2 to run our Locust script;
2) locust_sad.py: simulates alarm devices (sad) that send alarm messages to the ARS, and it writes the response times to a logfile;

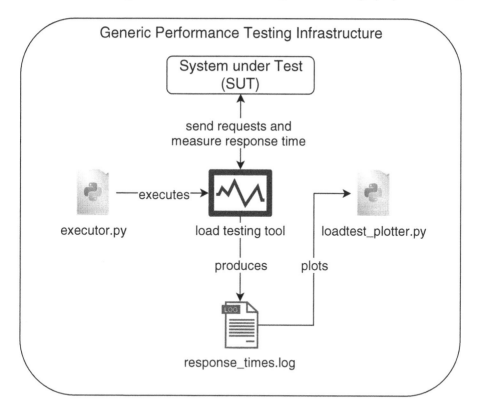

Fig. 6. Our Generic performance testing infrastructure

3) loadtest_plotter.py: reads the response times from the logfile, plots them and also visualizes our specific real-time requirements.

Listing 1.2 shows how we execute a Locust script: we set up a particular experiment by using the following parameters:

- the URL where the ARS is located (line 2);
- where to store the results (line 3);
- the number of alarm devices to simulate and the *hatch rate*—the number of devices to start per second (line 4);
- how long the test should run (line 5).

Listings 1.3 and 1.4 show the relevant parts of our Locust script *locust_sad.py* that simulates the behavior of a real alarm device. Here, class **AlarmDevice-Behavior** defines a single test task **test_alarm()** (Listing 1.3; lines 5–6)—Locust's way of annotating Python functions to be executed (line 4). Our task calls the **send_alarm()** function that implements the proprietary transmission protocol used by the legacy Alarm Receiving Software (ARS) and sends an alarm message using this protocol (line 6).

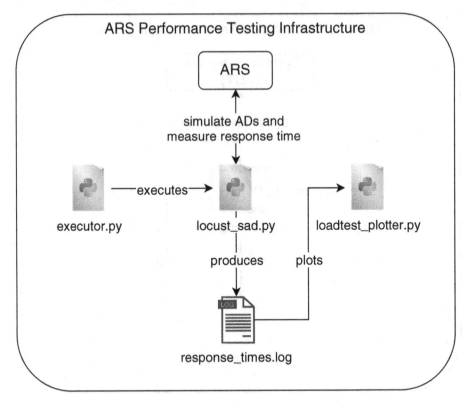

Fig. 7. Our Performance testing infrastructure using Locust

The behavior of a real alarm device consists in repeatedly trying to send an alarm message until a positive acknowledgment is received. This behavior has two reasons:

1. The response time, as explained in Sect. 2.3, spans the time between sending an alarm message and receiving a positive acknowledgment, so we have to measure it accordingly.
2. If the ARS is faulted, the AD keeps sending the alarm message until it has been successfully received and processed.

Listing 1.4 shows class `RepeatingHttpClient` that implements the described behavior (lines 9–15), tracks the response time appropriately (lines 8 and 17–18), and logs the measured times to a text file (line 19). To integrate `Repeating-HttpClient`, we implement a custom Locust client `RepeatingHttpLocust` as recommended by the Locust developers in [3] and we let class `AlarmDevice` inherit from it (Listing 1.3; line 13).

3.2   Preparations - Legacy Software Changes

As explained in Sect. 2.2, the legacy system is built using a database-centric architecture. This means that every alarm message sent to the ARS, triggers

```
1 $ locust -f locust_sad.py \
2 --host=http://<ip>:<port> --no-web \
3 --csv=loadtest_<no_clients>_client \
4 --clients=<no_clients> --hatch-rate=<hatch_rate>
5 --run-time=<total_runtime>
```

Listing 1.2. Shell-Command to execute Locust with our script from Listing 1.3

```
1 class AlarmDeviceBehavior(TaskSet):
2   ...
3
4   @task(1)
5   def test_alarm(self):
6     self.send_alarm()
7
8 class RepeatingHttpLocust(Locust):
9   def __init__(self, *args, **kwargs):
10    super(RepeatingHttpLocust, self).__init__(*args, **
        kwargs)
11    self.client = RepeatingHttpClient(self.host)
12
13 class AlarmDevice(RepeatingHttpLocust):
14   task_set = AlarmDeviceBehavior
15   ...
```

Listing 1.3. Locust script to simulate multiple alarm devices

a large amount of business logic in all programs of the system, resulting in database changes that also increase the size of the database. However, this logic and the particular database changes are sparsely documented: we do not know how changes in the database and the increased size affect the performance of the system. Furthermore, we have no way to reliably revert the database to the state in which it was before we started our performance test, because the database changes are undocumented and other programs of the system perform database changes simultaneously.

So, to measure the performance of the ARS in isolation and prevent database changes, we introduce the concept of a *fake alarm* by extending the original proprietary transmission protocol of the ARS. When the ARS receives a fake alarm, it immediately returns a positive acknowledgment, without storing the alarm in the database. Thus, fake alarms are not influenced by database operations performed by other programs. In particular, the alarm messages sent by Locust (Listing 1.3) are treated as fake alarms.

We perform our tests in the staging environment, to avoid disturbing the production environment of the company.

To make sure that we receive consistent measurements in our experiments, we let Locust send alarm messages always to the same colocation, because the computing resources of each colocation are different from each other. Furthermore,

```
1 class RepeatingHttpClient:
2   def __init__(self, base_url):
3     self.base_url = base_url
4
5   def post(self, endpoint, json_data):
6     url = self.base_url + endpoint
7
8     tau_trigger = time.time()
9     successfully_sent = False
10    while not successfully_sent:
11      try:
12        response = requests.post(url, json=json_data)
13        successfully_sent = 200 <= response.status_code <
              300
14      except RequestException:
15        pass
16
17    tau_ack = time.time()
18    total_time = int((tau_ack - tau_trigger) * 1000)
19    events.request_success.fire(request_type="POST", name=
              endpoint, response_time=total_time, response_length
              =0)
20
21    logger.info("Response time %s", total_time)
22
23    return response
```

Listing 1.4. Client simulating the behavior of an alarm device

because of the master-slave architecture, Locust always sends alarm messages to the active colocation.

3.3 Experimental Setup

In our experimental setup, the RMS has the following parameters for the fault detection mechanism: checkInterval = 8 s, timeout = 200 ms, and error-Threshold = 3. Currently, 10 programs are executed per colocation.

Figure 8 shows the measured timing behavior of the fault detection mechanism with these parameters. When the ARS fails, the first check will be performed within the next checkInterval sec. Consequently, to detect a fault of Colocation 1, the mechanism takes between 26 s and 34 s, and to detect a fault of Colocation 2, it takes between 28 s and 36 s. This means the fault detection mechanism may take more than the 30 s allowed by the standard.

To find out how the fault detection mechanism performs in practice, we experimentally evaluate it by simulating a fault in the ARS and measuring the minimum and maximum response time. We are not considering the fault recovery mechanism, because, as explained before, it takes minutes to perform and is out

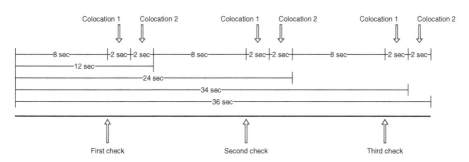

Fig. 8. Timing behavior of the fault detection mechanism of the RMS: Every 8 s, RMS checks the status of all programs running in a colocation, including ARS. Checking 10 programs sequentially with a timeout of 200 ms takes around 2 s. Once a colocation is checked for the third time and one of the programs is still unresponsive, the colocation is marked as faulted and an employee of ESC can see the status in RMS, although he is not notified. The colocations are checked sequentially, meaning the further the colocation is located in the list, the longer it takes until it is checked. Therefore, detecting if Colocation 2 is faulted takes 2 s longer than for Colocation 1.

of scope for this paper. Therefore, we idealize the fault recovery mechanism: we constantly monitor the RMS and, as soon as the fault detection mechanism triggers, we restart the ARS. By doing this, the response time we measure almost equals the fault detection time.

In our experiment, we measure the following times:

$$t_{min} = t_{transmission} + t_{processing} \tag{1}$$
$$t_{max} = t_{faulted} + t_{min} \tag{2}$$
$$t_{faulted} = t_{max} - t_{min} \tag{3}$$

The minimum response time t_{min} is the time the system needs to transmit the alarm message and the response $t_{transmission}$, and process an alarm message $t_{processing}$ as in Eq. (1). The maximum response time t_{max} includes the time $t_{faulted}$ which the RMS takes to detect a fault, and also the time t_{min} the ARS needs to receive an alarm, process it, and send an acknowledgment. So, to estimate how long the RMS takes to detect the fault, we subtract the minimum response time from the maximum response time as in Eq. (3).

Figure 9 illustrates how we perform the experiment. We, as the tester in the figure, start Locust with the required parameters to simulate one AD: Locust begins sending alarm messages. After Locust receives an acknowledgment from the ARS, it waits one second and then sends the next alarm message. By waiting for a second, we generate a minimal workload for the ARS, such that the response time we measure is the minimum response time t_{min}. Simultaneously, the RMS performs the fault detection.

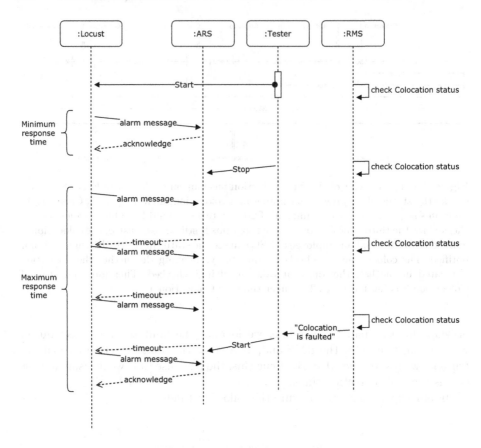

Fig. 9. Timing diagram of our experiment

Then we simulate a fault in the ARS by stopping it. Now, when Locust sends an alarm message, it receives a negative response (timeout), repeats the alarm message immediately and the measurement continues. After simulating the fault, we monitor the RMS that displays the system's status. The RMS continues checking the colocation's status. After the third check, the RMS reports that the colocation is faulted and we start the ARS again. Now, when Locust repeats the alarm message, it receives a positive response (acknowledgment) and the measurement stops, resulting in the maximum response time t_{max} expressed by Eq. (2). We repeat the procedure shown in Fig. 9 multiple times during one day to get reproducible results.

3.4   Experimental Results

Table 1 shows an excerpt of the results of our experiment while Fig. 10 shows full details: times when we stopped and started the ARS taken from the ARS' logfile, the time differences between these two timestamps, the times at which

Locust received the response from the ARS, the response times measured by Locust, and the recovery time, which is the difference between the response time and the Start-Stop Diff.

Table 1. Excerpt of our measurements

Stop	Start	Start-Stop Diff in sec	Locust received response	Response time in sec	Recovery time ARS in sec
09:25:26	09:25:59	33	09:25:59	35	2
09:26:26	09:27:01	35	09:27:02	35	1
09:27:37	09:28:16	39	09:28:21	43	4
11:26:28	11:27:06	38	11:27:09	43	5
11:28:02	11:28:36	34	11:28:37	35	1
12:20:23	12:21:03	40	12:21:05	42	2
12:21:36	12:22:09	33	12:22:09	35	2
12:22:42	12:23:14	32	12:23:16	35	3

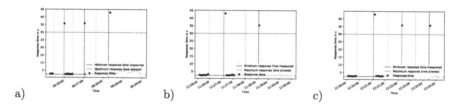

a)   b)   c)

Fig. 10. Times of stopping/ starting ARS and response times measured by Locust. The orange vertical lines are the times of stopping the ARS; after that, Locust receives no response anymore. The green vertical lines indicate the times of starting ARS again. (Color figure online)

After (re-)starting the ARS, it takes a variable amount of time until the ARS has recovered and Locust receives the response (Column 4). This is reasonable: 1) although Locust repeats the alarm message as soon as it receives a negative response (Listing 1.4; lines 9–15), the transmission time $t_{transmission}$ elapses between every repetition as the network request has to be sent through the network and the network error sent back, and 2) the ARS needs some time to start up again. The time difference (recovery time) between starting the ARS and receiving the response at Locust is shown in column 6. We expect that the recovery time is at least 2 s which is the minimum response time we measured. However, we can see that there are some values lower than 2 s. Our explanation is that Locust repeated the alarm message just before the ARS was restarted, thus reducing the transmission time $t_{transmission}$.

Figure 11 illustrates our results: whenever we simulate a fault, the maximum response time of 30 s (red line) (allowed according to the standard's real-time

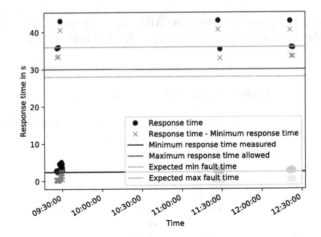

Fig. 11. Calculated fault times (Color figure online)

requirements) is exceeded. The maximum response times t_{max} we measure are in the range of 35 and 43 s (black dots). Subtracting the minimum response time t_{min} of 2 s (blue line), the time $t_{faulted}$ is most often 33 s (gray x's). In this test case, we connected Locust to Colocation 2 so we expect between 28 and 36 s (orange lines) as the fault time, according to the fault detection mechanism explained in Fig. 8, thus 33 s fits within our expected range.

In summary, our results confirm that even when the ARS is not under load and we exclude a realistic human reaction time, the ARS still cannot fully comply with the real-time requirements of the EN 50136 standard [5] when a fault occurs: the fault detection mechanism takes longer than 30 s.

4   Conclusion

We enable reproducing our measurement experiments or adapting our testing infrastructure to other use cases in that we provide a Bitbucket Repository [11], where the full source code of our infrastructure using Locust is available. The repository contains a program that simulates the workload of the ARS based on measurements in the production environment and also the fault management mechanism of the RMS. Some proprietary details, like the network protocol and the variables of the real environment, are omitted.

In this paper, we design and implement a novel approach to building a performance testing infrastructure for measuring the performance of mission-critical distributed legacy real-time software systems using the load testing tool Locust. Locust scripts implement the core load testing logic, like sending requests to the System under Test (SUT), measuring the response time, and logging it. Around the Locust scripts, we build Python scripts that execute Locust with the parameter set required for an experiment, as well as evaluate the measurements against real-time requirements and plot the results.

To showcase our testing infrastructure, we measure the performance of the legacy Alarm Receiving Software (ARS) provided by the GS company group in Germany and we evaluate whether the ARS meets the performance requirements of the current EN 50136 standard [5] under faults. Although our case study focuses on alarm systems, our testing infrastructure can easily be adapted for other use cases.

While developing the performance testing infrastructure, we faced the following problems, common for many database-centric legacy systems:

- undocumented business logic, database changes and software components that perform database changes simultaneously, leading to irreversible database changes;
- unknown effects of database changes on the performance.

In order to cope with these problems, we introduce test requests (fake alarm messages) to isolate the SUT and to prevent database changes. Our application case study has uncovered a major problem in the legacy system of the GS company group: the time it takes for the fault detection mechanism of the RMS to detect a fault exceeds the maximum acceptable response time of the EN 50136 standard, even when excluding the human reaction time. This applies to both the staging environment and the production environment.

In our future work, we will extend the performance testing infrastructure proposed in this paper to allow for evaluating the possible performance improvements of the legacy alarm system by means of the modern cloud techniques, in particular automatic failover. We expect that cloud-based automatic failover should accelerate the fault detection process and eliminate human reaction time, thus reducing the time to detect failures and handle them.

References

1. Avritzer, A., Kondek, J., Liu, D., Weyuker, E.J.: Software performance testing based on workload characterization. In: Proceedings of the 3rd International Workshop on Software and Performance, WOSP 2002, New York, NY, USA, pp. 17–24. Association for Computing Machinery (2002). https://doi.org/10.1145/584369.584373
2. Byström, C., Heyman, J., Hamrén, J., Heyman, H.: Locust. https://docs.locust.io/en/stable/what-is-locust.html
3. Byström, C., Heyman, J., Hamrén, J., Heyman, H.: Locust - Testing other systems using custom clients. https://docs.locust.io/en/stable/testing-other-systems.html
4. da Silva, P.P., Laender, A.H.F., Resende, R.S.F., Golgher, P.B.: Characterizing a synthetic workload for performance evaluation during the migration of a legacy system. In: Proceedings of the Fourth European Conference on Software Maintenance and Reengineering, pp. 173–181, March 2000. https://doi.org/10.1109/CSMR.2000.827325
5. DIN EN 50136–1:2012–08: Alarm systems - alarm transmission systems and equipment - part 1: General requirements for alarm transmission systems, August 2012
6. GS. https://www.gselectronic.com/

7. ISO/IEC: ISO/IEC 2382:2015: Information technology - Vocabulary. Technical report International Organization for Standardization (2015)
8. Jin, Y., Tang, A., Han, J., Liu, Y.: Performance evaluation and prediction for legacy information systems. In: 29th International Conference on Software Engineering (ICSE 2007), pp. 540–549, May 2007. https://doi.org/10.1109/ICSE.2007.64
9. Kumar, A., Yadav, R.S., Ranvijay, A.J.: Fault tolerance in real time distributed system. Int. J. Comput. Sci. Eng. **3**(2), 933–939 (2011)
10. Matthiesen, S., Bjørn, P.: Why replacing legacy systems is so hard in global software development: an information infrastructure perspective. In: Proceedings of the 18th ACM Conference on Computer Supported Cooperative Work & Social Computing. CSCW 2015, New York, NY, USA, pp. 876–890. Association for Computing Machinery (2015). https://doi.org/10.1145/2675133.2675232
11. Tomak, J.: Performance testing infrastructure (2020). https://bitbucket.org/JT1337/locust_scripts
12. Zhang, L.: Performance Models for Legacy System Migration and Multi-core Computers-an MVA Approach. Ph.D. thesis, MCMaster University (2015). http://hdl.handle.net/11375/18196

SHAMan: A Flexible Framework for Auto-tuning HPC Systems

Sophie Robert[1,2] (ID), Soraya Zertal[2(✉)] (ID), and Philippe Couvee[1] (ID)

[1] Atos BDS R&D Data Management, Échirolles, France
{sophie.robert,philippe.couvee}@atos.net
[2] Li-PaRAD, University of Versailles, Versailles, France
{sophie.robert2,soraya.zertal}@uvsq.fr

Abstract. Modern computer components, both hardware and software, come with many tunable parameters and their parametrization can have a strong impact on their performance. Auto-tuning methods relying on black-box optimization have delivered good results for finding the optimal parametrization of complex computer systems. In this paper, we present a new optimization framework, called the **S**mart **HPC** **MAN**ager. It provides an out-of-the-box Web application to perform black-box auto-tuning of computer components running on a distributed system for an application submitted by the user. This framework integrates three state-of-the-art heuristics, as well as resampling strategies to deal with the noise due to resource sharing, and pruning strategies to speed-up the convergence process. We demonstrate a possible use-case of this framework by tuning a software I/O accelerator.

Keywords: Auto-tuning · Black-box optimization · Optimization heuristics · I/O accelerators · HPC

1 Introduction

Modern computer components, both hardware and software, come with many tunable parameters and their parametrization can have a significant impact on their performance. Making sure that the parametrization of the system is optimal is thus crucial for maximizing the performance of computer systems. This is especially important for HPC systems, as many components of a cluster can be parametrized, such as Message Passing Interface libraries (MPI), storage bays or I/O (Input/Output) accelerators. For optimal performance, the most adapted parametrization for each application running on the cluster must be determined and used. But, this parametrization is difficult to find because of the complexity of the relationship between each component and the lack of insight on the system's behavior.

Auto-tuning methods relying on black-box optimization are a promising solution to find the optimal parameters of complex systems in various fields, by

© Springer Nature Switzerland AG 2021
M. C. Calzarossa et al. (Eds.): MASCOTS 2020, LNCS 12527, pp. 147–158, 2021.
https://doi.org/10.1007/978-3-030-68110-4_10

removing the complex task of tuning the system manually or through theoretical models.

In this paper, we present a new optimization framework, called the **S**mart **HPC MAN**ager, which provides an out-of-the-box Web application to perform black-box auto-tuning of custom computer components running on a distributed system, for an application submitted by the user. This framework integrates three state-of-art heuristics, as well as noise reduction strategies to deal with the possible interference of shared resources for large scale HPC systems, and pruning strategies to limit the time spent by the optimization process.

The rest of the paper is organized as follows. Section 2 describes works and tools related to ours and Sect. 3 highlights the advantages of our software compared to already existing ones. Section 4 introduces the principle of black-box optimization and its application to auto-tuning of computer systems. The main features available in SHAMan are described in Sect. 5 and the architecture of the software is described in Sect. 6. An example of use of the software to tune a software I/O accelerator is described in Sect. 7. We conclude and discuss further directions in Sect. 8.

2   Related Work

Auto-tuning using black-box optimization has been used in several domains in the last years. It has yielded good results in very diverse situations and has been particularly helpful in computer science for finding optimal configurations of various software and hardware systems [6,8], especially in the HPC [2,14] and I/O communities [3,4,11]. When it comes to auto-tuning frameworks, several have been proposed recently. Frameworks like *Google Vizier* presented in [7] provide black-box optimization as a service. Several innovative frameworks, like Optuna [1] and Autotune [9], have been developed to find the optimal parametrization of Machine Learning models. However, to our knowledge, no framework specific to HPC clusters' running in production has been suggested.

3   Advantages

Compared to already existing solutions, we provide these main advantages:

- *Accessibility:* the optimization engine is accessible through a Web Interface.
- *Easy to extend:* the optimization engine uses a plug-in architecture and the development of the heuristic is thus the only development cost.
- *Integrated within the HPC ecosystem:* the framework relies on the Slurm workload manager to run HPC applications. The microservice architecture enables it to have no concurrent interactions with the cluster and the application itself.
- *Flexible for a wide range of use-cases:* new components can be registered through a generalist configuration file.

– *Integrates noise reduction strategies:* because of their highly dynamic nature and the complexity of applications and software stacks, HPC systems are subject to many interference when running in production, which results in a different performance measure for each run even with the same system's parametrization. Noise reduction strategies are included in the framework to perform well even in the case of strong interference.
– *Integrates pruning strategies:* runs with unsuited parametrization are aborted, to speed-up the convergence process.

4   Auto-tuning of Computer Systems Using Black-Box Optimization

4.1   What Is Black-Box Optimization?

Black-box optimization refers to the optimization of a function f, possibly stochastic, with unknown properties in a minimum of evaluations, without making any assumption on f. The only available information is the history, which consists in the previously evaluated parameters and their corresponding objective value. Given a budget of n iterations, the problem can be transcribed as:

$$min \ \mathbb{E}(F(x)), \ x \in \mathcal{P}$$
$$F(x) = f(x) + \epsilon(x)$$

– f the function to optimize, F the observed values of the function.
– $\mathcal{P}$ the parameter space and ϵ a possible noise function.

Black-box optimization process consists in iteratively selecting a parametrization, evaluating the black-box function at this point and selecting accordingly the next data point to evaluate.

4.2   Adaptation for Auto-tuning of Computer Systems

When used for auto-tuning of computer systems, black-box optimization consists in treating the combination of the configurable component and the running application as a black-box, which takes as input the parametrization of the tuned component and outputs a performance measure, as depicted in Fig. 1. Given this new information, the optimization heuristic decides the next parametrization to evaluate by the system. This feedback loop is repeated until a convergence criterion is reached and the best found parametrization is deemed to be the best parametrization for the system.

4.3   Heuristics Available in the Framework

Among the black-box heuristics available in the literature, we have implemented surrogate models [10], simulated annealing [13] and genetic algorithms [5]. Our selection is motivated by their simplicity of implementation and their proven efficiency for various computer systems' tuning [4,12].

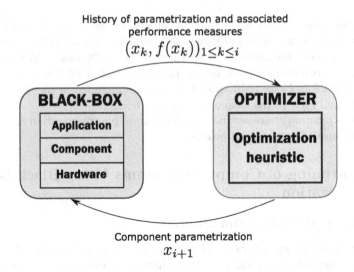

Fig. 1. Schematic representation of the black-box

5 Main Features

SHAMan is a framework to perform auto-tuning of configurable component running on HPC distributed systems. It performs the auto-tuning loop by parametrizing the component, submitting the job through the Slurm workload manager, and getting the corresponding execution time. Using the combination of the history (parametrization and execution time), the framework then uses black-box optimization to select the next most appropriate parametrization, up until the number of allocated runs is over.

5.1 Terminology

Throughout this section, we will use the following terms:

- **Component:** the component which optimum parameters must be found. It must be configurable, either through environment variable or command line arguments.
- **Target value:** the measurement that needs to be optimized. For now SHAMan only deals with the execution time.
- **Parametric grid:** the possible parametrization tested by SHAMan, defined as a minimum, maximum and a step value.
- **Application:** a program that can be run on the clusters' nodes through Slurm and for which we want to find the optimal parametrization of the component.
- **Budget:** the maximum number of evaluations the optimization algorithm can make to find the optimum value.
- **Experiment:** A combination of a component, a target value, an application and a budget that will output the best parametrization for the application and the component.

5.2   Declaring a New Component

Running the command `shaman-install` with a YAML file describing a component registers it to the application. This YAML file must describe how the component is launched and declares its different parameters and how they must be used to parametrize the component. After the installation process, the components are available in the launch menu, as seen in Fig. 2. This component can be activated through options passed on the job's command line, a command called at the top of the script or the setting of the LD_PRELOAD variable.

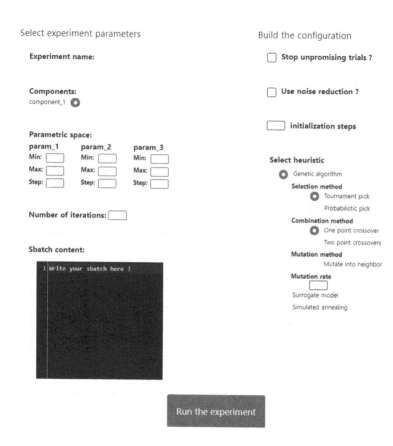

Fig. 2. Page for designing and launching an experiment

The `header` variable is a command written at the top of the script and that is called between each optimization round, before running the job. For instance, a clear cache command is called when tuning I/O accelerators to ensure independence between runs. The parameters with a default value, can be either passed:

- As an environment variable (`env_var=True`)
- As a variable appended to the command line variable with a flag (`cmd_var=True`)
- As a variable passed on the job's command line (`cli_var=True`).

```
components:
  component_1:
    cli_command: example_1
    header: example_header
    command: example_cmd
    ld_preload: example_lib
    parameters:
      param_1:
        env_var: True
        type: int
        default: 1
      param_2:
        cmd_var: True
        type: int
        default: 100
        flag: test
      param_3:
        cli_var: True
        type: int
        default: 1

  component_2:
    ...
```

5.3   Launching an Experiment

To launch an experiment through the menu depicted in Fig. 2, the user has to configure the black-box by:

1. Write an application according to Slurm sbatch format.
2. Select the component and the parametric grid through the radio buttons (minimal, maximal and step value).
3. Configure the optimization heuristic, chosen freely among available ones. Resampling parametrization and pruning strategies can also be activated.

5.4   Visualization of an Experiment

After the submission, the evolution of the running experiments can be visualized in real-time, by displaying the different tested parameters and the corresponding execution time, as well as the improvement brought by the best parametrization. If noise reduction is enabled, the user can either visualize a raw or aggregated views of the performance as shown on Fig. 3.

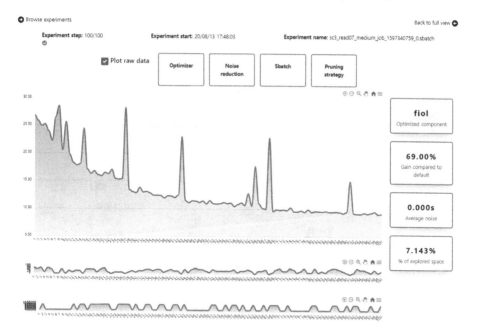

Fig. 3. Result page after FIOL experimentation.

6 Architecture

6.1 General Architecture

SHAMan relies on a microservice architecture (see Fig. 4) and integrates:

- A front-end Web application
- A back-end storage database
- An optimization engine, reached by the API through a message broker, and which uses runners to perform optimization tasks.

The several services communicate through a REST API.

6.2 Optimization Engine

The optimization engine is a stand-alone Python library. It is installed on a node, separate from the compute nodes, so that it does not interfere with the running application, but is able to communicate with the Slurm workload manager and share the same filesystem as the compute nodes.

The engine, schematically described in Fig. 5, is composed of a generic black-box library and a wrapper.

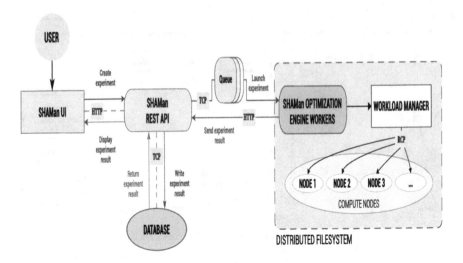

Fig. 4. General architecture of the tuning framework.

The Black-Box Optimizer. The black-box optimizer module performs the black-box optimization process. It can optimize any Python object with a .compute method that takes as input a vector corresponding to a parametrization and outputs a scalar corresponding to the target value.

The Black-Box Wrapper. The black-box wrapper module transforms the component undergoing tuning into a black-box. It is a Python object (called bb_wrapper) that configures and launches the component according to the specification given by the user in the configuration file. It builds a .compute method that takes as input the parameters of the component and the parameters of the experiment, edits the virtual environment and the sbatch file, submits the job through Slurm, parses the output of the Slurm program to get the execution time, and sends this information to the optimizer so that it can make the decision of the next parameters to use.

6.3 Implementation Choices

SHAMan uses *Nuxt.js* as a frontend framework. The optimization engine is written in Python. The database relies on the NoSQL database management system *MongoDB*. The message broker system uses Redis as a queuing system, manipulated with the ARQ Python library. The API is developed in Python, using the FastAPI framework.

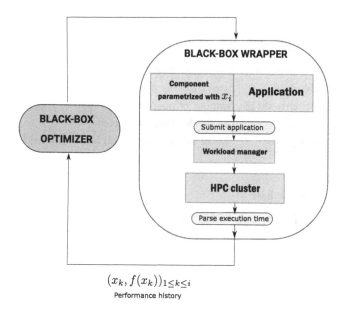

Fig. 5. Schematic representation of the optimization engine.

7   An Application to Auto-tuning an I/O Accelerator

We illustrate how a pure software I/O acceleration library developed by Atos, called the Fast I/O Libraries, FIOL has been optimized by the framework when used with an I/O benchmark.

7.1   The Small Read Optimizer Accelerator

This accelerator relies on a dynamic data preload strategy to prefetch in memory chunks of files that are regularly accessed, in order to speed-up pseudo-random file accesses. The file is conceptually cut into different zones of size `binsize` and the number of accesses within each is counted, up until a maximum value of `sequence_length`. Once the number of accesses in a zone reaches a certain threshold `cluster_threshold`, the pre-fetching mechanism loads a file zone of size `prefetch_size` in memory. These parameters are summarized in Table 1. The FIOL accelerator is highly sensitive to its parametrization, as a poorly set parametrization can trigger too many prefetches, slowing down the application, or too little, which limits the speed-up potential of the accelerator. It is important to find the right balance, in order to prefetch only zones of the file that will be accessed again.

Table 1. Fast I/O libraries parameters

Name of parameter	Description
sequence_length	Number of past accesses kept for counting
binsize	Size of the file zones
cluster_threshold	Number of operations required to trigger the pre-fetching mechanism
prefetch_size	Size of the zone that will be prefetched

7.2   Configuration File

The configuration file for registering the SRO with SHAMan is:

```
components:
  small_read_optimizer:
    cli_command: fastio=yes
    parameters:
      sequence_length:
        env_var: True
        type: int
        default: 100
      binsize:
        env_var: True
        type: int
        default: 1048576
      cluster_threshold:
        env_var: True
        type: int
        default: 2
      prefetch_size:
        env_var: True
        type: int
        default: 20971520
```

7.3   Test Experiment

Based on the results found in [12], we perform the following experiment:

- Test application: The test application is an in-house benchmarking application, running on a single node. This application performs a series of reads using a pseudo-random pattern.
- Initialization budget: The experiment is initialized with 20 iterations.
- Experiment parametric grid: The selected parametric grid is described in Table 2.
- Test black-box heuristic: The test is conducted using genetic algorithms with a tournament pick method for population selection and single point crossover, for a budget of 80 iterations. Noise reduction strategy is disabled and the pruning strategy uses the current median execution time as a threshold time.

Table 2. Description of the parametric grid

Parameter name	Lower limit	Upper limit	Step
Cluster threshold	2	100	20
Binsize	524288	1048576	262144
Sequence length	50	700	50
Prefetch size	1048576	10485760	1048576

7.4   Results

The result screen is displayed in Fig. 3. Compared to default parametrization, we find an improvement of 69%, after exploring only 7.14% of the specified parametric space. This result shows the strong impact of the parameters on the system's performance and the usefulness of auto-tuning to maximize the effect of this I/O accelerator.

8   Conclusion and Further Works

We present in this paper a new optimization software, called SHAMan, aimed at tuning configurable component of HPC systems for particular applications. It comes with several state-of-the-art heuristics, as well as resampling and pruning strategies, particularly adapted to the tuning of noisy and costly system. It is also easily configurable for a wide range of different components and use-cases, as we demonstrated by tuning an I/O accelerator. In terms of future works, we are planning on adding more sophisticated resampling and pruning strategies, to further enhance the efficiency of the optimization engine. We are also looking at adding stop criteria different than a budget-based one.

References

1. Akiba, T., Sano, S., Yanase, T., Ohta, T., Koyama, M.: Optuna: a next-generation hyperparameter optimization framework (2019)
2. Balaprakash, P., et al.: Autotuning in high-performance computing applications. Proc. IEEE **106**(11), 2068–2083 (2018)
3. Behzad, B., et al.: Taming parallel I/O complexity with auto-tuning. In: Proceedings of the International Conference on High Performance Computing, Networking, Storage and Analysis, SC 2013, pp. 68:1–68:12 (2013)
4. Cao, Z., Tarasov, V., Tiwari, S., Zadok, E.: Towards better understanding of black-box auto-tuning: a comparative analysis for storage systems. In: Proceedings of the 2018 USENIX Conference on USENIX Annual Technical Conference, USENIX ATC 2018, pp. 893–907 (2018)
5. Davis, L.: Handbook of Genetic Algorithms. Van Nostrand Reinhold, New York (1991)

6. Desani, D., Gil Costa, V., Marcondes, C.A.C., Senger, H.: Black-box optimization of hadoop parameters using derivative-free optimization. In: 2016 24th Euromicro International Conference on Parallel, Distributed, and Network-Based Processing (PDP), pp. 43–50 (2016)
7. Golovin, D., Solnik, B., Moitra, S., Kochanski, G., Karro, J.E., Sculley, D. (eds.): Google Vizier: A Service for Black-Box Optimization (2017)
8. Jamshidi, P., Casale, G.: An uncertainty-aware approach to optimal configuration of stream processing systems. CoRR, abs/1606.06543 (2016)
9. Koch, P., Golovidov, O., Gardner, S., Wujek, B., Griffin, J., Xu, Y.: Autotune. In: Proceedings of the 24th ACM SIGKDD International Conference on Knowledge Discovery & Data Mining, July 2018
10. Ky, V.K., D'Ambrosio, C., Hamadi, Y., Liberti, L.: Surrogate-based methods for black-box optimization. Int. Trans. Oper. Res. **24**, 393–424 (2016)
11. Li, Y., Chang, K., Bel, O., Miller, E.L., Long, D.D.E.: CAPES: unsupervised storage performance tuning using neural network-based deep reinforcement learning. In: Proceedings of the International Conference for High Performance Computing, Networking, Storage and Analysis, SC 2017, New York, NY, USA, pp. 42:1–42:14 (2017)
12. Robert, S., Zertal, S., Goret, G.: Auto-tuning of IO accelerators using black-box optimization. In: Proceedings of the International Conference on HighPerformance Computing & Simulation (HPCS) (2019)
13. Gelatt, C.D., Kirkpatrick, S., Vecchi, M.P.: Optimization by simulated annealing. Science **220**, 671–680 (1983)
14. Seymour, K., You, H., Dongarra, J.: A comparison of search heuristics for empirical code optimization. In: 2008 IEEE International Conference on Cluster Computing, pp. 421–429 (2008)

Balanced Gray Codes for Reduction of Bit-Flips in Phase Change Memories

Arockia David Roy Kulandai[1], Stella J[2], John Rose[2], and Thomas Schwarz[1(✉)]

[1] Marquette University, Milwaukee, WI, USA
{david.roy,thomas.schwarz}@marquette.edu
[2] Xavier Institute of Engineering, Mahim (West), Mumbai, India
{stella,johnrose}@xavier.ac.in

Abstract. Phase Change Memories combine byte addressability, non-volatility, and low energy consumption with densities comparable to storage devices and access speeds comparable to random access memory. This qualifies PCM as a successor technology to both DRAM and SSD. The only disadvantage is limited endurance (though still orders of magnitude higher than for Flash memory). Since PCM consume energy only when actively reading and writing and writing consumes much more energy than reading, reducing "bitflip pressure" is important not only in order to stretch endurance, but also to save energy.

We present two related contributions to relieve bitflip pressure. Many data structures use status or dirty bits that over the lifetime of a data structure such as a key value store can flip numerous times. We use balanced Gray codes to distribute the changes of a dirty bit across a whole byte. Our second construction offers a way to implement counters using Gray codes that have close to one bit-flip per increment.

Keywords: Phase change memories · Bit-flip reduction · Balanced gray codes

1 Introduction

Phase Change Memories (PCM) are one of several competing technologies with the potential to drastically change Computer Architecture. They combine the speed and byte addressability of Dynamic Random Access Memories (DRAM) with the non-volatility, storage density, storage capacity, and the low costs per Gigabyte of Solid State or Hard Disk Drives (SSD/HDD). The first versions of PCM are already on the market, but specialized to replace (or augment) either DRAM or SSD. Their only draw-back is limited endurance, even though their endurance is still orders of decadic magnitude larger than that of SSD.

To put endurance in perspective, assume we are writing to memory at a rate of 50 GB/sec, close to the current theoretical bandwidth of the data bus. Assume further that we are using the system at this rate for 10 years. Since there are only 3.15576×10^8 s in 10 years, we would write a total of 1.57788×10^{10} GB of

© Springer Nature Switzerland AG 2021
M. C. Calzarossa et al. (Eds.): MASCOTS 2020, LNCS 12527, pp. 159–171, 2021.
https://doi.org/10.1007/978-3-030-68110-4_11

data during a decade. There is currently a 1.5 TB PCM on the market (albeit only as an SSD and not as a memory replacement). A 1.5 TB PCM would see its bytes overwritten some 1.05×10^7 times, a number that is well within the endurance limits of such a future device. The simple, but important expedient of only overwriting bits that actually have to change (Data Comparison Write DCW [17]) additionally halves the number of overwrites of individual bits. This naive calculation assumes of course perfect load balancing. Without perfect load balancing, the systems community needs to find ways to prevent hot bits from being over-used. Here, we make a small contribution by lowering the bit flips needed for a "dirty bit", used in many lock-free data structures, and of counters. Finally, we investigate whether our solution based on balanced Gray codes [2, 10, 14–16] would also be useful for integer addition. We envision a close future where the bulk of memory in computer systems consists of PCM or one of its faster rival technologies, while caches have become even larger. We argue for the importance of reducing bitflips in data structures with a number of reasons.

1. Some data structures, for example those used in the file system, will perdure for the lifetime of a system, and are dangerous to move by a load balancer, which identifies heavily written blocks and swaps them for less often written blocks.
2. Some parts of a data structure will be accessed many times, resulting in "hot" regions with a large number of bit-flips. An example would be the root node of a B-tree.
3. Overusing a single bit in a block should force the load balancer to swap out the complete block, but a load balancer will not be able to track the use of each bit and would therefore be unable to diagnose the problem.
4. PCM use energy only for read and write operations. The costs of overwrites dominates its energy consumption. The less bitflips a data structure has, the less energy is spent on its maintenance. As CPU operations are fast compared to memory operations, we can trade a few additional instruction executions for fewer bitflips.
5. Not all PCM memories will be large. Sensors and embedded systems will be dimensioned as small and as cheap as possible. A combination of steady updates with a small memory can stress endurance.

Our work is speculative, based on a vision of a future that might never happen. If this future happens and if our contributions become reality, they will need support either in hardware (such as translating nibbles and bytes from the usual integer representation to Gray codes) or at the system level (such as implementing a counter class). Such changes will not come quickly, but if, and this is a big if, if PCM or one of its competing non-volatile storage technologies unify memory and storage, then they will need support at either the OS or the CPU architecture level and probably both.

The remainder of the paper is organized as follows. We first review related work on extending the longevity of PCM and similar non-volatile memories. The third section gives an overview of balanced and other Gray codes. In Sect. 4, we give our constructions first for implementing a dirty bit and then for implementing counters. We also prove experimentally that balanced Gray codes will not be able to lower bitflips for addition.

2   Related Work

Bit flip pressure can be alleviated at all levels of the storage hierarchy. At the PCM architecture level, the fundamental contribution avoids superfluous writes. Lee *et al.* and Yang *et al.* both observed that we only need to overwrite cells whose content has changed (Partial Write/Data Comparison and Write) [11], [17]. We can safely assume that this proposal is embedded in all current and future PCM devices.

A next group of proposals trades off *ad hoc* encoding with additional bits to be stored. Cho and Lee's *Flip-N-Write* adds a bit cell that determines whether a word is to be read as is or inverted [5]. Palangappa and Mohanram's *Adaptive Flip-N-Write* also stores some words in reversed form [13]. They combine their scheme with light-weigth compression proposed by Alameldeen and Wood and based on recognizing seven frequent patterns for words in memory [1]. Jalili and Sarbazi-Azad observe that bit-flips are not uniformly distributed and only use Flip-N-Write for hot locations. Their scheme, *Captopril*, identifies the hot bits in a block and stores this information as metadata with the block [8].

Just minimizing the number of bit-flips can backfire if the scheme just concentrates bit-flips into a hot set, because frequently written cells could then reach their limit of endurance before the economic lifespan of the system. *Flip-Min* by Jacobvitz, Calderbank and Sorin spreads out bitflips by using coset coding and only write the coset vector with the minimum number of bitflips [7]. Maddah and colleagues propose *Cost-Aware Flip Optimization* (CAFO), which organizes bits in a matrix with auxiliary bits for each row and column indicated whether a cell content is read as is or in inverted form [12]. Han *et al.* use a hardware shuffle to distribute bitflips evenly over a byte or a word [9].

Bittman's work comes closest to ours, as he and his colleagues alleviate bit flip pressure at the systems and data structure level. Besides showing that relatively minute changes in the design of a data structure can yield unexpected bitflip savings, they argue that common structures such as the OS stack should be redesigned [3,4].

Table 1. Recursive Gray Code for four bits.

Code	Binary	Hex	Bit flipped		Code	Binary	Hex	Bit flipped
r_0	0000	0	3		r_8	1100	c	3
r_1	0001	1	0		r_9	1101	d	0
r_2	0011	3	1		r_{10}	1111	f	1
r_3	0010	2	0		r_{11}	1110	e	0
r_4	0110	6	2		r_{12}	1010	a	2
r_5	0111	7	0		r_{13}	1011	b	0
r_6	0101	5	1		r_{14}	1001	9	1
r_7	0100	4	0		r_{15}	1000	8	0
r_{16}	0000	0	3					

$$\vdots \qquad\qquad\qquad\qquad \vdots$$

3   Balanced Gray Codes

A Gray code on n bits orders all the 2^n binary strings of length n in such a way that all consecutive strings differ by exactly one bit. Here we are only interested in codes such that the last and first element of the string differs also in exactly one bit. These are more properly called Gray cycles. Gray codes can be interpreted as Hamiltonian circuits on the edges of an n dimensional unit cube.

Probably the best-known Gray code is the Binary Reflected Gray Code (BRGC) presented in Table 1 for length 4. The second column represents the four-digit binary code, the next column the equivalent hexadecimal digit, and the last column gives the position of the single bit flipped between the current code and its predecessor (with 0 for the least significant bit and 3 for the most significant bit). For this code, the least significant bit is flipped eight times whereas the most significant bit is flipped only twice.

Each Gray code is given by the sequence of bits that are flipped, called the *delta sequence* [10] and the first element, customarily 0. In the case of the BRGC, the delta sequence is

$$\delta_{\mathrm{BRGC}} = (0, 1, 0, 2, 0, 1, 0, 3, 0, 1, 0, 2, 0, 1, 0, 3).$$

If we start with a different element or if we apply a permutation on the number representing the bit flipped, then we obtain a different, but equivalent Gray code. For example, if we start with 0111, and apply the same sequence of bits flipped, we obtain a code 0110, 0100, 0101, 0001, ... The delta sequence also allows us to store a Gray code in more compact form, since the size of the elements of the delta sequence is the binary logarithm of the number of different elements. Another way to create an equivalent Gray code is to permute the integers in the delta sequence. The delta sequence $(\delta_i)_{i \in \mathbb{Z}_{2^n}}$ would be replaced by $(\pi(\delta_i))_{i \in \mathbb{Z}_{2^n}}$ with π a permutation of $\{1, \ldots, n\}$.

The Gray code in Table 1 gets its name because of its typical construction. For $n = 1$, there is only one Gray code with bit flip sequence $\Gamma_1 = (0)$, i.e. with code sequence $0 \rightarrow 1 \rightarrow 0 \ldots$. For $n = 2$, we start with Γ_1, insert 1, and then

Table 2. All balanced Gray codes on four bits starting with 0

```
0,1,3,2,6,7,15,11,9,13,5,4,12,14,10,8
0,1,3,2,6,4,12,14,10,11,15,7,5,13,9,8
0,1,3,2,6,14,15,7,5,13,9,11,10,8,12,4
0,1,3,2,6,14,10,11,9,13,15,7,5,4,12,8
0,1,3,2,6,14,10,8,9,11,15,7,5,13,12,4
0,1,3,2,10,11,15,7,5,13,9,8,12,14,6,4
0,1,3,2,10,8,12,14,6,7,15,11,9,13,5,4
0,1,3,2,10,14,15,11,9,13,5,7,6,4,12,8
0,1,3,2,10,14,6,7,5,13,15,11,9,8,12,4
0,1,3,2,10,14,6,4,5,7,15,11,9,13,12,8
0,1,3,7,6,2,10,14,12,4,5,13,15,11,9,8
0,1,3,7,6,14,15,11,9,13,5,4,12,8,10,2
0,1,3,7,5,4,12,13,9,11,15,14,6,2,10,8
0,1,3,7,5,4,12,14,6,2,10,11,15,13,9,8
0,1,3,7,5,13,12,4,6,2,10,14,15,11,9,8
0,1,3,7,5,13,15,14,6,2,10,11,9,8,12,4
0,1,3,7,5,13,9,8,12,4,6,14,15,11,10,2
0,1,3,7,15,13,5,4,12,8,9,11,10,14,6,2
0,1,3,7,15,11,10,8,9,13,5,4,12,14,6,2
0,1,3,7,15,11,9,8,10,2,6,14,12,13,5,4
0,1,3,7,15,11,9,8,12,13,5,4,6,14,10,2
```

repeat Γ_1. This gives bit flip sequence $\Gamma_2 = (0,1,0)$ and Gray code sequence $00, 01, 11, 10$. Let the dot . denote concatenation of sequences. For the general case we then have

$$\Gamma_{n+1} = \Gamma_n.(n-1).\Gamma_n.$$

Thus, $\Gamma_3 = (0,1,0,2,0,1,0)$. For Γ_4, the delta sequence has 3 between two copies of Γ_3 resulting in the delta sequence above and the Gray code of Table 1.

If we use the binary reflected Gray code to increment a value in $0, 1, 2, \ldots, 15$ by one before rolling back to 0000, we flip only one bit at a time, but we do not flip each bit equally often. A Gray code is called *balanced* if it distributes the number of bit flips evenly over all bits. Let x denote this number. If a Gray code over n digits is balanced and has x bit flips in each bit, then $n \cdot x = 2^n$, which implies that both n and x are powers of two.

We look for balanced Gray codes for $n = 4$. We can assume the start to be zero and the first bit to be flipped to be 0. The next bit to be fliped cannot be 0, so we can assume it to be 1. This means, that we are looking for balanced Gray codes that start out with $0000, 0001, 0010$. For the next step, we can make a case distinction, namely whether the next bit to be flipped is among those already flipped or a new one. In the first case, the only possibility is to flip 0, in the second case, up to permutation of the set of bits flipped, we can assume that this is bit 2. This means that if a balanced Gray code exists, then it must begin with $0000, 0001, 0011, 0010$ or with $0000, 0001, 0011, 0111$. In the first case, we know that we have to now flip a different bit, and up to equivalence, this has to be bit three, Therefore, this family of balanced Gray codes starts out with $0000, 0001, 0011, 0010, 0110$. We can now use a computer search to find all balanced Gray codes of length 4, given in Table 2, subject to these restrictions.

Table 3. Balanced Gray code on eight bits [15].

```
00,01,03,02,06,0e,0a,0b,09,0d,0f,07,05,04,0c,08,
18,1c,14,15,17,1f,3f,37,35,34,3c,38,28,2c,24,25,
27,2f,2d,29,39,3d,1d,19,1b,3b,2b,2a,3a,1a,1e,16,
36,3e,2e,26,22,32,12,13,33,23,21,31,11,10,30,20,
60,70,50,51,71,61,63,73,53,52,72,62,66,6e,7e,76,
56,5e,5a,7a,6a,6b,eb,ea,fa,da,de,d6,f6,fe,ee,e6,
e2,f2,d2,d3,f3,e3,e1,f1,d1,d0,f0,e0,a0,b0,90,91,
b1,a1,a3,b3,93,92,b2,a2,a6,ae,be,b6,96,9e,9a,ba,
aa,ab,bb,9b,99,9d,dd,d9,db,fb,7b,5b,59,5d,7d,79,
f9,fd,bd,b9,a9,e9,69,6d,6f,67,65,64,e4,e5,e7,ef,
ed,ad,af,a7,a5,a4,ac,ec,6c,68,e8,a8,b8,f8,78,7c,
fc,bc,b4,b5,b7,f7,f5,f4,74,75,77,7f,ff,bf,9f,df,
5f,57,55,54,d4,d5,d7,97,95,94,9c,dc,5c,58,d8,98,
88,c8,48,4c,cc,8c,84,c4,44,45,c5,85,87,c7,47,4f,
cf,8f,8d,cd,4d,49,c9,89,8b,cb,4b,4a,ca,8a,8e,ce,
4e,46,c6,86,82,c2,42,43,c3,83,81,c1,41,40,c0,80
```

The first general existence proof for balanced Gray codes comes from Wagner and West for a number of digits that are powers of 2 [16] and extended to all length by Bhat and Savage [2]. Table 3 shows a balanced Gray code for length 8. We find them less useful in our context as translating an integer $i \in \{0, 1, \ldots, 255\}$ to the ith element of the code or calculating the next element in the Gray code – perhaps via the delta sequence – leads to larger circuits or more space consuming software implementations.

4 Implementing a Dirty Bit

Dirty bits are a common tool in designing lock-free data structures. The use of a *Compare-And-Swap* (CAS) or similar atomic instruction insures that updates to the dirty bit will be written directly to main memory bypassing the caches and invalidating their entries. Since there are only $10 \times 365.25 \times 24 \times 60 \approx 5 \times 10^6$ minutes in ten years, flipping a dirty bit regularly, even if it were for a data structure that persists over the lifetime of the system, is usually not a large issue. However, this consideration does not apply if the dirty bit belongs to a system data structure, e.g. for memory management, that is changed more often, since we then would be approaching the 10^7 to 10^8 endurance of PCM. For this rare, but important cases, we present here a solution to spread out the dirty bit over several bits.

Our first solution combines the dirty bit with a counter. This can be useful to evade the ABA problem [6]. Abstractly, it creates a data structure with an internal value field (such as a nibble, a byte or several bytes) that implements a *flip* function and an *evaluate* function which returns the value of the dirty bit, that is, either zero or one. Our first solution uses a balanced Gray code to store the value in a nibble or a byte. The evaluate method returns the parity of the value field. The flip operation just advances the Gray code by one. Since two

```
class DirtyBit:
  nextvector = [ ... ]
  def __init__(self):
     self.value = 0
  def getValue(self):
     ...

def next(self):
  right = self.value&1
  index = self.value>>1
  info = DirtyBit.nextvector[index]
  bit = info>>4 if right else info&0xf
  self.value^=0x1<<bit
```

Fig. 1. Python pseudo-code for the next function of a dirty bit implementation.

consecutive words in the Gray code differ by one bit, the parity of the value field is guaranteed to change.

To implement the advancement in software, we can use two methods. First, for all possible values, we store the next value in an array. If the values are bytes, there are 256 values, so that we need an array of 256 bytes. This array is read-only and can easily fit into a cache. At the cost of more calculation, we can save half the space by only adding the integer representation of the bit to be flipped. Since the bit number only needs 4b storage, we can store the information in half a byte. We therefore create a 128B array such that the left half of the byte at index i gives the bit to flip when the current value is $2i$ and the right half of the byte at index i gives the bit to flip when the current value is $2i + 1$. To extract it (Fig. 1), we divide the current value of the dirty bit into the trailing binary digit and into the current value shifted to the right. The first number tells us whether the desired information is in the left or in the right half of the byte, the second number gives us the address of the byte in the lookup array (DirtyBit.nextvector).

If the value is a nibble, we only need 8 bytes to encode the next array, which consists of 16 half-bytes. We can also use the delta sequence, which consists of 16 elements that can be encoded in two bits, for a total of 4 bytes.

The calculations are performed in CPU and do not need to write anything but the new value of the dirty bit. Since the code can be shared by all processes, we can even expect it to be always cache resident.

If we only use a single nibble, then it is very easy to implement the next function in hardware.

To determine the parity, we can also use a hardware solution, but software implementations are also readily available. One possibility would be a 256 bit look-up array of size 32B.

When we initialize a dirty bit in a byte, we do not have to change the value of the byte about half the time, namely when it already has the correct parity. If this is not the case, then we simply flip the dirty bit.

If we are only interested in flipping a dirty bit, the use of the balanced Gray code is overkill. An alternative is using a sequence like 000000000000,

```
if x&0x8000:
    x = (x<<1)&0xffff
else:
    x = ((x<<1)|0x01)&0xffff
```

Fig. 2. Python pseudo-code for implementing a dirty bit in 16 actual bits.

000000000001, 000000000011, 000000000111, ..., 011111111111, 111111111111, 111111111110, 111111111100, ..., 100000000000, 000000000000. This can also be implemented in software, as is examplified by the code fragment given in Fig. 2. Depending on the most significant bit, we either use a left shift or a left shift combined with setting the least significant bit. We can trade clarity for terseness by replacing the if-else construct with additional bit-wise operations.

5   Implementing a Counter

While the setting of our dirty bit can be simply evaluated by calculating the parity of the value field, we often need to calculate the value of a counter. This is not always necessary, as sometimes we just need to count to a given value. We represent a number as usual in binary format. We then break this number up into nibbles and replace each nibble i with the ith element of a Gray code $(\beta_i)_{i=0,\ldots 15}$ such as $B_4 = (0, 1, 3, 2, 6, 4, c, e, a, b, f, 7, 5, d, 9, 8)$. We assume that this translation happens in hardware. We can think of this encoding as encoding integers with base 16, but using a different representation for hexadecimal letters.

If we start at 0 and increment a n-bit counter until we roll over to 0 again, we flip the least significant digit 2^n times, the second least significant digit 2^{n-1} times, and so on. The most significant digit is flipped only twice. The total number of bit-flips is

$$\sum_{i=1}^{n} 2^i = 2^{n+1} - 2$$

times or per increment operation $2 - 2^{1-n}$ times. If we however use our encoding, we flip one bit in the least significant hexadecimal digit once per increment or a total of 2^n times, one bit in the second least significant hexadecimal digit every 16 increments or 2^{n-4} times, and one bit in the most significant hexadecimal digit 2^4 times. The total number of bit-flips is

$$\sum_{i=1}^{\frac{n}{4}} 2^{4i} = \frac{16}{15}(2^n - 1)$$

and the average per increment operation is now $\frac{1}{15}2^{4-n}(2^n - 1)$, which is only 8/15 of the previous numbers and close to the optimal number of 1 bitflip per increment.

If instead we represent the integer in base 256 and then use a balanced Gray code on eight binary digits, the number of bitflips goes down to 128/255, that is, we improve from a savings of 46.67% of bitflips to 49.80% of bitflips.

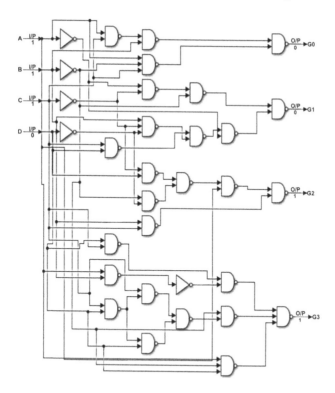

Fig. 3. Hardware implementation of a translation from 4-bit unsigned integer to Gray code.

5.1 Implementation

Somewhere on the way between the CPU and PCM memory, we need to transfer between the normal integer representation and the representation using a Gray code. In software, this is best done using a loopup table. Such a lookup table is likely to reside in cache, but in any case will not cause any writes to PCM. We can also look at hardware implementations. For this, we break each integer into nibbles, e.g. on a 64b architecture into 16 nibbles. For each nibble, we then have circuits translating between the standard unsigned integer and the Gray code. Figure 3 gives an example. The circuit implements the balanced Gray code $(0, 1, 5, 4, 12, 8, 10, 14, 6, 7, 15, 13, 9, 11, 3, 2)$ as a translation circuitry. If $ABCD$ is a nibble, then the corresponding element $(G_0 G_1 G_2 G_3)$ of the Gray code is $G_0 = B(\bar{A} + \bar{C}) + A\bar{B}C$, $G_1 = \bar{B}(A + C) + \bar{A}(CD + BC\bar{D})$, $G_2 = BC + A(\bar{C}D + \bar{B}D)$, $G_3 = AB(\bar{C} + \bar{D}) + \bar{B}(C \oplus D) + A\bar{B}D$. This can be implemented with 32 NAND gates. For a number of other codes that also save a few bitflips for addition (see below) in Table 4, we found implementations with 32 NAND gates.

Table 4. Good four-bit balanced Gray codes

Group A

```
[0, 1, 3, 2, 6, 4, 12, 14, 10, 11, 15, 7, 5, 13, 9, 8]
[0, 1, 3, 2, 10, 8, 12, 14, 6, 7, 15, 11, 9, 13, 5, 4]
[0, 1, 5, 4, 12, 8, 10, 14, 6, 7, 15, 13, 9, 11, 3, 2]
[0, 1, 9, 8, 10, 2, 6, 14, 12, 13, 15, 11, 3, 7, 5, 4]
[0, 1, 9, 8, 12, 4, 6, 14, 10, 11, 15, 13, 5, 7, 3, 2]
[0, 2, 3, 1, 5, 4, 12, 13, 9, 11, 15, 7, 6, 14, 10, 8]
[0, 2, 6, 4, 5, 1, 9, 13, 12, 14, 15, 7, 3, 11, 10, 8]
[0, 2, 6, 4, 12, 8, 9, 13, 5, 7, 15, 14, 10, 11, 3, 1]
[0, 2, 10, 8, 9, 1, 5, 13, 12, 14, 15, 11, 3, 7, 6, 4]
[0, 4, 6, 2, 10, 8, 9, 11, 3, 7, 15, 14, 12, 13, 5, 1]
[0, 4, 5, 1, 9, 8, 10, 11, 3, 7, 15, 13, 12, 14, 6, 2]
[0, 4, 12, 8, 10, 2, 3, 11, 9, 13, 15, 14, 6, 7, 5, 1]
[0, 4, 5, 1, 3, 2, 10, 11, 9, 13, 15, 7, 6, 14, 12, 8]
[0, 8, 9, 1, 5, 4, 6, 7, 3, 11, 15, 13, 12, 14, 10, 2]
[0, 8, 10, 2, 6, 4, 5, 7, 3, 11, 15, 14, 12, 13, 9, 1]
[0, 8, 12, 4, 5, 1, 3, 7, 6, 14, 15, 13, 9, 11, 10, 2]
```

Group B

```
[0, 1, 3, 2, 6, 14, 10, 8, 9, 11, 15, 7, 5, 13, 12, 4]
[0, 1, 3, 2, 10, 14, 6, 4, 5, 7, 15, 11, 9, 13, 12, 8]
[0, 1, 9, 8, 10, 14, 12, 4, 5, 13, 15, 11, 3, 7, 6, 2]
[0, 1, 9, 8, 12, 14, 10, 2, 3, 11, 15, 13, 5, 7, 6, 4]
[0, 2, 3, 1, 5, 13, 9, 8, 10, 11, 15, 7, 6, 14, 12, 4]
[0, 2, 3, 1, 9, 13, 5, 4, 6, 7, 15, 11, 10, 14, 12, 8]
[0, 2, 6, 4, 12, 13, 5, 1, 3, 7, 15, 14, 10, 11, 9, 8]
[0, 2, 10, 8, 12, 13, 9, 1, 3, 11, 15, 14, 6, 7, 5, 4]
[0, 4, 12, 8, 9, 11, 10, 2, 6, 14, 15, 13, 5, 7, 3, 1]
[0, 4, 6, 2, 10, 11, 3, 1, 5, 7, 15, 14, 12, 13, 9, 8]
[0, 4, 6, 2, 3, 11, 10, 8, 12, 14, 15, 7, 5, 13, 9, 1]
[0, 4, 5, 1, 9, 11, 3, 2, 6, 7, 15, 13, 12, 14, 10, 8]
[0, 8, 9, 1, 3, 7, 5, 4, 12, 13, 15, 11, 10, 14, 6, 2]
[0, 8, 10, 2, 6, 7, 3, 1, 9, 11, 15, 14, 12, 13, 5, 4]
[0, 8, 12, 4, 5, 7, 6, 2, 10, 14, 15, 13, 9, 11, 3, 1]
[0, 8, 12, 4, 6, 7, 5, 1, 9, 13, 15, 14, 10, 11, 3, 2]
```

5.2 Addition

Since encodings based on Gray codes lower the number of bitflips when employing a counter, we can ask whether the same ploy also works for addition. With a large cache, numerical results will only overwrite operands after involved calculations and encoding is unlikely to accrue savings, but this might not be the case for an embedded system with a small PCM and puny processor.

We experimented by determining the expected number of bitflips for addition under various encodings. In the absence of a better model, we assume that summands are according to a Zipfian distribution in a range $[0, 2^m]$. We calculated the expected number of bitflips in an immediate addition x += y, where x and y are taken from this range. As possible candidates for encodings we used all balanced Gray codes in Table 2 including those obtained by slicing the delta sequence into two parts and rejoining them in reverse order. Our search gave us two groups, A and B in Table 4 that reasonably consistently gave savings. The savings as well as the total number of expected bitflips using the normal binary encoding are given in Figure 4. As the savings are not consistent and on the order of 1%, the results are not encouraging.

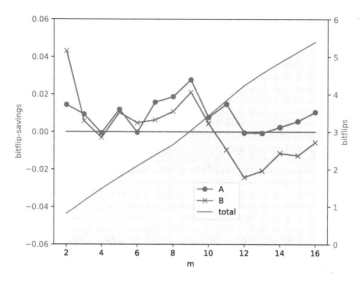

Fig. 4. Expected number of bitflips when adding using the traditional encoding (blue) and savings when using Codes from Groups A and B (red). The x-axis gives the range of the operands as $[0, 2^m]$.

Fig. 5. A load balanced counter with raw value 0010 0000 1001 1110 1011 or $15 \cdot 16^4 + 0 \cdot 16^3 + 12 \cdot 16^2 + 7 \cdot 16 + 13 = 986237$ if we use the 4-digit Gray code implemented in Figure 3. The first nibble points to the least significant digit of the counter value. (Color figure online)

5.3 Load Balancing

Using our or any of the many other schemes to save bitflips can backfire if we manage to concentrate a lesser number of bitflips in relatively few cells, which might reach the limit of their endurance before the end of the economic lifespan of the system.

A number of hardware based proposals [7], [9], [12] are effective in doing so, but it is unclear to us whether their hardware overhead will make them attractive to device manufacturers. History has shown that the cost-savings of large numbers mitigate optimizations for special cases. We therefore need a software solution. One possibility is to use the first nibble of a 32b word for load balancing, limiting of course the maximum value to which we can count to 2^{28}. The first nibble contains a value between zero and seven, which is interpreted as a pointer to the least significant nibble of the counter (see Figure 5). We advance the offset whenever the three least significant nibbles roll over zero, resulting in a burst of bitflips. When we advance, we have to move seven nibbles, however, three of them we know to be zero. Of the seven nibbles overwritten, thus two are overwriting a zero nibble with a zero nibble, so that with Data Comparison Write, we overwrite 5 nibbles, leading on average to 20 bit flips. For a counter that eventually reaches a large number N (less than 2^{24}), we therefore expect

$$\frac{20\,N}{16^3} = 0.00488N$$

additional bitflips caused by our load balancing scheme. This is an increase of less than half a percent.

To achieve load balancing for counters that are not heavily used, we can load the first nibble with a random number when initializing a counter.

6   Conclusions

PCM is one of a class of non-volatile storage technologies that is capable of uniting the role of memory and storage in current computer architectures. Of the many competing technologies, it is the first to be on the market in terabyte size. While it is still undergoing rapid technological development and while we still do not know whether it is going to be the winner in the current race, now is the time to think about its uses and the technological adaptions that are needed. Like many of its competitors, PCM have limited endurance. Therefore, reducing bitflip pressure is important, in particular if the size of the PCM is limited. An additional reason to limit the number of bitflips lies in the concentration of energy consumption of PCMs in the writes.

Here, we investigated situations where the limited endurance of PCM is an issue. We identified two issues. First, the "dirty bit" that is part of many important data structures, including system data structures that lasts for the lifetime of the system. Second, a counter such as might be implemented in PCM itself in order to gather the statistics on writes to a block so that load balancing becomes possible.

In both cases, we showed that using balanced Gray codes allows us to save bitflips and even more importantly, to distribute the bitflip load equally over the bits. In addition, we proposed a simple way of distributing the dirty bit over many bits.

References

1. Alameldeen, A., Wood, D.: Frequent pattern compression: a significance-based compression scheme for L2 caches. Technical Report, University of Wisconsin-Madison (2004)
2. Bhat, G., Savage, C.: Balanced gray codes. Electron. J. Comb. **3**, R25 (1996)
3. Bittman, D., et al.: Designing data STructures to minimize bit flips on NVM. In: 2018 IEEE 7th Non-Volatile Memory Systems and Applications Symposium, pp. 85–90 (2018)
4. Bittman, D., Long, D., Alvaro, P., Miller, E.: Optimizing systems for byte-addressable NVM by reducing bit flipping. In: 17th Conference on File and Storage Technologies, USENIX (2019)

5. Cho, S., Lee, H.: Flip-N-Write: A simple deterministic technique to improve PRAM write performance, energy and endurance. In: 42nd Annual IEEE/ACM International Symposium on Microarchitecture, pp. 347–357 (2009)
6. Dechev, D., Pierkelbauer, P., Stroustrup, D.: Understanding and effectively preventing the ABA problem in descriptor-based lock-free designs. In: 13th IEEE International Symposium on Object/Component/Service-Oriented Real-Time Distributed Computing, pp. 185–192 (2010)
7. Jacobvitz, A., Calderbank, R., Sorin, D.: Coset coding to extend the lifetime of memory. In: IEEE 19th International Symposium on High Performance Computer Architecture, pp. 222–233 (2013)
8. Jalili, M., Sarbazi-Azad, H.: Captopril: Reducing the pressure of bit flips on hot locations in non-volatile main memories. In: Conference on Design, Automation & Test in Europe, DATE 2016 (2016)
9. Han, M., Hun, Y., Ki, S.W., Lee, H., Park, I.: Content-aware bit shuffling for maximizing PCM endurance. ACM Trans. Des. Autom. Electron. Syst. **22**(3), 1–26 (2017)
10. Knuth, D.: The art of computer programming: Generating all combinations and permutations, vol. 4, Fac. 2, Addison Wesley (2005)
11. Lee, B., Ipek, E., Mutlu, O., Burger, D.: Architecting phase change memory as a scalable DRAM alternative, ACM SIGARCH Comput. Architect. News **37**(3), 2–13 (2009)
12. Maddah, R., Seyedzadeh, S., Melhem, R.: CAFO: cost aware flip optimization for asymmetric memories. In: IEEE 21st International Symposium on High Performance Computer Architecture, pp. 320–330 (2015)
13. Palangappa, P., Mohanram, K..: Flip-mirror-rotate: an architecture for bit-write reduction and wear leveling in non-volatile memories. In: Great Lakes Symposium on VLSI, pp. 221–224. ACM (2015)
14. Savage, C.: A survey of combinatorial Gray codes. SIAM Rev. **39**(4), 605–629 (1997)
15. Suparta, I.N.: Counting sequences, Gray codes and Lexicodes, Ph.D. thesis, TU Delft (2006)
16. Wagner, D., West, J.: Construction of uniform Gray codes. Congressus Numerantium **80**, 217–223 (1991)
17. Yang, B., Lee, J., Kim, J., Cho, J., Lee, S., Yu, B.: A low power phase-change random access memory using a data-comparison write scheme. In: 2007 IEEE International Symposium on Circuits and Systems, pp. 3014–3017 (2007)

Network and System Optimization

QUIC Throughput and Fairness over Dual Connectivity

David Hasselquist, Christoffer Lindström, Nikita Korzhitskii,
Niklas Carlsson[(✉)], and Andrei Gurtov

Linköping University, Linköping, Sweden
`niklas.carlsson@liu.se`

Abstract. Dual Connectivity (DC) is an important lower-layer feature
accelerating the transition from 4G to 5G that also is expected to play
an important role in standalone 5G. However, even though the packet
reordering introduced by DC can significantly impact the performance
of upper-layer protocols, no prior work has studied the impact of DC on
QUIC. In this paper, we present the first such performance study. Using
a series of throughput and fairness experiments, we show how QUIC is
affected by different DC parameters, network conditions, and whether
the DC implementation aims to improve throughput or reliability. Our
findings provide insights into the impacts of splitting QUIC traffic in a
DC environment. With reasonably selected DC parameters and increased
UDP receive buffers, QUIC over DC performs similarly to TCP over DC
and achieves optimal fairness under symmetric link conditions when DC
is not used for packet duplication.

Keywords: QUIC · Dual connectivity · Throughput · Fairness ·
Transport protocol · Multipath

1 Introduction

The end-to-end performance depends on the interactions between protocols in
different network layers. As new features are introduced on the lower layers, it
is therefore important to understand the impact that such features and their
parameters have on the upper layer protocols [5]. One such feature is Dual Connectivity (DC). DC was introduced in 4G, gained popularity with the introduction of 5G, and currently plays an integral role in accelerating the generational
transition from 4G to 5G [7].

With DC, users can transmit and receive data from two base stations concurrently. This allows users to use both 4G and 5G networks in parallel, simplifying
the above-mentioned generational transition. However, it has also been argued
that DC should be a part of future 5G solutions needed to meet the requirements
of Ultra-reliable and Low-Latency Communications (URLLC) [2,17]. Combined
with its increased usage, this has made DC an important 5G feature.

Like multi-path transport protocols [8,12,27], DC can be used to combine
WiFi with 4G and 5G solutions. Furthermore, like these protocols, DC can be
used to achieve improved throughput (by sending different data over different

M. C. Calzarossa et al. (Eds.): MASCOTS 2020, LNCS 12527, pp. 175–190, 2021.
https://doi.org/10.1007/978-3-030-68110-4_12

paths), to increase reliability (by transmitting the same data over the different paths), or both. However, in contrast to the transport-layer multipath solutions, DC is performed within the link layer of the network stack and is therefore in practice invisible to transport layer protocols such as TCP and QUIC. This is an important observation since DC may introduce jitter or reordering of packets that can significantly impact TCP and QUIC performance.

In parallel with the transitioning of different network generations, Google recently introduced QUIC as a next generation transport-layer solution aimed at addressing some shortcomings with TCP [16]. QUIC is implemented in the user-space, on top of UDP, and provides much improved stream multiplexing compared to TCP. This is important to speed up web connections in the presence of packet losses and/or modern HTTP/2 traffic. Initial research shows that QUIC allows performance improvements over TCP in several cases while providing an easy way to achieve fast incremental deployment [16]. Popular services that already today use QUIC include Google search services, Chrome, Chromium, YouTube and Facebook [10,16].

Due to the increasing use and popularity of both QUIC and DC, combined with the continuous rollout of 5G networks using DC, it is important to understand how QUIC performs over DC under different network conditions, and the impact that different DC parameters have on QUIC performance.

In this paper, we present the first performance evaluation of QUIC over DC. First, a testbed is set up to simulate DC. The testbed captures QUIC and TCP performance under a wide range of network behaviors (based on bandwidth, delay, and loss conditions) and the impact of different DC parameters. Second, using a series of throughput and fairness experiments, we show how QUIC is affected by different DC parameters, network conditions, and whether the DC implementation aims to improve throughput or reliability. For our throughput evaluation, we primarily compare the throughput of QUIC over DC with that of TCP over DC, and for our fairness comparisons we compare the throughput (and calculate a fairness index) of competing flows when using QUIC over DC. We also present results using different QUIC implementations (aioquic, ngtcp2) and congestion control algorithms (NewReno, CUBIC). Our findings provide insights into the impact that DC and its parameters have on QUIC performance. For example, we show the value of increasing the UDP receive buffers when running QUIC over DC, that QUIC over DC can achieve similar throughput as TCP over DC, and that QUIC over DC can achieve optimal fairness under symmetric link conditions, except if DC duplicates packets to increase reliability.

Outline: Sections 2 and 3 introduce DC and present related works, respectively. The following sections present our methodology (Sect. 4), performance results (Sect. 5), and conclusions (Sect. 6).

2   Dual Connectivity

DC, sometimes called inter-node radio resource aggregation, is a multi-connectivity technique introduced in release 12 of the third-generation partnership project (3GPP) [1]. The aim was to increase reliability, performance, and signaling due to frequent handovers in scenarios where macro and micro cells are connected with a non-ideal backhaul (X2) link. DC tries to achieve this by splitting the traffic over multiple paths.

Figure 1 shows an overview of DC in a Radio Access Network (RAN) environment. With DC, a User Equipment (UE) connects to two different Evolved Node Bs (eNBs) [2]. One of the nodes will serve as Master eNB (MeNB), and the other one will serve as Secondary eNB (SeNB). Each of the MeNB and SeNB contains a separate Radio Link Control (RLC) and Media Access Control (MAC) layer, while sharing the same Packet Data Convergence Protocol (PDCP) layer.

DC is similar to carrier aggregation [26], but is performed in the PDCP layer instead of the MAC layer. Carrier aggregation uses the same scheduler for the separate connections and requires an ideal X2 link. The split connections are therefore often transmitted from the same node. In contrast, DC uses two separate schedulers together with a non-ideal X2 link, and packets are often originating from two different nodes.

PDCP is a sublayer located inside the link layer, just below the network layer and above RLC and MAC. The main tasks of PDCP are header compression and decompression, ciphering, integrity protection, transfer of data, sequence numbering, reordering and in-order delivery [3]. The PDCP layer can be broken out into a unit called a Packet Processor (PP), which connects to Serving Gateway (SGW), MeNB and SeNB using a GTPU-tunnel. SGW is connected to the Packet Data Network Gateway (PGW), which connects to the public internet. The PP can also be a part of MeNB. In this case, MeNB splits the traffic and the link between MeNB and SeNB becomes the X2 link. In both scenarios, the traffic is split in the PDCP layer.

3   Related Work

Dual Connectivity: Unlike TCP, QUIC is relatively new, and there are few studies of it in specific scenarios such as DC. As QUIC shares similarities with TCP, we can obtain initial insights from research about DC that uses TCP as the transport protocol. Polese et al. [22] study the performance of TCP when using DC to perform mobile handovers for an UE and compare the performance with different single connection mobility management solutions. They show that DC can improve TCP goodput by quickly moving the traffic from one of the two DC links to the other.

Other studies have focused on specializations of DC; e.g., LTE-WLAN Aggregation (LWA) [14,15], which allows for network traffic over LTE and WLAN. Jin et al. [14] show that splitting TCP over LTE and WiFi at the PDCP layer can achieve similar throughput and better fairness than MP-TCP; demonstrating the value of lower-layer traffic splitting. Khadraoui et al. [15] investigate the effect of PDCP reordering when using TCP in LWA over heterogeneous links. Their results show that PDCP reordering can have adverse effects on TCP throughput, and that in some cases it is better to use only one link. While

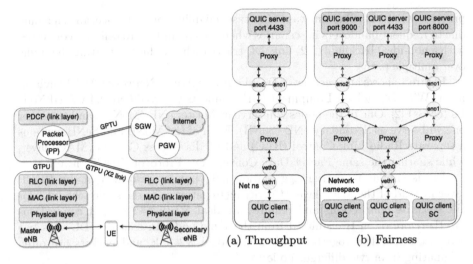

Fig. 1. Dual connectivity overview   Fig. 2. Testbed for throughput and fairness

some works have looked at TCP with DC, no prior work has studied QUIC performance over DC.

Upper-Layer Multipathing: Multipathing is similar to DC but performed higher up in the network stack. Most such solutions are implemented in the transport layer, e.g., SCTP [12] and MP-TCP [27], but some are implemented in the network layer [9]. Here, we focus on QUIC-based solutions. De Coninck and Bonaventure [8] implement Multipath QUIC (MP-QUIC) based on quic-go and lessons learned from MP-TCP, and show that serving QUIC over multiple paths is beneficial. Mogensen et al. [19] expands MP-QUIC to Selective Redundant MP-QUIC (SR-MPQUIC). Their solution modifies the congestion control algorithm, the scheduler, and the stream framer. SR-MPQUIC reduces latencies and improves reliability for priority data at a small increase in bandwidth usage and latencies for background data. The results show the importance of proper packet scheduling and the value of packet duplication. While additional cross-layer communication would be required to benefit DC, QUIC also includes some unique attributes to assist packet/flow scheduling [23].

Fairness: Fairness can be difficult to judge when there are multiple paths with different amount of resources. Becke et al. [6] study the fairness of different congestion control algorithms in multipath scenarios, focusing on two fairness types: link-centric and network-centric flow fairness. Raiciu et al. [25] study how MP-TCP can replace single connections and load balancing in data centers. For specific topologies, MP-TCP significantly improved fairness and provided throughput closer to optimal compared to single connectivity using random load balancing. To judge fairness, they and many others [25,27,28] evaluate multipathing using Jain's fairness index (JFI) [13]. Similar to these works, we use JFI here.

Table 1. Hardware and operating systems

Component	Client	Server
OS	Ubuntu 18.04.3 LTS	Ubuntu 18.04.3 LTS
Kernel	Linux 4.15.0-74-lowlatency	Linux 5.3.0-26-generic
Processor 1 & 2	Intel(R) Xeon(R) CPU E5-2690 v3	Intel(R) Xeon(R) CPU E5-2667 v3
eno1 & eno2	82599ES 10-Gigabit SFI/SFP+	82599ES 10-Gigabit SFI/SFP+

4   Methodology

4.1   Dual Connectivity Testbed

Figure 2 shows an overview of the testbed used for studying QUIC performance over DC. We used one machine to capture client-side behavior and performance, and one machine to capture server- and network-side effects. The two machines were connected via two network interface pairs, each supporting 10 Gbps full duplex. Hardware specifications are given in Table 1. We next describe the configurations used for our throughput and fairness tests, respectively, and our proxy implementation used to simulate DC and PDCP.

Throughput Test Configuration: For our throughput tests (Fig. 2(a)), we used one client, one server, and studied the performance impact of DC parameters and the network conditions between them. In our baseline tests, both the QUIC server and QUIC client used aioquic [4]. When running comparison tests with TCP, we used a Hypercorn server using HTTP/2 over TLS 1.3, and the client used curl to make HTTP/2 requests. As baseline, both TCP and QUIC used NewReno for congestion control.

Since traffic splitting with DC is implemented in the link layer, QUIC (and TCP) are unaware that the traffic is sent over multiple paths, and therefore do not need to be modified. However, as DC was introduced for radio technology, the link layer functions differ from the Ethernet links used here. To simulate the functionality of DC and PDCP, two proxies were implemented: one at the client and one at the server.

The QUIC client was launched inside a network namespace. Two virtual interfaces were created to forward data to and from the namespace. The server side does not require a network namespace as DC is only studied on the downlink. To simulate different network conditions, tc in Linux was used to add extra delay, jitter, loss, and bandwidth limitations.

Fairness Test Configuration: For our fairness tests (Fig. 2(b)), we used three clients and three servers. One end-to-end connection was performing DC, while the other two used single connectivity (SC) over interface eno1 and eno2, respectively. The server with port 8000 was operating only on eno1, while the server on port 9000 only on eno2. The QUIC server on port 4433 used DC and operated on both interfaces. Each server and client were equipped with its own proxy, simulating the PDCP functionality for each connection independently.

Proxy-Based Implementation: To capture the PDCP functionality, packets originating from the server are caught by iptables OUTPUT chain and delivered to a NFQUEUE, before being read by the server proxy. The server proxy then adds a 2-byte PDCP sequence number to each packet and routes the packets to the client over two interfaces. When running DC, the server proxy alternates between the two interfaces.

At the client proxy, packets are caught in the PREROUTING chain and delivered to NFQUEUE. The client proxy can then read from the queue, perform PDCP convergence of the two streams, do PDCP reordering, and remove the sequence numbers that were added by the server proxy.

If a packet is received in order, it is immediately forwarded to the client. However, if a packet is out of order, it is kept until the missing packets are processed or until a PDCP timer of 200 ms is reached. If the timer is reached, all packets before the missing packet and all consecutive packets after the missing packets are delivered. The reordering algorithm follows the PDCP standard described in 3GPP [3] and the testbed was developed in close consultation with Ericsson. Our proxy adds around 1ms to the total RTT, assuming that the packets arrive in order. Without PDCP, large reordering occurs, resulting in QUIC having a very low throughput.

4.2   Performance Testing

To understand how DC affects QUIC, a series of tests are performed that captures the impact of different DC parameters and network conditions. In our experiments, we vary one parameter at a time, starting with a default configuration, while keeping the others constant (as per the default configuration). In the throughput tests, the client downloads a 100 MB file, and in the fairness tests each client downloads a 1 GB file and we measure the clients' performance for the first three minutes of the download. For each test configuration, we run ten tests and calculate both average and standard deviation values for the metrics of interest.

DC Parameters and Default Configurations: The primary DC parameters we varied were the DC batch size and DC batch split. These parameters determine how many packets are sent over each interface before the server proxy switches to the other interface. For example, with a DC batch size of 100 and a DC ratio of 9:1 (90% eno1 and 10% eno2), the proxy would send 90 packets over eno1, before switching over to send 10 packets over eno2. In our default experiments, the default DC batch size and DC ratio was configured to 100 and 1:1, respectively.

Network Emulation Parameters and Default Configurations: To capture different network conditions, we primarily varied the bandwidths, delays, and loss rates of the links. For both the bandwidths and delays, we present experiments both where we vary the average values and where we vary the ratio between the two links. In the case we vary one of the ratios, we keep the average value of that metric constant. For example, a bandwidth ratio of 3:1 corresponds to 30 Mbps and 10 Mbps for the downlink interfaces eno1 and eno2, respectively. In our default experiments, each link operates at 20 Mbps and has normally distributed per-packet delays with a mean of 10 ms and a standard deviation of 10%.

QUIC and TCP Configurations/Versions: Throughput tests for QUIC are performed both with the default UDP receive socket buffer size and a larger receive buffer size. The larger size is used to give a fair comparison to TCP, as the kernel performs buffer autotuning for TCP [21]. When studying fairness, QUIC with modified buffer size is used and the fairness is calculated using JFI.

In our default scenarios we use aioquic with NewReno. However, as discussed by McMillan and Zuck [18], the QUIC RFC is ambiguous, open for interpretation, and differences between QUIC implementations following the RFC have been demonstrated using specification testing. We therefore repeated our experiments with both another QUIC implementation (ngtcp2 [20]) and congestion control algorithm (CUBIC).

Trace-based Evaluation: Finally, experiments were repeated using a real LTE bandwidth trace collected by Raca et al. [24]. The specific bandwidth trace (*Static A_2018.02.12_16.14.02*) has an average throughput of 4.5 Mbps for the first 200 s.

5   Evaluation Results

5.1   Dual Connectivity Parameters

DC Batch Size: When using DC, network operators must select a good DC batch size for each connection. To illustrate the impact of this choice on QUIC performance, Fig. 3(a) shows the throughput as a function of the DC batch size. (We omitted the standard deviations from all figures, as the they are small; e.g., well within 1Mbps in more than 90% of the cases.) In general, large DC batch sizes result in lower throughput. One reason for this is reduced link utilization. For example, Figs. 3(b) and 3(c) show the link utilization of the two links when using a DC batch size of 50 and 500, respectively. With a large DC batch size, we see significant periods during which one of the links is underutilized as almost all packets are being forwarded over the other interface. With smaller DC batch sizes, both links can better be used concurrently. However, there is also a penalty to using too small batch sizes, as this increases the number of re-order events. The best batch sizes are instead typically in the mid-range (e.g., around 100–150), with the sweet spot depending on the protocol being used. Finally, we note that QUIC with modified buffers perform similar to TCP for much of the parameter range.

Figure 4(a) shows summary results for our fairness tests with varying DC batch sizes. Here, we measure fairness using Jain's fairness index (JFI), shown using purple text, as averaged over 10 full runs. When discussing fairness, it is important to note that the relative throughput of the competing clients can vary significantly over time. This is illustrated in Fig. 4(b) where we show example throughput for the three competing clients over a 3-min long experiment with the default settings.

Similar to the throughput, the fairness is negatively affected by large DC batch sizes. In fact, the user using DC observe a significant throughput reduction

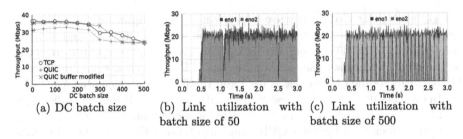

Fig. 3. Throughput and link utilization for different DC batch sizes

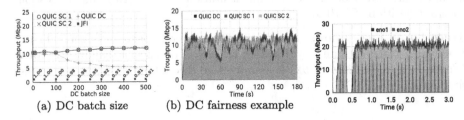

Fig. 4. Fairness for different DC batch sizes

Fig. 5. Link utilization example with unbalanced DC ratio of 9:1

with batch sizes of 150 and above. Here, SC clients can monopolize the links during the DC client's off periods, while DC is always sharing the link it is currently sending to at every point of time. This allows SC clients to increase their cwnd further than the DC client and to use a larger bandwidth share.

DC Batch Split: Operators also control the DC ratio. This parameter determines the split over the two links. Figure 5 illustrates an unbalanced example with a DC batch split of 9:1, in which 90% of the packets are sent over the main interface (eno1), and Fig. 6(a) shows the throughput as a function of the percent of packets sent over eno1. As per our default case, both links have the same network conditions. In this case, the throughput peaks when using a 50/50 split, and decreases as a convex function as the split becomes more uneven. This decrease is caused by poor link utilization of the less loaded link (eno2 in Fig. 5), but also demonstrates the value of DC.

Figure 7(a) shows our corresponding fairness results. When the ratio is significantly skewed (e.g., below 20% or above 80%), the throughput of the SC with the higher throughput increase/decrease at roughly the same rate as the DC's throughput increase/decrease, whereas the other SC has fairly constant throughput over these skewed splits. In this region, the DC compete (almost) fairly only over the more utilized interface. As the DC split becomes more even, the overall fairness improves, with optimal fairness and all connections having roughly equal throughput when perfectly balanced.

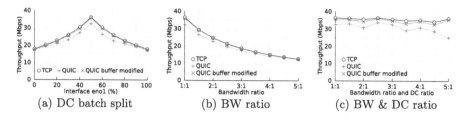

Fig. 6. Throughput for different batch splits and bandwidth ratios

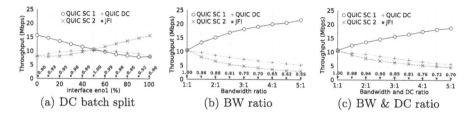

Fig. 7. Fairness for different batch splits and bandwidth ratios

5.2 Network Conditions

Bandwidth Ratio: Figures 6(b) and 6(c) show the throughput for different bandwidth ratios. Figure 6(b) shows results for the case when the batch split is 50/50, and Fig. 6(c) shows results for when the batch split is selected to match the bandwidth ratio. Figure 6(b) illustrates the importance of matching ratios, as the highest throughputs are achieved with a ratio of 1:1. As the ratio increases, a 50/50 batch split underutilizes the link with higher bandwidth. In contrast, when the DC batch split is selected to match the bandwidth ratio (Fig. 6(c)), a much better overall throughput is achieved. With QUIC buffer modified and TCP, the impact is very small. The reason for the worse performance of QUIC with default buffers is the higher burstiness caused by increased reordering. Despite PDCP mitigating reordering, it results in increasing RTTs.

The fairness results for the cases when we vary the bandwidth ratio of the two links are shown in Figs. 7(b) and 7(c). Similar to the throughput results, higher fairness is achieved when the DC split is selected based on the capacity of the two links. For example, even when the bandwidth ratio is 5:1, the scenario in which the DC split matches the bandwidth ratio achieves a JFI of 0.70, compared to 0.59 in the case a 50/50 split is used. In both cases, the bandwidth usage is dominated by the SC user with higher bandwidth and the DC user relies heavily on the throughput achieved via the weaker link. However, the fairness improves as DC moves more traffic to the link with the higher bandwidth.

Delay Ratio: Both the throughput and fairness are negatively affected by increasing delays, and in the case of a high average delay, these metrics are also negatively affected by an increasing delay ratio. This is illustrated by comparing the throughput Figs. 8(a) and 8(b) or fairness Figs. 9(a) and 9(b).

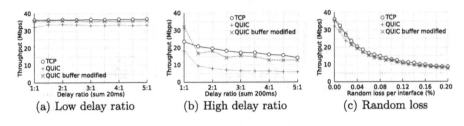

Fig. 8. Throughput for different delay and loss ratios

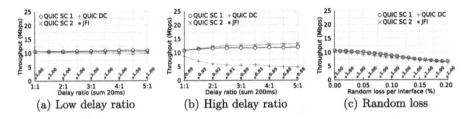

Fig. 9. Fairness for different delay and loss ratios

For both types of experiments, the two figures show results for low-delay and high-delay scenarios, respectively. In the low-delay scenarios, the sum of the delays over the two links is 20 ms, and in the high-delay scenario the sum is 200 ms.

The throughput decrease is mostly due to increased packet reordering caused by the higher delays. In these cases, the PDCP layer will buffer more packets before performing a batch delivery to the QUIC client, causing packet bursts as well as a higher RTT. Furthermore, after receiving a batch delivery, the clients will send a cumulative ACK for many packets, which will, for a short time, largely decrease the number of packets in flight when received at the server. The draft for QUIC [11] recommends a pacer, which helps the QUIC server recover from an ACK-burst by sending new packets at steadier pace. The advantage of more even pacing can be seen by the higher values observed with a delay ratio of 1:1 in Fig. 8(b).

The increasing delays and delay ratios also negatively impact fairness. For example, in the low-delay case (Fig. 9(a)), JFI reduces from 0.9996 to 0.9986 as the delay ratio increases from 1:1 to 5:1, whereas JFI drops from 0.9903 to 0.8758 for the high-delay case (Fig. 9(b)). The higher throughput of SC eno2 compared to that of SC eno1 is due to its lower RTT.

Loss Rates: While increased packet losses negatively impact the throughput (Fig. 8(c)), small packet losses have very limited impact on the fairness index (Fig. 9(c)).

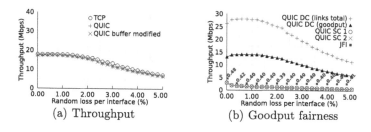

(a) Throughput   (b) Goodput fairness

Fig. 10. DC throughput and fairness with duplicate packets

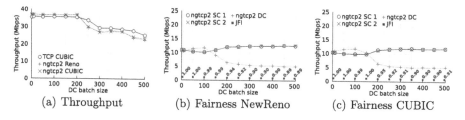

(a) Throughput   (b) Fairness NewReno   (c) Fairness CUBIC

Fig. 11. Impact of congestion control algorithm: Performance examples with ngtcp2 as QUIC version for different batch sizes

5.3 Use of Duplicate Packets

Besides improving throughput, DC can also be used to increase connection reliability. However, DC with packet duplication negatively effects fairness. For example, in fairness tests with loss rates of 0-to-5% (Fig. 10(b)) JFI is in the range from 0.39 to 0.48. For DC in Fig. 10(b), we show both the combined interface throughput (B) and the goodput (X), which under an independence model with retransmissions (after simplification) can be related as $X = B(1+p)/2$, where p is the loss rate. The low fairness stems from DC having a much higher end-to-end packet delivery probability (i.e., $1-p^2$ vs $1-p$ under independence assumptions) and lower end-to-end packet loss probability (i.e., p^2 vs p) compared to SC. This results in DC obtaining a larger share of the link bandwidths. These results show that duplication can provide much higher reliability at the cost of fairness and goodput.

5.4 QUIC Implementation and Congestion Control Algorithm

To explore the impact of other QUIC implementations and congestion control algorithms, experiments were repeated using ngtcp2 and CUBIC. Figure 11(a) shows little to no differences in the results between different congestion control algorithms when varying DC batch size. However, when compared to Fig. 3(a), differences can be observed between the QUIC implementations. While the results follow the same patterns for both implementations, the considerable throughput drop occurs at different batch sizes. Another noticeable difference is

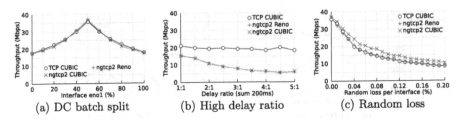

Fig. 12. Throughput when using ngtcp2 (as QUIC implementation) with NewReno and CUBIC for different parameters

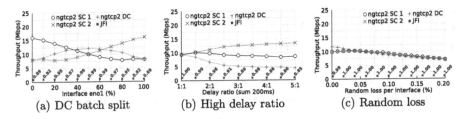

Fig. 13. Fairness when using ngtcp2 with NewReno for different parameters (CUBIC results very similar)

that ngtcp2 has a slightly higher throughput than aioquic at smaller batch sizes, exceeding the throughput for TCP.

Figures 11(b) and 11(c) show the corresponding fairness results. Again, only small differences between the NewReno and CUBIC results are observed. For example, the JFI differ by at most 0.02 (DC batch size of 500) between the algorithms. DC using CUBIC is initially slightly more resilient to performance drops occurring with a larger batch size. In contrast, NewReno allows the SC connections to achieve slightly higher throughput at larger batch sizes while the DC throughput is similar to CUBIC at higher batches. When comparing Figs. 11(b) and 11(c) to 4(a), some differences can be seen between the QUIC implementations. Ngtcp2 is more aggressive, leading to the DC connection having slightly higher throughput than the SC connections at smaller batch sizes and a drastic reduction in throughput when the batch size increases. Aioquic has a more balanced sharing of the bandwidths at smaller batch sizes and see a smaller reduction in throughput at larger batch sizes.

When studying the DC batch split using ngtcp2 and different congestion control algorithms (Fig. 12(a)), minimal difference in the overall throughput is observed. Compared to aioquic in Fig. 6(a), little differences are observed at more uneven ratios. Ngtcp2 achieves a higher throughput than aioquic and TCP at more balanced ratios. When comparing the corresponding fairness results in Fig. 13(a) to 7(a), larger differences can be seen between the QUIC implementations. While the two implementations exhibit similar behavior at the most uneven split, the DC connection using ngtcp2 grows more aggressively than the aioquic counterpart when the ratio becomes more balanced. This growth lead to optimal fairness for aioquic, but results in a slightly unfair bandwidth allocation for ngtcp2.

A significant throughput difference between the QUIC implementations can be seen when comparing the high delay ratio experiments in Figs. 12(b) and 8(b). Ngtcp2 achieves a significantly lower throughput than aioquic throughout the experiment. This is most likely due to differences in the pacer implementations. Differences can also be seen when comparing corresponding fairness tests (Fig. 13(b) and 9(b)). Here, the DC connection using ngtcp2 achieves more fair throughput than the aioquic counterpart at balanced ratios and sees a slower drop in throughput when the ratio gets skewed. However, after the 2:1 ratio point, the DC connections' throughputs become the same for the two implementations. The ngtcp2 SC connection with a higher delay has a much worse performance than the aioquic counterpart at more skewed ratios.

Finally, when studying the impact of loss rates using ngtcp2 and CUBIC, only small differences are observed (Figs. 12(c) and 13(c) compared to Figs. 8(c) and 9(c)). However, in contrast to the other experiments, ngtcp2 using CUBIC shows a noticeable better performance compared to TCP CUBIC. Looking closer at the 0.08% loss case, we have observed that the TCP implementation more often stays in CUBIC's TCP mode (used when detecting growth slower than Reno). This also explains why TCP CUBIC, TCP NewReno, and ngtcp2 NewReno perform similarly here.

In general, ngtcp2 achieves higher throughput than aioquic, even though both follow the same IETF recommendations. As discussed, differences can occur due to the RFC being open for interpretation. The execution speed and resources required by the two implementations also differ. Ngtcp2 is implemented in C and aioquic in Python. With ngtcp2, a larger receive buffer did not impact throughput, as the client buffer was quickly emptied. Ngtcp2 is also noted to be greedier than aioquic over DC, often introducing some unfairness to scenarios that were fair for aioquic. One potential reason is the difference in pacer implementation, as the IETF only recommends a pacer but does not specify it in detail. The difference in pacer implementation is also clearly shown in high delay ratio tests.

5.5   Bandwidth Variability Scenario

To capture a more realistic bandwidth user scenario, Figs. 14(a) to 14(c) show repeated experiments with aioquic for DC batch size, high delay ratio and loss rates performed over a LTE sampled bandwidth trace. Figures 14(d) to 14(f) show these results but using ngtcp2 with CUBIC. For DC batch size and loss rates, similar trends are observed as when using a fixed bandwidth capability. Similar trends are also observed in the case of delay ratio, but with the effect of the pacer more clearly shown. Lastly, we note that ngtcp2 is more aggressive than aioquic and that CUBIC achieves higher throughput.

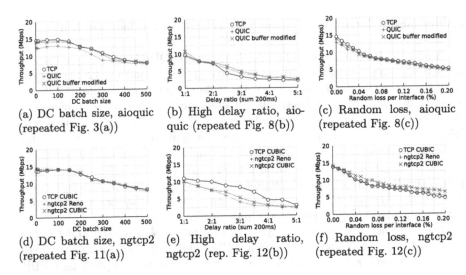

(a) DC batch size, aioquic (repeated Fig. 3(a))

(b) High delay ratio, aioquic (repeated Fig. 8(b))

(c) Random loss, aioquic (repeated Fig. 8(c))

(d) DC batch size, ngtcp2 (repeated Fig. 11(a))

(e) High delay ratio, ngtcp2 (rep. Fig. 12(b))

(f) Random loss, ngtcp2 (repeated Fig. 12(c))

Fig. 14. Trace-driven bandwidth variability tests using aioquic and ngtcp2 as QUIC implementations

6   Conclusions

In this paper, we present the first performance study of QUIC over DC. Key insights are given for network operators to understand how different DC parameters and network conditions affect QUIC performance. QUIC's throughput is found to be similar to that of TCP in general cases, provided that the UDP receive buffer (when using aioquic) has been increased to similar size as the corresponding TCP buffer. We show that QUIC can take advantage of DC when the links share similar properties, and the DC batch size is small. When the properties of the links are too far apart, QUIC performance suffers to the degree that the performance would be better if DC was turned off. Furthermore, we show that QUIC can achieve system-wide fairness, provided that the link properties are similar. We also show that packet duplication allows QUIC to improve throughput for lossy environments at the cost of substantially increased unfairness.

With aioquic, the QUIC throughput is considerably lower if the UDP receive buffer remains at default values for Linux, as PDCP introduces packet bursts, causing packet drops due to full buffers. This occurs especially often in asymmetric link scenarios with high throughput. With the increased use of QUIC, we emphasize the importance of studying and optimizing the resources provided by the kernel to QUIC.

Acknowledgement. This work was funded in part by the Swedish Research Council (VR).

References

1. 3GPP: Study on Small Cell enhancements for E-UTRA and E-UTRAN; Higher layer aspects. Technical Report 36.842 Release 12 (2013)
2. 3GPP: Summary of Rel-15. Technical Report 21.915 Release 15 (2019)
3. 3GPP: Evolved Universal Terrestrial Radio Access; Packet Data Convergence Protocol specification. Technical Report 36.323 Release 16 (2020)
4. aioquic: aioquic (2020). https://github.com/aiortc/aioquic
5. Alfredsson, S., Brunstrom, A., Sternad, M.: Cross-layer analysis of TCP performance in a 4G system. In: Proceedings of SoftCOM (2007)
6. Becke, M., Dreibholz, T., Adhari, H., Rathgeb, E.P.: On the fairness of transport protocols in a multi-path environment. In: Proceedings of IEEE ICC (2012)
7. Da Silva, I., Mildh, G., Rune, J., Wallentin, P., Vikberg, J., Schliwa-Bertling, P., Fan, R.: Tight integration of new 5G air interface and LTE to fulfill 5G requirements. In: Proceedings of VTC Spring (2015)
8. De Coninck, Q., Bonaventure, O.: Multipath QUIC: Design and Evaluation. In: Proceedings of ACM CoNEXT (2017)
9. Gurtov, A., Polishchuk, T.: Secure multipath transport for legacy Internet applications. In: Proceedings of IEEE Broadnets (2009)
10. IETF 106 Singapore: Some updates on QUIC deployment numbers (2019). https://datatracker.ietf.org/meeting/106/materials/slides-106-maprg-quic-deployment-update
11. Iyengar, J., Swett, I.: QUIC Loss Detection and Congestion Control. Internet-Draft draft-ietf-quic-recovery-29, IETF (2020)
12. Iyengar, J.R., Amer, P.D., Stewart, R.: Concurrent multipath transfer using SCTP multihoming over independent end-to-end paths. IEEE/ACM Trans. Networking (2006)
13. Jain, R.K., Chiu, D.M.W., Hawe, W.R.: A quantitative measure of fairness and discrimination for resource allocation in shared computer systems. Technical Report DEC-TR-301, Eastern Research Lab, Digital Equipment Corporation (1984)
14. Jin, B., Kim, S., Yun, D., Lee, H., Kim, W., Yi, Y.: Aggregating LTE and Wi-Fi: toward intra-Cell Fairness and High TCP Performance. IEEE Trans. Wirel. Commun. (2017)
15. Khadraoui, Y., Lagrange, X., Gravey, A.: TCP performance for practical implementation of very tight coupling between LTE and WiFi. In: Proceedings of IEEE VTC Fall (2016)
16. Langley, A., et al.: The QUIC transport protocol: design and internet-scale deployment. In: Proceedings of ACM SIGCOMM (2017)
17. Mahmood, N.H., Lopez, M., Laselva, D., Pedersen, K., Berardinelli, G.: Reliability oriented dual connectivity for URLLC services in 5G New Radio. In: Proceedings of ISWCS (2018)
18. McMillan, K.L., Zuck, L.D.: Formal specification and testing of QUIC. In: Proceedings of ACM SIGCOMM (2019)
19. Mogensen, R.S., et al.: Selective redundant MP-QUIC for 5G mission critical wireless applications. In: Proceedings of IEEE VTC Spring (2019)
20. ngtcp2: ngtcp2 (2020). https://github.com/ngtcp2/ngtcp2
21. Paasch, C., Khalili, R., Bonaventure, O.: On the benefits of applying experimental design to improve multipath TCP. In: Proceedings of ACM CoNEXT (2013)
22. Polese, M., Mezzavilla, M., Rangan, S., Zorzi, M.: Mobility management for TCP in mmWave networks. In: Proceedings ACM mmNets (2017)

23. Rabitsch, A., Hurtig, P., Brunstrom, A.: A stream-aware multipath QUIC scheduler for heterogeneous paths. In: Proceedings of ACM SIGCOMM Workshop EPIQ (2018)
24. Raca, D., Quinlan, J.J., Zahran, A.H., Sreenan, C.J.: Beyond throughput: A 4G LTE dataset with channel and context metrics. In: Proceedings of ACM MMSys (2018)
25. Raiciu, C., Pluntke, C., Barre, S., Greenhalgh, A., Wischik, D., Handley, M.: Data center networking with multipath TCP. In: Proceedings of ACM SIGCOMM Workshop HotNets (2010)
26. Ravanshid, A., et al.: Multi-connectivity functional architectures in 5G. In: Proceedings of IEEE ICC (2016)
27. Wischik, D., Raiciu, C., Greenhalgh, A., Handley, M.: Design, implementation and evaluation of congestion control for multipath TCP. In: Proceedings of USENIX Symposium on NSDI (2011)
28. Zhang, X., Li, B.: Dice: A game theoretic framework for wireless multipath network coding. In: Proceedings of ACM MobiHoc (2008)

Hypothesis-Based Comparison of IPv6 and IPv4 Path Distances

David Hasselquist[1], Christian Wahl[1,2], Otto Bergdal[1], and Niklas Carlsson[1(✉)]

[1] Linköping University, Linköping, Sweden
[2] Technische Universität München, Munich, Germany
niklas.carlsson@liu.se

Abstract. Short end-to-end path lengths and faster round-trip times (RTTs) are important for good client performance. While prior measurement studies related to IPv6 primarily focus on various adoption aspects, much less work have focused on performance metrics such as these. In this paper, we compare the relative end-to-end path distances and RTTs when using IPv6 and IPv4 between PlanetLab nodes in Europe and different subsets of popular domains. In addition to providing access to multiple measurement nodes, the use of PlanetLab also provides a use-case driven report of running IPv6 experiments on this previously prosperous experimental platform for academic research. In particular, the study provides a first report on performing IPv6 experiments on PlanetLab, highlights the lack of IP support among PlanetLab nodes and limitations of state-of-the-art traceroute tools used for IPv6 measurements, and provides a statistical methodology that uses hypothesis testing to derive insights while accounting for such testbed and traceroute shortcomings. Our performance analysis shows (among other things) that the relative RTTs of the IPv6 paths are currently faster than the corresponding IPv4 paths, and that the fraction of pairings for which this is the case is quickly increasing across a wide range of domain popularities and domain categories. These findings suggest that there is incentive to use IPv6, which may impact the rate of further IPv6 deployment.

Keywords: IPv4 vs IPv6 · Path distances · Traceroute · PlanetLab

1 Introduction

After a long, slow initial adoption period, IPv6 has finally started to see significant usage. For example, over the past ten years, the fraction of IPv6 connections to Google servers has increased from 0.25% (Jan. 2011) to 5% in Jan. 2015 and to 29–34% in Sept. 2020 [18]. A diminishing pool of IPv4 addresses and various flag days may have been contributing factors.

With increasing use of IPv6, it is becoming increasingly important to understand the performance that clients observe when accessing the web using IPv6. However, it has long been understood that the IPv6 and IPv4 routing topologies are non-overlapping (e.g., with IPv6 having a less connected core [16]) and

© Springer Nature Switzerland AG 2021
M. C. Calzarossa et al. (Eds.): MASCOTS 2020, LNCS 12527, pp. 191–208, 2021.
https://doi.org/10.1007/978-3-030-68110-4_13

that IPv6 tunnels can negatively impact the performance. In this paper, we use traceroute measurements from a number of European locations to measure the end-to-end path distances between these locations and different sets of popular web domains, perform statistical tests on the collected datasets, and report on similarities and differences in the relative distance differences observed when using IPv6 and IPv4, respectively. Of particular interest are the observed IP-hop counts, AS-hop counts, and end-to-end round-trip times (RTTs). These metrics are important to understand to what extent end-to-end routing differences (e.g., due to differences in connectivity and the use of tunnels) still cause significant differences in the end-to-end path distances observed with IPv6 and IPv4, and to what extent such differences impact the end-to-end RTT performance.

While many measurement studies have focused on IPv6 adoption [12,13, 16,21,23,30,31], less work has focused on the relative end-to-end performance of IPv6 and IPv4 connections and how it may be affected by the lack of full end-to-end adoption. Most closely related our work (Sect. 5), Giotsas et al. [16] showed in 2015 that the performance of IPv6 paths can be significantly hurt by IPv6 tunnels and a less connected transit-free clique. However, since then, further adoption has taken place, and one would expect that IPv6 paths and their performance would improve over time as tunneled paths are replaced with native paths and IPv6 AS relationships mature.

Motivated by the observations above and shortcomings of the basic traceroute tool (which has been shown to not capture the actual paths taken [3]), the popular Paris traceroute alternative (which we find does not work well for IPv6), and traceroutes in general (today often having many missing entries), in this paper we develop a methodology that combines basic traceroute measurements and statistical methods to determine whether there are statistically significant differences in paths lengths and RTTs between IPv6 and IPv4 paths, while accounting for the limitations of existing traceroute tools.

In contrast to prior work (Sect. 5), we focus on the relative end-to-end distances when connecting to different categories of domains when using IPv6 and IPv4, and how the RTT performance may be affected by the lack of full end-to-end adoption. Implementing our data collection on PlanetLab using different traceroute tools, we first provide some methodological insights regarding challenges (such as lack of IPv6 support among PlanetLab nodes and state-of-the-art traceroute tools) that complicate traceroute-based monitoring of IPv6 paths from PlanetLab. Second, we present a data collection (Sect. 3) and pairwise analysis (Sect. 4.1) methodology that allows head-to-head comparisons of the distances observed when using IPv6 and IPv4 from example locations in Europe. For data collection, we employ two different *traceroute* tools [2,3] on the full (but small) set of PlanetLab nodes located in Europe that run IPv6, and measure the network routes to popular website domains [1,29].

While Paris traceroute (used for a four-week measurement campaign) in theory should better capture the actual paths taken than the basic traceroute tool, we find the success rates of this tool unacceptably low (22%), and instead mostly focus our analysis on the datasets collected in May 2019 and Sept. 2019 using parallel instances of the basic traceroute tool (74–78% success rate). Using these datasets, we evaluate the differences and changes observed across different sets of domains (grouped based on popularity rank or domain category) and measurement locations, with regards to the measured RTTs and the number of IP and Autonomous Systems (AS) hops along the paths. For our quantitative analysis, we used three different statistics (mean, median, and 95% confidence tests) to determine which protocol version has the shorter distance for each end-to-end pairing, between PlanetLab node and domain, and then summarized the results on a per-category basis.

Our analysis provides a quantitative snapshot into the relative differences in the distances observed when using IPv6 and IPv4 to connect to different domain classes, and how these differences are changing. For example, there still appears to be significant use of IP tunnels (e.g., much lower IP and AS hop counts), the relative RTTs of the IPv6 paths (compared to the corresponding IPv4 paths) improved notably between the datasets (May 2019 and Sept. 2019) across all five rank categories considered (based on Alexa ranks) and across almost all 16 domain categories considered (each represented using the 50 top-ranked domains of that category). Overall, our findings are encouraging, since IPv6 already appears to outperform IPv4 and these advantages are increasing. This may further incentivize IPv6 deployment.

The remainder of the paper is organized as follows. Section 2 presents background and challenges comparing IPv6 and IPv4 paths from PlanetLab. The following sections present our collection methodology (Sect. 3), analysis methodology and results (Sect. 4), discussion of related works (Sect. 5), and conclusions (Sect. 6).

2   Background and Challenges

PlanetLab (Status and Challenges): At one point in time, PlanetLab provided an excellent testbed for running large-scale network experiments. However, today many PlanetLab nodes are old, out of date, and often not even reachable. Among the 295 PlanetLab Europe nodes that we had access to, only 66 nodes responded to at least one ping during an eight-day measurement (May 2019) in which we sent one ping every 10 min. Out of the 66 responding nodes, only 45 nodes responded every time and we could only login to 39 nodes using ssh. To make things worse, the current implementation of the virtual machine system used in PlanetLab lacks IPv6 support, preventing us from running IPv6 traceroutes from within our Planetlab slice even when a node was supporting IPv6. After contacting PlanetLab support, we found out that only nine (!) nodes on PlanetLab Europe support IPv6 in some way. In addition to limited maintenance, this shows that few members have upgraded their machines to support IPv6.

The lack of IPv6 support among the existing PlanetLab nodes captures a general inertia in deploying IPv6. While some PlanetLab participation requirements (e.g., that nodes should be placed in a DMZ, outside the local firewall, and typically need to be isolated from the institutions regular network) may be

Table 1. PlanetLab nodes used for experiments

Location	Node ID
Université Pierre et Marie Curie, Paris, France	**ple3**.planet-lab.eu (not "Sept 2019"), **ple42**.planet-lab.eu, **ple44**.planet-lab.eu, **nuc1**.planet-lab.eu
Univ. of Rostock, Germany	**pl1**.uni-rostock.de, **pl2**.uni-rostock.de
Univ. of Göttingen, Germany	**planetlab2**.informatik.uni-goettingen.de
CESNET, Prague, Czech Republic	**ple1**.cesnet.cz (not "Paris"), **ple2**.cesnet.cz (only "Sept. 2019")

a contributing factor to the low IPv6 support, one may still expect that research institutes such as those participating in PlanetLab would be among the "early" adopters of such technology. (Whatever "early" adopter means in the context of IPv6 deployment!) Fortunately, PlanetLab's excellent support team gave us direct access to all host machines that had IPv6 support and installed the necessary software on these machines. This allowed us to run our experiments (using both IPv6 and IPv4) from multiple locations in Europe.

While the IPv6 study presented in Sects. 3 and 4 would have benefited from more PlanetLab nodes in Europe deploying IPv6, these nine nodes provided us with access to multiple geographically diverse measurement locations and allowed us to demonstrate the use of our hypothesis-based methodology. In this regard, PlanetLab still offers some benefits over running experiments from only local machines.

Table 1 summarizes the nine machines that had support for IPv6. Already at this time, we note that one of the machines was not accessible during our May 2019 experiments and one machine was not accessible during our Sept. 2019 experiments. To allow comparison over time, we excluded measurements from these machines from the analysis in Sect. 4.

Traceroute (Versions, Limitations, and Challenges): Traceroute tools typically use a sequence of probe messages with increasing time-to-live (TTL) values, and leverage that ICMP "Time exceeded" messages are returned by the router at which the TTL value reaches zero to learn where each probe ended and measure the RTTs to each such router/node. Due to route changes and load balancing, for example, the end-to-end path during such sequence of probes may change over time. It is therefore important to note that such basic implementation does not necessarily return a specific route taken by a packet and may suggest false links (between unconnected routers). Furthermore, some routers do not respond with ICMP packets and/or make different decisions based on packet type, leaving holes in the path information [20]. These challenges have motivated the implementation of many traceroute versions and many designs allow different packet types to be used for the probes (e.g., UDP/DNS, TCP SYN, and ICMP Echo packets).

Augustin et al. [3] recognized that per-flow load balancing is often used to ensure end-to-end stability, and proposed the *Paris* traceroute tool as a means to mitigate network topology mapping anomalies that can occur due to such load balancing. With per-flow load balancing, packets from the same flow (defined as a *five-tuple* consisting of source IP, destination IP, source port, destination port, and protocol) are forwarded over the same route, while packets associated with other flows (same IP-pair) may be routed on different paths. This causes problems for the standard traceroute tool, since it uses randomized values for some IP header fields (e.g., ports) to distinguish responses from different probes. Paris traceroute tries to amend this problem by identifying probes using only IP header fields not used by per-flow load balancing.

Paris traceroute has been shown to provide more accurate paths than basic traceroute. However, due to a bug in the current implementation, simultaneous traceroutes are not possible with Paris traceroute (as routes gets mixed). The use of this tool therefore significantly limits the number of (accurate) traceroutes that can be performed within a time window. We have contacted the developers of the tool and a fix is expected. However, as of the writing of this paper, the authors only have a fix for IPv4 (on a separate version), not IPv6, and we are not able to install any such tools on the PlanetLab nodes ourselves. We therefore limit our study to using the basic traceroute tool and using Paris traceroute strictly sequentially. Paris traceroute was used for a four-week long single-threaded campaign, while we used the basic traceroute tool for two separate one-week long campaigns.

Naturally, the data collected with Paris traceroute should in theory enable somewhat deeper analysis, as the paths collected with this tool are more likely to correspond to actual paths. However, due to lack of parallelism and much lower success rates (Sect. 3.2), these datasets are much smaller in size and only capture paths to a smaller subset of the domains. For most of our analysis we instead focus on the end-to-end path lengths and RTTs reported by basic traceroute, and note that these metrics still are representative of the actual distances observed to these domains. For the analysis presented in this paper, this tool therefore provides sufficient accuracy.

Heterogeneous Environments with Competing Load: The run times of example measurements differ substantially between PlanetLab nodes and can vary over time as the mix of competing loads on the nodes change. For example, during the initial measurement campaign (see Sect. 3) the run times of a large batch of traceroutes (to a fixed set of sample domains) differed by more than six times, and the fastest nodes in these experiments were among the slowest in experiments we ran three months later. To account for these speed differences, while trying to capture potential time varying traceroute effects, we carefully scheduled traceoute measurements to account for the run times on each individual node (Sect. 3) and perform all analysis on a pairwise basis, allowing us to account for different source-destination pairs having more/less measurement samples.

Domain Dependent Path Distances: The route lengths and RTTs can differ substantially depending on the popularity of the sites. For example, the routes to popular services are typically shorter than the routes to less popular services [10], with the route lengths being closely related to the amount of traffic that they forward, and routes often differing both regionally and within the same AS. To compare path lengths of IPv6 and IPv4 routes, it is therefore important to measure the paths to domains associated with different popularity classes and service categories. For popularity-based domain selection, we leverage the commonly used Alexa top-million list [29] and 16 per-category top lists [1]. A subtle challenge we address when using the Alexa top-1M list, is how to downsample the list in easily reproducible way that result in the exact same sample set [29]. For this purpose, we present a simple, deterministic domain sampling technique that we applied on lists available in public repositories [29].

3   Collection Methodology

3.1   Measurement Framework

Overview: All campaigns run repeated traceroutes to the IP addresses returned by each PlanetLab's local DNS resolver for a pre-determined selection of domains. At the start of each campaign, we first distribute this domain list to every European PlanetLab node supporting IPv6. Throughout the duration of the measurement campaign, we then schedule multiple traceroute "batches" on each such node, where a "batch" includes a series of traceroutes to all IPv6 and IPv4 addresses that the local DNS resolver has returned for each domain. Domain-to-IP mappings are refreshed on a daily basis, with each batch job always starting off by checking whether new mappings have been obtained that day. If not, new mappings are obtained using the local DNS resolver of the node. At the end of each campaign, we run reverse DNS lookups and perform AS lookups to obtain additional information about all unique IP addresses observed. Finally, the data is downloaded from each node, merged into a single database, and analyzed. We next highlight some of the details associated with these steps and how they address the challenges discussed in Sect. 2.

Domain Sampling: Using the *Alexa 1M Global* list [29] from May 13, 2019, we selected the first 100 domains (ranks 1–100) and the last 100 domains from each additional magnitude sample (i.e., ranks 901–1,000, 9,901–10,000, 99,901–100,000, and 999,901–1,000,000), as well as the top-50 domains from the Alexa top sites of 16 top-category lists [1]: Adult, Shopping, Arts, Society, Business, Health, Computers, Home, Games, Kids & Teens, Reference, News, Regional, Recreation, Science, Sports. Ignoring a very small number of duplicates, this results in a list of 1,300 domains. The smaller sample set allows us to run traceroutes for each domain and location multiple times per day, and the diversity in sample classes allows us to compare routes to domains across both domain popularities and domain categories. Finally, we again note that this sampling method allows others to easily rerun the experiments (Sect. 4.1) with the exact same sample set.

Node Selection: As described in Sect. 2, PlanetLab's support team provided us with accounts and installed the necessary tools on the small, but full, set of

European PlanetLab nodes supporting IPv6. No further sampling criteria were used.

Daily DNS Resolution and Traceroute Scheduling within a Batch: In the case that the local DNS server returns several IP addresses, all returned addresses are stored and used. In the case that the DNS server cannot resolve an IP address corresponding to the domain name, a prefix of "www" is added to the domain name before repeating the DNS lookup procedure. If this secondary DNS query also yields no results, we discarded the domain from the study. In total, only 5 out of the 1,300 sampled domains needed to be discarded. Finally, to keep unknown duplication to a minimum, we did not include CNAME pointer records in our dataset. Given the set of IP addresses, traceroutes within a batch of traceroutes were scheduled one domain at a time. For each domain, we first scheduled traceroutes to IPv4 addresses and then to IPv6 addresses. This ensures that IPv6 and IPv4 traceroutes to the same domain runs relatively nearby in time (typically within less than a minute). We leverage this in our analysis, as path lengths always are compared for the same source-destination pair (for which we then have many nearby sample pairs).

Batch Scheduling: Due to time-varying loads and significant differences between the processing times on the different PlanetLab nodes, we decided to schedule batches at different intervals. In the first campaign ("May 2019"), we pre-scheduled periodic batch jobs (on 1, 2, 3 or 6 h intervals) based on the maximum run lengths that we had observed at each location the days leading up to the actual collection period, and interrupted the batch jobs that did not fully complete within one such interval. This pruning resulted in some missing data for one of the eight PlanetLab nodes available during the first campaign. When planning the next campaign, we observed substantially different run times for the different nodes, prompting us to improve the methodology somewhat for the final two campaigns. In particular, we schedule new batch jobs to start at the top of the next even hour (as measured locally) following the ending of the previous batch jobs. For most of the locations, this results in batch jobs starting every 2, 4, or 6 h with the basic traceroute tool ("Sept 2019"). However, for the second campaign (single threaded with Paris traceroute) we observed 12-h intervals.

Post Campaign Lookups: At the end of each campaign, we collected the reverse DNS entry for each observed IP address as well as the AS number (as provided by RIPEstat [27]). To reduce the number of calls to the later API and to speed up the IP-to-AS mapping, we (i) converted the unique set of IP addresses into their binary form, (ii) cached looked-up entries, and (iii) used the AS number of cached entries whenever there already exists an entry in the cache for which the IP address fitted within its IP network mask. The choice to only run the lookups once per campaign is motivated by the high resource usage during these lookups (that otherwise would impact the data collection itself). Also, note that such mappings change much less frequently than the IP routes themselves, and that this choice is expected to have negligible impact on our results.

Table 2. Summary of measurement campaigns

Short name	Duration	Dates (all 2019)	Method	Nodes	Traceroutes	Success
May 2019	1 week	May 14–20	Baseline	8	1,966,793	74%
Paris	4 weeks	Aug. 11–Sept. 8	Paris	6	265,206	22%
Sept. 2019	1 week	Sept. 18–24	Baseline	8	1,773,553	78%

3.2   Overview of Datasets

Table 2 summarizes some key differences and characteristics for the three measurement campaigns analyzed in this paper. Again, all three campaigns use the same sample list of domains (see "Domain sampling" above), are based on the same high-level methodology, and only differ by the adjustments made to account for differences in the traceroute tools (impacting parallelism) and how the run duration of individual samples differ across PlanetLab nodes and vary over time. For example, the "Paris" campaign lasted for four weeks (but only used one thread per node), while the other two campaigns used the basic traceroute tool and lasted a week each. Despite having much shorter collection duration, the two campaigns performed with the basic traceroute tool were able to perform many more traceroutes and resulted in 3.4–3.5 times higher success rates than when using Paris traceroute.

Given the far lower Paris traceroute success rate, we also ran Paris traceroute with alternative configurations. However, such alternative configurations resulted in even worse success rates. For example, in a 12 h experiment using the 9 active PlanetLab nodes at that time, we obtained the following success rates with the main configuration options: 20% (5,966/30,372) when using the default option (i.e., UDP probes with default destination port 33457), which also is the option we used in the above experiments, 5% (1,606/30,392) when using UDP probes with destination port 53, 0.6% (178/30,349) when using ICMP probes, and 0.14% (42/30,345) when using TCP probes.

Due to the small success rate of Paris traceroutes, as observed from our example locations, in the following, we focus only on the two datasets using the baseline traceroute implementation (i.e., "May 2019" and "Sept. 2019"). Again, note that this tool allows use of parallel traceroutes and provided much higher success rates, but that we cannot trust the exact paths reported. While this limits any accurate analysis to comparing distances rather than the exact "paths" reported by the tool, it should be emphasized that the type of statistics analysis we present here are designed for the purpose of looking only at path distances and RTTs, not the exact paths.

4   Evaluation Method and Results

4.1   High-Level Analysis Methodology

For the evaluation presented here, we use the measurements collected from the seven IPv6 enabled PlanetLab nodes that were active both in May 2019 and

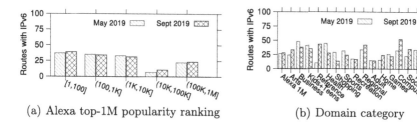

(a) Alexa top-1M popularity ranking   (b) Domain category

Fig. 1. Fraction of end-to-end pairings evaluated in different domain categories that were IPv6 enabled in May 2019 and Sept. 2019

Sept. 2019. By excluding the measurements for the two additional nodes, we ensure fairer longitudinal analysis of the changes that have happened over the four-month period between the datasets. First, note that this fixed set of PlanetLab nodes combined with using a fixed set of sample domains (see "Domain sampling" in Sect. 3) ensures that we use the same set of node-domain pairings for all the datasets. Second, to account for differences in the number of samples observed (to each domain) at each PlanetLab node, we apply a pairwise analysis and report summary statistics for sets of node-domain pairs. In particular, for most comparisons, we calculate the fraction of node-domain pairings of a subset of such pairings for which either IPv4 or IPv6 is deemed the "winner", as calculated using different pairwise statistics.

In addition to minimizing the effects of different nodes allowing for different number of measurements (e.g., due to load differences and their relative network speeds when performing the measurements) our pairwise analysis methodology also minimizes the effects of differences in the number of measurements per domain from a particular node (e.g., due to multiple IPs for some domains and one of the nodes not fully completing all of its batches in the first dataset). We also stress that the two dataset we focus on both were collected using the same traceroute tool, and only use Paris measurements for complementing analysis. Finally, while we only use a limited number of measurement nodes, we note that these nodes are public and therefore allow others to with some work (and extra help from the PlanetLab group) repeat our measurements and analysis (assuming those nodes remains active).

4.2   IPv6 Deployment

Much prior work has considered the IPv6 adoption from different perspectives. While this is not the focus of this paper, to provide some context of end-to-end paths that we evaluate, here, we briefly (i) note that all end-to-end pairings that we observed were IPv6 enabled also had corresponding IPv4 paths, and (ii) report the fraction of pairings that we observed were IPv6 enabled. Figure 1 summarizes these results.

Across the domain categories and locations that we used for the evaluation, the number of IPv6 enabled paths were typically below 50% (for each category). In May 2019, 27.8% of all observed pairings were IPv6 enabled and in Sept. 2019,

Table 3. Summary table of pairwise distance comparisons

	Metric	Median winner (%)			Average winner (%)			95% conf. win. (%)		
		v.4	v.6	tie	v.4	v.6	tie	v.4	v.6	none
May'19	IP hops	15.4	**77.5**	7.0	21.1	**78.7**	0.2	19.9	**77.5**	2.6
	AS hops	14.3	**59.3**	26.4	17.1	**79.6**	3.3	16.0	**78.0**	6.0
	RTTs	46.0	**54.0**	0.0	47.2	**52.8**	0.0	33.1	**44.7**	22.2
Sep'19	IP hops	14.4	**77.6**	8.0	20.2	**79.8**	0.0	19.4	**79.0**	1.6
	AS hops	10.3	**55.4**	34.3	15.4	**81.5**	3.1	13.3	**78.7**	8.1
	RTTs	36.2	**63.8**	0.0	31.3	**68.7**	0.0	25.7	**59.0**	15.3

29.2% of all observed pairings were IPv6 enabled, suggesting a small increase by 1.44% over this period. Within the Alexa top-1M dataset (Fig. 1(a)), the fraction of IPv6 enabled paths is highest for the subsets with domains ranked in the top-10K subset (i.e., [1,100], (100, 1K], and (1K,10K]). When instead considering the statistics for the top-50 domains of different domain categories (Fig. 1(b)), we observed individual categories with above ("Computers") or close to 50% IPv6 enabled pairings, including two categories ("References" and "Computers") for which the fraction of IPv6 enabled paths increased substantially between May 2019 and Sept. 2019: 323% (10.2%→43.2%) and 61% (32.5%→52.4%), respectively.

4.3   High-Level Distance Comparisons

Table 3 summarizes the percent of pairings for which IPv4 and IPv6 are deemed the "winner" in the two datasets ("May 2019" and "Sept. 2019"), using three distance metrics (IP hops, AS hops, and RTTs) and three statistics (median, average, and a 95% confidence test on the average difference).

Statistics: For each pair, the median and average statistics are trivially calculated over all observations. Here, we simply report the percent of pairings for which these statistics are lower (i.e., fewer hops or shorter RTTs) for IPv4 and IPv6, respectively, as the fraction of "winners". In the case that the statistics are the same, we report a "tie" for that pairing. With the exception for the median number of AS hops, ties are relatively rare for these metrics.

For the 95% confidence tests, we use one-sided t-tests for the paths associated with each of the two protocol versions and report the percent of cases where the null-hypothesis that the metrics are the same can be rejected in favour of the alternative hypothesis that the (average) paths associated with that particular protocol are shorter with a confidence level of 95%. In the case that both tests fail, we list the pairings under the "none" column (indicating that neither is a significant winner). Note that the fraction of "none" entries always should be greater than the fraction of "ties" for the average statistic and that the 95% confidence test in general provides greater statistical insights into which differences are significant than the other two statistics. The average statistics

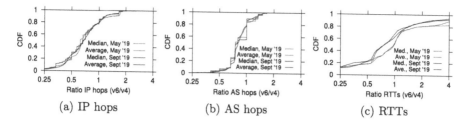

Fig. 2. CDFs of the ratio of the pairwise distances using IPv6 and IPv4, as measured using (a) IP hops, (b) AS hops, and (c) RTTs

provide insights regarding in which direction the "none" cases are leaning, and the median statistics (typically considered more robust to outliers than averages) provides a complementing perspective into which set of paths are shorter more robust to outliers.

IPv6 Most Frequent Winner in All Cases: The IPv6 paths have the largest fraction of pairwise winners across all three metrics, all three statistics, and for both datasets. To highlight this, the table uses bold text to indicate the set of paths with the most winners for each of the 18 cases ($3 \times 3 \times 2$). Furthermore, while we observe an increase in the fraction of IPv6 winners in 8 out of 9 cases (median AS hops being the exception), the differences between the datasets are only substantial for the three RTT cases, for which we see the following increases: 54.0%→63.8%, 52.8%→68.7%, and 44.7%→59.0%. We next analyze each distance metric separately.

IP and AS Hops: Both the number of IP hops and AS hops are significantly shorter (95% confidence) in a 77–79% of the pairwise cases observed. The shorter hop-count lengths can also be observed when considering the ratios of the pairwise IP hop counts (Fig. 2(a)) and AS hop counts (Fig. 2(b)) using IPv6 and IPv4. Here, smaller ratios mean that the IPv6 paths has less visible hops. We also note that the values reported for the median and average statistics in Table 3 simply refers to the point at which the curves in Fig. 2 have a ratio of 1. These figures not only emphasize that IPv6 paths are shorter, but that they in some cases are substantially shorter. For example, in nearly 20% of the cases the number of IP hops are half of what was observed using IPv4. Again, we expect that these cases often correspond to cases where IP tunnels have been used; something we have manually validated for some cases. Furthermore, we note that the median and average curves follow each other relatively closely (with the average curves being smoother) across the two datasets.

RTTs: Interestingly, when considering the RTTs, we see a relatively lower but increasing fraction of paths for which IPv6 is deemed the winner (Table 3). For example, using the median statistic the fraction increases from 54.0% to 63.8%; with the average statistic the fraction increases from 52.8% to 68.7%, and with the 95% confidence test statistic the fraction increases from 44.7% to 59.0%. The improving IPv6 RTTs are perhaps even more visible in Fig. 2(c), as they result in in a clear shift of the relative RTT ratios. Comparing this with the

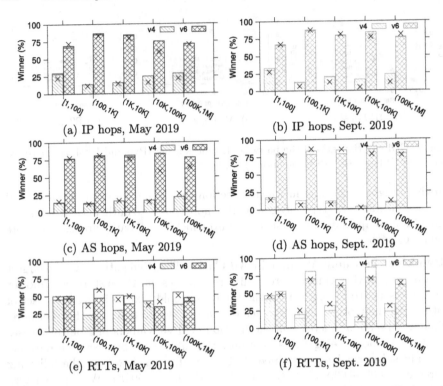

Fig. 3. Fraction of instances that the IPv6 path (blue/purple) and IPv4 path (red/orange) is the winner, as broken down per the rank of the top-1M domains (Color figure online)

(typically higher, but stable fractions) for the IP and AS hop metrics (which remained relatively stable), the IPv6 paths' relative RTTs improve significantly. Overall, the lower IPv6 RTTs (skew towards lower ratios observed in Fig. 2(c)) and further improvements of the IPv6 RTTs (slight shift to the left of curves) suggest that the IPv6 paths perform very well and that current deployment examples are encouraging.

4.4 Rank-Based Distance Comparisons

Figure 3 shows the fraction of pairings that the IPv6 path (blue/purple) and IPv4 path (red/orange) is the winner for domains with different ranking. The full bars show the results using the average statistic, the filled region of the bars shows the winners using the 95% confidence tests, and the crosses (×) show the results for the median statistic. Here, we include a pair of plots for each of the three metrics: IP path lengths ((a) and (b)), AS path lengths ((c) and (d)), and RTTs ((e) and (f)). Changes over time are seen by comparing the left (May 2019) and right (Sept. 2019) figure.

In general, our previous observations are consistent across the different domain ranks. First, the IP hop counts and AS hop counts are the clear winner

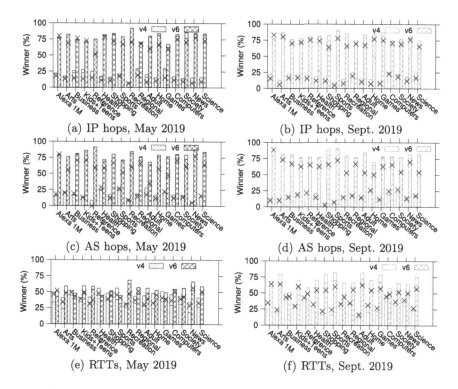

Fig. 4. Fraction of instances that the IPv6 path (blue/purple) and IPv4 path (red/orange) is the winner, as broken down per the domain category (Color figure online)

in most cases, and these ratios do not change much over time. Second, when considering the RTTs, with exception of the top-100 ranked domains (for which there are small differences), we observe a significant increase in pairings for which IPv6 is the winner.

4.5   Category-Based Distance Comparisons

The corresponding results for the 50 top ranked domains of 16 Alexa domain categories (plus the top-1M set itself) are shown in Fig. 4. Here, we again break down the results per dataset (column), metric (row), and statistic (bars, filled bars, and crosses). Similar as for the rank-based results, our main observations are relatively consistent across the different categories. First, the fraction of paths for which the IPv6 paths have shorter IP and AS hop counts than the corresponding IPv4 hop counts are consistently (much) higher for all categories than the fraction of pairs that IPv4 would be the winner, and the differences remained relatively consistent between the two snapshots. Second, across the domain categories, we observe an increasing fraction of pairings for which the IPv6 RTTs are lower than the corresponding IPv4 RTTs. This has also resulted in an increase in the number of categories for which there are more IPv6 winners

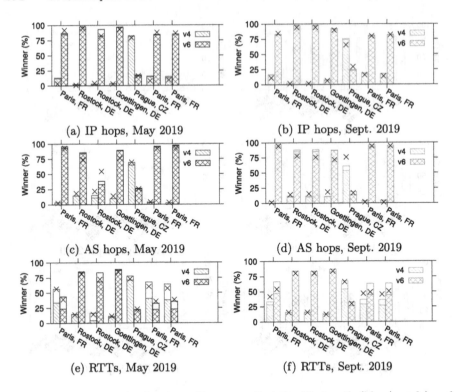

Fig. 5. Differences in the fraction of instances that the IPv6 path (blue/purple) and IPv4 path (red/orange) is the winner, as broken down per PlanetLab node (Color figure online)

than IPv4 winners. For example, IPv6 has gone from having more winners in 13 out of the 17 categories (May 2019) to having more winners in all of the categories (Sept. 2019), regardless of statistic.

4.6 Impact of PlanetLab Node

To better understand the impact of the selection of origin sources, we next discuss to what degree the results also were consistent across the PlanetLab nodes used for our analysis. While we did observe some significant differences in the fraction of IPv6 winners at each node, the observations were relatively consistent. For example, for the hop-count based results, IPv6 had a larger fraction of winners for 6 out of 7 of the nodes in both May 2019 and Sept. 2019, whereas the fraction of nodes for which IPv6 had more winners when using the RTT as the metric increased from 3/7 to 6/7. The node that stood out the most was `ple1.cesnet.cz` (located in Prague, CZ), which consistently had IPv4 as the winner across all metrics and datasets. However, also for this node, the relative changes in the fraction of IPv6 winners when using the RTTs metric increased noticeably from May 2019 to Sept. 2019. Figure 5 shows a per-node breakdown.

5 Related Work

Over the years, many measurement studies have focused on IPv6 adoption [12,13,16,21,23,30,31]. Although many such studies are a few years old, they combine for a good picture of the slow IPv6 adoption across geographic regions, user equipment technologies, edge networks, ISPs, content providers, and other entities in the end-to-end ecosystem. However, less work has focused on the relative end-to-end IPv6 performance and how it may be affected by the lack of full end-to-end adoption.

As discussed in the introduction, Giotsas et al. [16] showed in 2015 that the performance of IPv6 paths can be significantly hurt by IPv6 tunnels and a less connected transit-free clique. However, since then, further adoption has taken place. As validated by our study, the IPv6 paths and their performance are therefore expected to improve over time as tunneled paths are replaced with native paths and IPv6 AS relationships mature. Giotsas et al. [16] also showed that Hurricane Electric (HE), a prominent provider of this technique, already at that time significantly contributed to the AS connectivity and that the use of their peerings was quickly increasing.

Bajpai et al. [4] investigated the time it takes to complete the initial TCP handshake over an IPv6 and IPv4 network to the top-100 dual-stack websites. Using measurements from both residential and research networks, they identified several cases where CDN caches were present at the edge networks for IPv4, but not for IPv6. This resulted in relatively higher connection establishment times with IPv6. While they observed some improvements in IPv6 connection times over time, more recent TCP connection establishment measurements towards YouTube media servers suggest that both TCP connection establishment times and startup delays are higher over IPv6 [5].

In other recent work, Goel et al. [17] measure RTTs, DNS lookup times, and page load times using the Akamai monitoring system, and show that IPv6 performs better than IPv4 in US cellular networks. Pujol et al. [26] use DNS and flow-level statistics from an ISP to show that RTTs observed in the backbone are similar for IPv6 and IPv4 (e.g., 80% of RTTs within 10ms of corresponding IPv4 RTTs).

Other, somewhat older studies, have evaluated the IPv6 performance using HTTP requests to experimental Google web service hostnames [11], using pings from three US locations to globally distributed dual-stack name servers [6], by performing download speed tests [24], and by measuring page load times [13] of popular websites. Although older, we note that the two later studies (i.e., [13,24]) made some interesting observations that suggest that IPv6 performance typically was comparable to IPv4 performance when AS-level forwarding paths were the same, but that the performance typically was much worse otherwise. Based on the adoption trends observed by Giotas et al. [16], which suggest that the IPv6 AS-level topology (at least in 2015) slowly is converging towards the IPv4 topology, we would therefore expect that IPv6 performance will improve relative to IPv4 performance over time. This is also supported by taking a (close to) 10-year perspective and comparing our average, median, and 95%-ile results with those obtained by Berger [6] in 2010. While the IPv4 ping times that they measured between their three US-based locations and dual-stack name servers associated with different geographic regions were almost always faster than the corresponding IPv6 ping times, we observe IPv6 to be the winner in most of cases today (from our measurement locations). While some of the above papers give a glimpse into the relative performance that clients may see when using IPv6 rather than IPv4, most of these works are old, and none of the works capture, compare, or contrast the status observed for different domain categories. Furthermore, none of the previous works use pairwise hypothesis testing to quantify the number of paths for which IPv6 (or IPv4) is the winner.

Finally, we note that yet others have developed techniques to scan the IPv6 address space [14,15,28], to study the stability of IPv6 in the control/data planes [22], to discover the IPv6 topology [9] or address space [25], and to pair addresses of dual-stacked DNS resolvers or IP end points [7,8]. We consider these works orthogonal to ours.

6   Conclusions

In this paper we presented the methodological challenges and results from a measurement study in which we compared the relative end-to-end distances when using IPv6 and IPv4 between PlanetLab nodes in Europe and selected domain sets. The paper provides a use-case driven report of running IPv6 experiments on PlanetLab, highlights the lack of IP support among PlanetLab nodes, and provides a statistical methodology that uses hypothesis testing and pairwise comparisons to provide insights into the current IPv6 paths performance, relative to that of IPv4, while accounting for current testbed and traceroute limitations. Our analysis shows (among other things) that despite significant use of IP tunnels (e.g., much shorter IP and AS hop counts), the RTTs of the IPv6 paths are now relatively faster than the corresponding IPv4 paths in the majority of cases when they are available, and the fraction of pairings for which this is the case has increased notably between May 2019 and Sept. 2019 across all five rank categories and almost all 16 domain categories considered. These findings suggest that the IPv6 end-to-end path performance is continuing to improve and most often already outperform IPv4 path performance. These performance improvements may be due to careful deployment by individual operators, but may also help incentivize further deployment by others.

The limited IPv6 deployment among PlanetLab nodes in Europe restricted us to a smaller number of measurement locations. Interesting future work include applying the pairwise hypothesis-based methodology presented here on similar datasets collected from other locations and/or collected at different points in time. An interesting measurement effort worth mentioning here is an online tool created by Geoff Huston [19], which provides country-by-country statistics and data that potentially could be used for such analysis.

Acknowledgement. We thank Burim Ljuma at PlanetLab for helping us setting up PlanetLab with IPv6 connectivity. We also thank the developers of Paris traceroute for their continuing efforts to improve the tool.

References

1. Alexa - top sites by category: Top. https://www.alexa.com/topsites/category. Accessed 07 Mar 2019
2. traceroute(8) - Linux manual page. http://man7.org/linux/man-pages/man8/traceroute.8.html. Accesssed 14 Feb 2019
3. Augustin, B., et al.: Avoiding traceroute anomalies with Paris traceroute. In: Proceedings IMC (2006)
4. Bajpai, V., Schönwälder, J.: IPv4 versus IPv6-who connects faster? In: Proceedings IFIP Networking (2015)
5. Bajpai, V., Ahsan, S., Schönwälder, J., Ott, J.: Measuring YouTube content delivery over IPv6. In: ACM CCR, October 2017
6. Berger, A.: Working paper on comparison of performance over IPv6 versus IPv4. Technical report, Akamai Technologies (2011)
7. Berger, A., Weaver, N., Beverly, R., Campbell, L.: Internet nameserver IPv4 and IPv6 address relationships. In: Proceedings IMC (2013)
8. Beverly, R., Berger, A.: Server siblings: Identifying shared IPv4/IPv6 infrastructure via active fingerprinting. In: Proceedings PAM (2015)
9. Beverly, R., Durairajan, R., Plonka, D., Rohrer, J.P.: In the IP of the beholder: strategies for active IPv6 topology discovery. In: Proceedings IMC (2018)
10. Chiu, Y.C., Schlinker, B., Radhakrishnan, A.B., Katz-bassett, E., Govindan, R.: Are we one hop away from a better internet? In: Proceedings IMC (2015)
11. Colitti, L., Gunderson, S.H., Kline, E., Refice, T.: Evaluating IPv6 adoption in the internet. In: Proceedings PAM (2010)
12. Czyz, J., Allman, M., Zhang, J., Iekel-Johnson, S., Osterweil, E., Bailey, M.: Measuring IPv6 adoption. In: Proceedings ACM SIGCOMM (2014)
13. Dhamdhere, A., Luckie, M., Huffaker, B., kc claffy, Elmokashfi, A., Aben, E.: Measuring the deployment of IPv6: topology, routing and performance. In: Proceedings IMC (2012)
14. Fukuda, K., Heidemann, J.: Who knocks at the IPv6 door?: Detecting IPv6 scanning. In: Proceedings IMC (2018)
15. Gasser, O., Scheitle, Q., Gebhard, S., Carle, G.: Scanning the IPv6 internet: towards a comprehensive hitlist. In: Proceedings IFIP TMA (2016)
16. Giotsas, V., Luckie, M., Huffaker, B., kc Claffy: IPv6 AS relationships, cliques, and congruence. In: Proceedings PAM (2015)
17. Goel, U., Steiner, M., Wittie, M.P., Flack, M., Ludin, S.: A case for faster mobile web in cellular IPv6 networks. In: Proceedings ACM MobiCom (2016)
18. Google: Google IPv6 adoption statistics. http://www.google.com/intl/en/ipv6/statistics.html. Accessed 01 Oct 2020
19. Huston, G.: V6/v4 RTT comparison by country (ms) (2020). https://stats.labs.apnic.net/v6perf. Accessed 01 Oct 2020
20. Jobst, M.E.: Traceroute anomalies. In: Seminar Future Internet (2013)
21. Karir, M., Huston, G., Michaelson, G., Bailey, M.: Understanding IPv6 populations in the wild. In: Proceedings PAM (2013)
22. Livadariu, I., Elmokashfi, A., Dhamdhere, A.: Characterizing IPv6 control and data plane stability. In: Proceedings IEEE INFOCOM (2016)

23. Nikkhah, M., Guerin, R., Nikkhah, M.: Migrating the internet to IPv6: an exploration of the when and why. IEEE/ACM Trans. Network, August 2016
24. Nikkhah, M., Guérin, R., Lee, Y., Woundy, R.: Assessing IPv6 through web access a measurement study and its findings. In: Proceedings ACM CoNEXT (2011)
25. Plonka, D., Berger, A.: Temporal and spatial classification of active IPv6 addresses. In: Proceedings IMC (2015)
26. Pujol, E., Richter, P., Feldmann, A.: Understanding the share of IPv6 traffic in a dual-stack ISP. In: Proceedings PAM (2017)
27. RIPE NCC: RIPEstat data API. https://stat.ripe.net/docs/data_api#network-info. Accessed 03 May 2019
28. Rohrer, J.P., LaFever, B., Beverly, R.: Empirical study of router IPv6 interface address distributions. In: IEEE Internet Computer, July/August 2016
29. Scheitle, Q., et al.: A long way to the top: significance, structure, and stability of internet top lists. In: Proceedings IMC (2018)
30. Zander, S., Andrew, L.L., Armitage, G., Huston, G., Michaelson, G.: Investigating the IPv6 teredo tunnelling capability and performance of internet clients. In: ACM CCR, October 2012
31. Zander, S., Andrew, L.L., Armitage, G., Huston, G., Michaelson, G.: Mitigating sampling error when measuring internet client IPv6 capabilities. In: Proceedings IMC (2012)

LP WAN Gateway Location Selection Using Modified K-Dominating Set Algorithm

Artur Frankiewicz[2], Adam Glos[1], Krzysztof Grochla[1(✉)],
Zbigniew Łaskarzewski[2], Jarosław Miszczak[1], Konrad Połys[1],
Przemysław Sadowski[1], and Anna Strzoda[1]

[1] Institute of Theoretical and Applied Informatics, Polish Academy of Sciences,
Bałtycka 5, Gliwice, Poland
{aglos,kgrochla,jmiszczak,kpolys,psadowski,astrzoda}@iitis.pl
[2] AIUT Sp. z o.o., Wyczółkowskiego 113, Gliwice, Poland
{afrankiewicz,zlaskarzewski}@aiut.com

Abstract. The LP WAN networks use gateways or base stations to communicate with devices distributed on large distances, up to tens of kilometres. The selection of optimal gateway locations in wireless networks should allow providing the complete coverage for a given set of nodes, taking into account the limitations, such as the number of nodes served per access point or required redundancy. In this paper, we describe the problem of selecting the base stations in a network using the concept of k-dominating set. In our model, we include information about the required redundancy and spectral efficiency. We consider the additional requirements on the resulting connections and provide the greedy algorithm for solving the problem. The algorithm is evaluated in randomly generated network topologies and using the coordinates of sample real smart metering networks.

Keywords: LP WAN · Radio planing · Gateway location · Redundancy

1 Introduction

The introduction of Low Power WAN network concept, with devices communicating over distances of tens of kilometers using low power radio interface, has generated multitude of novel use cases based on long life battery powered devices. The LoRa (Long Range) is one of the most widely adopted LP WAN standards, which is based on ISM (Industrial, Scientific and Medical) frequencies and chirp spectrum modulation. The LoRa communication now is being deployed in devices such as smart meters, sensors or actuators executing smart

This work has been partially funded by the Polish National Center for Research and Development grant no. POIR.04.01.04-00-0005/17.

city functions. The LoRa can provide cheap and very energy efficient communication with thousands of devices per one access point, at the cost of low data rate. To facilitate the deployment of LoRa devices, the LoRaWAN standard has been proposed, which defines the packet format and communication architecture allowing to forward the information from the devices to the internet servers.

Traditionally radio planning technologies are used to select location of base stations in long range wireless networks. This approach is not always feasible in LP WAN, as due to the low cost of access point (few hundred dollars) and the simplicity of its deployment it is more efficient to deploy the access points in less efficient manner, but without the costly radio planning procedures. Traditionally, the gateway location selection problem was solved by radio planning engineers, using radio signal propagation models and simulation software and tested through the drive tests [1,2]. This method is to expensive for the LP WAN networks, which employ very large number of low cost devices, as it requires both engineering time to plan the radio and execution of time consuming drive tests. The number and locations of gateways need to be dynamically modified basing on the growth of the network, to provide coverage appropriate to the endpoints' density, as more end nodes generate more traffic which needs to be served.

In this work, we propose an algorithm to select the suboptimal location for the LP WAN gateway location for a given set of endpoint location. The gateway location is selected from a set of location candidates, which may be the same as the set of end node location. The selection of a set of gateways must meet the requirement to provide connectivity to all end nodes and to provide the required redundancy. We assume that the connectivity graph estimated from the distances between the nodes is the input. We treat the problem as a problem of selection of a dominating set, which is an NP-complete decision problem in computational complexity theory [3]. Thus the problem is complex and it is hard to solve.

There are a few differences between other popular radio networks (e.g. LTE) and LoRa. LoRa end devices are typically battery powered devices so they transmit data rarely, but usually in a constant time window. LoRa uses ALOHA media access control so collisions are more probable. LoRa devices also use all possible channels uniformly, there is no "colouring" of areas and LoRa uses spreading factors, thus the capacity of the gateway may vary depending on the spatial distribution of the nodes. We assume the set of client locations and the traffic characteristics are known and is an input for the proposed algorithm, which is a case e.g. for advanced metering infrastructure (AMI) networks.

The rest of the paper is organized as follows: the second section describes the state of the art regarding the planning and dimensioning of LP WAN networks and the selection of AP location. Next, we describe the network model used in the study. In the following section, we show the pseudocode of the proposed optimization algorithm. Next we present the analysis of the performance of the algorithm for different types of topologies. We finish the paper with a short conclusion.

2   Literature Review

The radio network planning has been investigated for more than twenty years, however most of the work is dedicated to cellular networks - see e.g. [1] or [2]. However, there is very little research results available considering the specifics of the LP WAN radio network planning, where the cost of network deployment is much smaller, thus it does not justify the costly drive tests and radio signal propagation analysis. One of the few tools which allow to estimate the coverage of a LoRa gateway on a map is CloudRF [4]. There are some other tools allowing to simulate radio signal propagation, of which most support ISM frequencies and allow to estimate the range of LP WAN access points, such as e.g. Radio Mobile Online [5]. These tools are very useful in analysis of network coverage for a given set of access points, but require large knowledge of RF signal propagation and do not select automatically the gateway location, requiring the experience of the operator. While this is effective for a small number of access points, for large networks which need to match the restraints of number of nodes services by an access point use of such tools is ineffective. In the previous work by part of the authors [6] two of us have proposed a heuristic algorithm for gateway location selection, which however do not support redundancy.

3   Gateway Location Selection Procedure

3.1   Problem Formulation

To describe the problem of selecting the set of gateways for the given set of stations (end points), we assume that we have for our disposal the graph describing the visibility between the stations. In such graph two stations are connected only if it is possible to transmit packets between them. We assume that different connections may have different costs. We also make some assumption on capabilities of the resulting network. First, we assume that each gateway has a fixed maximal capacity, the same for each of them, representing the maximal number of stations it can connect to simultaneously. This ensures that the transmission load will not exceed the capacity of the gateway. Second, we assume that each non-station has to be connected at least to some fixed number of gateways. This condition describes the redundancy requirements for the resulting network. Finally, we would like to find the smallest possible set of gateway, which expresses the requirement of using the smallest possible number of gateways.

To represent this situation we use a triple (G, c, k), where G is undirected weighted graph $G = (V, E)$, with the set of vertices V and the set of edges E, c is the maximal capacity of the gateways, and k is the domination number describing the minimal number of gateways each station is connected to. In this description each vertex represents a station, and stations are connected if they are within their radius of visibility. To each edge, $(v, w) \in E$, we assign a weight C_{vw}, representing the cost of the connection between the station represented by vertices v and w. The connection cost between nodes v and w is equal to

$\frac{1}{2^{12-SF_{vw}}}$, where SF_{vw} is equal to the value of spreading factor in the communication between nodes v and w. Values of SF in the communication between two
nodes are determined on the basis of a signal propagation model that takes into
account the distance between nodes and random attenuation. The higher the SF
value, the higher the transmission cost. The domination number k is used for
representing the required redundancy.

3.2   Description of the Solution

To describe our approach we first consider a simplified sub-problem, defined as
follows.

Problem 1 (Gateways). For a given set of stations, described by (G, c, k), find
the set D of stations such that each station is in this set or it has a direct
connection to a station from this set.

One can note that, as the only requirement here is to assure the visibility
between the stations, the solution of the above problem is given a subset of
stations. Thus, no information about the connections is given.

The stations from the set D, obtained as a solution of the above problem,
are called gateways. The set D is called a dominating set of G. If we impose the
condition that each element station should be connected to at least k gateways,
the solution of the above problem is equivalent to finding k-dominating set, D_k,
of a graph G.

Definition 1. *For a graph $G = (V, E)$, the k-dominating set of G, denoted by
D_k, is any subset of vertices such that each vertex from V is connected to at
least k nodes from D_k or belongs to D_k.*

The notion of k-dominating set captures the redundancy requirement. Still
the information about the D_k alone is not sufficient to describe the allocation of
connection between stations and gateways.

A similar approach has been used previously for constructing routing algorithms in *ad hoc* networks [7], and various methods have been developed in this
context [8–10]. However, one should keep in mind that in our scenario we assume
that not only the resulting network has to be redundant, but also the resulting
gateways have limited capacities. On the other hand, in contrast to the routing
problem, we do not require the subgraph with vertex set consisting of gateways
to be connected.

One should note, that if we assume the capacity c in our problem to be
infinite, then an arbitrary connection scheme with a gateway D_k would be a
proper solution. In particular, gateway can serve all of the neighbouring nodes.
However, since capacity is finite, each gateway cannot serve all neighbouring
nodes, thus we may need to add gateways in order to serve not-served one. Thus,
the solution of our problem is given by the solution of k-domination problem,
which is to find the minimal k-dominating set, with fixed capacity c.

Taking all this into account, we define our problem as follows.

Algorithm 1. Greedy algorithm for finding k-dominating scheme and its connection scheme. The stop condition is that every vertex is either a gateway or is served by k gateways. If the stop condition is not fulfilled, new gateway according to NEW_GATEWAY is chosen. Here G is input graph, C is the cost function, k is the domination parameter and c is the common capacity for all gateway nodes

```
1: function CREATE_CONNECTION_GRAPH(G = (V, E), C, k, c)
2:     E_H ← ∅
3:     D ← ∅
4:     H := (V, E_H, f)
5:     while {v ∈ V : deg_H(v) < k} \ D ≠ ∅  do
6:         w, S ← NEW_GATEWAY(G, H, C, D, k, c)
7:         D ← D ∪ {w}.
8:         for all v ∈ S do
9:             E_H ← E_H ∪ {{v, w}}
10:    return D, H
```

Problem 2 (Gateways with constrains). For a given graph, $G = (V, E)$, find the set of gateways D_k, forming a k-dominating set $D_k \subset V$, and a graph, $H = (V, E_H)$, which is a subgraph of G, $H \subset G$, satisfying the following conditions,

1. each edge from E_H connects gatewas and stations,
2. each end point is connected to at least k gateways,
3. the sum of weights for edges for each gateway v is at most c,

$$\sum_{w \in V, \{w,v\} \in E_H} C_{vw} \le c. \qquad (1)$$

The last conditions assures that the redundancy requirement is fulfilled, and even if for given station $k - 1$ neighbouring gateway would be unavailable, it is promised that kth gateway will have enough resources for serving the station.

3.3   Greedy Algorithm

Let $G = (V, E)$ be an undirected graph with $n = |V|$ vertices. The algorithm is an extension of the greedy algorithm for k-dominating set creation [11]. It is a greedy algorithm that starts with $D = \emptyset$, and adds a new vertex w minimizing current value of $a(G, D \cup \{w\})$ of the form

$$a(G, D) = nk - \sum_{v \in V} d_k(v, D), \qquad (2)$$

where

$$d_k(v, D) = \begin{cases} \min(k, N(v) \cap D), & v \notin D, \\ k, & v \in D, \end{cases} \qquad (3)$$

where $N(v)$ is the neighbourhood of v in G. The algorithm stops when $a(G, D) = 0$, which implies that D is a k-dominating set. Note that function $a(G, D)$

Algorithm 2. The algorithm which chooses best end point to be new gateway. It is chosen to be the end point, which can serve maximal possible stations. Here G is input graph, H is the subgraph of G, C is the cost function, D is the collection of gateways, k is the domination parameter and c is the common capacity for all gateway nodes. A degree of vertex v in graph H is denoted as $\deg_H(v)$.

1: **function** NEW_GATEWAY$(G = (V, E), H = (V, E_H), C, D, k, c)$
2:     **for** $w \in V$ **do**
3:         **if** $w \in D$ **then**
4:             value$[w] \leftarrow 0$
5:         **else**
6:             $T \leftarrow N_G(w)$ ▷ $N_G(w)$ returns neighbouring nodes
7:             $T \leftarrow T \setminus D$ ▷ remove gateways
8:             $T \leftarrow \{v \in T : \deg_H(v) < k\}$ ▷ remove served nodes
9:             $S \leftarrow \emptyset$
10:            **while** $\sum_{v \in S} C_{vw} \leq c$ **do**   ▷ check if the station can still serve more stations
11:                $v \leftarrow \arg\min_{v \in T} C_{vw}$ ▷ choose neighbour with smallest connection cost
12:                $S \leftarrow S \cup \{v\}$
13:                $T \leftarrow T \setminus \{v\}$
14:                value$[w] \leftarrow 1 + |S|$ ▷ because marking w makes it served
15:        $w \leftarrow \arg\max_{v \in V}$ value$[v]$
16:        **return** w, S

---

describes how many nodes are already in D, or in the case of non-gateways how many gateways are within their radius.

In our scenario the gateways, which are elements of a k-dominating set, have limited capacity. Thus, we need to store which end points connect to newly added gateway. Hence, we start with empty gateway collection D and empty graph $H = (V, E_H = \emptyset)$.

We choose gateways until (D, H) is a proper solution of our problem. The procedure to provide the solution is provided in Algorithm 1. At each step, new gateway is chosen to be the one maximizing the number of end point stations that it can serve and that requires service S. The details are provided in Algorithm 2. When the gateway w is chosen, it is added to current gateway collection $D = D \cup \{w\}$, and the edges set E_H is updated with edges connecting w and nodes it promised to serve by $E_H = E_H \cup \{\{w, v\} : v \in S\}$.

4   Performance Evaluation

The proposed algorithm has been evaluated using the randomly generated topologies and the real topologies of smart metering networks in two Polish cities which datasets we have access to, but are not in public domain. The algorithms are compared primarily in terms of the number of base stations selected for a given network topology, method operation time and spreading factors in the communication between selected base stations and end devices assigned to them by each of two algorithms. Experiments have been carried out for algorithm parameter sample values such as $k \in \{1, 2, 3\}$ and fixed maximal capacity of the gateway. The value of the maximal capacity parameter has been determined on the basis of our calculations taking into account transmission parameters such as the probability of packet delivery, the transmission time of a single packet and the transmission window.

As a reference method, we've used an implementation of the algorithm from [12], as the most similar to our approach. To be more precise, we've applied the heuristic method named accelerated dynamic weighted greedy algorithm (ADWGA) which is algorithm edition based on the recommendations of the authors of [12] this version of the algorithm for large–scale cases. In this app-roach, the base stations are not limited to the maximum number of end devices that can be assigned to a single base station. The authors of [12] do not provide exacts values of input algorithm parameters, marked in [12] as α and β, but only appoint the ranges within which the parameter values should be. Searching for the reference method parameter values has a significant impact on the algo-rithm's operation time. Due to the long–running calculations of the reference method, we conducted the experiments using the reference method [12] for two real–life network topologies and for some small random data sets. The results of both methods are compared with each other in Table 1 (for real network topolo-gies) and Table 2 (for random network topologies).

Figure 1 depicts the distribution of nodes for two real–life IoT deployment topologies of two sample cities A and B, being the subject of experiments. City A is a typical small city topology and city B consists of nodes divided in two separate regions – a double city estate topology.

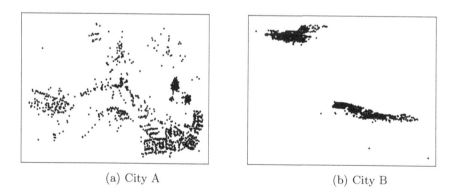

(a) City A   (b) City B

Fig. 1. Real–life IoT deployment network topologies of two sample cities A and B.

In Table 1 the results of both greedy and reference method [12] for real net-work topologies are summarized. The results in the Table 1 include an amount of selected gateways ('number of gateways'), algorithm operation time in which the result was obtained ('time [s]') and the average spreading factor to the gateway ('avg. SF'). Even though in most cases the reference algorithm found a smaller number of base stations than our method, the difference is very small. However, the difference in the time of operation of both methods is huge. For these two real network topologies our algorithm finds comparable number of base stations in much less time than reference method.

Table 1. Results of the proposed greedy algorithm and reference method [12] (ADWGA) for two real–life network topologies A and B.

City	Nodes	Area [m]	k	Number of gateways		Time [s]		Avg. SF	
				Greedy	Reference [12]	Greedy	Reference [12]	Greedy	Reference [12]
A	1719	2490 × 4090	1	6	6	4.95	253.08	9.19	9.18
			2	12	11	8.86	3118.27	9.2	8.92
			3	17	15	12.58	7603.15	9.17	8.88
B	1760	1260 × 3060	1	8	7	2.47	169.45	7.8	8.06
			2	15	14	4.57	363.16	7.84	7.86
			3	20	19	6.72	2249.87	7.84	7.89

Experimental results presented below include proposed algorithm performance statistics for various scenarios assuming the different number of network nodes randomly positioned in accordance with the uniform distribution in changing areas. The algorithm has been tested on network topologies with different density of nodes distribution in space. The statistics presented in tables below were obtained based on 30 runs of the algorithm for each number of nodes equals 1000, 2500, 5000, 10000 and 20000 distributed in a rectangle with dimensions 5000 m × 7500 m, 10000 m × 15000 m, 15000 m × 22500 m and 20000 m × 30000 m. Before each running of the algorithm positions of nodes were selected randomly. Tables 3, 4 and 5 contain statistics such as the average number of selected gateways, the average algorithm running time and the average spreading factor occurring between gateways and their clients (end point nodes) for redundancy factor $k \in \{1, 2, 3\}$ respectively and with fixed maximal capacity.

In Table 2 greedy and reference method statistics, described above, for small data sets are contained. It can be seen that in each case the running time of the greedy algorithm is much shorter than the running time of the reference method, especially for network topologies characterized by a dense distribution of nodes in space. In cases where the reference algorithm returns a smaller number of base stations than our method, which is on the plus side for the ADWGA, because it generates lower costs, then the greedy algorithm returns a little more base stations in a much shorter time. Moreover, for less dense network topologies our algorithm finds significantly fewer base stations much faster than reference method. The speed of the greedy algorithm allows us to obtain results for large–scale network topologies in a relatively short time.

Table 2. Results of the greedy and reference [12] method for sample topology scenarios.

Nodes	Area [m]	k	Avg. number of gateways		Avg. time [s]		Avg. SF	
			Greedy	Reference [12]	Greedy	reference [12]	Greedy	Reference [12]
1000	5000 × 7500	1	16.31	15.37	0.75	71.74	9.52	9.44
		2	29.9	27.5	1.41	640.51	9.54	9.58
		3	42.38	38.31	2.03	1139.58	9.57	9.56
1000	10000 × 15000	1	47.66	47.94	0.23	64.58	9.62	9.61
		2	86.03	83.2	0.43	733.19	9.67	9.66
		3	123.34	117.69	0.61	933.72	9.7	9.68
1000	15000 × 22500	1	91.34	92.59	0.13	80.6	9.69	9.69
		2	166.45	166.41	0.25	939.71	9.74	9.71
		3	236.34	249.41	0.34	1074.58	9.77	9.7
1000	20000 × 30000	1	145.38	153.93	0.1	348.31	9.74	9.74
		2	264.31	296.03	0.19	739.93	9.78	9.71
		3	373.38	566.28	0.27	896.88	9.78	10.02
2500	5000 × 7500	1	18.14	16.59	5.4	624.57	9.46	9.38
		2	32.52	30.24	9.94	8496.08	9.48	9.52
		2	46.72	41.14	14.39	18170.28	9.5	9.5

Figure 2 is the graphic interpretation of results for the average number of selected gateways presented in Table 2. To make the charts more transparent, the dimensions of the network topology area are presented in units of kilometers instead of meters, as in the tables.

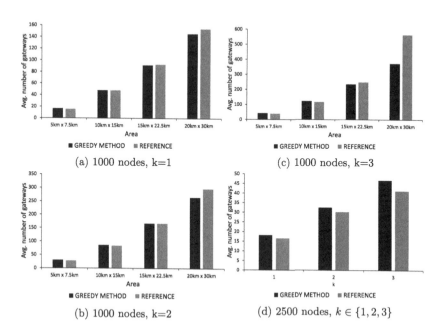

Fig. 2. Comparison of the average number of selected gateways for $k \in \{1, 2, 3\}$ for both methods; the proposed greedy algorithm and reference method [12] for 1000 number of nodes deployed in all areas (a), (b), (c) and for 2500 number of nodes deployed in the smallest of considered areas (d).

On Figs. 3, 4 and 5 a graphic interpretation of the greedy method has been shown to ilustrate the results presented in the Tables 2, 3, 4, 5 for $k \in \{1, 2\}$.

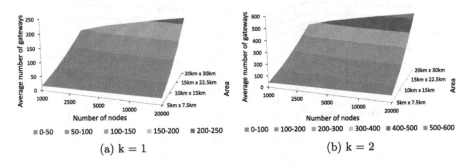

(a) k = 1   (b) k = 2

Fig. 3. Average number of selected gateways for each scenario for redundancy factor $k \in \{1, 2\}$.

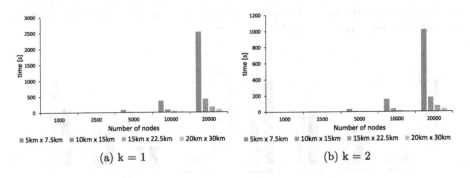

(a) k = 1   (b) k = 2

Fig. 4. Average greedy algorithm run time for each scenario for redundancy factor $k \in \{1, 2\}$.

Table 3. Statistics of the proposed greedy algorithm of finding k – dominating set for $k = 1$.

Nodes	Area [m]	Avg. number of gateways	Avg. time [s]	Avg. SF
2500	10000 × 15000	53.9	1.97	9.54
	15000 × 22500	105.9	0.97	9.64
	20000 × 30000	170.6	0.61	9.7
5000	5000 × 7500	19.53	34.79	9.43
	10000 × 15000	58.73	8.74	9.49
	15000 × 22500	115.53	4.06	9.57
	20000 × 30000	188.03	2.51	9.64
10000	5000 × 7500	20.97	155.8	9.41
	10000 × 15000	62.53	36.39	9.45
	15000 × 22500	124.4	15.07	9.52
	20000 × 30000	203.8	8.78	9.58
20000	5000 × 7500	22.73	1015.3	9.21
	10000 × 15000	67.1	177.7	9.43
	15000 × 22500	132.7	72.3	9.47
	20000 × 30000	218.9	36.3	9.52

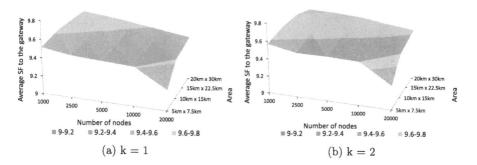

(a) k = 1   (b) k = 2

Fig. 5. Average Spreading Factor to the gateway for each scenario for redundancy factor $k \in \{1, 2\}$.

The distribution plots shown in the Fig. 6 present how the percentage number of non – gateway having a given spreading factor to the gateway is distributed for a sample consisting of specified network topologies. A single sample consists of 150 topologies with an amount of nodes equal to 1000, 2500, 5000, 10000, 20000 distributed in a given area, where 30 random topologies were generated for each of the five number of nodes. Each of the plots Fig. 6a, 6b, 6c, 6d was created on the basis of described 150 topologies generated for each area separately.

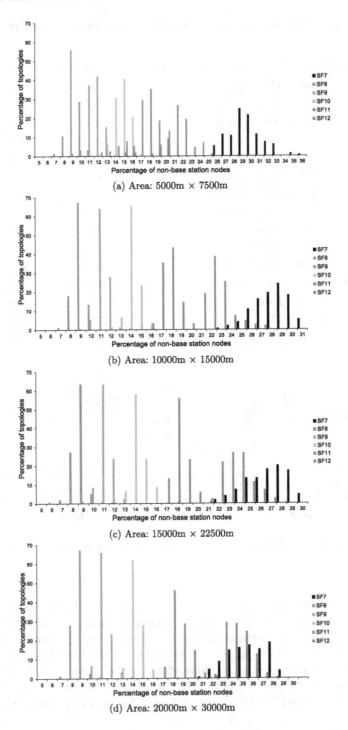

Fig. 6. Distributions of the percentage number of nodes having a specific SF to the gateway for different sizes of the node distribution area.

Table 4. Statistics of the proposed greedy algorithm of finding k – dominating set for $k = 2$.

Nodes	Area [m]		Avg. number of gateways	Avg. time [s]	Avg. SF
2500	10000 × 15000	97.1		3.41	9.61
	15000 × 22500	188.43		1.60	9.7
	20000 × 30000	305.07		1.08	9.75
5000	5000 × 7500	35.43		59.42	9.48
	10000 × 15000	104.80		14.84	9.55
	15000 × 22500	206.03		7.07	9.65
	20000 × 30000	333.27		4.31	9.71
10000	5000 × 7500m	37.57		264.52	9.45
	10000 × 15000	111.63		61.24	9.52
	15000 × 22500	220.3		25.55	9.59
	20000 × 30000	361.53		14.91	9.65
20000	5000 × 7500m	40.83		1735.58	9.25
	10000 × 15000	117.23		301.56	9.48
	15000 × 22500	233.81		121.46	9.54
	20000 × 30000	385.35		61.6	9.59

The distributions of percentage number of non – gateway nodes having a spreading factor equal to SF8, SF9, SF10 or SF11 to the target gateway are in very similar ranges of values, regardless of the size of the area. For instance, the percentage of the number of nodes having SF8 to gateway from topologies distributed on area 5000 m × 7500 m is in the range from 6% to 11% and stays within similar limits despite the increasing area and, consequently, the decreasing network density. The same phenomena can be observed for percentage of number of nodes that have spreading factor to gateway equals to SF9, SF10 and SF11. The algorithm selects the locations of gateway in such a way that the percentage of clients with a given SF to the gateway is very similar, regardless of the density of the network. Around each gateway, there are areas within there are non – gateway nodes having a given spreading factor SF7, SF8, etc. The higher the density, the proportionally higher percentage of nodes is in the area with spreading factor SF7 and less in the area with SF12. Similarly, the lower the density, the proportionally smaller percentage of nodes falls into the area with spreading factor SF7 to the gateway and more into the area with spreading factor SF12. In the remaining areas, the number of nodes in each of them is proportionally comparable regardless of the density of the network. In the Fig. 6 can be observed that as the area increases and, as a consequence, the network density decreases, the values of the bins in distributions of nodes with SF7 to the gateway decrease. In the subsequent charts, the percentage range of nodes having SF7 to the gateway moves left along the horizontal axis, simultaneously the percentage range of nodes with SF12 to the gateway moves right along the

Table 5. Statistics of the proposed greedy algorithm of finding k – dominating set for $k = 3$.

Nodes	Area [m]	Avg. number of gateways	Avg. time [s]	Avg. SF
2500	10000 × 15000	137.43	4.62	9.58
	15000 × 22500	266.5	2.21	9.68
	20000 × 30000	430.87	1.54	9.74
5000	5000 × 7500	50.27	81.38	9.49
	10000 × 15000	147.63	20.66	9.58
	15000 × 22500	289.57	9.82	9.68
	20000 × 30000	470.13	6.07	9.74
10000	5000 × 7500	53.33	366.6	9.47
	10000 × 15000	157.63	84.68	9.54
	15000 × 22500	309.2	35.47	9.62
	20000 × 30000	506.96	20.9	9.68
20000	5000 × 7500m	58.3	2532.12	9.26
	10000 × 15000	165.62	422.78	9.5
	15000 × 22500	327.15	171.19	9.57
	20000 × 30000	539.58	86.86	9.62

same axis. In other words, the lower the network density, the lower the percentage of nodes having SF7 and higher percentage of nodes with SF12 to the gateway (Fig. 7).

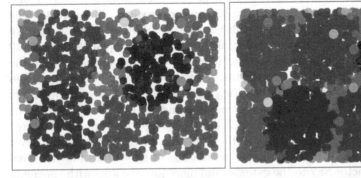

(a) 1000 nodes on 5000m × 7500m area   (b) 2500 nodes on 5000m × 7500m area

Fig. 7. Maps of areas served by gateways selected by the proposed algorithm for two sample random topologies for redundancy factor $k = 1$.

5   Conclusion

We have proposed and evaluated an algorithm for sub-optimal selection of LP WAN gateway locations based on k-dominating set. The proposed algorithm provides the complete coverage for a given set of nodes, taking into account the maximum number of nodes served by a gateway and required redundancy. The performance evaluation using excesive simulations in both real-life topologies and regular topologies proved that the algorithm is able to select near-optimal locations with a low computing time.

References

1. Laiho, J., Wacker, A., Novosad, T.: Radio network planning and optimisation for UMTS, vol. 2. Wiley Online Library (2002)
2. Hurley, S.: Planning effective cellular mobile radio networks. IEEE Trans. Veh. Technol. **51**(2), 243–253 (2002)
3. Alber, J., Fellows, M.R., Niedermeier, R.: Polynomial-time data reduction for dominating set. J. ACM (JACM) **51**(3), 363–384 (2004)
4. CloudRF. https://cloudrf.com/LoRa_planning
5. Radio Mobile Online. https://www.ve2dbe.com/rmonline_s.asp
6. Grochla, K.P.K.: Heuristic algorithm for gateway location selection in large scale LoRa networks. In: Proceedings of the 2020 International Conference on Wireless Communications & Mobile Computing (IWCMC 2020). IEEE (2020)
7. Das, B., Bharghavan, V.: Routing in ad-hoc networks using minimum connected dominating sets. In: 1997 IEEE International Conference on Communications, 1997. ICC 1997 Montreal, Towards the Knowledge Millennium, vol. 1, pp. 376–380. IEEE (1997)
8. Hochbaum, D.S., Shmoys, D.B.: A best possible heuristic for the k-center problem. Math. Oper. Res. **10**(2), 180–184 (1985)
9. Wan, P.J., Alzoubi, K.M., Frieder, O.: Distributed construction of connected dominating set in wireless ad hoc networks. Mob. Networks Appl. **9**(2), 141–149 (2004)
10. Dai, F., Wu, J.: On constructing k-connected k-dominating set in wireless networks. In: Parallel and Distributed Processing Symposium, 2005. Proceedings. 19th IEEE International, 10-pp. IEEE (2005)
11. Foerster, K.T.: Approximating fault-tolerant domination in general graphs. In: Proceedings of the Meeting on Analytic Algorithmics and Combinatorics. Society for Industrial and Applied Mathematics, pp. 25–32 (2013)
12. Zhou, T., Sun, Y., He, S., Shi, Z., Chen, J., Tao, Z.: Gateway planning for hybrid LoRa networks. In: 2019 International Conference on Internet of Things (iThings) and IEEE Green Computing and Communications (GreenCom) and IEEE Cyber, Physical and Social Computing (CPSCom) and IEEE Smart Data (SmartData), pp. 1071–1079. IEEE (2019)

Toolset for Run-Time Dataset Collection of Deep-Scene Information

Gustav Aaro, Daniel Roos, and Niklas Carlsson[✉]

Linköping University, Linköping, Sweden
niklas.carlsson@liu.se

Abstract. Virtual reality (VR) provides many exciting new application opportunities, but also present new challenges. In contrast to 360° videos that only allow a user to select its viewing direction, in fully immersive VR, users can also move around and interact with objects in the virtual world. To most effectively deliver such services it is therefore important to understand how users move around in relation to such objects. In this paper, we present a methodology and software tool for generating run-time datasets capturing a user's interactions with such 3D environments, evaluate and compare different object identification methods that we implement within the tool, and use datasets collected with the tool to demonstrate example uses. The tool was developed in Unity, easily integrates with existing Unity applications through the use of periodic calls that extracts information about the environment using different ray-casting methods. The software tool and example datasets are made available with this paper.

Keywords: Deep-scene data collection · Virtual reality · Unity · Light-weight ray-casting

1 Introduction

Virtual reality (VR) provides a safe way to explore environments that otherwise may not be easily accessible or safe for users. For example, VR can be used to train and prepare people for rare but mission critical situations, explore disaster areas, or simply visit places that otherwise would not be accessible to the user. With current technological advancements, the potential applications of VR appear limited only by our imagination. However, to most effectively deliver such services (e.g., over resource constrained networks and/or by offloading computing to edge-cloud servers) and to make the most appropriate system optimizations, it is important to understand how users interact with these environments.

In this paper, we present a methodology and software tool for generating run-time datasets capturing a user's interactions with such 3D environments. In particular, the tool collects time-series information about the *user's movements* (head position and rotation in the 3D environment) together with *deep-scene information* about the objects visible to the user, including each objects' identifier, the user's distance to the object, the angle offset between the center of the user's field

© Springer Nature Switzerland AG 2021
M. C. Calzarossa et al. (Eds.): MASCOTS 2020, LNCS 12527, pp. 224–236, 2021.
https://doi.org/10.1007/978-3-030-68110-4_15

of view to the closest recorded point on the object, the volume of the object, and a ray-based metric that estimates how visible the object is to the user.

The tool was developed in Unity, easily integrates with existing Unity applications through the use of periodic calls that extracts information about the environment. To collect deep scene information in a game engine, we implement different *ray-casting methods*. First, to provide a close to constant overhead while prioritizing objects close to the center of the user's field of view, we implement an algorithm that uses a Gaussian distribution to carefully distribute the rays over the user's field of view. We then implement lightweight refinement methods to further improve the recall rates of this baseline (at a limited additional overhead) and provide an extension that allows rays to be cast also in other directions. The methods are evaluated against a gold standard that uses a dense grid to capture all objects in static example scenes.

While the tool is developed for the VR context, we note that the data-driven approach enabled by the tool (and VR) potentially also can be used for both qualitative and quantitative studies aiming to better understand how people explore and interact within new environments in general.

To demonstrate how the tool can be used to help understand the user's interactions in the environment, we use the tool to collect a few use-case-driven datasets and use relatively simple methods to illustrate example uses of these datasets[1]. While other papers have produced head-movement datasets for 360° videos [3,4,7–9,12,13], these works typically only focus on the viewing direction within a video, do not consider users movement within 3D environments, and do not collect deep-scene information about the objects visible to the user. This paper addresses this void and presents a novel toolset to capture how users explore these exciting new environments.

Outline: Section 2 presents our general framework, Sect. 3 presents the ray-casting methods used, and Sect. 4 evaluates these methods. We then use datasets to demonstrate example uses (Sect. 5). Finally, we present related works (Sect. 6) and our conclusions (Sect. 7).

2   Methodology Framework

2.1   Environment and Tools

We use the Oculus Rift[2] Head Mounted Display (HMD), consumer version 1, together with the Unity[3] 3D game engine that renders the scenes to the user. Oculus Rift provides a rich open-source SDK, including a specific SDK for Unity. For the experiments and collection of the datasets, we used a Windows 10 workstation (Intel Xeon CPU E5-1620 V4 3.50 GHz) with NVIDIA GeForce GTX 1080 graphics card with a dedicated HDMI video output, and 32.0 GB RAM.

---

[1] Scripts and example datasets are made available here: https://www.ida.liu.se/nikca89/papers/deep-scene-2020.html.
[2] https://www.oculus.com.
[3] https://unity3d.com/.

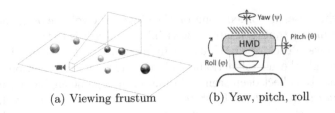

(a) Viewing frustum   (b) Yaw, pitch, roll

Fig. 1. Viewing frustum and direction (relative headset).

2.2 High-Level Framework

Our methodology provides light-weight data collection of time-series traces that for each time instance captures (i) the user's head position, (ii) the user's viewing direction, and (iii) information about the visible objects within the user's field of view. For this purpose, we place a Unity *player camera*[4] at the position of the user's head location and point it in the user's viewing direction. From this location we then use *ray-casting*[5] to determine objects that are visible to the user (and count how many rays hit each visible object). As the name implies, ray-casting is a method used in the Unity game engine that casts a ray in a predetermined direction from a point of origin, and if an object is hit by the ray it returns detailed information about the object that was hit. While this is a very useful method to discover object, it comes at a high computational cost. It is therefore important to limit the number of rays used. In this paper we implement and test different methods to determine the directions to cast rays. Of particular interest are the objects within the *view frustum*, defined as the region of the 3D world that appears on the screen for the user (Fig. 1(a)). For the identified objects, we then collect deep-scene information and record them into a trace file.

Sampling Frequency: While the Oculus headset updates its data at a frequency of 1,000 Hz and has a refresh-rate 90 Hz, through our experiments, we have determined that a reasonable sweet spot to collect sample data about in-engine generated content (such as objects visible to the user) is 50 Hz, which we use for our default settings here. Due to high computational complexity, higher sample frequency can easily result in performance problems (which slow down rendering and can result in user sickness [10]) and lower sample frequency may not be sufficient to track all the objects that a client interacts with.

To trigger all physics-related operations needed for the data collection we use the hook-in method `FixedUpdate`[6] associated with Unity's C#-scripting interface. In particular, we set the *fixed timestep* variable in Unity's `TimeManager` to 0.02 s; providing us 50 Hz "heartbeat".

---

[4] https://docs.unity3d.com/ScriptReference/Camera.html.

[5] https://docs.unity3d.com/ScriptReference/Physics.Raycast.html.

[6] https://docs.unity3d.com/ScriptReference/MonoBehaviour.FixedUpdate.html.

Positional and Rotational Information: We import the *Oculus Platform SDK* assets into Unity and use an `OVRPlayerController` object to gather information about the headset's position (in world coordinates provided by Unity) and rotation (in *yaw, pitch,* and *roll*). Figure 1(b) illustrates these rotations.

2.3 Dataset Structure

Our application saves all sample points in *JSON*-format [5]. Each such JSON entry contains the following:

- The `timestamp` of the sample point.
- Player `position`, using Unity's world coordinates.
- Player `rotation`, using yaw, pitch and roll.
- The collection speed in frames-per-second (`fps`) possible at that specific sample point.
- An array (`visibleObjects`) of visible objects, where each entry contains detailed object information, including (i) a `name` descriptor for the object, (ii) a unique object identifier `id`, (iii) the `distance` between the center point of the player and the object, (iv) the smallest `angle` between the closest observed point of the object and the player, (v) the number of rays that hit the object during the sample point, and (vi) the `volume` of the object's bounding box, as given by the `size` property of the renderer's bounds[7].

3 Object Detection Methods

Determining all objects visible to a user is highly computationally expensive. We therefore design and use relatively light-weight sampling methods that may miss some objects within the user's field of view, but that allows us to sample at a much higher frequency. In this section we describe some key tradeoffs considered (Sect. 3.1), a constant-ray baseline heuristic that prioritizes finding objects closer to the center of the users' viewing direction (Sect. 3.2), and a few refinement methods (Sect. 3.3) that help improve the results.

3.1 Per-Object Vs Constant-Ray Approaches

Two fundamental approaches to identify visible objects are (i) to go through the list of all objects and check whether they appear visible, and (ii) to cast rays within the viewer's viewing frustum and record the objects hit by such rays.

Basic Implementations: Our simplest implementation of the first approach (called *per-object ray-casting*) first performs frustum culling, followed by ray-casting in the center direction of each of the remaining objects. If an object is hit by at least one such a ray, the object is included in the list of visible objects; otherwise it is assumed hidden. We have also considered extensions that cast

---

[7] https://docs.unity3d.com/ScriptReference/Bounds.html.

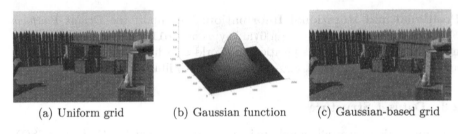

(a) Uniform grid   (b) Gaussian function   (c) Gaussian-based grid

Fig. 2. Per-view ray grid examples using 1700 rays.

additional rays towards different locations within the object's bounding box. In contrast, our implementation of the second approach (called *per-view ray grid*) uses the ScreenPointToRay method built into Unity to map rays within the user's view field according to some distribution. Through experiments, we have found that the second approach typically performs and scales better.

Scaling Problem with Per-Object Rays: Clearly, even a small object can obstruct a ray cast towards a much bigger object, and there may be many objects hidden behind a big object. With the first approach, an important tradeoff therefore arises when determining how many rays should be cast before considering an object hidden. However, in scenes with many objects, the time casting just one ray per object can be substantial and have typically been all that the system can handle 50 Hz for the basic scenes considered here.

In general, this method is not scalable to scenes with many objects (many of which may be hidden). Clearly, in the ideal case, the sampling method should not depend on the number objects in the scene. Therefore, in the following, we focus on the second baseline approach (that uses a constant number of rays, regardless of the number of objects) and optional refinement methods that limit the number of additional objects to consider based on the findings from this baseline approach.

3.2   Baseline Approach: Per-View Ray Grid

To ensure that the number of rays that are cast is independent of the number of objects in the scene, we distribute rays across the user's current view. Figure 2(a) presents a simple example in which we have used a uniform grid of 1,700 rays.

While the uniform distribution is good at detecting objects within the field of view, it does not account for users being more likely to see (and interact with) objects closer to their viewing center. To increase the likelihood that objects closer to the center of the field of view (e.g., the mug in the center of Fig. 2(a)) are not missed, while keeping the same budget of rays fixed, we therefore selected to use a two-dimensional Gaussian distribution function to adjust the grid points. In particular, we use the general expression of a multivariate Gaussian distribution function:

$$f(x,y) = A \cdot e^{-\left(\frac{(x-x_0)^2}{2 \cdot \sigma_x^2} + \frac{(y-y_0)^2}{2 \cdot \sigma_y^2}\right)}, \tag{1}$$

where A is the amplitude of the function, (x_0, y_0) are the median coordinates, and σ_x and σ_y represent the deviations in the x and y dimensions, respectively. First, we empirically searched for good parameters choices, resulting in the following parameter choices: $A = 0.8$, $x_0 = W/2$, $y_0 = H/2$, $\sigma_x = W/8$, and $\sigma_y = H/8$, where W and H represent the width and height of the screen. Second, we used this perturbation function to move all points in the grid towards the center of the screen by a distance proportional to the Gaussian value (Fig. 2(b)) of each coordinate. Figure 2(c) shows the result using the same scene and number of rays as before. We note that the mug that earlier was missed is now hit by multiple rays, illustrating the higher weight given to trying to find objects close to the user's viewing center. Of course, this comes at the cost of potentially missing some objects in the periphery of the viewing field.

3.3   Ray-Casting Refinement Methods

While we have found the *per-view ray grid* method desirable over the *per-object ray* method, in some instances, it clearly misses some objects that a per-object method would find. To reduce the chance of (mis)labeling visible objects as hidden, we developed and tested different enhancement algorithms. Here, we describe two light-weight algorithms and a more computationally expensive algorithm to select a set of objects to perform additional *per-object* ray castings on.

All three methods are designed to enhance the results of the *per-view ray grid* method and the combination can be seen as a hybrid approach. In particular, they all identify a small subset of additional objects, which has not yet been found (using the *per-view ray grid* method), and then (similar to the *per-object ray* method) check the objects in this subset one by one, to see if their center points are visible to the user. We also briefly discuss how the low-cost algorithms can be modified to require a constant number of ray castings.

Delaunay Surface (DS): This method leverages the 3D point cloud defined by the coordinates where each of the original rays cast by the *per-view ray grid* method first hit an object to delimit the set of candidate objects to consider. In particular, the method only considers objects that (i) have not yet been deemed visible, (ii) are within the viewing frustum, and (iii) have a center point closer to the camera than the Delaunay surface defined by these points. The Delaunay 3D surface (exemplified in Fig. 3(a)) is made up by triangles from a Delaunay triangulation with the points in the point cloud making up the vertices on the surface. A Delaunay triangulation maximizes the minimum angle in each triangle and allows us to loop trough all objects meeting the first two criteria above to check whether the intersection between the line passing through the camera and the object's center point would intersect this surface before or after passing through the objects center point. To do so, we first determine the intersection triangle, and then calculate the point where the projection line intersects the plane defined by this triangle. If this point is further away from the user then the candidate object's center point (i.e. the object is between the 3D surface and the user), the object is included in the candidate set of objects to check

(a) 3D Delaunay surface   (b) RoI using DT, $P = 0.5$

Fig. 3. Example boundaries for region of interest (RoI). (Color figure online)

further. While this method nicely can prune the search space of objects, it is computationally expensive.

Percentile-Based Distance Threshold (DT): To reduce the complexity and allow users to tune the number of rays that need to be cast, we implemented a *percentile-based distance threshold* (DT) method. First, all distances between the camera and the points in the point cloud are sorted. Second, a distance threshold D_P is determined that corresponds to a specific percentile P of these distances. Third, we only include the objects that (i) have not yet been deemed visible, (ii) are within the viewing frustum, and (iii) have a distance $d < D_P$ to its center point. Figure 3(b) shows the point cloud (red line) and region of interest (blue area) when using $P = 0.5$, for a simple 2D example. It is important to note that in comparison to ray-casting, determining which objects fall within the viewing frustum is inexpensive.

Finally, we note that DT easily can be modified to return no more than a constant number of objects. For example, simply sort the distances to the center points of all objects that satisfy the first two (or three) criteria and select the K closest such objects. In this paper, we focus on the hybrid version of DT, described more carefully above.

Angular Threshold (AT): This method is similar to DT, but uses a threshold α on the angle offset θ_i of object i to determine which objects to consider further. In particular, the method selects the set of objects that (i) have not yet been deemed visible, (ii) are within the viewing frustum, and (iii) have an angular offset $\theta_i < \alpha$. We note that many hidden objects may be included by this method, and that a maximum distance (as used with DT, for example) therefore ideally also should be used. As with DT, this method can also easily be modified to bound the number of objects to (at most) K, using the offset angle θ_i to rank candidates.

4   Methodology Evaluation

While our system is designed to capture the objects within the user's view also in dynamic environments with lots of movement, for our ground-truth-based

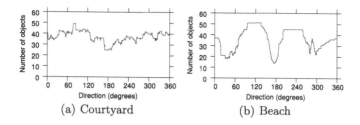

(a) Courtyard   (b) Beach

Fig. 4. Number of visible objects in each direction using the gold standard approach.

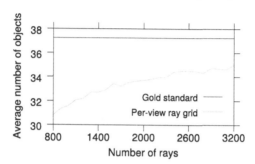

Fig. 5. Average number of objects detected as a function of the number of rays used by *per-view ray grid*. (Courtyard)

validation we used two scenes supplied by a third party[8]: *Courtyard* and *Beach*. The Courtyard scene (e.g., Fig. 3(b)) is densely populated with objects close to the user, whereas the objects in the Beach scene are significantly further away and more clustered. For each scene, we placed the player in the center of the scene, spun the player 360° at a constant speed, and recorded the objects identified under different parameter settings.

Gold Standard: To generate a type of ground-truth, called the *gold standard* here, we slowly moved the camera around its z-axis while casting vertically spaced rays. By slow rotation of these even spaced rays we created a 9,000 × 2,000 grid of rays, spanning the full 360° view, giving us higher than per-pixel granularity of the objects in the scene. Through post-processing we then recreated exactly which objects are visible within the field of view of each viewing direction. Figure 4 shows the number of objects possible to observe using this approach for each viewing direction.

4.1   Impact of Grid Density

Figure 5 shows the average number of objects detected over all (sample) directions as a function of the number of rays used with the *per-view ray grid*

---

[8] Mega Fantasy Props Pack: https://assetstore.unity.com/packages/3d/environments/fantasy/mega-fantasy-props-pack-87811.

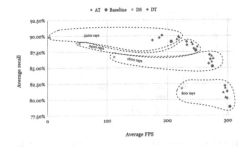
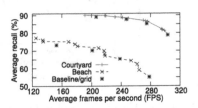

Fig. 6. FPS and recall scores for each method, with points grouped based on the number of rays by the original baseline.

Fig. 7. Recall-FPS tradeoff frontiers.

approach. As a comparison, we also include the average number of visible objects as determined by the *gold standard*. We note that the *per-view ray grid* baseline performs well and achieve within 7% of the gold standard when using a grid with 3,200 rays. However, we also observe diminishing recall returns, motivating the use of refinement methods such as those considered here.

4.2   Refinement Method Comparison

To compare the different refinement algorithms, we started with using the *per-view ray grid* method with grids of 800, 1600, 2400 and 3200 rays. For DT we used percentile thresholds of $P = 0.5$, 0.7, and 0.9, and for AT we used the angular thresholds: $\alpha = 20°$, 30°, and 40°. Figure 6 shows a scatter plot of the average recall rate versus the average frames per seconds (FPS) across the samples of each of these methods and settings. Here, the recall rate (of each sample) is equal to the fraction of objects identified by the gold standard that the method tagged correctly, and we group the data points based on the number of rays used in the original grid.

The baseline and refinement methods did not discover any object that the gold standard did not discover. The precision is therefore always 100% and the F1-score is always $2r/(1 + r)$, where r is the recall. Of this reason, throughout, we only use recall (not precision or F1 scores).

Significant variations in the FPS metric caused some anomalies. For example, there are instances where the refinement methods have higher FPS than the corresponding baseline alone. These cases can be explained by unrelated background processes (running on the same Windows-PC). Some caution should hence be taken when interpreting the FPS values. However, in general we clearly see that additional rays tends to increase the recall and decrease the FPS. Therefore, it is perhaps not surprising that DS typically have the lowest FPS and among the highest recall. The simplicity of both DT and AT provide more attractive trade-offs, with DT typically giving slightly better recall scores. This is most apparent with increased ray counts. Finally, we note that the gap in recall between the best methods in the 800 ray cluster and the baseline in the 1,600 ray cluster is

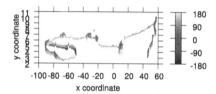
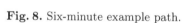

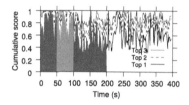

Fig. 8. Six-minute example path.

Fig. 9. Example scores of the top-3 objects over time.

due to many of the missed objects having hidden centers, showing that additional rays (e.g., with a denser grid or with more per-object rays) are needed to find these objects. Overall, we have found that the hybrid approaches analyzed here provides a nice tradeoff, pushing up the recall at a very limit overhead.

In general, the beach scene is much more challenging than the courtyard scene. Figure 7 plots the recall-FPS tradeoff frontiers (using the analogy of a Pareto frontier) for the two scenes. We note a substantial shift of the tradeoff curve, with the maximum recall differing by 14%. To put the frontiers in perspective, we also include markers for the four baseline experiments, again demonstrating the improvements provided by the lightweight refinement methods.

5   Example Use Case

The tool has many use cases and can be used for both qualitative and quantitative studies. For example, consider a crime scene analysis. Using a 3D map of a city, for example, an investigator can use test users to better understand what witnesses or victims are more or less likely to have seen. For example, a test user may be asked to walk the path of an actual witness or victim (potentially recreated using GPS, base station IDs, and/or other network operator related data). Qualitatively, example paths such as the one in Fig. 8 (in which we walked through a Viking village[9] looking for swords) of multiple test users can corroborate witness statements.

To aid in better understanding what objects a person is more likely to have seen, per-object ray counts and other scoring criteria can be used. Figure 9 shows the cumulative score associated with the top-three objects on a second-per-second basis. Here, we use a basic scoring function $\sum_{t \in T}(w_d \frac{1}{d_t} + w_\alpha \frac{1}{\alpha_t} + w_n n_t)$, where T is a time interval of interest, w_d, w_α, w_n are weights, d_t is the distance to the object at time t, α_t is the smallest angle to the object at time t, and n_t is the number of rays that hit the object at time t. For our example results, we set the weights so that the three factors are roughly equally weighted. First, without loss of generality, we chose $w_d = 1$. Second, we express the other weights relative to

---

[9] https://assetstore.unity.com/packages/essentials/tutorial-projects/viking-village-29140.

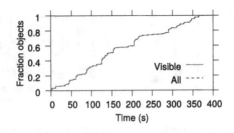

Fig. 10. Objects observed over time.

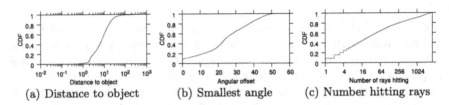

(a) Distance to object   (b) Smallest angle   (c) Number hitting rays

Fig. 11. Example CDFs.

this: $w_\alpha = \sum_{t,i} \frac{1}{d_t} / \sum_{t,i} \frac{1}{\alpha_t}$ and $w_n = \sum_{t,i} \frac{1}{d_t} / \sum_{t,i} n_t$, where the sums are over all observed samples (i.e., both over time t and visible objects i). Furthermore, for the first 200 s we use colors to indicate when the identity of the highest scored object changes.

Finally, note that various distribution statistics may be useful to better understand the rate that new objects appear (Fig. 10), the objects relative locations (Figs. 11(a) and 11(b)), or the number of rays that hits the objects (Fig. 11(c)). Comparing these statistics with the corresponding values (and scores) for specific objects may provide insight into the relative presence certain objects have. Of course, this does not account for color differences, contrast, and other aspects that may cause certain objects to stick out to an observer. Furthermore, the tool we use does not capture eye gaze [2], which could further improve the use of this type of tool.

6   Related Work

While there is a significant amount of use-case-driven research leveraging VR, there is a lack of generic tools to collect deep-scene information. In early work (2004), Chittaro and Ieronutti [6] present a tool for analyzing users' interactions with virtual environments through tracking of their position and orientation. However, they focus on the visualization aspects and do not collect any deep-scene information about the objects. Others have collected avatar traces and similar for virtual worlds [15] and games [11]. Since the official Oculus Rift release in March 2016, there have been many dataset papers and research studies using head movement [3,4,7–9,12,13] or eye gaze [2] data for 360° video. However, these works typically only focus on the viewing direction, as these videos do not

(a) View from above   (b) Side view

Fig. 12. Third-person example of 360 peripheral: forward-facing rays (magenta), backward-facing rays (green). (Color figure online)

allow users to move around within the environment. In contrast, in our context, users can move around and their interactions can change the scene itself (e.g., as both objects and users move). None of the prior works collect deep-scene information about the objects visible to the user.

Finally, we note that the data link between the HMD and the computer has extremely high data rate requirement and delay constraints. This complicates creating an untethered experience [1] and how to best deliver remote service [14]. Such important efforts to provide improved VR experiences are orthogonal to the work presented here.

7   Conclusions

This paper presents a methodology and software tool for generating run-time datasets capturing user movements and visible objects in immersive 3D environments. Collecting deep-scene information in a game engine such as Unity is non-trivial and requires careful ray casting. Our tool implements baseline methods to carefully distribute the rays over the user's field of view and refinement methods that improves the recall rates at limited additional processing overhead. The methods are evaluated against a gold standard.

Our tool collects information about the users' movements (position, rotation) at a tunable time granularity together with information about the objects visible to the user, including each object's identifier, distance, angle offset, volume, and how many rays hit the object at each time instance. While our validation is done with two static environments, our tool also works for dynamic environments with moving objects.

Finally, we use example datasets and relatively simple methods to illustrate example use cases. Interesting future work include user studies (using the tool) to be better understand users' interactions with selected example objects, but also the development of methods (based on extensions of the tool) for improving user experiences and system performance. For example, while the algorithms used here focus on objects within the viewing frustum, our tool also includes an extension that collects information about peripheral objects. Figure 12 illustrates the rays cast when operating in this extended mode. Future work will evaluate the use of such extensions for predicting objects that are likely to appear for the user.

Acknowledgments. This work was funded in part by the Swedish Research Council (VR).

References

1. Abari, O.: Enabling high-quality untethered virtual reality. In: Proceedings ACM Workshop on Millimeter-Wave Networks and Sensing Systems (2017)
2. Agtzidis, I., Startsev, M., Dorr, M.: 360° video gaze behaviour: a ground-truth data set and a classification algorithm for eye movements. In: Proceedings ACM Multimedia (2019)
3. Almquist, M., Almquist, V., Krishnamoorthi, V., Carlsson, N., Eager, D.: The prefetch aggressiveness tradeoff in 360° video streaming. In: Proceedings ACM MMSys (2018)
4. Bao, Y., Wu, H., Zhang, T., Ramli, A., Liu, X.: Shooting a moving target: motion-prediction-based transmission for 360° videos. In: Proceedings IEEE Big Data (2016)
5. Bray, T.: The JavaScript object notation (JSON) data interchange format. RFC 8259, Internet standard, IETF (2017)
6. Chittaro, L., Ieronutti, L.: A visual tool for tracing users' behavior in virtual environments. In: Proceedings AVI (2004)
7. Corbillon, X., Simone, F.D., Simon, G.: 360° video head movement dataset. In: Proceedings ACM MMSys (2017)
8. David, E.J., Gutiérrez, J., Coutrot, A., Da Silva, M.P., Callet, P.L.: A dataset of head and eye movements for 360° videos. In: Proceedings ACM MMSys (2018)
9. Fremerey, S., Singla, A., Meseberg, K., Raake, A.: AVtrack360: an open dataset and software recording people's head rotations watching 360° videos on an HMD. In: Proceedings ACM MMSys (2018)
10. LaViola Jr, J.J.: A discussion of cyber sickness in virtual environments. ACM SIGCHI Bull. (2000)
11. Lee, Y.T., Chen, K.T., Cheng, Y.M., Lei, C.L.: World of Warcraft avatar history dataset. In: Proceedings ACM MMSys (2011)
12. Lo, W., Fan, C., Lee, J., Huang, C., Chen, K., Hsu, C.: 360° video viewing dataset in head-mounted virtual reality. In: Proceedings ACM MMSys (2017)
13. Qian, F., Han, B., Xiao, Q., Gopalakrishnan, V.: Flare: Practical viewport-adaptive 360° video streaming for mobile devices. In: Proceedings ACM MobiCom (2018)
14. Tan, Z., Li, Y., Li, Q., Zhang, Z., Li, Z., Lu, S.: Supporting mobile VR in LTE networks: How close are we? In: Proceedings of ACM SIGMETRICS (2018)
15. Varvello, M., Ferrari, S., Biersack, E., Diot, C.: Exploring second life. IEEE/ACM Trans. Networking (2010)

Measurement and Modeling of Tumblr Traffic

Rachel Mclean$^{(\boxtimes)}$, Mehdi Karamollahi, and Carey Williamson

University of Calgary, Calgary, AB, Canada
{rarmclea,mehdi.karamollahi,cwill}@ucalgary.ca

Abstract. Tumblr is a popular microblogging platform that allows users to share content and interact with other users. This paper focuses on the measurement and modeling of Tumblr network traffic characteristics, since few studies have focused on Tumblr from this perspective. Our work uses a combination of active and passive approaches to network traffic measurement. Using Wireshark and mitmproxy, we identify the primary hosts associated with Tumblr traffic, the traffic patterns associated with specific user actions, and the TCP connection behaviour. We then study Tumblr usage by our campus community for one week, using passively collected connection summaries. As a frame of reference, we also compare this traffic with several other popular social media platforms with user-generated content, namely Facebook, Instagram, and Twitter. Our work identifies several similarities and differences in the network traffic patterns for these social networking sites. We also develop and calibrate a synthetic workload model for Tumblr network traffic.

Keywords: Network traffic measurement · Internet traffic characterization · Workload modeling · Online social networks · Tumblr · TCP/IP

1 Introduction

Today's Internet supports many different online social network (OSN) communities. Facebook is the most well-known OSN, with nearly 26 billion monthly visits worldwide. Its familiar structure focuses on creating networks of people, organizing social events, and providing user-specific services. However, there is a wide variety of other social media platforms, including microblogging platforms like Twitter and Tumblr. The latter two examples focus more on providing a platform for curating and sharing user-generated content.

OSN sites with user-generated content have experienced tremendous growth in popularity over the past decade. Instagram [16] is a particularly interesting example; owned by Facebook, Instagram began as a photo and video sharing site, but has since grown into an immensely popular social media platform, with recently added functionality for voice calls, instant messaging, and live video streaming. Currently, Instagram has over one billion users who are active on

© Springer Nature Switzerland AG 2021
M. C. Calzarossa et al. (Eds.): MASCOTS 2020, LNCS 12527, pp. 237–253, 2021.
https://doi.org/10.1007/978-3-030-68110-4_16

at least a monthly basis. A typical day has more than 500 million users active, posting more than 400 million stories [6].

Tumblr is another example of a social media platform with user-generated content. Tumblr is organized around the concept of the blogosphere, but with microblogging as its key idea. On Tumblr, users can create and curate their own microblogs, with any topic or media content type of their choosing. The microblogs in Tumblr span many diverse topics, including anime, cooking, fitness, gardening, hiking, movies, music, sports, yoga, and more.

In this paper, we focus on characterizing the usage of Tumblr by our campus community (i.e., faculty, staff, and students), and comparing its usage patterns with those of Facebook, Instagram, and Twitter, which have been well-studied in the prior literature. One motivation for our work is the lack of recent measurement studies of Tumblr, especially from a networking viewpoint. Another motivation is a desire to compare and contrast Tumblr with other OSN applications. Although existing social media platforms each serve different niches, we find several similarities in their underlying usage. For example, OSNs tend to generate long-duration sessions, often involving media objects with heavy-tailed transfer sizes.

The primary research questions examined in this paper are:

– What are the key characteristics of Tumblr traffic?
– How does Tumblr compare to other OSN applications in terms of network traffic usage patterns?

For our study, we collected information about Tumblr and other OSN sites for a one-week period in February 2020. We analyze this traffic in terms of usage patterns at the application, transport, and network layers. First, we characterize the network traffic patterns for Tumblr and other popular OSN sites. Second, we characterize the TCP connections and transfer sizes used. Third, we identify several characteristics that appear similar or different across these OSN sites. Finally, we design and implement a synthetic workload model for Tumblr traffic that can be used in network simulations or capacity planning studies.

The remainder of this paper is organized as follows. Section 2 provides background information on Tumblr, and reviews related research on Internet traffic measurement. Section 3 describes our measurement methodology. Section 4 provides a workload characterization of Tumblr traffic on our campus network, and compares these findings to the other OSN traffic observed. Section 5 presents our synthetic workload model for Tumblr network traffic. Finally, Section 6 concludes the paper.

2   Background and Related Work

This section provides some background information on Tumblr and network traffic measurement research.

2.1   Tumblr

Tumblr is a short-form blogging platform [15] that was launched in 2007. It currently has nearly 500 million blogs and 17 million daily posts [14].

Tumblr shares many features with Twitter and Instagram, but with fewer limitations on post type and length, allowing for highly diverse content. Each user has at least one dedicated blog with its own associated Tumblr URL.

Tumblr blogs are generally accessible to anyone, including non-Tumblr users. These blogs typically contain a chronological list of all posts published on that blog (including original and reblogged content), along with a brief user bio, a customized theme, and a set of links for navigating that user's blog. However, for Tumblr users, most of the interaction with other users is not done via their individual blogs, but via the functionality in the Tumblr 'dashboard'. The dashboard is only accessible to authenticated Tumblr users, and contains a time-ordered feed of content from all the blogs being followed.

Tumblr allows several different types of original posts, including text, audio, video, images, and external links. However, text posts may (and frequently do) include photos, links, and videos. Similarly, any user may append additional content of various types as a comment when reblogging a post.

Users may interact with a post in many different ways:

- *reblog*: copying a post to the user's own blog [19];
- *queue*: adding a copy of the post to a queue for later publication according to some user-specified time interval;
- *schedule*: setting a specific day and time for the post to be published to the user's blog;
- *save draft*: adding a copy of the post to a collection of drafts to be reviewed, posted, or deleted at a later time;
- *share*: allowing users to share a link to the post via Twitter or Facebook, or by sending a direct link to another Tumblr user using Tumblr's instant messenger;
- *like*: adding the post to a collection of 'liked' posts; and
- *reply*: adding a message that appears in the notifications for the post creator, and in the post's public history, but is not itself published to anyone's dashboard.

2.2   Related Work

Many papers in the literature have explored the complexities of online social networks [3–5,8,9,13]. As the total population of social media users continues to grow, the ability to accurately characterize OSN user behaviour is increasingly valuable. Developing a clear understanding of network usage, number of requests, and data traffic volume can provide useful insights on how to improve protocol efficiency and user experience on a given platform or network.

One common approach to OSN research is to focus on the social aspects of interactions. For example, researchers have examined the structure and behaviour of social networks [9], analyzed click-stream data of browsing sessions [13], and characterized the behaviour of the users themselves [3,8].

Relatively few papers have dealt with Tumblr specifically. In 2014, Xu *et al.* [20] analyzed 23.2 million users and 10.2 billion posts over four months. They found that the majority of content in Tumblr is recirculated in the form of reblogged posts. They also found that Tumblr posts tended to have a longer lifespan on average than posts on other social media and microblogging platforms. By cross-referencing both implicit and explicit links on Twitter and Tumblr, they identified more than 6.5 million cross-linked pairs of users on the two platforms. Also in 2014, Chang *et al.* [4] characterized Tumblr in terms of user content, connections, and activity. A year later, in 2015, Alrajebah [1] examined content propagation across Tumblr by characterizing the cascade structure of reblogs.

While many of these papers prioritize analysis of OSN content, a higher level analysis of traffic patterns in terms of volume and connection characteristics can reveal useful insights into network performance. In 2018, Roy *et al.* [12] conducted a network measurement study of Learning Management System (LMS) traffic, identifying several issues at the transport layer that resulted in sluggish network performance. More recently, in 2019, Klenow *et al.* [7] measured Instagram traffic on a campus network, showing that this traffic averaged approximately 1 TB of data per day, and had very consistent usage patterns from one weekday to the next. Our work is similar in flavour to these latter two studies, but with a focus on Tumblr network traffic.

3   Methodology

Our research methodology involved a combination of active and passive approaches to network traffic measurement [17]. The active approach was applied to study micro-scale aspects of Tumblr traffic for specific user test sessions conducted by us. The passive approach was used to provide a macro-scale view of Tumblr usage by our campus community as a whole.

3.1   Active Measurements

We conducted active measurements using our own client laptop in order to test Tumblr features and study browsing sessions on both Google Chrome and Mozilla Firefox. During these scripted test sessions, two existing network traffic analysis tools were used to passively capture network-level data, namely Wireshark and mitmproxy.

Wireshark [18] is an open-source network protocol analyzer. It captures packets as they pass through the network and displays them in a human-readable format, including IP addresses, port numbers, content length, and flags. Wireshark has powerful filtering capability and statistical analysis tools, which are helpful for identifying TCP connection behaviour associated with Tumblr and specific user actions.

Figure 1 shows an example of a Tumblr browsing session, based on a Wireshark capture that lasted just over one minute. This graph shows a time-series representation of the user activity on a single TCP connection to Tumblr. The vertical axis shows the bursts of network traffic (in bytes) as Tumblr pages and objects are accessed, while the horizontal axis illustrates the timing structure for the user's interactions as indicated on the graph. Tumblr sessions generate bursty on-off patterns in the network traffic because of the think times between user interactions, such as page downloads, uploads, or reblogging events.

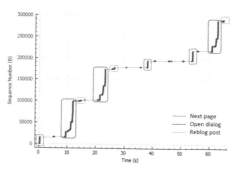

Fig. 1. Annotated TCP sequence number plot of a Tumblr browsing session

Because Tumblr's network traffic is encrypted (HTTPS), data collection was supplemented by the use of mitmproxy [10], a tool for intercepting secure network traffic between the server and client. We used this tool to identify traffic to and from Tumblr. During these test sessions, two IP addresses (152.199.24.192 and 152.195.50.59) were identified as responsible for the majority of Tumblr traffic.

Table 1 summarizes all of the Tumblr-related IP addresses identified during our active measurements. Some of the domain names (e.g., Yahoo, Oath, Verizon) and IP addresses reflect the historical evolution of Tumblr as a social media platform [14,15].

Table 1. IP addresses observed for Tumblr traffic

Domain name	IP address
www.tumblr.com	152.199.24.192
assets.tumblr.com	
px.srvcs.tumblr.com	
api.tumblr.com	
66.media.tumblr.com	152.195.50.59
static.tumblr.com	
tspmagic.tumblr.com	35.211.245.42
fc.yahoo.com	216.115.100.124
opus.analytics.yahoo.com	152.199.24.48
consent.cmp.oath.com	152.195.55.192
(unknown Verizon/ANS)	152.195.14.41

3.2 Passive Measurements

The primary network traffic dataset for our research was obtained using the connection logs from Zeek (formerly known as Bro [11]). This network monitor passively records connection-level summaries of traffic between our campus network and the Internet. These summaries do not include packet payloads, but do include source and destination IP addresses, port numbers, connection duration, connection state, as well as the number of packets and bytes that are sent and received on each TCP connection.

Our research used connection logs from a one-week period between Sunday, February 2 and Saturday, February 8, 2020. This period is well into the regular Winter semester, but before the COVID-19 pandemic that led to the University of Calgary switching to distance learning mode on March 15, 2020. These logs were filtered by IP address to consider only the relevant addresses that were identified during active measurements.

4 Network Traffic Characterization

This section presents our workload characterization of Tumblr network traffic. We begin with an overview of the OSN traffic on our campus network, and then proceed to study Tumblr's diurnal traffic patterns, connection-level characteristics, and session-level characteristics. We also highlight similarities and differences compared to other OSN traffic.

4.1 OSN Traffic Overview

A measurement study of Tumblr and other OSN applications provides an opportunity to compare their characteristics and to gain a better perspective on Tumblr's traffic. For this purpose, we selected three of the most popular OSNs (Facebook, Instagram, and Twitter), and collected measurements for the exact same one-week period (February 2–8, 2020). Prior to collecting this empirical data, we used active measurements to determine the main IP addresses used by these OSNs, whether connecting via a Web browser or their mobile applications.

Unlike Tumblr, most other OSNs use cloud-based services like Amazon Web Services (AWS) and/or Content Distribution Networks (CDNs) to deliver a lot of their content, such as multimedia files. It is non-trivial to find the exact IP addresses of the CDNs used by these OSNs, since depending on the time of the day, type of content, and other characteristics of the content, the IPs change frequently. For example, depending on the Twitter account page from which content is being retrieved, the CDN may vary. Furthermore, it is difficult to determine whether the observed IPs are being used for any other non-OSN services on the Internet. Therefore, for this study, we have only used the IP addresses that are owned and managed by these OSNs, and used consistently in all the traces.

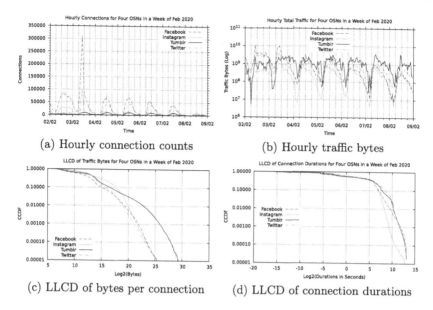

(a) Hourly connection counts

(b) Hourly traffic bytes

(c) LLCD of bytes per connection

(d) LLCD of connection durations

Fig. 2. Comparison between traffic characteristics of four OSNs over one week (Feb 2–8, 2020)

Figure 2(a) shows a comparison between the four OSN sites in terms of the number of TCP connections per hour. As one might expect, Facebook received more connections than the other three OSNs in this week. Twitter had the second most connections, with Instagram third, and Tumblr having the fewest connections. Facebook also had the greatest variability in its connection activity, with a pronounced spike on the Monday, and a slight decline in activity throughout the week. The other three OSNs are much more consistent in their day-to-day traffic patterns, except for the weekends.

Figure 2(b) shows the hourly data traffic volume (in bytes) for the four OSNs under consideration. Surprisingly, the data traffic volume for Tumblr is comparable to, and sometimes higher than, the data volumes for the other three OSNs during the week, even though the number of TCP connections is much lower for Tumblr. This observation reflects larger media objects being transferred over Tumblr, as is evident from the Log-Log Complementary Distribution (LLCD) plot of transfer sizes in Fig. 2(c). Specifically, Tumblr has some transfer sizes that exceed 500 MB, while the transfer sizes for the other three OSNs rarely exceed 50 MB. Another contributing factor is the use of CDNs (e.g., Akamai, Fastly) for storing and delivering large media objects for some OSNs, like Facebook. At the time of our study, Tumblr did not seem to use any CDNs at all.

Figure 2(d) shows the LLCD plots of connection durations for the four OSNs. These distributions look quite similar across the four OSN sites, even in the tails. However, Instagram has a slightly shorter tail to the distribution than Tumblr.

4.2   Tumblr Traffic Overview

Figure 3 provides a graphical overview of the Tumblr traffic characteristics, using the same format as Fig. 2. The four lines on these graphs correspond to the four main IP addresses associated with Tumblr, namely the Web server (152.199.24.192), the media server (152.195.50.59), oath.com (152.195.55.192), and Verizon/ANS (152.195.14.41). We discuss these traffic characteristics over the next few subsections.

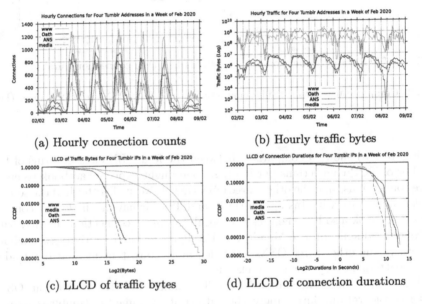

(a) Hourly connection counts   (b) Hourly traffic bytes

(c) LLCD of traffic bytes   (d) LLCD of connection durations

Fig. 3. Tumblr traffic characteristics for one week (Feb 2–8, 2020) (Color figure online)

Table 2 shows the total volume of data transferred to and from the two primary Tumblr IP addresses identified earlier in Sect. 3. Two observations are evident from this table. First, the volume of inbound traffic dominates the outbound traffic, with nearly 98% of Tumblr traffic being inbound. This asymmetric traffic pattern is similar to that observed for other OSNs, such as Instagram [7]. Second, the media server for Tumblr (IP 152.195.50.59) is responsible for approximately three times as much data traffic volume as the main Web server (IP 152.199.24.192), despite having fewer TCP connections.

4.3   Tumblr Traffic Patterns

We next study the pattern of Tumblr traffic over time, in terms of hourly connections and hourly data traffic volume.

Figure 3(a) plots the number of new TCP connections initiated to Tumblr in every one-hour interval for one week of observation. These plots show clear diurnal patterns: the number of connections is lowest in the early hours of the morning, rises sharply to a peak around noon, then falls again in the evening. The number of Tumblr connections drops off markedly on the weekends, since fewer people are on campus.

Table 2. Summary of Tumblr traffic asymmetry

IP address	Pkts out	Bytes out	Pkts in	Bytes in
152.199.24.192	21,335,822	1.7 GB	33,635,987	43.8 GB
152.195.50.59	51,700,867	2.4 GB	100,808,104	143.4 GB
Total	73,036,689	4.1 GB	134,444,091	187.2 GB

The weekday traffic for Tumblr is fairly consistent on a day-to-day basis, suggesting that Tumblr users are creatures of habit. This consistency of usage is stronger than that seen in our earlier studies of LMS traffic on our campus network [12], but not quite as pronounced as the consistency seen for Instagram traffic [7]. One small difference in the Tumblr traffic is the "shoulder" effect in the late evenings, which is most evident for the Web server traffic. This plateau is possibly due to students in the campus residences who access Tumblr after classes have ended for the day.

Another interesting observation from Fig. 3 is the relative number of connections to each Tumblr server address. The main Web server has the highest number of connections. The numbers of connections to Oath and Verizon/ANS are smaller; furthermore, the activity to each of these two sites seems to move in tandem, suggesting that they are closely related. Finally, the media server consistently has fewer daily TCP connections than the other three Tumblr addresses, although it is responsible for the largest proportion of the byte traffic in Fig. 3(b). The latter observation implies that it tends to deliver larger objects; this observation will be confirmed shortly in our upcoming traffic analyses.

Figure 3(b) plots the hourly total data volume (in bytes) for Tumblr traffic. The total amount of data transferred varies widely across the four main IP addresses, so the number of traffic bytes is shown on a log scale (base 10), to more clearly display the hourly traffic patterns. As mentioned earlier, the Web server (yellow line) and media object server (pink line) account for substantially more data volume than the other two server addresses (shown in blue and green).

4.4   Tumblr Transfer Sizes

Figure 3(c) shows LLCD plots of the bytes per connection for the four Tumblr-associated IP addresses. This value demonstrates substantial variation, with some connections transferring very few bytes, and others approaching 1 GB. In the graph, the number of bytes per connection is shown on a log scale (base 2). This figure shows clear differences between the primary IP addresses (shown in pink and yellow) and the secondary addresses (shown in blue and green). The primary addresses have a pronounced tail to the transfer size distribution, with a slow and gradual decline similar to a LogNormal distribution. In contrast, the data volumes for the secondary addresses decline earlier and more sharply, suggesting a lighter tail to these distributions.

4.5   Tumblr Connection Durations

We next examine the duration of TCP connections to Tumblr recorded in the Zeek connection logs. This value measures the time elapsed between the first and last observed packet over a single connection. The TCP connection durations vary widely, with many connections lasting less than a second while others last a few hours. The average connection durations for the primary IP addresses were 100.2 s for the media server, and 110.1 s for the Web server. These durations are even longer than the 72-s average observed for Instagram, which also uses persistent connections [7].

Figure 3(d) shows LLCD plots of TCP connection duration for the four main addresses associated with Tumblr, with the durations shown on a log scale (base 2). These plots show that the distribution of connection duration is similar for all four addresses measured, suggesting that Tumblr connection durations are not directly related to transfer sizes. A more detailed statistical analysis (not shown here) confirms that the correlation between transfer size and connection duration is rather weak.

Two particularly interesting observations from our Tumblr datasets are the large sizes of some of the transfers for a "microblogging" site (e.g., 320 MB), and the extremely low throughputs achieved (e.g., about 5 Mbps). Since the transfers are encrypted, we do not know the types of the objects involved. We speculate that the low throughput is attributable to both the persistent connection timeouts being used, as well as the window-limited TCP performance between Calgary and Tumblr (e.g., 64 KB of data every RTT).

To better understand the long-lasting TCP connections, some additional active measurement experiments were performed. These test sessions revealed a regular "API ping" between the client and the Tumblr Web server every 30 s, to update status information for the user. This "keep-alive" feature is unique to Tumblr, and helps explain some of the long-lasting connections with very little data volume.

4.6   Tumblr Connection State

We next analyze the TCP connection states recorded in the connection logs. A typical TCP connection, opened with a SYN flag and terminated with a FIN flag, will have a recorded final state SF, while a connection that is terminated with a RST flag may have a recorded final state of RSTO (reset by the originator) or RSTR (reset by the responder). Other connections may be only partially[1] observed, including connections that are attempted but not established (S0), connections that are established but not terminated (S1), or connections where only midstream traffic is observed without opening or closing handshakes (OTH).

Table 3 shows the relative frequency of different connection states in the dataset of Tumblr connections. SF connections are the most common, accounting for approximately 25% of connections to the Web server and 30% of those to the media server. Among the remaining connections, RSTO, OTH, and S1 are the most frequent final states for both addresses. The RSTO connections may be due to user actions interrupting TCP connections, or resource management policies that use resets to terminate idle TCP connections. One explanation for the unusually high frequency of OTH and S1 states may be the repeated API pings and long connection durations described in Sect. 4.5.

Table 3. TCP connection states for Tumblr traffic

Connection state	152.199.24.192 (www)		152.195.50.59 (media)	
	Conns (%)	Bytes (%)	Conns (%)	Bytes (%)
SF	26.36%	39.42%	32.23%	34.35%
RSTO	22.10%	24.11%	19.36%	22.98%
OTH	16.56%	12.24%	15.83%	14.75%
S1	15.29%	12.74%	15.04%	16.01%
RSTOS0	7.01%	4.08%	5.43%	5.88%
RSTRH	3.61%	0.49%	1.08%	0.65%
SHR	2.65%	0.52%	6.45%	0.45%
RSTR	2.62%	2.96%	1.61%	2.54%
S3	1.78%	2.98%	1.53%	1.90%
S0	1.24%	0.00%	0.59%	0.00%
S2	0.42%	0.31%	0.52%	0.34%
SH	0.27%	0.09%	0.28%	0.15%
REJ	0.09%	0.05%	0.04%	0.01%
Total	100.0%	100.0%	100.0%	100.0%

4.7   Session-Level Characteristics

Figure 4(a) shows an example of the Tumblr connection activity for one user during a session that lasted about 45 min. The horizontal axis is time, and the vertical axis shows the TCP source port number used by the campus NAT. In general, the port numbers increase monotonically upward with time, until they

---

[1] Our network traffic monitor is restarted every 3 h to reduce the risks of data loss.

reach the maximum possible port value in the range, and wrap around to the lower end of the range again. Each '+' on the plot indicates the start time of a TCP connection to a Tumblr server (www or media). The horizontal lines, when present, indicate the time duration of the connection. A solid line is used for connections to the Tumblr Web server, and a dashed line for connections to the Tumblr media server.

Several observations are evident from Fig. 4(a). First, about 75% of the 78 connections in this session were to the Tumblr Web server, with the rest to the Tumblr media server. Second, most of the connection durations are short, but there are a few long ones, as evident from the lines on the graph. Third, there are several examples of multiple TCP connections in parallel, either to the Web server, or to the media server, or to both servers concurrently. In most cases, there are clear timing dependencies between these connections, which either start at very similar times, or end at very similar times.

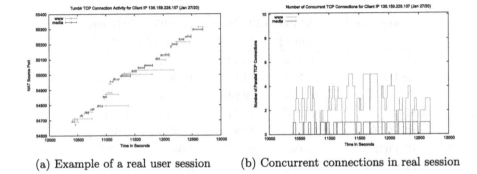

(a) Example of a real user session   (b) Concurrent connections in real session

Fig. 4. Example of connection-level characteristics for a real Tumblr session

Figure 4(b) provides a detailed look at the use of parallel TCP connections during this user session with the Tumblr site. This user maintains up to five TCP connections in parallel with the Tumblr Web server, and at most one TCP connection with the media server. The number of concurrent connections fluctuates with time, as the user navigates to different pages and takes different actions on the Tumblr site.

5   Tumblr Traffic Model

As the final component of our work, we have designed and implemented a synthetic workload model for Tumblr network traffic. The model is written in C, and consists of just over 300 lines of code.

Our synthetic workload model for Tumblr is conceptually similar to Web browsing models from the mid-1990's [2]. Specifically, we use a hierarchical workload model, with three conceptual layers. The topmost layer models a single user *session* in Tumblr. This session consists of one or more *conversations* with a Tumblr server[2] (e.g., 75% to Web server and 25% to media server) at the intermediate layer, with random think times in between. Each conversation with a server in turn involves one or more TCP *connections*, with either independent or correlated start times, and randomly generated transfer sizes. The TCP connection layer constitutes the lowest layer of the Tumblr model; we do not model the IP packet layer, or the dynamics of TCP congestion control. Concurrent TCP connections are allowed to both of the Tumblr servers, with connection start times slightly staggered to reflect processing overheads and non-deterministic user interactions.

The Tumblr workload model has been calibrated based on the empirical measurement data reported in the previous section. We use a geometric distribution for the number of connections, and hybrid distributions for the numbers of bytes sent and received on each connection. Connection durations depend on data transfer sizes, network bandwidth for uploading/downloading, TCP handshaking, and the timeout values used for persistent connections. Table 4 provides a summary of the main parameters in our Tumblr model, and the default settings for these parameters. The default settings produce Tumblr sessions with an average of 50 TCP connections, and lasting just under half an hour on average.

Table 4. Parameters and settings for Tumblr traffic model

Parameter	Setting
Session IAT	Exponential (120)
Conversations	Geometric (5)
Web Server Prob	0.70
Media Server Prob	0.20
Dual Server Prob	0.10
Connections	Geometric (10)
Persistent Conn Prob	0.20
Persistent Conn Timeout	60 s
Tail Prob	0.50
Bytes Sent	LogNormal (12,2)
Bytes Received (www)	LogNormal (14,2)
Bytes Received (media)	LogNormal (15,2)
Upload Bandwidth	1.5 Mbps
Download Bandwidth	4.0 Mbps
User Think Time	Uniform (0,60)

---

[2] We ignore the Oath and Verizon/ANS servers, which contribute negligibly to the connection count and data volume in the empirical Tumblr traffic.

When building a synthetic workload model for Tumblr traffic, it is important to model the cross-correlations in TCP connections, which are clearly not independent. For this purpose, the conversation model allows some shared state between Web and media server connections, with the data volumes randomly split between the two connections, while the connection durations are harmonized.

Figure 5 shows an example of the output from this model for a 50-min user session with about 84 TCP connections. About two-thirds of these connections go to the Web server, and about one-third to the media server. These graphs use the same style and format as Fig. 4. Specifically, Fig. 5(a) represents the time series evolution of TCP connection usage, while Fig. 5(b) shows the concurrent connection usage across the two main Tumblr servers. These graphs are visually similar to those for the empirical user session shown in Fig. 4. However, we have not modeled the API ping feature, which likely causes some of the longer Web server connections in Fig. 4(a).

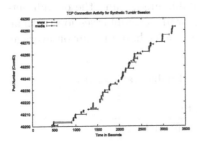 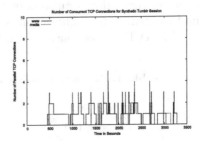

(a) Example of a synthetic user session   (b) Concurrent connections in synthetic session

Fig. 5. Example of connection-level characteristics for a synthetic Tumblr session

Figure 6 provides a more detailed look at how transfer sizes for connections are modeled. In the example shown here, we use a hybrid distribution, with 50% of the transfer sizes being in the body of the distribution (e.g., less than 64 KB), and 50% of the transfer sizes being in the tail of the distribution. The tail is modeled using a LogNormal distribution, as indicated earlier. We explicitly model the asymmetry of the traffic, with received bytes on average being about four times larger than sent bytes. We also increase the average transfer size for the media server, which has a more pronounced tail to the distribution for received bytes. The modeling results in Fig. 6 are structurally similar to those shown for the empirical workload in Fig. 3(c), though the latter did not explicitly separate the two directions of traffic.

By combining the foregoing Tumblr session model with a time-varying Poisson arrival process, we have generated one synthetic week of Tumblr traffic, as shown in Fig. 7. In this particular example, we used a mean session arrival rate of 30 Tumblr sessions per hour during the main part of the work day (8:00 am

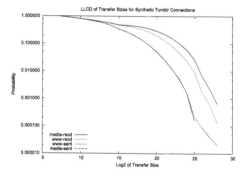

Fig. 6. Distribution of transfer sizes for synthetic Tumblr connections

to 4:00 pm), but only 20% of this rate in the evening, and only 10% of the base rate in the early morning hours. (We also ignored the notion of weekends.) The graph shows the instantaneous number of Tumblr sessions that are concurrently active at each time throughout the week. With these example settings, there are about 15 active Tumblr sessions in steady state during the main part of each day.

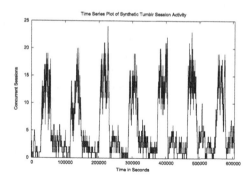

Fig. 7. Diurnal profile for one week of synthetic Tumblr sessions

Figure 8 provides a more detailed breakdown for our synthetic week of Tumblr traffic, in a format similar to that of Fig. 3(a) and (b). Figure 8(a) shows the synthetic connection arrival pattern on a per-hour basis, while Fig. 8(b) shows the corresponding byte transfer information, again on a per-hour basis. This aggregate model captures the diurnal structure well, while still reflecting the stochastic nature of connection arrivals and transfer size variability.

In the future, we plan to incorporate our Tumblr model into network simulations of OSN usage on mobile wireless networks. Our synthetic traffic model for Tumblr is currently available online from the Web site of the third author (Williamson) at the University of Calgary.

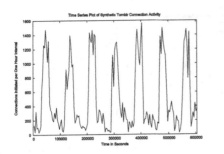

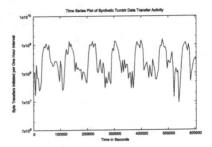

(a) Synthetic connections per hour   (b) Synthetic bytes per hour

Fig. 8. Traffic profile for one week of synthetic Tumblr connections

6   Conclusions

In this paper, we have presented a detailed workload characterization study of Tumblr traffic on our campus network. Furthermore, we have built upon the insights gained from our study to identify similarities and differences compared to other popular social media applications.

The main highlights from our paper are summarized as follows. First, Tumblr usage is seemingly much lower than Instagram and other OSNs, when measured in users or TCP connections, but it is actually comparable in data traffic volume. Second, despite relative differences in popularity, the structural properties of network traffic for OSN sites are qualitatively similar in many ways, including diurnal profile, asymmetry, long-lived connections, and heavy-tailed transfer size distributions. Third, there are some distinct features of Tumblr traffic that differ from other OSNs. These include the session keep-alive behavior, dual server usage, low TCP throughput, and the absence of CDNs.

Our campus-level study provides a glimpse of possible future demands for OSN usage on enterprise, ISP, and mobile networks. We hope that our measurement and modeling results are of value to researchers, network operators, protocol designers, and content providers as they consider how to handle future growth in OSN traffic, especially on mobile networks.

Acknowledgements. The authors thank the anonymous reviewers from IEEE MASCOTS 2020 for their constructive feedback and suggestions on an earlier version of this paper. Financial support for this research was provided in part by the Department of Computer Science at the University of Calgary, and by Canada's Natural Sciences and Engineering Research Council (NSERC). The authors are also grateful to University of Calgary Information Technologies (UCIT) for facilitating our collection and analysis of the campus-level network traffic.

References

1. Alrajebah, N.: Investigating the structural characteristics of cascades on tumblr. In: Proceedings of IEEE/ACM International Conference on Advances in Social Network Analysis and Mining (ASONAM), Paris, France, pp. 910–917 (2015)
2. Arlitt, M., Williamson, C.: A synthetic workload model for internet mosaic traffic. In: Proceedings of the 1995 Summer Computer Simulation Conference, Ottawa, ON, Canada, pp. 852–857 (1995)
3. Benevenuto, F., Rodrigues, T., Cha, M., Almeida, V.: Characterizing user behavior in online social networks. In: Proceedings of the 9th ACM Internet Measurement Conference (IMC), Chicago, IL, pp. 49–62 (2009)
4. Chang, Y., Tang, L., Inagaki, Y., Liu, Y.: What is tumblr: a statistical overview and comparison. ACM SIGKDD Explor. Newslett. **16**(1), 21–29 (2014)
5. Deng, Q., Li, Z., Wu, Q., Xu, C., Xie, G.: An empirical study of the wechat mobile instant messaging service. In: IEEE INFOCOM Workshops, Atlanta, USA, pp. 390–395, May 2017
6. Instagram. A quick walk through our history as a company, March 2019. https://instagram-press.com/our-story
7. Klenow, S., Williamson, C., Arlitt, M., Keshvadi, S.: Campus-level instagram traffic: a case study. In: Proceedings of IEEE International Symposium on Modeling, Analysis, and Simulation of Computer and Telecommunication Systems (MASCOTS), Rennes, France, pp. 228–234 (2019)
8. Maia, M., Almeida, J., Almeida, V.: Identifying user behavior in online social networks. In: Proceedings of 1st Workshop on Social Network Systems, Glasgow, Scotland, pp. 1–6 (2008)
9. Mislove, A., Marcon, M., Gummadi, K., Druschel, P., Bhattacharjee, B.: Measurement and analysis of online social networks. In: Proceedings of ACM Internet Measurement Conference (IMC), San Diego, CA, pp. 29–42 (2007)
10. Mitmproxy (2020). https://www.mitmproxy.org
11. Paxson, V.: Bro: a system for detecting network intruders in real time. Comput. Netw. **31**(23–24), 2435–2463 (1999)
12. Roy, S., Williamson, C., Mclean, R.: LMS performance issues: a case study of D2L. ISCA Int. J. Comput. Appl. **25**(3), 113–122 (2018)
13. Schneider, F., Feldmann, A., Krishnamurthy, B., Willinger, W.: Understanding online social network usage from a network perspective. In: Proceedings of ACM Internet Measurement Conference (IMC), Chicago, IL, pp. 35–48 (2009)
14. Tumblr. About, May 2020. https://www.tumblr.com/about
15. Wikipedia. Tumblr, May 2020. https://en.wikipedia.org/wiki/Tumblr
16. Wikipedia. Instagram, May 2020. https://en.wikipedia.org/wiki/Instagram
17. Williamson, C.: Internet traffic measurement. IEEE Internet Comput. **5**(6), 70–74 (2001)
18. Wireshark (2020). https://www.wireshark.org
19. XKit (2020). https://new-xkit-extension.tumblr.com
20. Xu, J., Compton, R., Lu, T., Allen, D.: Rolling through tumblr: characterizing behavioral patterns of the microblogging platform. In: Proceedings of ACM Conference on Web Science, Bloomington, IN, pp. 13–22, June 2014

Tail Latency in Datacenter Networks

Assad Althoubi[1(✉)], Reem Alshahrani[2], and Hssan Peyravi[1]

[1] Department of Computer Science, Kent State University, Kent, OH 44242, USA
aalthoub@kent.edu, peyravi@cs.kent.edu
[2] Department of Computer Science, Taif University,
Taif 26571, Kingdom of Saudi Arabia
rashahrani@tu.edu.sa

Abstract. One of the major challenges in cloud service data centers is to satisfy service-level agreements without significant over-provisioning. Achieving predictable performance is critical for many interactive applications. While the focus, particularly in theoretical models, has been on reducing average latency, the skewed tail of the latency distribution is much harder to reduce despite over-provisioning. In this paper, we take two approaches to mitigate tail latency in data centers. The first approach is based on bridging selected edge and aggregate switches to reduce east-west traffic latency. The second approach is based on task scheduling dependent tasks via their dependency acyclic graph. A queuing network model has been developed which can be used to reduce the average latency. Numerical and simulation results have shown the techniques are effective in terms of reducing the average tail latency within a data center network.

Keywords: Data centers · Cloud computing · Tail latency

1 Introduction

The emergence of cloud computing in recent years has led to the development of various cloud services including Business Process as a Service (BPaaS), Platform as a Service (PaaS), Software as a Service (SaaS), Management/Security as a Service (MaaS), and Infrastructure as a Service (IaaS). The growth of these services has also been remarkable in recent years and the trend continues. The fastest-growing market segment will be cloud system infrastructure services or infrastructure as a service (IaaS). The second-highest growth rate will be cloud application infrastructure services or platform as a service (PaaS) [19].

These applications service several millions of queries and instructions on several thousands of machines and are concerned with *tail latency*. Optimizing data center networks for tail latency is a shift from previous designs, where the performance metrics of interest were throughput or average latency. Still, optimizing average throughput for latency-insensitive traffic is an important performance metric. Optimizing for tail latency has already been considered in the design of new operating systems, cluster managers, and data services [14–16].

© Springer Nature Switzerland AG 2021
M. C. Calzarossa et al. (Eds.): MASCOTS 2020, LNCS 12527, pp. 254–272, 2021.
https://doi.org/10.1007/978-3-030-68110-4_17

It is important to understand what causes the latency problem and what it means to the applications. First, request latency is a user-perceived time and could vary from one user to the other. It reflects how long it takes from sending a request to receiving the reply which is the time spent waiting in the queue plus the time spent executing the corresponding instructions. Second, the significant portion of latency is dominated by the network transfer time, and that in turn is dominated by queuing delay which is probabilistic. There is also the variation of latency to be concerned about. The variation in network latency is caused by network traffic types which include background traffic and request/response traffic with tight deadlines. The background traffic can be latency-sensitive and short control messages or large replicated transfer files. Third, the absence of priority scheduling for latency-sensitive traffic when latency-sensitive and non-latency-sensitive share the network equally. Additionally, uneven load balancing and bursty traffic all contribute to variation in network transfer times. Forth, increasing buffer size to reduce loss rate introduces variable buffer latency. As predictability of response time becomes more critical for latency-sensitive cloud services, finding a balance between expected response time and deployment of computation/communication resources becomes more critical.

Historically, data center workloads were dominated by North-South traffic which carried mostly online transaction processing jobs in which client requests were responded by servers through a simple 3-tier architecture, Fig. 1 (a). With the hyper exponential growth of social media and mobile apps, traffic patterns have dramatically shifted from North-South to East-West in which a query may generate only a little amount of traffic between the client and data center, but, the response may require generating a massive amount of traffic within the data center, Fig. 1 (b).

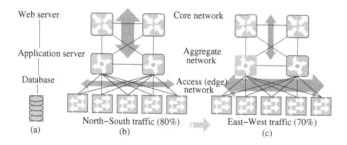

Fig. 1. Traffic shift from North-South (NS) to East-West (EW).

A significant portion of East-West traffic is internal queries related to the core advertising business model behind many of the social media and mobile apps. These include but not limited to browsing history, interests, and recent purchases, user demographics, and real-time auctions to grant the highest bids.

The traffic shift from North-South to East-West along with responses assembles from internal micro activities have made hyper-scale cloud and web providers to shift from the traditional article to the microservices architecture. The drawback of microservices architecture is the massive multiplication of tasks and instances generated within the data center. Some studies have shown a single online query can generate hundreds or even thousands of internal queries within the data center. The cumulative effect is a long (tail) latency response in which thousands of microservice tasks (or instances) simultaneously and the overall response time is determined by the slowest tasks (or instances). Studies [2] have shown that considerable dependencies exist between individual tasks which limit processing the chain in parallel and tail-latency becomes the weakest link in the chain. Therefore, worst-case latency is the most important determining overall performance, particularly for latency-sensitive traffic, and this the focus of this paper.

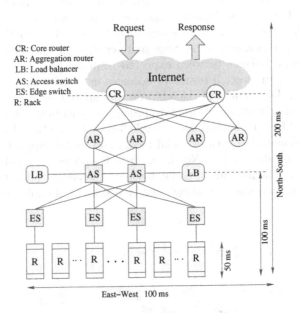

Fig. 2. Latency components.

Figure 2 shows the conventional architecture of a data center. Requests arriving from the Internet are IP packets routed through a core router (CR) to access an aggregator router (AR), all in layer 3 (L3) domain. A load balancer (LB) which is connected to a top-level access switch (AS) spread requests evenly across multiple servers. The dominant portion of response time is consumed by the access network. Traffic moves north-south and east-west (cross-rack communications) and generally, it is asymmetric in terms of latency. Spreading out reducers, while offers load balancing and reduce computing times, it increases communication time, congestion, and tail latency. Network latency alone can consume data retrieval time. Additionally, scalability will be bottlenecked by communication overhead. As the number of servers is increased, by provisioning or scale, communication time is increased faster than computation time decreased.

From the user's perspective, latency and its variation (jitter) are primary performance metrics. From the provider's perspective, utilization and cost are primary performance metrics. There are a few questions we try to answer in this article including how tail latency can be mitigated without overprovisioning, how to schedule different user requests, and how these decisions help the desire to minimize energy consumption. While answers to these questions often come from detailed experiments, it is of great value to have an analytical framework which can identify major trade-offs and challenges supporting latency-sensitive services in data center networks.

The rest of the paper is organized as follows. Section 2 present challenges facing tail latency reduction. Section 3 presents modeling speed-up and latency from the queuing theory perspective. It also shows one of the contributions concerning modeling and latency analysis in data centers. It describes a queuing network model, *Multi-stage network* (MSN), which can be used to model average latency and how to use it effectively to reduce both the mean and mitigate tail latency at a high load. Section 4 describes the sources of tail latency as a result of network infrastructure or traffic distributions. Section 5 presents ways to reduce tail latency. It presents two approaches, mitigation via bridging, and mitigation via dependency acyclic graph (DAG) scheduling. Section 6 describes the simulation and numerical evaluations of the methods used. Section 7 provides a short survey of related work in modeling and analysis of data center networks. Finally, conclusions, limitations, and remarks are presented in Sect. 8.

2 Challenges

The challenges facing data centers include a variety of network-specific real-time analytics, heterogeneous resources, scalability of many detailed data, tail latency, and sub-millisecond response time requirements. Small jobs, typically generated by interactive and exploratory data analyses, are held disproportionately by long-running jobs (called stragglers [6]). Studies have shown that stragglers increase the average job duration by 47% despite applying straggler mitigation techniques [6]. Stragglers run much slower than other tasks. Since a job finishes only when its longest task finishes, job completion suffers significantly from stragglers. A flow is useful only if it satisfies its deadline. However, stragglers increase tail latency which can be also affected by resource contention with background jobs, device failure, uneven-split of data between tasks, and network congestion.

A simple way to curb latency variability is to issue the same request to multiple replicas and use the results from whichever replica responds first. This is known as task replication [28]. The downside is the higher utilization of computing and communication resources. Delivering CPU-intensive and seamlessly interactive cloud services requires micro-partitioning of resources and prediction of certain behaviors that are likely to cause load imbalances. In [26], rather than breaking jobs into tasks that pipeline many resources, it is proposed to break jobs into mono tasks, which are units of work that each uses a single CPU, network, or disk, to identify bottlenecks.

A viable solution is to use distributed schedulers; in which a set of concurrent schedulers map incoming jobs into available servers [31]. Deployment of distributed schedulers to support job parallelism has become a common practice to meet the design goals of data analytics frameworks [10,13,27,32].

3   Modeling Data Centers

To get better insight, we build upon ideas from queuing theory, which provides a framework to measure task-arrival rates, service times, and end-to-end response times. Providers can utilize the model to analyze and manage their computing and communication resources in data centers in a more effective and cost-efficient way while mitigating tail latency.

While parallelism mitigates tail latency, there is a limit as how much it can improve tail latency when microservices with fork-and-join are used. Amdahl's law describes the speedup (s) of a task when a fraction (f) of the computation is accelerated by a factor (k).

$$s = \frac{1}{f/k + (1 - f)} \tag{1}$$

Equation (1) says that the amount of parallel speedup in a given problem is limited by the sequential portion of the problem, which are stragglers and dependent tasks. Figure 3 illustrates how stragglers can limit the speed-up gained by parallelism. While Amdahl's law captures the average performance from multiple cores, it does not describe tail latency. Simple models such as $M/M/1$ and $M/M/k$ are particularly attractive for performance calculations in closed-form

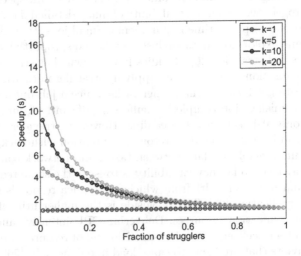

Fig. 3. Speed-up in $M/M/k$ limited by Amdhal's law.

expressions. In [16], the previous analyses on Amdahl's law for parallel and multi-core systems [5, 21] has been extended to develop an analytical framework based on $M/M/k$ queuing model to predict tail latency. The tail latency for $M/M/1$ can be described as q-percentile of the response time. The mean response time of an $M/M/1$ queue is $E[r] = \frac{1}{\mu-\lambda}$, where λ is the mean arrival rate and μ is the mean service rate. Hence, the probability density and distribution functions for the latency in $M/M/1$ can be expressed as:

$$f_r(t) = (\mu - \lambda)e^{-(\mu-\lambda)t}, \quad F_r(t) = 1 - e^{-\mu(1-\rho)t} \tag{2}$$

Now, the q-percentile of the latency can be expressed as:

$$1 - F_r(t) = \frac{q}{100} \Rightarrow t_q = \frac{-1}{\mu(1-\rho)} \ln(1 - \frac{q}{100}) \tag{3}$$

For $M/M/k$, the probability density and distribution functions for the latency can be computed in a similar way but more efforts. However, computing the cumulative distribution function of waiting is more tractable.

$$F_r(t) = 1 - P_w e^{-k\mu(1-\rho)t} \Rightarrow t_q = \frac{-\ln(\frac{100-q}{100P_w})}{k\mu(1-\rho)} \tag{4}$$

where P_w is the Erlang-C probability of waiting.

While eliminating the sources of latency variability in large-scale systems is impractical, especially in shared environments, prediction and mitigation of tail latency are possible through queuing analysis. In the following subsection, we describe a multi-stage tandem queuing network (MSN) model with distributed schedulers and parallel servers, which one of the contributions in this paper, to derive the average and tail latency.

3.1 Multi-stage Network Model (MSN)

In this section, we develop a multi-stage tandem queuing model to represent the fat-tree network in data centers. It is based on architecture described in Figs. 1 and 2, with an additional level which represent servers. Figure 4 (a) represent a miniature fat-tree replica of a data center interconnection network. Core routers (layer 3) are interconnected with aggregate routers in a systematic block-structured form. Aggregate routers and edge switches form pods that host servers.

While the $M/M/1$ and $M/M/k$ described in Sect. 3 are helpful and simple to analyze a data center, they are not sufficient when the bottleneck is within the data center interconnection network. Hence a network of queues is more representative to describe a data center. The model is described in the following section.

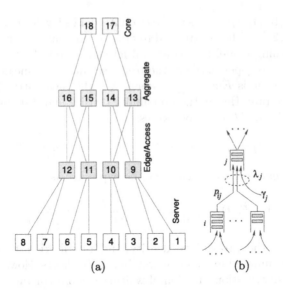

Fig. 4. (a) A 4×16 fat-tree, (b) a node model.

3.2 Queuing Networks

A Jackson queuing network [22] is a network of N $M/M/1$ state-independent queuing system. Upon receiving its service at node i, a packet will proceed to node j with a probability p_{ij}. This is shown in Fig. 4(b). The queue capacity at each node is assumed to be infinite, so there is no packet dropping. Figure 4 (b) illustrates a node model for Jackson network.

Let N be the number of nodes in a Jackson [22] network, and $\mathbf{P_{N \times N}}$ be a probability matrix describing routing within a Jackson network [22], where $\overrightarrow{\gamma} = (\gamma_1, \gamma_2, \cdots, \gamma_N)$ is a vector of the exogenous mean arrival rates, and $\overrightarrow{\lambda} = (\lambda_1, \lambda_2, \cdots, \lambda_N)$ is a vector of mean arrival rates of the traffic aggregates. Unlike the state transition used for Markov chains, the rows of $\mathbf{P}$ matrix need not necessarily sum up to one, i.e., $\sum_j p_{ij} \leq 1$. The routing matrix $\mathbf{P}$ cab be generated by the underlying data center interconnectivity. Assuming the network reaches equilibrium, then we can write the following traffic equation using the *flow conservation principle*, in which the total sum of arrival rates entering the system is equal to the total departure rate under steady-state condition.

$$\lambda_j = \gamma_j + \sum_i^N \lambda_i p_{ij}, \quad j = 1, 2, \cdots, N. \tag{5}$$

In the steady state,

$$\overrightarrow{\lambda} = \overrightarrow{\gamma} + \overrightarrow{\lambda} \mathbf{P}, \tag{6}$$

and the aggregate arrival rate vector can be solved by:

$$\overrightarrow{\lambda} = \overrightarrow{\gamma} (\mathbf{I} - \mathbf{P})^{-1} < \overrightarrow{\mu}, \tag{7}$$

where vector **I** is an identity matrix. $\vec{\mu} = (\mu_1, \mu_2, \cdots, \mu_N)$ is a vector representing service rates. The service times are assumed to be mutually independent, and also independent of the arrival process at that queue, regardless of the previous service times of the same packet in other nodes.

3.3   Response Time Analysis

In this section, we will use the model described in Sect. 3 to develop a closed-form solution for the mean response time of traffic moving up on the fat-tree. Generally, joint traffic (South-North) contribute more to the tail of latency than forked traffic (North-South). A similar approach can also be used for the traffic moving South.

Let $\lambda_{\ell j}$ be the aggregated traffic arrival at node j in stage ℓ. Given the regularity and hierarchical structure of fat-tree, we can directly compute the load on each node at each level. Assuming a uniform distribution of traffic governed by the load balancers, we can formulate aggregated traffic at each level as,

$$
\lambda_\ell = \begin{cases}
\vec{\lambda_h} = (\gamma_1, \gamma_2 \cdots \gamma_n) & \ell = 1 \\
\vec{\lambda_e} = \vec{\lambda_h} \times \mathbf{P}, & \ell = 2 \\
\vec{\lambda_a} = \vec{\lambda_h} \times \mathbf{P}^2, & \ell = 3 \\
\vec{\lambda_c} = \vec{\lambda_h} \times \mathbf{P}^3, & \ell = 4
\end{cases}
\tag{8}
$$

where, n is the number of hosts and h, e, a, c, are indices for hosts, edge switches, aggregators, and core servers, respectively.

$$
T_\ell = \begin{cases}
(\mu_h - \gamma_h)^{-1}, \ell = 1, \gamma_h < \mu_h, \\
(\mu_e - \lambda_h)^{-1}, \ell = 2, \lambda_h < \mu_e, \\
(\mu_a - \lambda_a)^{-1}, \ell = 3, \lambda_a < \mu_a, \\
(\mu_c - \lambda_c)^{-1}, \ell = 4, \lambda_c < \mu_c,
\end{cases}
\tag{9}
$$

The shortest(unique path) gives us the response time as cumulative individual delays at each level.

$$
T_{SN} = \sum_{\ell=1}^{L} T_\ell
\tag{10}
$$

To illustrate the above formulation with an example, consider an 8×2 fat-tree with 8 hosts, 4 edge switches, 4 aggregator switches and 2 core switches. Further assume $\gamma_i = \gamma$ and $\mu_i = \mu$, for an illustration purpose,

$$\lambda_\ell = \begin{cases} \lambda_h = \gamma \\ \lambda_e = 2\gamma \\ \lambda_a = 2\gamma \\ \lambda_c = 4\gamma \end{cases} T_\ell = \begin{cases} (\mu - \gamma)^{-1} & \ell = 1 \\ (\mu - 2\gamma)^{-1} & \ell = 2 \\ (\mu - 2\gamma)^{-1} & \ell = 3 \\ (\mu - 4\gamma)^{-1} & \ell = 4 \end{cases} \tag{11}$$

$$T_{SN} = \sum_{\ell=1}^{L} T_\ell = \frac{(2\mu - 3\gamma)(2\mu - 6\gamma) - \mu\gamma}{(\mu - \gamma)(\mu - 2\gamma)(\mu - 4\gamma)}. \tag{12}$$

The above queuing system is stable only if $\rho = 4\gamma/\mu < 1$. While analytical models give insights, they run the risk of not accurately reflecting the complex operation of a real system. In Fig. 5, we show a brief validation study of the queuing model against real traces. We set the mean interarrival rate and service time according to the statistics obtained from the traces [2]. There were $K = 3$ sources (schedulers) and $N = 4043$ servers. In both cases, when providing the system with exponentially distributed input load, the measured request latency is very close to the one estimated by the queuing model across load levels.

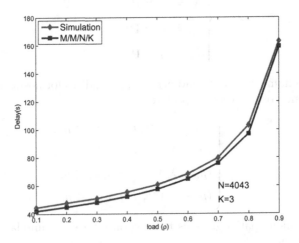

Fig. 5. $M/M/K/N$ model vs. Alibaba simulated traces.

While modeling data centers with average performance metrics (e.g., delay, throughput, etc.) to assess their long term operational performance has been studied with great interest in recent literatures [7,8,18,20,24,29,35], the tail latency is typical of much greater interest than the average latency for some data center applications. In modern data centers, sometimes a seemingly unimportant factor or an infrequent event can determine the overall performance.

4   Sources of Tail Latency

With the increasing demand and scale for diverse services, cloud service providers have turned to distributed platforms with distributed scheduling and parallel microservices architectures in which *instances* of a task are executed in parallel and/or instances of a job (tasks) are scheduled and executed concurrently to support more sophisticated online services. Often tasks that belong to the same job are inter-dependent. These distributed platforms result in a level of parallelism that makes response times much less predictable as some less frequent minor events can govern overall response times. The process relates to a fork-and-join problem while a small task (straggler) can hold the join operation before a job can be completed. Tail latency is expressed in terms of a percentile. A long-tail latency refers to a higher percentile (e.g., 99th) of latency in comparison to the average latency time. Studies [12] have shown that as a system grows in scale, the wider the degree of variability in latency. Since no infrastructure is designed with infinite resources, to some extent tail latency is experienced from time to time mainly due to unexpected traffic peak loads or unexpected failures or events.

4.1   Micro Service Architecture

A job consists of one or more tasks of which completion of one task may depend on completion of some other tasks expressed by a directed acyclic graph as shown in Fig. 6, obtained from Alibaba traces [2]. Each task has several instances. When all the instances of a task are completed, then the task is considered as "finished". If task 2 is depending on task 1, any instance of task 2 cannot be started before all the instances of task 1 are completed. Figure 7 shows the density and the distribution task dependencies obtained from Alibaba data center traces [2]. The other contributor to tail latency is the distribution of the number of instances per task. Given these instances are assigned to various servers with different queue lengths, they negatively impact the job response time according to Amdahl law [5], Eq. (1). Figure 7 shows the density and distribution functions

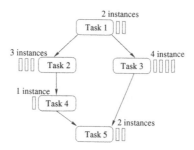

Fig. 6. An example of Dependency Acyclic Graph (DAG).

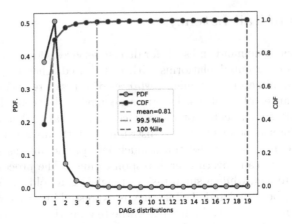

Fig. 7. PDF and CDF, and tail of task dependencies Alibaba traces [2].

of task dependencies in Alibaba traces [2]. While tail latency cannot be eliminated entirely, it can be minimized by identifying and managing the bottlenecks in jobs/tasks/instances as well in network configuration.

5   Tail Latency Mitigating

This paper does not intend to address all sources of tail latency and provide solutions for each. Rather, it intends to develop an analytical model that identifies network bottlenecks inside data centers and uses the model to reduce tail latencies caused by North-South and East-West traffic aggregations. It also uses the model to mitigate tail latencies caused by task dependencies via distributed task scheduling. Studies have shown that data center networks significantly contribute to end-to-end latency, and hence the overall tail latency. While the model is generic and scalable, for presentation and simulation purposes, we chose networks of size $a \times b$, where, a is the number of schedulers (core nodes), and b is the number of servers. We experimented with $a = \{1, 2, 4\}$ and $b = \{8, 16, 24, 32\}$.

Figure 8 illustrates the impact of East-West traffic on the average and tail latency when East-West traffic contributes 10% of the total traffic in the network. Longer tails were observed when the network size increases or the percentage of East-West traffic increases. We took two approaches to reduce tail latencies and compared their performance with existing practices which is a random task assignment. The first approach is mainly hardware by bridging pods via edge and aggregate switches. Second, we used a distributed scheduling algorithm in which dependent tasks (DAGs) were assigned to neighboring servers or neighboring pods.

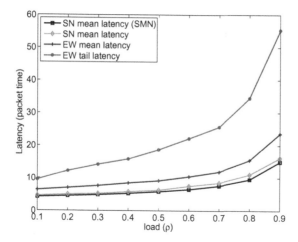

Fig. 8. Average and tail latency of 4×16 in Fig. 9.

5.1 Reducing Tail Latency by Bridging

First, we bridge some edge and core routers to shorten the East-West traffic paths. This is shown by edges marked "red" in Fig. 9. In this approach, the East-West delay is considerably reduced, particularly at higher loads which contribute to the tail latency. Figure 10 shows latency reduction when bridging is used.

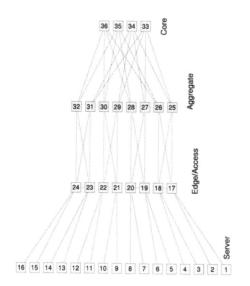

Fig. 9. A 4×16 network. (Color figure online)

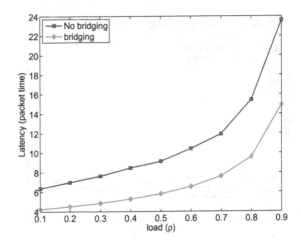

Fig. 10. Latency reduction by bridging, $N = 16, K = 4$.

5.2 Reducing Tail Latency by DAG

A job typically consists of several tasks whose dependencies are expressed by DAG (Directed Acyclic Graph) as shown in Fig. 6. Scheduling these dependent tasks in one or a few nearby servers reduces the volume of traffic being exchanged and the distance they travel. In distributed scheduling, different schedulers are responsible for scheduling different classes of traffic. Figure 11 show how the tail latency can be reduced, particularly at higher loads, by assigning DAG takes to nearby servers. In this scenario, 4 schedulers and 32 servers were used. Jobs arrived in the system according to an exponential inter-arrival time. Each job consisted of k geometrically distributed tasks. In the first approach (red), tasks that belong to the same job were randomly assigned to the servers in the cluster. In the second scenario, the tasks that belong to the same job were assigned to neighboring servers. This has reduced the East-West latency and overall tail latency. Figure 11 shows latency reduction when DAG is used during a task assignment.

6   Numerical Results

To verify the accuracy and effectiveness of the MSN model, several fat-tree networks with various sizes were simulated under various workloads both with synthetic data and traffic traces, and the results were compared. Figure 12 illustrates the performance of the MSN model theoretically and when the model simulated with synthetic data.

6.1   Simulation Configuration and Parameters

A discrete-event continuous-time simulation model based on SimPy [1] has been developed with standard queuing libraries to verify the theoretical results under various traffic load and network size. The simulation model consists of four stages representing servers, edge/access switches, aggregate switches/routers, and core routers.

For North-South traffic, Jobs arrive at core routers according to a Poisson process with different rates and distributed through aggregation and edge routers to the servers. The reverse process has been used for South-North traffic. For web services, the North-South traffic is generally quarries distributed across servers by a fork operation. The South-North traffic is responses combined by a join operation. Both fat-tree architecture and join (merge) operations increase the volume of South-North traffic higher and that in turn contribute to tail latency. Another tail latency contributor is East-West traffic normally generated by the transfer of data packets between servers. The volume of east-west traffic grows as a result of virtualization and data center trends such as converged infrastructure. East-west traffic analysis via queuing theoretical model is more complicated to be addressed in this context.

Queuing delays for North-South and South-Norths were measured and recorded at each stage and the end-to-end delays were calculated accordingly. For each load ($0 < \rho < 1$), 20 simulation runs were performed. We choose a 1 Gbps link with 1500 bytes packets. The average service time is set to be $1500 \times 8/1\,\text{Gpbs} = 0.012\,\mu\text{s}$. The stationary conditions for queuing stability, $\rho < \lambda/\mu$, and conditions in Eq. (9) were enforced for each node. The queue size was chosen sufficiently large to prevent tail drop and observe tail latency more accurately. Figure 12 compares the delay performance of the MSN theoretical model versus the simulation of 24 hosts with 8 cores.

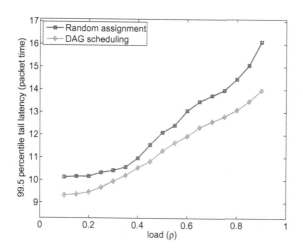

Fig. 11. DAG tail latency reduction, $N = 32, K = 4$.

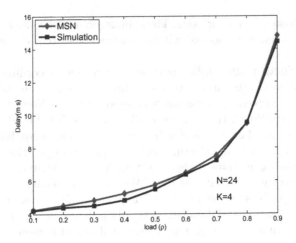

Fig. 12. Delay performance, MSN model vs. simulation, $N = 24, K = 4$.

7 Related Work

In recent years, several schemes [30] have been developed to reduce latency in data center networks such as DCTCP [3], HULL [4] and DeTail [9,25,33,37] have tried to speed up the network to reduce tail delay. Others such as Orchestra [11] have tried to exploit patterns in big-data transfers to optimize network utilization and reduce transfer time.

The work in [23] surveys the research efforts conducted on applying queuing theory to model and analyze cloud computing. Preliminary work in [36] captures the distribution of response times for a homogeneous cloud data center based on a $M/M/m/m + r$ queuing system. The jobs inter-arrival time and service times were assumed to follow an exponential distribution, and the system had a capacitated buffer of size $m + r$. The response time is broken down into waiting time, service time, and total execution times, assuming that all three times are statistically independent which may not be realistic, particularly for batch arrival.

A similar approach in the context of $M/G/m/m + r$ queues was developed in [24] to analyze a data center with heterogeneous servers. In this model, the analysis was extended to approximate the response time distributions, the mean number of tasks in the system, and the blocking probability. An interesting finding in this work is that a cloud data center that accommodates heterogeneous servers may impose longer waiting times for the incoming jobs compared to its homogeneous counterpart with the same traffic intensity. Although the results appear consistent with the prior research, the model is limited to jobs with a single task.

Another work that considers delay analysis in heterogeneous data centers is presented in [8]. The heterogeneity of servers is defined as the servers having different service rates, hence, different processing speeds. The authors have analyzed the mean response and waiting times by constructing an open queuing model that consists of two concatenated queuing systems; a master scheduling server and a set of multi-core parallel servers. The scheduling node is an FCFS capacitated $M/M/1/k$ while each computing node is modeled as an FCFS $M/M/c$ queuing system, where c represents the number of cores per server. Although this analysis provides an efficient approximation, it is reasonably accurate only when the number of servers is relatively small, typically two servers, which makes it unsuitable for performance analysis of cloud data centers. Besides, the model ignores the scheduling activity of the main server and the different dispatching probabilities. Thus, it treats all servers in the cluster identically, regardless of the servers' utilization.

An approximate solution for steady-state queue length in a $M/M/m$ system with a finite buffer has been described in [17]. A cloud platform with homogeneous servers and capacitated buffers has been modeled as a $M/M/m/C$ queuing system to estimate the number of Virtual Machines (VMs) needed to satisfy the QoS requirements. Each server can host up to m VM instances, where C is the maximum queue length of a server. A load balancer, the point of entry for the system, is modeled as a $M/M/1/C$ queue.

In [34], a cloud platform is modeled by an open Jackson network [22] to study QoS requirements. The system consists of a $M/M/1$ queue, representing an entry node as a load balancer, followed by a $M/M/m$ queue, which represents a set of homogeneous servers running an application. The proposed model aims to characterize the QoS guarantees a cloud provider can offer based on the response time of the service. Although the model analyzed the global cloud architecture, it neglects the concurrency of an application's task execution, which is most problematic to applications running in the cloud.

8   Conclusions

Achieving predictable performance is critical for many distributed applications, particularly interactive jobs. While resource provisioning such as parallel storage and multi-core servers can pull tail latency, they may not be sufficient in the absence of identifying traffic characteristics and network bottlenecks. In this paper, first, we introduced a theoretical queuing network model which can be used to allocate necessary resources to reduce average latency and pull tail latency. Second, we used a limited hardware solution, mainly bridging some edge and aggregate switches to reduce east-west traffic and mitigate tail latency. Lastly, we use a distributed scheduling technique that takes the task dependency acyclic graph and schedules dependent tasks in nearby servers to reduce both North-South and East-West tail latency. The results show considerable tail latency improvement, particularly when the load is high. We use traffic traces from Alibaba data centers for numerical and simulation evaluations. While parallelism mitigates tail latency, there is a limit as how much it can improve tail latency when microservices with fork-and-join are used.

References

1. Simpy. https://simpy.readthedocs.io/en/latest/contents.html#
2. Alibaba.com: Alibaba production cluster data (2018). https://github.com/alibaba/clusterdata
3. Alizadeh, M., et al.: Data center TCP (DCTCP). In: Kalyanaraman, S., Padmanabhan, V.N., Ramakrishnan, K.K., Shorey, R., Voelker, G.M. (eds.) SIGCOMM, pp. 63–74. ACM (2010)
4. Alizadeh, M., Kabbani, A., Edsall, T., Prabhakar, B., Vahdat, A., Yasuda, M.: Less is more: trading a little bandwidth for ultra-low latency in the data center. In: Gribble, S.D., Katabi, D. (eds.) Proceedings of the 9th USENIX Symposium on Networked Systems Design and Implementation, NSDI 2012, San Jose, CA, USA, 25–27 April 2012, pp. 253–266. USENIX Association (2012)
5. Amdahl, G.: Validity of the single-processor approach to achieving large-scale computing requirements. Comput. Des. **6**(12), 39–40 (1967)
6. Ananthanarayanan, G., Ghodsi, A., Shenker, S., Stoica, I.: Effective straggler mitigation: Attack of the clones. In: Feamster, N., Mogul, J.C. (eds.) Proceedings of the 10th USENIX Symposium on Networked Systems Design and Implementation, NSDI 2013, Lombard, IL, USA, 2–5 April 2013, pp. 185–198. USENIX Association (2013)
7. Ardagna, D., et al.: Performance prediction of cloud-based big data applications. In: Proceedings of the 2018 ACM/SPEC International Conference on Performance Engineering, pp. 192–199. ACM (2018)
8. Bai, W.H., Xi, J.Q., Zhu, J.X., Huang, S.W.: Performance analysis of heterogeneous data centers in cloud computing using a complex queuing model. Math. Probl. Eng. **2015**, 1–15 (2015)
9. Berger, D.S., Berg, B., Zhu, T., Sen, S., Harchol-Balter, M.: Robinhood: tail latency aware caching - dynamic reallocation from cache-rich to cache-poor. In: Arpaci-Dusseau, A.C., Voelker, G. (eds.) 13th USENIX Symposium on Operating Systems Design and Implementation, OSDI 2018, Carlsbad, CA, USA, 8–10 October 2018, pp. 195–212. USENIX Association (2018)
10. Boutin, E., et al.: Apollo: scalable and coordinated scheduling for cloud-scale computing. In: Flinn, J., Levy, H. (eds.) 11th USENIX Symposium on Operating Systems Design and Implementation, OSDI 2014, Broomfield, CO, USA, 6–8 October 2014, pp. 285–300. USENIX Association (2014)
11. Chowdhury, M., Zaharia, M., Ma, J., Jordan, M.I., Stoica, I.: Managing data transfers in computer clusters with orchestra. In: Keshav, S., Liebeherr, J., Byers, J.W., Mogul, J.C. (eds.) Proceedings of the ACM SIGCOMM 2011 Conference on Applications, Technologies, Architectures, and Protocols for Computer Communications, Toronto, ON, Canada, 15–19 August 2011, pp. 98–109. ACM (2011)
12. Dean, J., Barroso, L.A.: The tail at scale. Commun. ACM **56**(2), 74–80 (2013)
13. Delimitrou, C., Sanchez, D., Kozyrakis, C.: Tarcil: reconciling scheduling speed and quality in large shared clusters. In: Ghandeharizadeh, S., Barahmand, S., Balazinska, M., Freedman, M.J. (eds.) SoCC, pp. 97–110. ACM (2015)
14. Delimitrou, C., Kozyrakis, C.: QoS-aware scheduling in heterogeneous datacenters with paragon. ACM Trans. Comput. Syst **31**(4), 12:1–12:34 (2013)
15. Delimitrou, C., Kozyrakis, C.: Quasar: resource-efficient and QoS-aware cluster management. In: Balasubramonian, R., Davis, A., Adve, S.V. (eds.) Architectural Support for Programming Languages and Operating Systems, ASPLOS 2014, Salt Lake City, UT, USA, 1–5 March 2014, pp. 127–144. ACM (2014)

16. Delimitrou, C., Kozyrakis, C.: Amdahl's law for tail latency. Commun. ACM **61**(8), 65–72 (2018)
17. El Kafhali, S., Salah, K.: Stochastic modelling and analysis of cloud computing data center. In: 2017 20th Conference on Innovations in Clouds, Internet and Networks (ICIN), pp. 122–126. IEEE (2017)
18. Feitelson, D.G.: Workload Modeling for Computer Systems Performance Evaluation, 1st edn. Cambridge University Press, New York (2015)
19. Graham, C., Buest, R., Ackerman, D., Nag, S.: Forecast analysis: cloud managed services, worldwide, February 2020. https://www.gartner.com/en/documents/3981360
20. Gupta, V., Burroughs, M., Harchol-Balter, M.: Analysis of scheduling policies under correlated job sizes. Perform. Eval. **67**(11), 996–1013 (2010)
21. Hill, M.D., Marty, M.R.: Amdahl's law in the multicore era. IEEE Comput. **41**(7), 33–38 (2008)
22. Jackson, J.R.: Networks of waiting lines. Oper. Res. **5**(4), 518–521 (1957)
23. Jafarnejad Ghomi, E., Rahmani, A.M., Qader, N.N.: Applying queue theory for modeling of cloud computing: a systematic review. Concurr. Comput. Pract. Exp. **31**, e5186 (2019)
24. Khazaei, H., Misic, J.V., Misic, V.B.: Performance analysis of cloud computing centers using m/g/m/m+r queuing systems. IEEE Trans. Parallel Distrib. Syst **23**(5), 936–943 (2012)
25. Li, J., Sharma, N.K., Ports, D.R.K., Gribble, S.D.: Tales of the tail: hardware, OS, and application-level sources of tail latency. In: Lazowska, E., Terry, D., Arpaci-Dusseau, R.H., Gehrke, J. (eds.) Proceedings of the ACM Symposium on Cloud Computing, Seattle, WA, USA, 3–5 November 2014. pp. 9:1–9:14. ACM (2014)
26. Ousterhout, K., Canel, C., Ratnasamy, S., Shenker, S.: Monotasks: architecting for performance clarity in data analytics frameworks. In: SOSP, pp. 184–200. ACM (2017)
27. Ousterhout, K., Wendell, P., Zaharia, M., Stoica, I.: Sparrow: distributed, low latency scheduling. In: Proceedings of the Twenty-Fourth ACM Symposium on Operating Systems Principles, pp. 69–84. ACM (2013)
28. Poola, D., Ramamohanarao, K., Buyya, R.: Enhancing reliability of workflow execution using task replication and spot instances. ACM Trans. Auton. Adapt. Syst. **10**(4) (2016)
29. Qi, H., Shiraz, M., Liu, J., Gani, A., Rahman, Z.A., Altameem, T.A.: Data center network architecture in cloud computing: review, taxonomy, and open research issues. J. Zhejiang Univ. Sci. C **15**(9), 776–793 (2014)
30. Rojas-Cessa, R., Kaymak, Y., Dong, Z.: Schemes for fast transmission of flows in data center networks. IEEE Commun. Surv. Tutor. **17**(3), 1391–1422 (2015)
31. Schwarzkopf, M., Bailis, P.: Research for practice: cluster scheduling for datacenters. Commun. ACM **61**(5), 50–53 (2018)
32. Schwarzkopf, M., Konwinski, A., Abd-El-Malek, M., Wilkes, J.: Omega: flexible, scalable schedulers for large compute clusters. In: Proceedings of the 8th ACM European Conference on Computer Systems, pp. 351–364. ACM (2013)
33. Suresh, P.L., Canini, M., Schmid, S., Feldmann, A.: C3: cutting tail latency in cloud data stores via adaptive replica selection. In: NSDI, pp. 513–527. USENIX Association (2015)
34. Vilaplana, J., Solsona, F., Teixidó, I., Mateo, J., Abella, F., Rius, J.: A queuing theory model for cloud computing. J. Supercomput. **69**(1), 492–507 (2014)

35. Wang, W., Harchol-Balter, M., Jiang, H., Scheller-Wolf, A., Srikant, R.: Delay asymptotics and bounds for multi-task parallel jobs. ACM SIGMETRICS Perform. Eval. Rev. **46**(3), 2–7 (2019)
36. Yang, B., Tan, F., Dai, Y.S.: Performance evaluation of cloud service considering fault recovery. J. Supercomput. **65**(1), 426–444 (2013). https://doi.org/10.1007/s11227-011-0551-2
37. Zats, D., Das, T., Mohan, P., Borthakur, D., Katz, R.H.: Detail: reducing the flow completion time tail in datacenter networks. In: Eggert, L., Ott, J., Padmanabhan, V.N., Varghese, G. (eds.) ACM SIGCOMM 2012 Conference, SIGCOMM 2012, Helsinki, Finland - 13–17 August 2012, pp. 139–150. ACM (2012)

Author Index

Printed in the United States
By Bookmasters